THE FINAL WHISTLE

THE FINAL WHISTLE

WHISTLE

THE GREAT WAR IN FIFTEEN PLAYERS

STEPHEN COOPER

*To my grandfather, William, who fought and lived through it,
to my parents who grew up during the next
and to Sam and Ben, that they should never*

First published 2012
This paperback edition published 2013
by Spellmount, an imprint of The History Press
The Mill, Brimscombe Port
Stroud, Gloucestershire, GL5 2QG
www.thehistorypress.co.uk

British Library Cataloguing in Publication Data.
A catalogue record for this book is available from the British Library.

ISBN 978 0 7524 9900 0

Typesetting and origination by The History Press
Printed in Great Britain
Manufacturing Managed by Jellyfish Solutions Ltd

CONTENTS

Stephen Cooper has played and coached rugby for over forty years. After Cambridge, he worked in advertising and now runs a military charity. His grandfather survived the Battle of the Somme and inspired in him a lifelong fascination with the First World War. He lives in London.

'A fresh and fascinating take on the impact of the Great War with a novel and moving focus.'

Ian Hislop

'This is a deeply moving book about the loss of fifteen members of Rosslyn Park rugby club during the Great War. A war that scarred Britain and took so many fine men, who had they lived would have enriched this country. The lives of these young men, all so promising, are poignantly and vividly recalled by historian Stephen Cooper.'

Max Arthur

'Stephen Cooper has written a haunting and beautiful book. Here we see the grinding slaughter and the everyday humanity of men hurled into the abyss of modern warfare at its most terrible. His book tells the story of men from one rugby club but it is a universal narrative of heroism and loss. He writes superbly and has produced a book of commendable scholarship. I cannot recommend it enough.'

Fergal Keane

'Having played against Rosslyn Park Rugby Football Club over the years, you always got the impression of a friendly, welcoming club with a great history. (Stephen Cooper has written) ... a book of beauty and sadness about fifteen men who lost their lives for their country in the Great War. People use the word hero to describe sportsmen but the guys in this book are true heroes. A fantastic and inspiring read from the first page to the last.'

Jason Leonard, England & British Lions

'This is a portrait of an age where boys grew to be men driven by certainties, where today we have only doubts. And for those certainties they fought and died. Sensitive, original and profoundly moving'

Anthony Seldon

'A fitting tribute not simply to 15 individuals cut down in their prime, but a paean to all those who died in the First World War' –

Mark Souster, *The Times*

'An inspired idea ... brings home the pathos of these ardently lived lives... An original and illuminating approach to this endlessly fascinating subject.'

Edward Stourton

FOREWORD

I was delighted to be asked to write the foreword to this excellent book.

While our armed forces are currently engaged in Afghanistan and previously in Iraq, we should also remember the hundreds of thousands before them who gave their lives in the Great War just a two-hour car journey from Calais or a sea voyage away in Turkey or Mesopotamia.

Stephen's book tells the story of that war through the lives of one rugby club's players all sadly lost in those four years.

I hope you enjoy the book as much as I did.

Bill Beaumont CBE DL

THE FIRST BLOW

When the time came for the whistle to blow they were glad.

The shrill note hung in the damp air and in the moment's hesitation before they started, all time was suspended and every breath was held. The waiting was finally over and all they had trained for now lay in front of them. Their great game was now about to kick off on this field and their greatest hope was for victory.

The captain looked along his line to the left and right and saw that his men were ready. They had all worked hard for this since training had begun; they were fit in wind and limb, and eager to get stuck in. The mud on their boots, which they never could shake off, no longer felt so heavy.

He had talked to them quietly, each man in his turn; no need for big words as each knew his job and what he had to do. The big men felt strong, relishing the scrimmage to come, their faces set and determined. The faster men were looking to stretch their legs and show their pace in attack. In their eyes, he could see the excitement and the nervousness; no man on his team wanted to let the side down – if they had fears, this was the worst of them.

Most of all they were eager to take the fight to the opposition. This was their first taste of the game. The side they faced was unknown to them, although its reputation was fearsome. Their captain raised his arm to signal readiness, to steady the impatient, and waited for the moment, his own heart battering so loud in his chest he wondered that his men could not hear it.

He placed the whistle to his lips.

And blew.

THE FINAL WHISTLE

This is the story of fifteen men and more who heard that first shrill blast and answered its call to arms; they did not live to hear the final whistle that ended the game.

All were members of one sporting club, Rosslyn Park, then in Henry VIII's ancient Deer Park in Richmond to the south-west of London. In their youth they flocked together from all parts of the land and from the furthest ends of the earth to play the game of rugby. They stepped forward again in 1914 to fight a war that would last four long seasons.

Some were still in their playing prime; others had long since hung up their boots in favour of gentler pursuits, professions and families. These now took second place to war. The Victory Medal issued in 1919 sought to ennoble this brutal struggle as 'The Great War for Civilisation'; but these men never wore this medal or celebrated the victory: every one was killed in that Great War.

The whistle marked a beginning, but it also signalled an end: it blew away the old civilisation. On 4 August 1914, western imperial time was divided into 'before the whistle' and after – the time before the whistle would never return. This war did not end all wars, as optimists fervently hoped, but it did forever change the world. Combatants and civilians alike knew that they were living through an unprecedented transformation: the breakdown of one epoch and the uncertain stirrings of a new age. Wartime nurse Vera Brittain wrote in 1916: 'It seems to me that the War will make a big division of "before" and "after" in the history of the World, almost if not quite as big as the "B.C." and "A.D." division made by the birth of Christ.'[1] It took four years before the final whistle could sound and 'After War' time could begin.

The history of these men begins with their names lost in mystery. Rosslyn Park Football Club was established in 1879. In that year of the nineteenth century British soldiers died at Rorke's Drift; they also fought and died in Afghanistan, as they do again in the twenty-first. For relaxation they played rugby, with rudimentary pitch and posts, shown in a Victorian periodical engraving, at Khelat-i-Gilzai, near Kandahar.[2] In 2007 a prince and future vice-patron of the Rugby Football Union (RFU) kicked an oval ball about with his Household Cavalry unit in Helmand Province, Afghanistan. These colour images now flash worldwide on the internet and satellite television – our media have made progress even if our civilisation hasn't.

In 1914, with a new war looming, Rosslyn Park already had thirty-five seasons of mud on its shorts; successive waves of players had worn its red-and-white hooped jersey and would now don khaki. Any club of young, physically fit men will naturally suffer losses in wartime; those killed in the 'Second Great War' of the century, including the Russian Prince Alex Obolensky, the flying winger killed in his RAF Hurricane in 1940, are rightly revered on a club-house plaque. But why is there no memorial to its first war dead? Was it somehow lost in the move from Richmond to Roehampton in 1956? A few short miles but a careless slip by clumsy movers and a slab of broken marble consigned in muttering embarrassment to a skip; without a memorial there was no Roll of Honour, no record of the club's pain and pride.

So began the first work to piece together the list of men who died. The sole clue was a yellowed press cutting of the club's 1919 annual general meeting, reporting sixty-six members killed and six missing. No names were mentioned. Thankfully the club's membership records survive; the meticulous copperplate entries for name, address and school attended were checked against Commonwealth War Graves Commission (CWGC) records of those who died.[3] Some names took several more hours of trawling through census, school and university records, newspaper microfiche and National Archives to achieve conclusive matches. The total has already surpassed the stated seventy-two;[4] several more sit 'on the bench', tantalisingly short of the perfect match of name, address or initial that would select them definitively for the side lost by history.

Many names were already linked through shared friendships at school and university. In varying permutations, they bob to the surface time and again in a stream of match reports, school magazine articles, team sheets and photograph captions. Rosslyn Park would unite them again – friends naturally flock together in rugby – and prolong those masculine bonds into adult life. So, fleetingly, would military service in war, until it tore their brief lives and friendships violently apart. Muscular rugby bodies were reduced to sandbags of body parts: lungs drowned in gas froth; tendons and ligaments shredded and twitching; limbs sheared and snapped by pressure waves from passing shells; skulls splintered by steel, stripped of flesh and bleached. In their hour of dying their median age would be 23.

Young men, whether from the Australian outback, Indian railway or industrial Wales, were drawn by education or profession to London's metropolis and found companionship there with like-minded rugby players; they became teammates and close friends. Some passed through the club only briefly for a season or two and might not recognise a common allegiance if they later stumbled across a fellow 'Park-ite' at the front. Guy du Maurier had first played for the club in its earliest North London incarnation, when just 16 in 1881; he became the oldest to die, aged 49, in 1915. Much younger men than Guy were looking forward to a new season and a life of promise when war broke out; the youngest, Gerald David Lomax, was to die at just 20 years of age.

Some displayed exceptional talent in sporting arenas (not just the rugby field) that won them national honours. Others discovered talents and passions they scarce suspected – among them a poet and a playwright – to confound those who cherish the fixed image of rugby 'hearties' who could destroy Christopher Isherwood's college room for kicks. Some achieved distinction in death: the first player lost in August 1914 was the first airman downed by enemy fire; one of the last won the Victoria Cross in 1918. Many more were unsung battlers who hardly aspired to international sporting glory but volunteered enthusiastically to represent their country in the field.

Perhaps these players had absorbed some martial spirit from the *terroir* of Richmond Old Deer Park, in the manner of fine French wines. The 'splendidly quick-drying springy turf'[5] had once been used as an archery range by Queen Elizabeth I, that 'weak and feeble woman, with the heart and stomach of a king'. Just as these fresh recruits came from all corners of Britain and the empire for trial on the rugby field, so they were sent out to fight in every theatre of this war. On its second day the writer Henry James could write privately of 'the plunge of civilisation into this abyss of blood and darkness';[6] public hubbub, on the other hand, was of heroic adventure. The early clashes, roared on by armchair spectators reading sanitised match reports from the battlefield, had the flavour of one huge game. Plucky defence to the last man against superior opposition, defiant goal-line stands and, in true sporting headline fashion, the 'Race to the Sea', as both sides attempted to outflank the opposition by running wide around the wings.

A series of last-ditch tackles, at the cost of thousands dead and wounded, stopped every attack until the Germans were squeezed out of play at the topographic touchlines of the North Sea and Swiss border. Both sides then settled down to a full-frontal forwards game in the mud, rolling on interminable replacements as men went off injured and dying. The thoroughbreds were forever left in reserve, starved of action, waiting for the opportunity to burst through a gap in the opposition line which, in those four hard years, only appeared very late as its German defenders died on their feet – or surrendered on their knees.

However, the stark image of the Western Front is only part of the story. What emerges from the lives of these rugby men is a remarkable history in miniature of the entire war, across all fronts, arms, theatres and engagements. Some went to 'quiet shows' that proved just as deadly as the celebrated set pieces of Ypres and the Somme. They would die in Dublin and Lincolnshire. Some were honoured for their bravery, with one achieving the nation's highest award; far more fought in obscurity, their feats of arms rarely recorded and their death in 'some corner of a foreign field' marked only by the prosaic marginal notes of overworked War Office clerks. Not for them the gleam of the Military or Victoria Cross, or even the dignity of a named grave, only the shadow of the Cross of Sacrifice or granite memorial.

Some inherent quality of bravery or natural leadership saw many rugby men take the lead, as they had on the field, whether as reckless

pilots in frail biplane or balloon, as officers of doomed infantry companies or at the head of desperate naval storming parties. Youthful
hopes – the promise of life, adventure, love – turned swiftly to fears
of death, dismemberment, squalor and insanity. In callous mockery
of the club motto, fortune did not always favour the brave.

Their names are now scattered on public war memorials in home
towns where they lived and were loved, and on battlefields where
they perished. They were also engraved on the rim of the Victory
Medal, its rainbow ribbon emptily promising 'never again'. This
award was not automatic; service medals were issued to other ranks,
but officers or their next of kin had to apply for them. The family
also received a circular bronze plaque, known blackly as the 'Death
Penny', and a printed scroll from the king. These too are scattered
or lost. I have been privileged to view the plaque and medal trio
of 'first-class rugby forward' Arnold Huckett, dead at Gallipoli,
touchingly reunited by a collector with those of his brother Oliver,
killed in France. Aussie Syd Burdekin's medals are safe in a Sydney
museum. As for the rest, who knows.

For many parents, the loss of a young son (or two, even three),
heart-breaking in its own right, could also mean the death of the
family name, as the male lineage was violently severed. Thus it could
be said that whole families died at Ypres, Suvla Bay or Kut. Kipling
borrowed from Ecclesiasticus to promise that 'their Name Liveth for
Evermore', but with no descendants to preserve them, the living stories behind those dead names have rarely been handed down. Nor
are they collected in one place that unites them, as the rugby club
once did. Occasionally photographs emerge from family albums that
speak more eloquently than the formal portraits in memorial books.
However, some sons have left no trace of a face and remain invisible
and lost as men. It is the author's hope that more knowledge will
rise from the depths when readers chance upon these pages.

Almost a century later, why do we write so many books about
the Great War? And why do they invariably focus on those who
died? Gertrude Stein's oft-quoted 'lost generation' referred not to
the dead of the war, but to its war-interrupted survivors, damaged
and drifting in the 1920s. Many died but three-quarters of Park's
estimated 350 members who fought came through alive, although

not always untouched in body or mind. There are as many heroic stories to be told of players who survived. In his 1918 VC citation, Captain Reginald Hayward:

> … displayed almost superhuman powers of endurance. In spite of the fact that he was buried, wounded in the head and rendered deaf on the first day of operations and had his arm shattered two days later, he refused to leave his men, even though he received a third serious injury to his head, until he collapsed from sheer exhaustion.[7]

In hearty disregard for mortality, the superhuman Hayward lived until 1978. Yet it is Arthur Harrison VC, who died sixty years earlier in a storm of bullets at Zeebrugge, who fascinates and whose equally vivid story is told here.

This book tells of fifteen lives cut short, and touches on many others. Few of these mostly young men had time to marry and father children who would live after them and tend the flame of memory. If they wrote letters home, as surely they did, only a few have been spared by time; those glimpses into the thoughts of Alec Todd, John (Jack) Bodenham, Jimmy Dingle and Guy du Maurier are precious. Many did not even leave mortal remains: thirty-four bodies – two entire teams and more – were never found and have no known resting place. The only true death is to be forgotten; these pages hope to resurrect the ghosts of men lost and buried in the mass tomb of the Unknown Soldier that is the Great War.

A fortunate few achieved some small measure of youthful fame before the whistle, but rarely did it last, overwhelmed by the cataclysmic wave that washed away their world. None lived to write the memoirs and autobiographies which flooded on to the market in the 1920s and by which we know of the survivors' experiences. None were interviewed as forgotten voices in their declining years by historians rushing to preserve their accounts before the virus of death deleted them. While their names crumble on cold monuments, the warm-blooded stories of these vigorous, energetic and talented rugby-playing men have never been told.

Until now.

THE BOYS WHO WON THE WAR

Soldiers do not start wars. They fight them under orders. It is politicians who start wars and leave soldiers to endure them until they end. Then in the 'Great War to end all wars', once the fighting had stopped, the politicians again stepped forward, flags flying, to create the Treaty of Versailles and its vindictive reparations against Germany which led inexorably to another great war. And so it goes.

This fight was one of attrition. The generals' dreams and experience lay in wars of movement: sweeping flanking manoeuvres and gallant cavalry charges against brave but poorly equipped adversaries in colonial campaigns. Once outflanking was blocked by trenches stretching 460 miles from the Channel to the Alps, they had no Plan B. Gallipoli and Mesopotamia represented flanking moves on a grand scale, but soon regressed to the unimaginative mean of Western Front siege warfare.

Troops battered themselves senseless and lifeless against enemy defences because of the generals' instinct to attack, to break through and renew mobile warfare – otherwise why have generals? Even if there was no strategic offensive, there was an insistence on 'activity' or demonstration of aggressive intent, with artillery 'hates' and trench raids by night and day. The question 'Are we being as offensive as we might be?' was deservedly satirised in the pages of the *Wipers Times* trench journal; offence simply brought counter-offence, bombardment and death.

The presumption of attack created the trench conditions suffered by the British in cold Flanders mud, Turkish scrub and Mesopotamian sand. If victory was just over the ridge (and at least three cunningly laid and strongly built defensive lines) then why build permanent trench systems? So reasoned the generals. There was no need for fortification or durability according to the *Field Service Pocket Book*: 'The choice of a position and its preparation must be made with a view to economising the power expended on defence in order that the power of offence be increased.' So while the Germans on the Somme could emerge unscathed from their concreted bunkers after seven days of artillery barrage, the British crouched in dugouts, or 'funk holes', scraped into the trench wall and occasionally covered with thin sheets of corrugated 'elephant iron'.

Germany had swiftly taken territory in France. With her eastern front competing for resources (and, in the view of the High Command, more likely to bring a result over Russia), she was content to hunker down in well-engineered defensive systems and let machine gun, gas and wire do the job. The British attacked time and again, while the Germans simply bided their own time and quickly counter-attacked. From September 1914, when the French turned them back within sight of Paris, to the desperate last fling of spring 1918 which so nearly succeeded, the only sustained German attacks were at Second Ypres and on the French at Verdun. Even there the objective was not breakthrough but bloodshed – to 'bleed the French Army white' – knowing that France would never relinquish this symbolic fortress.

Untroubled by any obsession with attack, Germany made tactical withdrawals to better positions, like the Siegfried Line in 1917. British line officers like du Maurier could see the wisdom of such flexibility as early as February 1915 when trying to protect the indefensible trenches east of Ypres. However, Field Marshal Haig, faced with the 1918 German offensive, could still issue his famous Order of the Day on 12 April mandating that 'every position must be held to the last man. There must be no retirement. With our backs to the wall and believing in the justice of our cause, each one must fight on to the end.'

It was attrition, economic and military, that won the war. The Royal Navy's blockade finally choked the German people and war machine into submission. Germany's response of unrestricted submarine warfare only served to bring America's might and manpower into the war in 1917. What allowed the Allies to stay in the war so long despite appalling losses, however, was the dogged persistence of troops fed in successive waves into the maw of the guns. They came from all over France, Britain, its empire and dominions and, eventually, its former colonies in America. They rarely saw the generals and visits by staff officers wearing the 'Red Badge of Funk' on collar tab and cap band were brief. Lieutenant General Sir Lancelot Kiggell famously burst into tears when first confronted with the Passchendaele battlefield from his staff car, blurting, 'Good God, did we really send men out to fight in that?' He was assured it was much worse further up. Military discipline required that line officers showed strict public respect; in private they could be scathing and the men more openly scornful. What kept them fighting for four long years was those line officers, greatest in their number the young subalterns fresh from school or university. These were the boys who won the war.

Poet Sir Henry Newbolt believed that Clifton (Haig's school) gave boys the 'virtues of leadership, courage and independence; the sacrifice of selfish interests to the ideal of fellowship and the future of the race'. It was good form 'to be in all things decent, orderly, self-mastering: in action to follow up the coolest common sense with the most unflinching endurance; in public affairs to be devoted as a matter of course, self-sacrificing, without any appearance of enthusiasm'. Christian schoolboys happily took classical pagans as role models to become 'the Horatian man of the world, the Gentleman after the high Roman fashion, making a fine art, almost a religion of Stoicism'.[1] Their learning commanded respect from those with little or no education. Schooling had prepared them for a life of service to empire or business. Profession or family background gave them the authority of gentlemen over commoners, an order then accepted as entirely natural and certainly necessary for military discipline. They were mostly young (but not always, as we shall see), brought up as decent, compassionate men, with clear values of chivalry, godliness and sportsmanship that intermingled. This seems almost incomprehensible now in our hardened and questioning age. They had certainties where today we have doubts.

Guy du Maurier, a professional commanding a fusilier battalion said of one exemplary subaltern, a gentleman amateur: 'Absolutely no previous training as a soldier is wanted at this game – only a stout heart – a grip of men and a calm cheerful nature.' If their relationship to authority – whether house, school, regiment, king or country – was one of unquestioning obedience, then these boys also took thoughtful responsibility for the men on their team and felt genuine obligation towards those less privileged than themselves. Arguably, war exposed them as never before to the lower classes and trench life had a levelling effect. Energetic and youthful, they led enthusiastic games of rugby or football to keep up morale and break down social barriers. Many had flaws and weaknesses, if only from inexperience, which war would magnify and sometimes fatally expose, but they played the game as best they could. There were more Stanhopes than Flashmans.

These line officers shared dismal living conditions, starving for days with their men, carried the same weight of equipment and fought bravely alongside them. Witness how many rugby-playing officers receive fatal wounds to the head; they were shot peering over parapets, leading raids, or picked off by snipers when checking on their men. They were the first over the top in attack, their well-cut uniforms standing out from the baggy, shapeless Tommy to mark them as primary targets. As honorary horsemen – even in infantry regiments – they wore leather belts, boots and tight riding breeches. German snipers were instructed to target the soldiers with 'thin knees'; once the leaders were cut down, they were told, their men – who were not trained professionals like the Germans – would be lost in headless confusion. The officer casualty rates of 1915 were nearly double those of other ranks; if honoured to serve with the regular regiments, which were thrown into every important attack, junior officers could expect six weeks at the front before being wounded or killed.

Private soldiers and non-commissioned officers (NCOs) felt for their 'young gentlemen' a genuine, unashamed affection that crossed the class divide. Their letters of condolence to bereaved parents of junior officers may trail the stock phrases coached by chaplains in their pragmatic ministering (when talk of God might fall on deafened ears), but no more so than their educated officers, who invariably 'cannot tell you how deeply I feel his death'. As censors reading letters home, subalterns learned to understand – and share – the intimate hopes and fears of men they would never meet in peacetime. The servant valet was retained even under battlefield conditions as a comforting reminder of the peacetime class structure; his main role was to maintain a reasonable table and standard of dress for his officer. Of Charles Alvarez Vaughan, winger for Park, Surrey and the Barbarians, killed at Loos, his servant wrote:

> I never served a better Officer. The morning of the attack he went round his Platoon as cool as if we were on parade, giving them all a cheery word, and there was not one of them that morning but would have done anything for him, for they always declared that he was the best little Officer in the Battalion … We knew he was offered leave just before the attack came off, but he refused, he said he would take it after we were relieved, and I can assure you his Platoon were proud of him, as the Jocks say, 'he was the best wee spud that ever wore a kilt'.[2]

Vaughan remembered his man, Private Robert Ireland, in his will; the money from the 'young master' was gratefully sent to his sister. Even the statements dragged out of damaged memories for later Courts of Inquiry bear witness to the mutual respect of decent men and their line officers, united in common vulnerability under threat from bullet, bomb and bayonet. Lieutenant Dingle at Gallipoli, in the highest form of shared English humanity for his men, was 'a gentleman and made tea for ten of us'.

Did a generation truly die? The myriad names at Thiepval or Tyne Cot and the memorial on every village green might persuade us so. Of 8 million who served, some 723,000[3] died, of which half a million were under 30. Census returns in 1921 showed a 14 per cent decline since 1911 in males of military age, with the influenza epidemic of 1918 playing its own deadly part. Upper- and middle-class officers suffered disproportionate war casualties. So, accordingly, did the rugby clubs: of Park's men who marched away, a quarter failed to return[4] – a heavy blow on a single club. However, glance at the roll of pre-war Barbarians in Wemyss' history[5] and the black cross of sacrifice is only lightly sprinkled over its index. The scale of the slaughter is undeniable but men did survive in surprisingly high numbers, albeit many carrying wounds physical and psychological into their post-war lives. Some, unable to find adequate words or simply unwilling to discuss the horrors with anyone who had not been there, would become strangers in their own families.

In close communities which had joined up en masse in 1914, the death toll was so high that it would indeed have felt like a generation wiped out. The Pals battalions rushed to war from factory towns in a wave of patriotic fervour and workers' friendship. Complete new service battalions were drawn from city districts, like the Blackheath and Woolwich (20/London Regiment), or from common pursuits, like the Sportsmen's Battalion (23/Middlesex). One May morning in 1915, twenty-five men from the village of Wadhurst in Sussex were killed at Aubers Ridge; among them, Roy Fazan, who had played rugby in Germany with Park two years earlier. His brother and fellow clubman, Eric, survived the massacre to record in his diary: 'About mid-day the CO [commanding officer] told me poor Roy was killed ... All poor old Roy's men say he was very cool & shouted "come on boys".'[6]

Then there were the public schools. After a shaky, sometimes violent start to the nineteenth century, they became 'Builders of Character by Appointment to the British Empire'. The Clarendon Commission of 1864, set up after widespread criticism of the public school system, declared:

> It is not easy to estimate the degree in which the English people are indebted to these schools for the qualities on which they pique themselves most – for their capacity to govern others and control themselves, their aptitude for combining freedom with order, their public spirit, their vigour and manliness of character, their strong but not slavish respect for public opinion, their love of healthy sports and exercise.

Previous wars, or at least the Battle of Waterloo, according to the victorious Wellington, had been won on the playing fields of Eton. Of 5,650 Etonians who served in this war, 1,157 were killed. Quick to join up in August 1914 or already commissioned, the flower of

Etonian youth from the best families was crushed in the brutal first months. Peers and baronets fell like titled ninepins. So great was this toppling of sons of the ruling classes that Debrett's was unable to publish an updated edition in spring 1915.

Eton, however, was (and is) untypical even in the public school system of the age; Victorian Britain needed more than landed gentry with fluency in Latin and Greek. The rapid expansion of the empire required increasing numbers of trained military leaders, colonial administrators and civilising missionaries. With one exception (and that a brief one), Rosslyn Park players were not sons of Eton, but drawn from the industrious and professional middle classes, sons of doctors, lawyers, bankers, teachers and even (whisper it softly) men in trade. By the early twentieth century, birth and breeding were just one part of an evolving class structure that would undergo its most radical transformation as a result of war. Fifteen of the eighty-odd who died were sons of clergymen who lived on the verge of poverty, sustained by their vocation and the moral leadership of their flock. In this war, this would be as good an example as any military academy could give.

These boys attended the host of 'new' public schools that had flourished since Clarendon's endorsement and the founding of the Headmasters' Conference in 1860. Old Etonian George Orwell noted: 'At such schools the greatest stress is laid on sport, which forms, so to speak, a lordly, tough and gentlemanly outlook.'[7] When these boys left school and university they generally worked for a living, often following in fatherly footsteps. Through tribalism and tradition more than locality, certain schools dominated Rosslyn Park's membership: Bedford, Marlborough, Haileybury and Uppingham. Schools were recorded in the membership ledger as irrefutable proof of a 'fit and proper person' (and invaluable help to this book). They still appear on the club's honour boards; a continuing tradition in changing times where the late, great Andy Ripley's Greenway Comprehensive now rubs shoulders with Marlborough and Uppingham.

These boards are a mournful register of schools which racked up losses to stretch comparisons with cricket scores and matched Orwell's observation that at public schools 'the duty of dying for your country, if necessary, is laid down as one of the first and greatest of the Commandments'.[8] One in three Haileybury boys entering the school between 1905 and 1912 died in the war. There were 447 lost from Uppingham, whose alumni could easily have formed a 'pals' side at Park and make up fully a quarter of its roll call of dead. Its headmaster, lacking prescience, was a vocal hardliner, pronouncing: 'if a man can't serve his country, he's better dead.'[9] Schoolboys at Charterhouse today know there are as many *in statu pupillari* as names (686) engraved on the walls of its Gilbert Scott-designed memorial chapel. Wellington lost 699 alumni, Dulwich, 518, and Marlborough, 733. These birds of a social and educational feather later flocked together as students at Oxford, Cambridge, Sandhurst and the London teaching hospitals, where most first played for the club which binds their lives and early deaths into this volume.

Many became leaders at an early age: Jimmy Dingle and Nowell Oxland at Durham, Arnold Huckett at St George's Harpenden captained their school. Dozens more led the XV or XI, or both. Invariably their sporting prowess and leadership qualities brought them to the first rank of their school's Officer Training Corps (OTC). In 1804, well before its eponymous football game and Tom Brown, Rugby School formed a volunteer force to repel Bonaparte from Warwickshire. The spoilsports Nelson and Wellington ensured that it was not called into action and public school OTCs only started in earnest in 1860 when Rugby, Rossall, Eton, Harrow, Marlborough and Winchester all begat rifle corps. The Boer War and breathless tales in the *Boys' Own Paper* (like Park, first opened in 1879) and its legion of imitators gave OTCs a major boost. Haldane incorporated them into his Army Reforms from 1908; by 1911, 153 schools had them and 100,000 of some 250,000 officers commissioned in wartime had passed through an OTC.

By 1909 half of Harrow's boys were in the corps, its headmaster urging parents that 'attendance at Camp is a real engagement demanded of them, not a mere school matter, but as a duty to their country'. Objectors at Marlborough, noted poet Charles Sorley, were barely tolerated and 'inevitably come in for a certain amount of chaff as mere civilians'. By June 1914, Westminster was even more emphatic: 'it is the duty of every able-bodied cadet to consider seriously whether he cannot give up a small part of the holidays to maintaining the honour of the School, even at some slight personal inconvenience.'[10] Many boys continued after school, enlisting at university OTCs or in pre-war military, sporting and social 'gentlemen's clubs' like the Inns of Court, Artists' Rifles or London Rifle Brigade on Bunhill Row, which charged a guinea subscription.

The bolt of war hardly strikes out of the cloudless blue of August 1914; there had already been a decade of fevered speculation in parliament, the press, theatre and popular fiction. However, outside the small, well-trained regular army and in the absence of conscription, the best prepared to fight this war were those who had long been schooled for it. Vera Brittain, writing fifty years after the war that buried both her fiancé and brother, still hears an abiding echo:

> … of a boy's laughing voice on a school playing field in the golden summer. And gradually the voice becomes one of many; the sound of the Uppingham school choir marching up the chapel for the Speech day service in July 1914, and singing the Commemoration hymn … there was a thrilling, a poignant quality in those boys' voices, as though they were singing their own requiem – as indeed many of them were.[11]

Their names, picked out in gold leaf for scholarships, team captaincies and school prizes on mahogany boards, appear but a few years later carved on chapel walls or crosses on village greens. Just as poignant are the boys in their thousands who won no distinction at school, but are honoured on their war memorials.

At these highly competitive schools, alumni in wartime service were garlanded with acclaim, much as prestigious university entrants are today. Many used precious time on leave to visit the institution they had only just left and which still dominated their social circle. But these triumphal returns soon diminished. The school magazine edged in black its lengthening lists of names under the heading 'Pro Patria' yet lauded its fallen champions, thereby guaranteeing a succession of classmates moving swiftly from sixth form into uniform, through the trenches and into communal or unmarked graves.

In October 1915, Westminster proclaimed 930 Old Boys serving or already killed and swelled with satisfaction: 'It is a record of
which we may be justly proud, for it should be remembered that
Westminster, which has contributed more than three times its own
size, is the smallest of the great Public Schools, and that not more
than about eighty Old Westminsters were in the Regular Army
when war was declared.'[12] Editors' sentiments and language were
identical wherever public school values flourished, from English
shire to rural New South Wales. George Llewellyn Davies, nephew
of Guy du Maurier (and model for Peter Pan), was swiftly ushered
into a king's commission on the strength of his knock of 59 in the
Eton *v*. Harrow cricket game at Lords three years earlier, recalled in
admiration by the recruiting colonel at his interview. These lost boys
might also have heard Wendy's words: 'Dear boys, I feel that I have a
message for you from your real mothers, and it is this, "We hope our
sons will die like English gentlemen".'

In the dubious judgement of the War Office, these youngsters
had the right family and school background, strength of character
and sufficient OTC experience to lead men to war. Those without
the privilege of public school education faced a barrier. Kingston
Grammar School product R.C. Sherriff wrote later of his first
encounter with the recruiting office:

> An officer, I realised, had to be a bit above the others, but I had
> a sound education at the grammar school and could speak good
> English. I had had some experience of responsibility. I had been
> captain of games at school. I was fit and strong. I was surely one of
> the 'suitable young men' they were calling for.[13]

However, the future author of *Journey's End* was rejected, an experience which surely tinged his portrayal of Raleigh and Stanhope.
Pragmatism and the butcher's bill soon overwhelmed class prejudice; the events in France that he dramatised in his 1929 Savoy
Theatre hit meant he did not have to wait long for his commission. Conversely, many of the predestined 'officer class' were less
fussed about status and only too happy to join the ranks in their
haste to reach the front.

Britain's regular army was some 250,000 strong at the outbreak of war. Tiny by conscripted European standards (4 million Frenchmen and 5 million Germans), it was further weakened for a continental war by one battalion in each regiment being stationed overseas to guard the outposts of the furthest-flung empire the world had seen. South African war veterans like Lord Roberts had ardently lobbied for National Service, but to no avail. The Army Reserve – men who had served time with the colours and could be recalled in time of war – numbered some 213,000 former officers and soldiers of varying ages, many without experience of fighting. The part-time Territorial Force, established by Haldane, was viewed with suspicion by some, notably Lord Kitchener: they were 'Saturday soldiers' who had signed up for home defence only, with a clause that specifically precluded them being posted abroad, and were thought unreliable when the chips were down.

Many Park players had joined a Territorial regiment in readiness for hostilities that were, in most minds, simply a matter of 'when', not 'if'. Other ranks had more straightforward motivations. The 10/London (Kensington) Battalion was packed with men from grand department stores like Derry & Toms and Barkers; the regiment was a social extension of their workplace and the only means to weekend camps and paid annual holiday. Most 'Terriers' volunteered for service overseas in 1914, but not all; while Robert Dale's 1/9 Manchesters fought, the 2/9 stayed at home in training, until conscription took away any choice. Few who opted for active service received the full six months of training they were promised.

In England's July sunshine, a shadow fell across Territorial, OTC and corps summer camps, as regular army instructors and cooks suddenly departed. Newspaper headlines cast doubt over a 1914/15 rugby season; many players, itching to get into training, wasted no time in joining up for the new adventure – many Parkite applications were signed in the early days of August. There was real fear that the affair would be over before they reached the front; God had matched them with this short hour and they were dashed if they were going to miss it.

On 7 August, Lord Kitchener pointed his finger from that celebrated poster and called for men aged 19–30 to join up. These would be the 'First Hundred Thousand' (or K1) of the million men he envisaged being needed for 'three years or the duration of the war' in his New Army, quickly known as Kitchener's Army. Innocent boys in their teens and indignant men over 30 tried to lie their way in, many with facile success as the recruiting sergeant made another easy shilling. His lordship had his million by the end of 1914 – 1,186,375 to be precise – with over a million more in 1915. In London they flocked to recruiting stations from Dukes Road to Lincoln's Inn Fields, while some travelled from distant shores to answer the call. After his last Park game in March against Royal Naval College Osborne, Charles Vaughan had shipped out to Colombia to work on his father's cattle and tobacco estates. Hardly had he arrived than he did an abrupt about-face on to the river steamer from Honda to Baranquilla, starting the long voyage back to take up his post in the Reserve in October.

Such wildly successful recruiting brought immediate problems: there were more men than uniforms, equipment or guns. New Army battalions wore civilian clothes, or the embarrassing early dress of bright blue, with broom-handles and pitchforks at the slope. Officers for these ramshackle ranks were in even shorter supply. Indian army men home on leave, like Major Jonathan Bruce, did not return to their experienced battalions, but were requisitioned for novice units. Retired officers in their forties, like Alec Todd, returned to the colours. Students and schoolboys swapped one uniform for another.

Some older chaps, 'between thirty and thirty-five, absolutely fit and game for active service', wrote to *The Times* on 26 August, demanding an elite contingent be established entirely from public school and university-educated men. They met at Claridges (where else?) to draw up their proposal to the War Office, being 'anxious to serve their country, but at the same time somewhat chary of joining the regular army with the ordinary run of recruits'. The University & Public Schools (UPS) Battalion protested that:

There is no trace of snobbishness. Everyone accepts he is merely a 'Tommy Atkins' and is proud to be one. The reason for forming battalions of ourselves is *esprit de corps*. Every man will remember his old school, and do his utmost to keep it level with the others in this undertaking.[14]

Nonetheless this war was as much about upholding the honour of the schools as king and country – and those fellows from St Cakes couldn't be allowed to steal a march.

Certainly the army had a familiar feel for many former public schoolboys. Sassoon's alter ego, Sherston, found that being in the army was very much like being back at school. Charles Sorley, another Marlburian and angry critic of war from the outset, remarked that his Suffolk regimental colours matched his school house's. Absurd rules, ill-fitting uniforms with discreet badges of status, harsh discipline and compulsory exercise were nothing new; even the food harped back to the refectory. Many ex-schoolboys were delighted to be back in a regime where individuality was suppressed in favour of conformity and where routine duties banished the uncomfortable freedoms of adulthood. Rifleman Jack Bodenham positively enjoyed the refuge from responsibility afforded by private soldiering in the ranks – his diary shows him perfectly content as 'one of the lads'. But the great majority willingly took a commission in His Majesty's army, happy to be prefects once again.

Sherriff, who initially resented the public school exclusion zone, was eventually magnanimous. The testimony of one who was at the Somme and Ypres and won the Military Cross is worth that of many latter-day armchair historians and academics. He judged that:

> … most of the generals had been public schoolboys before they went to military academies. They knew from firsthand experience that a public school gave something to its boys that had the ingredients of leadership … Pride in their schools would easily translate into pride for a regiment. Above all without conceit or snobbery, they were conscious of a personal superiority that placed on their shoulders an obligation towards those less privileged than themselves. All this, together with the ability to speak good English, carried the public schoolboy a considerable way towards the ideals that the generals aimed at for good officers.[15]

In his view, it was the line officers' achievement to sustain a fighting force that would soak up punishment for four whole years until the weakened opponent was too exhausted and demoralised to carry on.

Ranker Alfred Burrage concurred in his memoir: 'I who was a Private, and a bad one at that, freely own that it was the British subaltern who won the war.'[16] As nervous conscripts young and old latterly replaced volunteers in their prime who had been obliterated, damaged or driven mad in the first two years, these officers' humane compassion and sense of responsibility led them to take care of the men in their charge.[17]

British officers averted the widespread mutinies that almost derailed the French Army in 1917, saw Italian mass desertions after Caporetto and the catastrophic collapse in German morale of 1918 'by keeping the men good-humoured and obedient in the face of their interminable ill treatment and well-nigh insufferable ordeals'. The headmaster of Cheltenham College went further: 'They have led them like faithful and good shepherds, caring for their souls and bodies, tending them, helping them and laying down their lives for them. They have loved their men and their men have loved them.'[18]

Companionship, fatalism, tobacco and the rum ration played supporting parts. Individuals had bitter personal experiences, of which they later wrote vividly, but the morale of the team – from platoon to division – remained steady and resilient, apart from an isolated late wobble at Étaples base camp. Sherriff and du Maurier agreed that these officers 'led them, not through military skill, for no military skill was needed':

> They led them from personal example, from their reserves of patience and good humour. They won the trust and respect of their men, not merely through the willingness to share the physical privations, but through an understanding of their spiritual loneliness. Many of the younger ones had never been away from home before.

Like Stanhope these were the team players, 'always up in the front-line with the men, cheering them on with jokes, and making them keen about things, like he did the kids at school',[19] even if it was in low murmurs through clenched teeth. Their commissions may have been temporary, but they carried them out with abiding durability. Finally the hour was theirs, in understated British fashion: 'through their patience and courage and endurance [they] carried the Army to victory after the generals had brought it within a hairsbreadth of defeat.' Sherriff concluded of these young men: 'The common soldier liked them because they were "young swells", and with few exceptions the young swells delivered the goods.'

After all, they had new junior boys to keep in line, new teams to captain, new games to win. They did not yet know about the 'hell where youth and laughter go'.[20]

CHARLES GEORGE GORDON BAYLY
THE FIRST OF THE GANG

Charles George Gordon Bayly, in Royal Engineers uniform. *(Royal Aero Club)*

In St Paul's Cathedral, a boy of 15 pauses before the marble figure of a soldier, laid at rest like a medieval knight. He knows this monument is hollow, empty of its corpse; he gazes in disbelief that this great hero of empire should be his relative, although he has spent his youthful life in the daunting certainty.

The boy stands on the verge of manhood; a distinguished scholar at a famous school, an all-round sportsman with colours in rugby and cricket, and newly enlisted in the Cadet Corps. He is also popular, according to an obituary which the school magazine will print only eight years hence: his 'pleasant temper and fine character made him a general favourite'. His is the first of 500 such notices published by St Paul's school.

Today his schoolmates are restive after the underground railway journey that has brought them from their terracotta temple of learning in West Kensington to the great domed cathedral that gave its name to the school. The boys nudge and jostle and exchange knowing looks, daring each other to rib their solemn friend, lost in his reverie. Sensing their amusement, he pulls back his shoulders, lifts his chin and stiffens to attention. His companions hush in shame and sidle away, leaving him alone to muse upon his own destiny.

Charles George Gordon Bayly was born to be a soldier. Named after his famed great-uncle, General Charles George Gordon, he was perhaps equally destined to die a soldier, as his 'Eminent Victorian' ancestor had famously done at Khartoum. His military breeding was as impeccable as the naming instincts of his family: one grandfather was Major Neville Saltren Keats Bayly of the Royal Artillery, the other Colonel William Jesser Coope of the 57th Regiment. Their valises were much travelled; the recruiting slogan 'Join the Army, see the world' never rang so true as in the Victorian era.

Both officers fought in the Crimean War and the Indian Mutiny. Coope then served with the Red Cross in the Russo-Turkish War of 1878, when he was taken prisoner at the fall of Plevna, being at that time an officer in the Imperial Ottoman Gendarmerie – he was suitably honoured with exotic Turkish decorations. Not content with his globe-trotting campaigning, he volunteered in 1899 for a three-year stint in the South African war. There he added the King's and Queen's Medals to the assortment of ribbons on his chest.

Major Bayly, wounded at Aden, married the sister of General Gordon. His son, Charles' father, Brackenbury, an electrical engineer by training, joined the Cape Civil Service. Unable to resist the familial martial urge, he saw service as a civilian under the military authorities in the Zulu War of 1879, and the Tembu campaign of 1881 to annex the territory of a clan whose most famous future son would be Nelson Mandela. After these military exploits, the civil servant Brackenbury could stand tall within his family of professional soldiers and proudly wear the Zulu War and General Service medals, both with clasp.

Meanwhile at the other end of Africa, in the Sudan, Great-Uncle Charles was having his celebrated spot of bother with the fanatical Muslim leader, the Mahdi Mohammed Ahmed. Gordon had been Governor General of the Sudan in the 1870s, but trouble had brewed since and two British expeditions had been defeated. Unwisely dispatched by Gladstone to conduct an orderly withdrawal (not in his nature), the stubborn Gordon broke his orders and stayed bottled up in Khartoum. This ultimately resulted in his death and decapitation, two days (and at least several inches) short of his fifty-second birth-day in 1885. A relief column of the Camel Corps would finally reach the besieged city that very day, but too late to save him, or indeed to recover either missing head or body.

General Gordon was Queen Victoria's favourite soldier and was widely mourned throughout the empire, from Windsor to Sydney. Gordon Boys Clubs sprang up all over Britain; Gloucester's Gordon League rugby club, founded in 1888, is still scrummaging strongly today. When young Charles was born at Rondebosch, Cape Colony, on 30 May 1891, he was named in memory of the martyred hero. He shared the honour with a school near Woking, a Gravesend prom-enade, several Australian parks, colleges and suburbs from Brisbane to Geelong, and a square in Gordon's Woolwich birthplace. Beatrice Mary, mother of the infant Charles, presumably felt a great sense of maternal achievement if she kept him out of uniform past his second birthday.

A Christian evangelist, Gordon held profound but eccentric views (one being that the Earth was inside a hollow sphere with God's throne directly above the altar of the temple in Jerusalem) and was a firm believer in reincarnation. In 1877, he wrote in a letter: 'I have little doubt of our having pre-existed; and that also in the time of our pre-existence we were actively employed. So, therefore, I believe in our active employment in a future life, and I like the thought.' This would certainly come in handy for an ascetic bach-elor missing an earthly body. Charles George Gordon Bayly, if not his great-uncle's reincarnation (as far as we are ever likely to know), would find himself on many occasions treading in the footsteps of his renowned ancestor – or, more accurately, standing in his shadow.

After the reconquest of the Sudan in 1898 by Field Marshal Horatio Herbert (subsequently ennobled as) Kitchener of Khartoum, several attempts were made to locate Gordon's remains, all in vain. Denied the chance of a proper funeral with full military honours, the Victorian myth-making machine had already swung into action on its own monumental expression of national grief, in a manner that would have impressed even the ancient Egyptian masters. By the time young Charles arrived in England from Cape Colony to attend first St Edmunds, Hindhead, and then St Paul's school, he could hardly turn a corner in London without being confronted by Great-Uncle Charles, immortalised in landmark effigy of stone or bronze. There were statues of Gordon to be found in all the great spaces at the heart of empire: Trafalgar Square, Westminster Abbey and St Paul's Cathedral, where the teenage Bayly would stand before his gloomy memorial. No pressure there, then, for a young man in a new country.

Away from his vacant sepulchre at the cathedral, General Gordon was suitably upright and commanding in Trafalgar Square, outdoor home of national heroes, before moving south in 1943. He now ponders the Victoria Embankment by the Ministry of Defence, supported by female figures of Fortitude and Faith, Charity and Justice. Sculpted in bronze by Sir William Thornycroft (uncle of Siegfried Sassoon), he stands in contemplative pose, his foot resting on a shattered gun barrel, wondering at the memorial to the Royal Air Force (no such thing in his day) and utterly bemused by the London Eye on the far riverbank. In the everyday jacket and long boots of a patrol officer, his chin is sunk in his right hand. The left clasps a pocket Bible and tucked beneath his arm is the short cane known, during his campaign leading the Chinese emperor's 'Ever Victorious Army', as his wand of victory. We see a cerebral soldier, not a gung-ho warrior (or driven megalomaniac). Wreaths are still laid there by the many institutions that bear his name.

Not to be outdone, Gordon's own corps, the Royal Engineers, also commissioned a statue of the hero general, this time astride a camel. It was exhibited at the Royal Academy in 1890 and then erected in Brompton Barracks, Chatham, home of the Royal School of Military Engineering, where it still stands. A second casting was erected at the junction of St Martin's Lane and Charing Cross Road in London's West End. At least Charles did not have to face this reminder of his family heritage: in 1903 it was moved to Khartoum, where it stood at the intersection of Gordon and Victoria Avenues, just south of the new palace built in 1899. After Sudanese independence in 1956, the well-travelled bronze returned to stand in the Gordon school grounds near Woking.

Charles was not tall but did outgrow his surprisingly diminutive relative, who was only 5ft 5in head to toe, even before his violent abbreviation. The young boy was toughened by sport: he first boxed for Botting's House at the weight of '6 Stone or Under (84 lbs), and beat TH Solomon of Mathew's with his good left, keeping going well'.[1] In Cape Town, he briefly attended Diocesan College, the nursery of South African rugby; the myrtle green of its Old Boys jersey was borrowed by the national team in their first victory over the British at Newlands in 1896. The lucky colour was then permanently adopted by the Springboks, a nickname hastily chosen to avoid being known, All Blacks-style, as the 'Myrtles' after the shirt. At St Paul's, playing on the spectacular 'Big Side' pitch, Charles grew into a pocket halfback for the XV who 'made very good openings; made the most of his pace. A fair collar, but could not stop a rush effectively.'[2] On leaving school he would play in the same position for Rosslyn Park.

His debut for Park was against Guy's Hospital on 8 January 1910. He was 19 years old, compact and wiry; he partnered the 23-year-old Wilfred Jesson at halfback. In this era there was no defined scrum-half or fly-half, but two halfbacks operating behind the forwards as play dictated, although one of the two would often decide to stand a little away from the scrum, hence 'stand-off half'. In the team photograph the two sit cross-legged and solemn at the front, boys among men, Bayly with the merest hint of upper-lip fluff. He stares at the lens, open-faced and optimistic, with no sense of the fate that awaits him three years later.

Five of Bayly's teammates would die by 1917: Jesson, a first-class cricketer for Hampshire, in Mesopotamia; another halfback partner, Australian Syd Burdekin, missing at Loos and never found; centre Denis Monaghan would lose his head commanding his tank section at Cambrai; forward Frank Purser would fight on the same battlefield and perish a month later at Villers-Pluich; and the tall, moustachioed lock-forward Noel Houghton would command the 16/Sherwood Foresters until his death at Ypres. Facing them for the 'medicoes' was Owen Parry-Jones, known as 'P.J.' and 'possessed of a very fine baritone voice',[3] who would bring his talents to Park when Hospital duty allowed. He would die of wounds received outside his own Royal Army Medical Corps (RAMC) Advance Aid Post in the third month of fighting at the Somme in 1916. Their war lasted as long as three years; Charles Bayly, by contrast, would not survive even three weeks.

Bayly's years at St Paul's from 1905 to 1909 were successful in every field: a senior scholar, winning both football and cricket colours, he rose to sergeant in the corps, taking his Certificate A, the first step to a regular commission. He won the shooting cup for his house in his final year and gained the School Exhibition award to the Royal Military Academy. In so doing he followed the example set by General Gordon himself, who had graduated from the RMA in his home town of Woolwich some sixty years previously. Rugby football at the academy was put on hold when Charles broke his wrist during his first season, although this did not stop him from getting his Rifleman's Certificate. Denied the oval ball in his hands, he excelled in non-contact athletics and won several prizes including the intriguingly named swimming obstacle race. He was also one of a dozen selected to compete for the prize saddle awarded to the best rider amongst the cadets.

The next step on the inexorable path set by heredity was naturally enough a commission with Gordon's Royal Engineers. Bayly passed seventh out of RMA Woolwich; in August 1911, as Gordon had been in 1852, he was gazetted second lieutenant. At Chatham's School of Military Engineering, he completed his training in the shadow of the camel-borne statue of his relative. His sporting prowess won him football colours for the Engineers, as well as a place on their cricket team. The young sporty officer who was effortlessly collecting distinctions in every pursuit to which he turned his hand could be the model for the improbably talented fictional heroes of G.A. Henty (25 million books sold) or Herbert Strang.

It was at Chatham, however, that Charles rose above the earthly path trodden by his forebear when he decided to learn to fly. The joys of powered flight had not been available to Gordon of Khartoum, as the American Wright brothers had been inconsiderate enough to delay their invention until 1903. It was still a brave pioneer who, ten years later, ventured into the air in flimsy frames of ash held together by wire and doped canvas. Lack of stature was an advantage when every pound of weight counted – hulking forwards need not apply. The driven Bayly lost no time in adding a new string to his bow of burnished gold, one that would fascinate both the soldier and engineer in him. Nor did he spare any expense, as flying qualifications had to be achieved at civilian schools with lessons entirely at the novice's cost until 1915. A statutory £75 was reimbursed on joining the Royal Flying Corps (RFC).

Flying offered Charles the chance to make a distinctive mark in the army, and to go one step beyond his illustrious namesake. It would indeed give him a place in history, if not exactly the one he coveted. He passed the test for his Pilot's Certificate in a Caudron biplane at the Ewen school, Hendon Aerodrome, in March 1913. After reaching an altitude of 400ft – a dizzy height at the time – and showing an ability to land safely again (always beneficial to a pilot's career), he received his Aero Club Aviator's Certificate, Number 441. He was now indisputably a Magnificent Man in a Flying Machine. His sister Beatrice also discovered her own passion for piloting, in the handsome form of his Woolwich Royal Engineer friend, Lanoe Hawker who qualified just six places ahead of Charles. Hawker became the first British 'ace', winning the VC before falling victim to Baron von Richtofen in 1916.

By summer, the newly promoted Lieutenant Bayly was posted to the 56th Field Company stationed at Bulford Camp on Salisbury Plain. His sporting pursuits in the Wiltshire countryside were very much of the 'field' variety: he rode in the Royal Artillery Harriers' Point-to-Point Light Weight Hunt Cup and placed second. Here at least he could be confident that no statues of General Gordon lurked behind the haystacks.

Bayly, father and son, were men of a modern age. Engineering knowledge from his father (Member of the Institute of Electrical Engineers), from Chatham and his aviator's training made Charles the perfect candidate for the new Flying Corps, formed from the Air Battalion of the Royal Engineers in 1912, and still firmly part of the army. Its application form made specific enquiry of electrical or mechanical engineering experience. Charles' scholarly mind was fascinated by the new-fangled idea of wireless telegraphy from aeroplanes. This was a science in its highly experimental infancy, in an aviation field that had itself only just reached early adolescence, but would soon be forcibly matured by experience over the trenches of Belgium and France. In May 1914, as the storm clouds of war gathered far beyond the Wiltshire horizon, he polished his aviation skills at the Central Flying School at Upavon on Salisbury Plain and talked of telegraphy and strut-wire tension in the mock Tudor-style officers' mess.

This was a superb summer for flying aeroplanes. The sportsman Bayly took his point-to-point talents into the blue heavens above the rolling farmland, wheeling and soaring closer to God in this new miracle of man's creation. As at St Paul's, Woolwich and Chatham, he excelled: his confidential report declared him 'very good indeed as a pilot and his capabilities as an officer being above the average', and added special praise for 'a very keen officer with plenty of initiative'. Major Trenchard, the disciplinarian second-in-command and future head of the corps, known as 'Boom' from his manner of speaking, expected all officers including himself to have a detailed grasp of the academic science of aeronautics. The 23-year-old Charles was quickly turning into a chip off the old Gordon marble block. Would the coming conflict bring him his own extensive collection of personal statuary?

That summer Archduke Franz Ferdinand stopped his fateful bullet in Sarajevo, and the Central Powers careered into war. On 4 August Britain declared war on Germany and Lord Grey, watching the gas streetlights being doused in Westminster, observed that 'the lamps have gone out all over Europe'. A life was extinguished in the Bayly household too, as Brackenbury died that same inauspicious day. His son had little time for grieving: as the Schlieffen Plan swung into action with Prussian precision, Lieutenant Bayly joined 5 Squadron RFC. The full array of squadrons could be counted on one hand and was now gathered at a new aerodrome at Netheravon; he had only a week to prepare for his flight to France on 12 August. The young RFC pilots were excited and eager to prove themselves, although their precise wartime role was not yet clear. Most important was to get into the fight before it was finished: British pundits were predicting peace by Christmas while the Kaiser told his Prussian Guard that they would be home before the leaves turned.

Bayly flew his machine from Dover to Amiens in France, and then onwards to Maubeuge, a key fortified town and railway centre near the Belgian border, hard by Marlborough's old battlefield of Malplaquet. This was no sudden choice: eight years ago, in the wake of the *entente cordiale*, the British and French military staff had agreed Maubeuge as the assembly point for an Expeditionary Force of 100,000 British troops sent to combat any invasion of neutral Belgium.

With half its regular battalions scattered throughout the empire, Britain could not make good its promise in August, but the eager RFC showed willing, despite scepticism on high. The cavalry officer Douglas Haig told a meeting that summer: 'I hope none of you gentlemen is so foolish as to think that aeroplanes will be able to be usefully employed for reconnaissance in the air.' By 1915, when General Trenchard took command, they were playing a vital part, but the average life expectancy of a new RFC pilot arriving in France was just seventeen days. For the first and last time in his life, Charles Bayly would post a score well below average.

Thrust into the war ahead of the land Expeditionary Force rushing by sea, train and route march, the RFC swiftly mobilised some 860 officers and men at Maubeuge with all twenty of its remaining planes – two from 5 Squadron had crashed en route – but was already frantically improvising with its manpower and machines. The baggage train of lorries hastily assembled in Regent's Park included one bright scarlet commercial vehicle from a sauce manufacturer, which was handily visible from the air.

As British forces hurried across France, civilians reported that German troops in large numbers were advancing through Brussels south-west towards Mons, 30 miles away. The RFC was tasked to confirm rumour by observation. At 10.16 a.m. on 22 August, Lieutenant Bayly took off from Maubeuge in Avro 504 No. 390 flying as observer, with Second Lieutenant Vincent Waterfall, another keen sportsman formerly of the East Yorkshires, as his pilot. The rule that two pilots must not fly together had already been overridden by the need for qualified observers. Their mission was to reconnoitre an advancing German infantry column near Enghien. Their all-wooden biplane, its curious skid protecting the propeller on landing if the tail was too high (a common novice error), was the familiar training workhorse from Upavon. The stable aircraft would train pilots for decades, but would soon be obsolete for active front-line duty.

To the observer fell the duty of defence. At best, he would have carried a carbine, shotgun or Colt Browning revolver, or made do with a flare pistol; the first Lewis gun would not be mounted on an Avro until October. However, at this early stage of the war, armed only with a keen pair of eyes, Bayly's hands gripped his binoculars as firmly as they had a rugby ball at the put-in. Tales abound of this new airborne fraternity saluting each other with courteous waves, before graduating to vigorous shaking of the fist, lobbing of bricks and then small arms fire. Throughout the war most missions were flown not for bombing or combat but for reconnaissance and artillery observation. The advent of mounted machine guns gave these sitting ducks some chance to fight back, but reconnaissance casualties were still high, furnishing over half of ace von Richtofen's eighty victims. Aerial dogfights captured the public imagination but the reality of wartime aviation was far more pragmatic.

In August, however, the threat was not yet in the air but from the ground. Until the 'target' roundel was added to the underside of wings in October (reversing the French order of colours) fire often came from friendly troops, unsure of who was above their heads. In these first days of flying bravado, recalled RFC intelligence officer Maurice Baring:

> … warfare in the air was still in the gentleman-like stage, and I have a note in my diary under September 15th, 1914 that No. 5 Squadron call the anti-aircraft gun (there seemed to be only one which gave them trouble in those days) Archibald, from the song '*Archibald, certainly not*' [by music-hall entertainer George Robey]. This was the origin of the word *archie* which was soon to be adopted by the British Army [as slang for all anti-aircraft guns] and to pass into the language.[4]

Pilots in high spirits reportedly sang the song as they careered through the smoke puffs of exploding shells.

The humourless Archibald did not take to his nickname and clearly had it in for Bayly's disrespectful 5 Squadron. Flying at 2,000ft, Avro No. 390 was first fired upon ineffectually by an infantry column and then downed by cannon fire over the German lines.

The two airmen flew over the Enghien-Soignies area at around 10.50 a.m., making a very low pass at just over 20m, taking the Germans by surprise so that they failed to fire a single shot at such an easy target, flying low and slow. The plane banked and returned towards one of the columns; the reception was ready this time. The Avro crashed by the roadside.

At a time when untrained anti-aircraft fire was more beginners' luck than judgement, the gunners must have been dumbfounded by their kill. The excited German infantry of the 12th Grenadiers were quick to claim the credit for themselves. Their captain, novelist Walter Bloem, wrote:

> We were crossing Enghien, going along a never-ending park wall … suddenly a plane flew over us … I ordered the two groups to fire at it … the plane started a half-turn … but it was too late: it went into a dive, spun around several times then fell like a stone about a mile from here.[5]

Bayly and Waterfall had no choice but to go down with their ship. Parachutes were not worn: the Air Board saw them as un-British and likely to undermine the crew's fighting spirit and desire to stay with their machine 'which might otherwise be capable of returning to base for repair'. The two men died on impact in a mess of splintered wood and propeller blades. There was little wreckage left after burning fuel incinerated the doped canvas and ash frame. A grisly photograph shows curious German soldiers keeping a respectful distance from two charred corpses – the fallen fliers they called 'Black Angels'.

Hector Durand, then a 14-year-old boy, guarding his grain cart from pilfering invaders, witnessed the crash at close hand, throwing himself beneath his wagon for safety. What struck him most was that throughout the plane's fatal descent he could clearly see the airmen's heads.[6] Waterfall and Bayly were unlucky. A fellow squadron officer described his own better fortune and Bayly's (anonymous) fate to *The Times* a few weeks later:

> We were shelled and shot at about 100 times, but only 13 shots went through the planes, and fortunately neither of us was

touched. Under fire it is loathly to go up as passenger. The corps has been very lucky, losing only one pilot (Waterfall) and his passenger to date. We have been shot at and shelled by friend and enemy every time we have been up.[7]

For the German commander, von Kluck, the wrecked Avro behind his lines and the bodies of two aviators in flying tunics with the winged RFC badge gave the first sure proof that British troops were present on the continent of Europe. As Germany's armies wheeled on their way to Paris, instead of open space beyond the French Army, they found the trained regulars of the British Expeditionary Force (BEF). Those hesitant soldiers at Marcq-Lez-Enghien who found the broken and burnt bodies of Waterfall and Bayly were unsure what to do with their first dead foe. They doffed their caps, fired a volley in salute over the smoking wreckage and hastily covered them with a scant 4in of soil. The local Belgians placed flowers on the mounds out of respect for those who had flown to rescue them from invasion. The local landowner, M. Louviau, later exhumed the corpses and placed them in zinc coffins, hidden in his distillery cellar to await a decent burial.

New York Tribune correspondent Richard Harding Davis recorded the place in a letter to a British newspaper. He was unable to identify the pilot, but gave very precise co-ordinates of the location:

Sir, Last week in Belgium I saw a wrecked British aeroplane and beside it the grave of the aviator. At the time I was prisoner with the Germans, and could not stop or ask questions … Should after the war the family of the officer desire to remove the body I am writing this that they should know where it is now buried … on a twisted plate I found the words 'Avro Manufacturing Company, Manchester, England'. At the head of the grave the Germans had put a wooden cross on which they had written 'Herr Flier, 22nd August 1914' … it should not be difficult to find. It is on the left hand side of the road as one walks from Enghien to Ath in a pear orchard, near a very old brick house with a square tower.[8]

Many families would never receive any such comfort. In this compassionate letter, Harding's presumption is that 'after the war' would surely not be long and that individual deaths were noteworthy. Very soon the army's insufficient 'clerk power' would struggle to record the slaughtered in their overwhelming thousands.

Bayly's reconnaissance report, unfinished and fatally interrupted, was picked up near the crash site by Belgian peasants, who hid it before smuggling the papers through the German lines to the Military Governor of East Flanders. His last words, scrawled at 11.00 a.m., note: 'cavalry, 4 columns infantry, other group of horses and column turning left to Silly.' By the time the report reached Command HQ it was of no practical use: the war had moved swiftly on and the retreat from Mons was in full flight. In any case, Field Marshal Sir John French, commanding the BEF had disbelieved RFC reports of advancing forces, until the Battle of Mons proved they were only too accurate. He would later become a great supporter, describing the RFC as of 'incalculable value' and writing in his dispatch from Ypres: 'I feel sure that no effort should be spared to increase their numbers and perfect their equipment and efficiency.'[9] It was one of many points of disagreement with Haig.

On this very same August day that Charles Bayly crashed to his death from the sky, another man beating out a fateful sound made lasting history. Outside Mons, Corporal Edward Thomas, a drummer in the Royal Irish Dragoon Guards, was the first British soldier to fire his rifle at the Germans. The last shot in 1918, after four years of bloody struggle, would be fired only 50 yards away – pure coincidence but an ironic comment on a Western Front congealed in futile stagnation. The two points almost opposite each other are now marked by bronze plaques. After his famed first shot, Thomas would fight through the war, winning the Military Medal and – a more exceptional achievement over four years – would survive, to become a cinema commissionaire. He fought as a cavalryman in an ancient regiment, and fired his rifle from his horse; Bayly was an aviator in an untried machine in a fledgling air force. By 1918 this Great War would transform the order of battle.

Charles George Gordon Bayly of the famous name has his own uncelebrated place in history: he can claim the doubtful honour of flying in the first British aeroplane to be shot down by enemy fire. But there is more. Britain had already taken casualties in other ranks:

the first in wartime, Private Joseph Viles, knocked off his bicycle in Bristol on the very first day and sailors of HMS *Amphion* killed by a mine on 6 August. The first two airmen, friends in Bayly's 5 Squadron, were killed in an accident as they took off from Netheravon on an Inglorious Twelfth. Private Bai of the Gold Coast Regiment died in Africa on 15 August. Another cyclist, Private John Parr, was the first soldier to die by enemy fire on the Western Front – by 21 August two wings were statistically as dangerous as two wheels. Lieutenants Bayly and Waterfall, therefore, were the first British Army officers to die in action in the Great War, noted in de Ruvigny[10] but largely overlooked in histories since. Their Saturday morning flight to destruction narrowly preceded the death of Royal Scots Lieutenant George Thompson on the same day in far-off Togoland, West Africa.

This was already a war like no other: on this August day alone, 27,000 Frenchmen were slaughtered. Bayly was the first player from Rosslyn Park to die in the Great War, his body broken and burned before Britain formally joined battle on the ground. There would be many more. Within a month, forward and career soldier Lt Basil Ash of the Sherwood Foresters was cut down by deadly machine guns on the Aisne. Another four club-mates – Bruce, Costin, Moore and Walker – would not survive 1914, as Britain's regular army officers took the brunt. Charles Bayly still lies in Belgian soil, his formal grave next to his fellow pilot, Waterfall, in Tournai Communal Cemetery since 1924.

He has no statue.

GUY DU MAURIER
THE ACCIDENTAL PLAYWRIGHT

Guy du Maurier in 1912. *(Great Ormond Street Hospital Children's Charity)*

The slaughter of young subalterns is a poignant tale but not the whole story. Also among those who rushed from club to colours in 1914 were senior men, long retired from the rugby field and even from military service, who heeded the bugle call and returned to fight. Lifetime soldiers saw an opportunity for one last hurrah before being put out to pasture in the Shires; some saw only Elysian Fields. Guy Louis Busson du Maurier DSO, veteran of Burma and South Africa, led his Royal Fusilier battalion to war and died aged 49 near Ypres in 1915. He is 'Father of the House' and the senior officer of this history.

Guy du Maurier joined Rosslyn Park Football Club in 1881, only two years after its founding, when it was little more than a group of friends playing winter rugby to tide them over until the cricket season. They leased a farmer's field at Gospel Oak. Guy was just 16 and played halfback. He came from a celebrated artistic family: his father George was an illustrator, despite the handicap of one blind eye, and later novelist creator of Trilby and Svengali. While still a struggling young cartoonist for *Punch* living in Belgium he writes to his 'dear Mamma' on 13 May 1865, announcing the arrival of the future rugby player:

> Pern [his pet name for wife Emma] was delivered of a boy to-day at 2 o'clock; it has been a terrible labour worse than the first as the child is so enormously large; much larger than Tricksy [sister Beatrix]. She is dreadfully faint and exhausted.[1]

Pern recovers well. Four days later, proud father Kicky (his own pet name derived obscurely from artists' mannequin figures) is able to reassure Mamma:

> Pern's rapid recovery is quite astonishing, considering … that the child is so enormous in size like a child six weeks old. He will be a good-looking fellow; quite a different sort to Tricksy though; I shall be proud of him … Trixy from her hands and feet will be a large and tall woman, like her mother. Guy Louis, in spite of his gigantic proportions will not depass me.

Kicky and Pern would have five children: Beatrix, Guy, Sylvia, Marie-Louise (May) and Gerald. Trixy, who sounds – unthinkably in 1865 – like a fine rugby prospect herself, would later influence her 16-year-old sibling's choice of club. She became engaged to Charles Hoyer Millar, founder and historian of Rosslyn Park, then in North London, where the du Mauriers were then comfortably nestled.

For Guy, being the brother of the founder's fiancée was as good a way as any to win an XV place. Charlie's relationship with Trixy, however, had damaging consequences for his own playing career, as his club history recounted in the third person:

> … missing only six matches in five seasons, he … ceased to be a playing member owing to his marriage in the following summer [1884]. In those days it was exceptional to play after marriage and to be still playing football at about twenty-eight was considered remarkable. He was presented with a carriage clock with a suitable inscription on it.[2]

The clock is lost but rugby readers will speculate on those 'suitable' words (perhaps including 'thumb' and 'under'). Guy's niece, the novelist Daphne, noted that his marrying into the family was done on their terms: 'the mocking critical tolerance of poor Charlie Millar ... suited tribal law.' Hoyer Millar observed that 'the family in general had a rooted dislike to serious topics of any kind, at all events in the presence of each other'. A mining engineer by profession, he would be the straight man in their creative Camelot. His acceptance by the clannish du Mauriers was qualified; Trixy grew tired of him and his first love remained Rosslyn Park.

The exotic family name originated from one Robert Mathurin Busson, a charming fraudster who arrived from France in 1789, on the run from the law. He became 'du Maurier' to endear himself to Englishmen easily charmed by aristocrats escaping the French Revolution. Not only did he fabricate a name, but a matching lineage back to the twelfth century. Daphne later discovered that the Bussons were actually humble glassblowers and 'les Mauriers' merely the farmhouse where Robert was born.[3] Coincidentally, a less charming Czechoslovakian fraudster, who was never all he seemed, also purloined 'du Maurier' as an alias for his clandestine work during the Second World War from his preferred brand of cigarettes, named after Guy's thespian brother Gerald in an innovative licensing deal. He later changed both nationality and name (again) to Robert Maxwell, and embarked on a life of deception on a grander scale.

Guy's father George, born in Paris, was a friend of Millais, Burne-Jones, Whistler and Rossetti. The novelist Henry James turned up every Sunday for lunch at George's New Grove House in Hampstead, the Montmartre of North London. The influence of the du Mauriers' arty set may be seen in the rather camp Park team photograph of 1883: the players pose against a backdrop of heavy theatrical drapes, some seated on a carved settle, others on a fur rug made of several indeterminate animals. Amid a forest of muscled arms folded across manly chests, a fresh-cheeked Guy sits casually at the front, without regulation club socks but in what appears to be early lycra tights – that's Hampstead bohemia for you.

In his pre-celebrity days, George had daringly struck out for a higher rate of pay for his *Punch* cartoons. Successful, he exults in a letter: 'Harrow and Oxford for Master Guy Louis.' In fact, it would be Marlborough and Sandhurst (it is Gerald who goes to Harrow). Guy was the first of many to play for Park while undergoing leadership training at the Royal Military College (now Academy). A photograph shows him solemn in ceremonial uniform, carrying his sword. At the tender age of 17, Guy was already vice-captain and honorary secretary of the Park second XV and sat on the Club Committee – clearly a man destined for exalted and responsible office.

Rugby has always embraced enthusiastic socialising. Before the war the Park secretary:

> conceived the idea of establishing the annual dinners on a higher plane than was then customary for such Club events, partly by arranging them at the best restaurants of the day, partly by having a Guards band play during the proceedings, and in particular by insisting that everyone should wear full evening dress. The result was that the Park dinner became known as the chief Social event of the Rugger season, invitations to which were welcomed and appreciated by all in the highest circles of Rugby Football.[4]

Hampstead, still a village apart from the metropolis, added its own flavour. Of the Park social scene in the 'wild' 1880s, Hoyer Millar wrote:

> In the first five years of the Club most of the members were personal friends. The Hampstead element was a strong factor and in addition to the annual Smoking Concerts, which were always held at the Hollybush Hotel, there were other local functions held there and elsewhere in Hampstead to which many of the London members were invited. Those who were in the City used to make the Lombard Restaurant a meeting place on Wednesdays throughout the year and during the football season the old Gaiety Restaurant served the same purpose on Saturday evenings. The pits of the Comedy Theatre, where dress musical plays were given, and of the Gaiety were favourite places of amusement and when later on the new Pavilion was opened in Piccadilly Circus, the

club played a not inconspicuous part in the inaugural celebrations of the first night.

The du Maurier family graced the annual smokers: Gerald, actor and impresario, 'sang to his own accompaniments at several of our informal suppers, but was never a member of the Club like his eldest brother Guy'.[5] Even father George added a Gallic flavour in 1884 with a programme including two French songs which were 'much to the delight of the audience'. According to the clearly smitten Dorothea Parry, daughter of composer Sir Hubert, famous for his setting of Blake's *Jerusalem*, Guy himself played the piano and sang, 'delicious comic songs in a soft, low voice and accompaniments in the minor keys, made up by himself ... a little dear, one of the cleverest and most delightful human beings. He is like Sylvia and has her crooked mouth which is a great attraction.'

For a rugby club it all sounds too decorous to be true, and even an account of larks after dinner at the Holborn Restaurant records that 'practice games were held round Leicester Square much to the amusement of the police who never interfered and often had kicks at the flying ball, generally Mr Thompson's squash hat. The young men of those days were very joyous often noisy in their nocturnal frolics but never a nuisance or rowdy.' While there will always be exceptions to any rule (mainly Welsh and English internationals today) this spirit of 'acceptable limits' to riotous behaviour in rugby still prevails. Compare the number of police on duty at Twickenham with the average Premiership football game – there is already enough violence on the pitch for most tastes, and the gratuitous spilling of beer is never encouraged.

A Park regular for four years, Guy crossed the whitewash for a last try against Maidstone in 1885, but was then distracted from rugby by an overseas tour with his new employer, Her Majesty the Queen Empress. He was gazetted to the Royal Fusiliers (City of London) Regiment as a lieutenant, and saw service in the Third Burma War of 1886–87, whereby Burma was forcibly annexed to the Raj. In the long haul for peacetime promotion, when frustrated subalterns would toast 'bloody wars and dread disease', he was not made captain until ten years later in 1896. The Boer War in South

Africa happily accelerated his career advancement with command of a mounted infantry battalion, raised from the City of London Yeomanry. As distinct from cavalry, who fought mounted, these units rode to battle and then dismounted to fight with carbines and bayonets. In a very un-English flourish they adopted the nickname of 'Rough Riders' after a volunteer US cavalry regiment in the recent Spanish-American War.

Guy missed the big battles and only arrived in time for 'mopping-up' operations in 1901. He came under fire for the first time ('not the jolliest thing in the world') and command was pressured: 'I'm too highly wrought, and the sense of responsibility is too much developed in me … I think I should enjoy it more as private soldier.'[6] A month later he shot his first Boer, but was more affected by the death of his soldier, Besley; he conducted a gentlemanly truce while the wounded were taken to safety. A picture emerges of a humane professional soldier, not enthusiastic about the 'unpleasant task of war-waging' and the 'Siren Song of the bullet'.[7]

Guy was mentioned in Kitchener's final dispatches[8] alongside names later familiar to every British household over four hard years and notorious in subsequent histories. They include a lieutenant colonel in the 17th Lancers: 'one of the most thoughtful and best educated of our Cavalry Officers in their own rank. He has also shown considerable skill in handling men in the field.' Later verdicts on Douglas Haig would be less complimentary about his military man management. With the privilege of hindsight, this dispatch makes interesting reading, to the accompaniment of hollow laughter. Kitchener, in all innocence, was able to say of the peace settlement with the Boers: 'I feel confident that a new era of complete reconciliation between all races has now dawned in South Africa.' Not even great men can read the future and Kitchener, in the waspish judgement of Margot Asquith, was 'a great poster, but not a great man'.

Guy was promoted, awarded the Queen's Medal with five clasps and DSO: 'Guy Louis Busson du Maurier, Major, The Royal Fusiliers, City of London Regiment, in recognition of services during the operations in South Africa.'[9] Although his reputation as a soldier was made at the age of 37, he was disillusioned. He firmly declares to his mother:

I do not like fighting ... I've thoroughly enjoyed it out here and
I wouldn't have missed it for anything. But I've seen the absolute
rottenness of our system, or rather want of system – and the hopeless amateurishness of the whole profession and I'm convinced it's
no place for a grown-up person.[10]

War had other effects on him, not least in his physical appearance.
His hair reportedly turned white in shock after he witnessed a shell
take the head off the man next to him. There is no such medical
condition, so it may have been exaggeration for dramatic effect –
not unusual in the family.

On his return to England, he discovered (and shared) an under-
current of feeling that the Boer War was less a glorious victory than
a symptom of deep malaise within the British military. He agreed
with his outspoken African leader, Field Marshal Lord Roberts, now
army commander-in-chief, that England's unchallenged prosperity
had made it flabby. Roberts advocated universal military training and
wrote prolifically on the subject of preparedness. In 1905 he told the
House of Commons: 'our armed forces ... are as absolutely unfitted
and unprepared for war as they were in 1899–1900.' However, it was
Guy who would one day find the voice to deliver this message to
the English-speaking world, with unexpected impact.

He had spent his childhood in the glare of celebrity. In *Punch*, his
father captured the essence of Victorian life in a popular illustrated
series, *English Society at Home*, about an upper-middle-class family
with five children. Readers avidly followed the 'Browns' – or the du
Mauriers in paper-thin disguise. One 1875 cartoon shows five children, playing trains in the garden. Breathless Trixy explains to her
mother: 'I'm the engine and Guy's a first class carriage, and Sylvia's a
second class carriage & May's a second-class carriage & Gerald, he's
a third-class carriage too – that is he's really only a truck, you know,
only you mustn't tell him so, it would offend him'. One can imagine
Guy's mortification if these cartoons appeared on noticeboards at
Marlborough, as surely they did – no wonder he left school to join
the army. Family situation comedy would improve with the advent
of television, but the Browns were then all the rage; we will meet
them again under altogether different circumstances.

George's eyesight was failing and he turned to writing. The novels *Peter Ibbetson* (1889) and *Trilby* (1894) brought late riches and lasting fame from his pen, far more than from his illustrator's brush. Despite leaving it late in the game, *Trilby* became the bestselling novel of the nineteenth century, beating off lightweight competition from Dickens, Eliot, Balzac and Flaubert. However, George died suddenly in 1896. In a last bohemian gesture, he was cremated at Woking – this was not legally approved by parliament (cremation, not Woking) for another six years. Youngest son Gerald, despite being 'only a truck', carried the creative torch via the Rosslyn Park smokers on to the London stage. A series of small parts were eclipsed by major roles in two world premières: as Ernest in *The Admirable Crichton* of 1902; and in the dual role of George Darling and Captain Hook in *Peter Pan, or the Boy who Wouldn't Grow Up*, first played at the Duke of York's Theatre on 27 December 1904. Both productions were the work of the Scottish playwright J.M. Barrie and made his name worldwide.

In 1897, Barrie famously met the children of Guy's sister, Sylvia, in Kensington Gardens. He soon became a regular visitor at the home of Sylvia, her husband, Arthur Llewellyn Davies, and their five sons, George, John, Peter, Michael and Nicholas. Their names and the adventures they shared with 'Uncle Jim' inspired *Peter Pan*, which also made Gerald's acting reputation. Barrie's influence would henceforth pervade the life of the entire du Maurier family.[11] He and Sylvia became close, despite both being married, and on Arthur's death in 1907 Barrie became financial protector to her and the boys, *Peter Pan* having made him a very wealthy man.

With George dead and Gerald ever more prominent in the theatre, the family's social circle moved from the visual arts to the literary as they were drawn under Barrie's mesmeric spell. Even mining engineer Charlie Hoyer Millar became a biographer of his father-in-law. Henry James still visited and Barrie's circle included George Bernard Shaw, Jerome K. Jerome and H.G. Wells. He ran a cricket team, the 'Allahakbarries', which featured Arthur Conan Doyle, G.K. Chesterton, P.G. Wodehouse and A.A. Milne (Barrie, J.M., might have named it the 'Double Initials XI').

Guy had declared to Emma from Africa: 'I should be inclined to bet against [marriage]. Much as I love many of them I am incapable of a whole-souled devotion to one only.' But in 1905, aged 40, he married Gwendolen, 28, eldest daughter of Edward Price of Godalming. The couple decamped the following year to officer's quarters in a now peaceable South Africa; Guy had again been given command of a battalion of mounted infantry. Without a war to fight, the patriotic soldier had time on his hands and wider military and national concerns on his mind. Emboldened by the family's London literary and dramatic circle, he now gave voice to his concerns about England's military preparedness: he decided to write a play.

Guy was not alone in his fears that England was poorly prepared for war, or in expressing them. Long before 1914, the British public was exposed to a flood of popular fiction and journalism that fore-shadowed the advent of cataclysmic war, and identified the likely foe as German. As early as 1899, Headon Hill's novel *The Spies of Wight* prefigured the more celebrated Erskine Childers' 1903 yarn, *The Riddle of the Sands*, with tales of sinister German spies and invasion plots against Britain. Instead of responding to this threat the golden young Edwardians showed distinct signs of physical soft-ness: heavy rugby defeats by touring New Zealanders in 1905 and South Africans the following year flashed warning signals for impe-rial leadership and competitiveness in Europe – let alone domestic rugby standards.

In 1906 the *Daily Mail* serialised William Le Queux's *The Invasion of 1910*, a story of a successful invasion by a German Army, 40,000 strong, which became a bestseller in book form. It was written in collaboration with Lord Roberts, by now President of the National Service League. That the government failed to prepare for a threatened invasion is frequently repeated, as is the phrase, 'they should have listened to Lord Roberts'. *Daily Mail* proprietor Lord Northcliffe deployed sandwich-board men to patrol Oxford Street, clad in Prussian uniforms and spiked *pick-elhaube* helmets, causing uproar with fake invasion headlines. Obligingly, the fictional German force marched through towns where the *Daily Mail*'s circulation needed a boost.

The temperature of 'spy fever' was raised further by E. Phillips Oppenheim's *A Maker of History* and Walter Wood's *The Enemy in our Midst*, which pointed the finger of suspicion at waiters,

hairdressers and shopkeepers as a network of Teutonic fifth columnists in London. Years later, the conviction that the enemy was always
one step ahead through their spies would be widespread in the
trenches from Ypres to Gallipoli, and 'one has to make an effort to
shake off the spell of their astounding efficiency and preparedness'.[12]
The seeds of this groundless belief were sown a decade before.

In 1909, the mood of alarm and Germanophobia reached its
peak. Scaremonger-in-chief Le Queux, clearly on to a good thing,
published his *Spies of the Kaiser*, about a secret network in Britain;
ironically, its undercover agents communicated via small ads in the
Daily Mail. In Captain Curties' *When England Slept*, London is occupied overnight by a German army which has stealthily infiltrated
the country over several weeks. The *Daily Mail* printed a warning
from an anonymous army officer: 'The risks of Britain's position
unarmed in the face of a Europe armed to the teeth cannot be too
clearly realized by the British public.'[13] This was the year when a
'Special Intelligence Bureau' was recommended as the fifth branch
of the War Office's Military Operations Directorate, initially designated MO5. In his *Britain at Bay*, journalist Spenser Wilkinson,
another friend of Lord Roberts, wrote:

> The Englishman ... remembers from his school lessons or reads
> in the newspapers of England in past centuries, and naturally feels
> that with such a past and with such an Empire existing today, his
> country should be a very great Power. But as he discovers what
> the actual performance of Germany is, and becomes acquainted
> with the results of her efforts in science, education, trade, and
> industry, and the way in which the influence of the German
> Government predominates in the affairs of Europe, he is puzzled
> and indignant, and feel that in some way Great Britain has been
> surpassed and outdone.[14]

This was also the year that H.G. Wells wrote the prophetic *War in
the Air*, and Bleriot's successful flight across the Channel sparked a
wave of 'scareship' hysteria, with phantom Zeppelin airships 'sighted'
all over the kingdom and even as far away as New Zealand.[15] The
newly popular cinema seized upon this photogenic threat and spread

the scare to the working classes. Films such as Walter Booth's *The Airship Destroyer* and Percy Stow's *The Invaders* mingled fearsome modern weaponry with plucky human resistance, usually with a romantic couple providing the love interest – there is nothing new in Hollywood. Leon Stormont's multimedia drama *England Invaded*, mixing fictional and factual film with live action, song and recitation, opened at the London Coliseum, followed by a sell-out national tour. The stage was set, quite literally, for Guy's contribution. His play, *An Englishman's Home*, opened at Wyndham's Theatre in January, produced and directed by Gerald with assistance from J.M. Barrie.

The author was initially credited anonymously as 'A Patriot'. Was he conscious of his rank and professional position, or simply nervous of risking his name on a stage failure? Was he so wary of the 'luvvie' theatre world which had embraced his family? The truth is that, far off in Africa, he was simply not involved in the production; its arrival on Charing Cross Road was down to the commercial instincts of Barrie and Gerald, who was looking for a hit for Wyndham's where he would soon become actor-manager. In the play, Guy's fictional Brown family (the name revived from Kicky's *Punch* cartoons) is faced with an invading force from 'Nearland' – closer to home than Barrie's 'Neverland' and instantly identified as Germany by theatregoers and critics. The play was an immediate sensation: 'it ran simultaneously in two London theatres, which is almost unprecedented, and several companies were sent to the provinces.'[16]

Guy, the accidental playwright, was not even in the country. Gerald, an instinctive publicist, quickly spotted the value of mystique in the author's identity, but it was not the best-kept secret. Sylvia wrote to her beloved Guy: 'the world is writing and talking of nothing else but your play … Mummie tells people the author's name is a profound secret, but in my heart I know she tells everyone she meets!'[17] News travelled fast by 'Special Cable' that the anonymous author was 'Major Guy du Maurier of the Royal Fusiliers, now in Africa'. The *New York Times* commented: 'He will probably be as much surprised when he learns of its success as was his father, George du Maurier at the unexpected fortune he made from *Trilby*.' Richard Harding Davis retold Barrie's account of how the news reached Guy and Gwen:

Barrie asked himself to lunch yesterday and was very entertaining. He told us of a letter he received from Guy Du Maurier who wrote 'An Englishman's Home' which has made a sensation second to nothing in ten years. He is an officer stationed at a small post in South Africa. He wrote Barrie he was at home, very blue and homesick, and outside it was raining. Then came Barrie's long cable, at 75 cents a word, saying his play was the success of the year. He did not know even it had been ACCEPTED. He shouted to his wife, and they tried to dance but the hut was too small, so they ran out into the compound and danced in the rain. Then he sent the Kaffir boys to the mess to bring all the officers and all the champagne and they did not go to bed at all. The next day, cables still at three shillings a word came from papers and magazines and publishers, managers, syndicates. And, in his letter he says, still not appreciating what a fuss it has made, 'I suppose all it needs now is to be made a question in the House,' when already it has been the text of half a dozen speeches by Cabinet Ministers, and three companies are playing it in the provinces. What fun to have a success come in such a way, not even to know it was being rehearsed?[18]

The play tells of a Territorial soldier who seeks the hand of Joan Brown but does not have her father's approval; only when the 'Nearlanders' invade and shoot his own son before his eyes does Mr Brown come to appreciate the value of the Territorials. The impact was more than Guy could have dreamed. Recruiting officers were stationed outside theatres; the new Territorial Force recently created by Haldane in his Army Reforms had a sudden influx of volunteers. Guy's support for the 'Terriers' was in direct opposition to the political agenda of Le Queux and Northcliffe, who were determined to scupper the proposed new force, considering it ineffective compared to conscription. The message swiftly spread beyond Britain's shores. In New York, the *Times* journalist observed, with the spirit (and spelling) of American independence:

The growing party of advocates of conscription consider it a remarkable object lesson in their favor ... the hold which the question of national defense has taken on the thoughts and

imagination of the English public was significantly emphasized by
the instant popularity that attended its production. It is all about
national shortcomings – the ignorance of volunteer troops, the
incompetence of officers, the complacency and worthlessness
of the idle classes. At first all this is amusing. It becomes serious
when the smug Englishman's domesticity is brought face to face
with the reality of war … In the end the invaders are overcome,
for a British theatre audience is British, but the lesson of unpreparedness has been vigorously enforced and the self-satisfaction of
the Englishman made the subject of stinging satire.

In England the play, hailed by Lord Roberts (predictably enough),
polarised public opinion: in Southampton critics raved that 'it
should be seen by all – men and women – not only for the great and
valuable lesson it teaches, but also because it is a powerful, real and
interesting play',[19] while in Norwich a speaker at the Peace Society
objected to the military's use of 'every means to entrap the young
fellows of our country … to be prepared against an enemy that does
not exist'.[20]

One city was less amused. When the play transferred in April to
the Neues-Theater Berlin, reports as far away as America warned
that 'troublous scenes are expected'.[21] Herr Schmieden, the coura-
geous theatre manager, was attacked in German newspapers, 'and
it will be necessary for the Kaiser's Police Department to send a
squadron of bluecoats to the theatre for riot duty on the first night'.
The report, important enough to transmit to New York by the
Marconi Transatlantic Wireless Telegraph, continues:

The manager has sent the newspapers advance copies of the text
of the play with a view to convincing them that it is of real dramatic merit; but they decline to view with favour a theatrical
piece which ends with the rout of Germany's invincible battalions … the newspapers ridicule du Maurier's contention that
the invaders in his play cannot possibly represent Germans. 'We
suppose,' remarks the *Lokalanzieger*, 'du Maurier wishes to warn
Englishmen against the danger of invasion by Servia [sic] or
Montenegro, or some other great power.'

No less a playwright than George Bernard Shaw, who would oppose the forthcoming war with uncompromising vigour, makes his own complaint, when his own counterbalancing play is banned by the Lord Chamberlain:

> The German press has got hold of the fact that my forbidden play makes hay of the anti-German war scare. It immediately scents anti-German opinions in St. James's Palace. In vain do I protest that to suspect the Lord Chamberlain's department of political ideas, or of any ideas whatsoever is to shew the grossest ignorance of our censorship. When An Englishman's Home, by Guy Du Maurier, a really good play which represents a German invasion, is not only licensed by the Lord Chamberlain, but that burlesques of it are forbidden, and a play which disparages the war scare has been refused a license on a pretext, what do you expect the German press to think?[22]

Art historian Stanley Casson recalled that in 1915, at a London restaurant, 'an orderly knocked at the door and handed me a pink army telegraphic form. My orders to leave the following day for France with a draft. The manner of my going was as dramatic as *The Englishman's Home*.'[23]

The stage play became a film in 1914. As war clouds again loomed over London in May 1939 it was revived at the Prince's Theatre; in the early days of that second conflagration, propagandists seized on the patriotic theme and adapted it for a new film, pointedly titled *Mad Men of Europe*, starring Paul Henreid (Viktor Laszlo in *Casablanca*). Guy's contribution to the invasion literature genre can also be traced in the work of his niece Daphne, Gerald's daughter. *The Birds* is a British Cold War invasion allegory, although Hitchcock chose instead to elaborate on the horror and suspense elements in his movie set in California. Her final novel, *Rule Britannia*, written post-Vietnam, imagines America seeking to annex Britain through an invasion of Cornwall.

In photographs from this era, Guy is a genial and gently smiling figure in tweeds and bow tie, and with his fabled grey hair, more university professor than professional soldier. They have the look of

Hollywood publicity stills. Still in the army despite his doubts, he must have found playwriting a strange second career, but it bought him a place on the memorial at the Theatre Royal, Drury Lane, alongside 'Actors, Musicians Writers & Workers for the Stage'. Or, more theatrically, 'that great white company of shining souls who gave their youth that the world might grow old in peace':

> These nobly played their parts, these heard the call
> For God, King and Home, they gave their all.

Guy was now secure in his military tenure, his newfound celebrity and an unexpected financial windfall. He and Gwen returned from the hut in South Africa to a rented residence in Church Street, Chelsea – as would befit this new member of the literary classes – and sadly in time for Sylvia's death in 1910 (not quite as portrayed by Kate Winslet in *Finding Neverland*). At her express request, Guy became guardian to her boys, along with Granny Emma, Arthur's brother, Crompton, and Uncle Jim – her will was explicit that 'JMB' should be one of the guardians. The family had reason to be grateful to Barrie, and Sylvia's boys clearly enjoyed his company and correspondence.

For a soldier, the beds in Chelsea were soft. Overseas postings to Africa (again), Crete and India followed, which made Uncle Guy rather a remote guardian to the boys. In August 1914 the lieutenant colonel and his beloved 3rd Battalion of Royal Fusiliers were stationed in Lucknow. They returned to a month under canvas outside Winchester before crossing to Le Havre on the SS *Atlantian* on 18 January 1915, just two weeks after Emma's death. As fresh regular troops were much in demand, they set off for Belgium immediately after disembarking, although 25 per cent were down with illness from the change of climate. A train journey in the trucks famously marked '40 hommes, 8 chevaux' took the battalion to Hazebrouck, where it detrained and marched to Caëstre. Several clashes with the enemy occurred as the battalion occupied front-line positions where Bedford House Cemetery (Ypres) is now located.

His letters to Gwen give a vivid account of an officer's life during this appalling winter. She read them to Henry James, who visited her regularly in the house she rented on Cheyne Walk. So touched was James by the account of life in the Salient and Guy's concern for his men that he had them printed for private circulation.[24]

Guy did not endure the physical labour of his men but his officer's daily grind left an average of three hours' sleep. On top of organising fatigues, inspecting the men, often under fire and in mud and waist-deep water, visiting sentries at night and leading patrols, he had volumes of staff work to process and reports to write. The permanent trench stores needed tracking: planks, props, duckboards, wire, sandbags, bombs, picks, shovels, blankets, gas gongs, sniper rifles, tin helmets, Very pistols, ammunition, trench waders. Daily 'returns' were mandatory and a detailed inventory would be needed for the unit that would relieve them. Cartoonist Bruce Bairnsfather's harassed colonel in a dugout under siege from 'whizz-bangs', 'coal-boxes' and 'Jack Johnsons' fields a GHQ signal: 'Please let us know, as soon as possible, the number of tins of raspberry jam issued to you last Friday.' It may be a cartoon, but the only joke is that jam was always plum and apple – never raspberry.

Nightly casualty reports and records of trench activity were compiled, letters of condolence written to next of kin, and a stream of memoranda, directives and orders digested. To Guy would also fall the censoring of his officers' letters home, although many refused to read the correspondence of their social equals. His own bluntness and anger on occasions makes it quite clear he did not expect interference from any censor.

Out of the line, things were no less busy; his men were billeted in ten different farms so he did his rounds on horseback. His HQ was a gamekeeper's cottage in the grounds of 'a lone and much-shelled chateau, looking picturesque in the rising moonlight'. By day German aeroplanes added a new tension to any movement in the open and lighting of fires was forbidden, even out of the front line. The relief cycle of four days in the trenches and four in reserve, with no more than thirty-six hours in the front line, became increasingly theoretical. He was wearied by the sapping conditions and incessant demands of the job:

The shrapnel bullets must be raining down somewhere close to us as our shells are bursting right over our heads – but the men enjoy looking, for them it is a tamasha [Hindi for spectacle]. Only uninteresting details eternally rained down on me. I'm getting tired of demands for boots, shirts, rifle oil etc., all the hundred things that the soldier must have and that always seem the most difficult to get.

Standard issue stores were never enough. Guy sends a stream of requests: waders from Fortnum & Mason, shaving bowls and brushes, socks in vast quantities, loofahs and several hundred Huckaback towels. His concern was always for his men, that they should have whatever they needed to recover after the mud and freezing water, to feel human again. Gwen acted as London quarter-master and armourer: he requested his Männlicher sniper rifle with telescopic sight and a box of oil paints in earth colours, so that he could camouflage a sniper shield. Siegfried Sassoon, on leave in 1916, purchased two pairs of rubber-handled wire cutters at the Army & Navy Stores as 'my private contribution to the Great Offensive'.[25] Harrods had a dedicated 'War Comforts Room'. Soldiers today bound for Afghanistan still buy personal kit by mail order.

Guy's affection for his junior officers and men is real; he was not just on first-name terms, but used the fond diminutives and nick-names of male companionship. Massa, Kim, Andy Boy and Nobby are mourned as one by one they are killed, wounded or break down with 'nervous prostration', leaving Guy 'fretting and worrying over my poor men and a bit jaded with it all'. He grieves for one lost subaltern, buried in the ramparts of Ypres without ceremony but with German shells dropping all round:

[Sam] was shot through the head on Sunday afternoon. The shot came right through the rotten parapet and of course death was practically instantaneous. He's a great loss. He turned up big trumps at this game; was absolutely calm and had a soothing effect on the nerves of all his company who thought no end of him – and did splendidly all through a very trying time … he was splendid under fire – so cool – and the men would take their cue from him and were as steady as rocks … all the men were touchingly anxious to have something out of his kit when I distributed it.

He repeatedly expresses sorrow for Sam's wife, 'poor Booty', but is less sympathetic to the cloud of busy auxiliaries swarming around his men:

> As far as I can see for every fighting soldier in the real front, it takes about 10 people driving about in motor cars to look after his food or clothing, or to censor his letters, or just to do nothing but rush up and down the road – scattering mud over the infantry as they move along.

He has harsh words too for the relative of a friend (anonymous for the censor, although Gwen would have known him) who was 'very stupid and obstinate and really responsible for a lot of our troubles … a proper failure and … ought to be outed'. While frank about the prospects of new officers coming to the front who were clearly not up to it, he approves the 'natural good qualities' of the Territorial troops arriving in numbers; his public stage praise of 1909 was repeated in theatre. The regular officer in him notes that they might not be so good 'in operations of war that demand some professional knowledge and experience' but this trench war, in his opinion, was no such thing.

As battalion commander, he was unimpressed by his seniors, as he was in Africa: 'Told that we had lost a bit of trench and we were to go up and help re-take it. Great rejoicings.' The battalion rushed to the front only to find that:

> The General commanding the Brigade which had been attacked and to help whom we had come about 10 miles in the night, was quite vague as to what he wanted – and didn't seem to know whether he had lost a trench or not. So I couldn't get any exact news of the situation and no orders as to what I was required to do or when; so I went back to the Battalion.

By mid-February 'my beautiful battalion' was reduced to 200 men, more by trench conditions than by enemy shelling. One day, 200 men went to hospital with frostbitten feet and gangrene, compared to fifty casualties from fire. Bitter cynicism set in as insidiously as a case of trench foot for Guy:

The Staff and unemployed generally each one of whom gets mentioned in despatches – in comparison to about 3% of the men who have done the fighting, may like it. We don't. There is no lust for battle, because you can't call it battle – it's a duel from ditches and the duellist is wet through and cold and feeling rotten ...

As winter dragged on, his anger intensified. Bear in mind this was no school-fresh subaltern but a seasoned professional with a lifetime of service:

I am getting bored stiff with papers of literature which roll up in the shape of hints, recommendations, what to do, and what not to do, all emanating from people who never come near the trenches. Personally I haven't seen a General or a General Staff Officer within a mile of them; and they haven't a notion what it is like but they write and write the most appalling rubbish. Then we get hauled over the coals for using too many sandbags and are accused of wasting them – but again no one ever comes to see them. It's like the Chef of the Ritz sitting down to write a cookery book in Nyasaland ... Never have I admired the regimental officer more, or thought less of the Staff and the higher commanders. I don't say the higher commanders can <u>do</u> anything – they can't – much – but in God's name let them stop writing ... tripe.

Apologists for the generals have sought to temper any suggestion that they were somehow 'absent without leave' from the front, both mentally and physically. The damning evidence from Guy at Ypres in 1915 is that they were indeed armchair warriors. It is tempting to speculate how Guy might have used his new-found stage voice if he had survived the war – he was sure there would be no military employment for him after it was over.

There was growing unease that the deck was stacked against the British. The Germans overlooked them and had deep communicating trenches where they could move safely, while Guy's fusiliers were exposed whenever they left their fire trench. The Germans used Belgian workers to dig their trenches, saving their soldiers for fighting, while the British felt unable to press allied civilians into forced labour. The flooded ditches made life unbearable and men incapable. Du Maurier was frustrated that better, drier ones could not be dug, even if it meant giving up ground: 'it's better to lose a 100 yards than a 1,000 men.' The exhausting struggle through the mud was compounded by the sheer weight of equipment, 'thick vest, shirt, wooly [sic] serge jacket, fur coat, great coat and carrying about 75lbs dead weight on your shoulders'. The army greatcoat could be the greatest liability: already weighing 7lb, it could absorb some 20lb of water. One officer at the Somme examined his men's coats as they came out of the line and found that one sodden, mud-clogged sample actually weighed 58lb.

Amidst the misery, Guy's affection for Gwen found expression in his letters. There is intimacy in his casual use of Hindi with his '*memsahib*'. He promises a gift of genuine Valenciennes lace which he had seen hand made. His love was reciprocated; Gwen even planned to motor out in a little red car, which Guy tactfully discouraged. There was even time for flirting: 'I loved your photograph – it made you look very chaste and demure – couldn't for a moment suspect you of the least vestige of impropriety, Miss Price.' As the commanding officer's wife, Gwen also supported her husband at the front by comforting bereaved wives at home. Their marriage was childless and she would live a widow until 1958.

In early March, the 3rd Battalion found itself east of Kemmel, in 'trenches that aren't trenches at all but just small hollows in the ground where you lie in liquid mud and pray'. In Kensington Gardens, show trenches had been constructed for the edification of civilians, with neatly stacked sandbags, dry floors and plumb vertical walls – no soldier would recognise this Ideal Trench Exhibition. Battalion HQ in Flanders was a ruined farm cellar too low for standing and without daylight, where fifteen officers and men worked by the light of a single candle. Food brought up at night – at the cost of lives each time – was eaten cold; thirst was a major problem and scarce water was carried through communication trenches in jars, then stored in ammunition boxes. Guy's mood was low:

The cursed close confinement of this life is the worst of it and depresses me fearfully, and it's hard not to take a gloomy view and sitting in a trench isn't much relief. The stink is so awful. There are many dead Highlanders just in front – killed in December I think – and they aren't very pleasant.

In one of his last letters, we see not only the human cost of trench life but also Guy's true colours, as a man of compassion, who rises above his own plight in his concern for his men:

A touchingly young soldier was brought before me to-day for a very serious offence i.e. quitting his look-out post when a sentry in the trenches – and his story was (true as a fact) that the man had been shot quite close to him – and it so un-nerved him that he had had to sit down and put his hands over his eyes – and he added that he couldn't get the sight out of his memory – I had to overlook the offence. He was so young – and I want to do it so much myself. A dirty business war …

His humanity and consideration for others would shine through even in his ending. However, for Royal Irish Rifles Captain Burgoyne (less full of the milk of human kindness than Guy) such compassion bred laxity in the Fusiliers: 'I hear that they were awfully slack in the trenches and the enemy used to stroll up and look over into their trenches, so to speak, and when our Brigade went up there, they stopped all that nonsense.'[26]

Orders had been given that 'considerable activity' had to be shown by the troops in the trenches. No soldier ever welcomed these instructions for showy belligerence: genuine attacks are understandable, but 'hates' merely led to 'counter-hates'. Raids and patrols simply added to the casualty count and the 'intelligence' gathered was often inconsequential. The aim of this faked activity was to preoccupy the Germans during the (failed) attack on Neuve Chapelle further south. But it simply resulted in the Fusiliers' positions being badly shelled in predictable retaliation and in the death of their avuncular commanding officer. The regimental history states the plain facts:

On the night of March 9th battalion headquarters were shelled and burned. Official correspondence, a machine gun, rifles and eighty

sets of equipment were destroyed. It was on this occasion that
Lt Col Guy du Maurier DSO was killed. L/Cpl Fovargue who was
at HQ at the time, stated they were asleep when a shell suddenly
tore off part of the roof. The Colonel rushed to the doorway, and
just as he reached it a shell fell on the spot and killed him instantly.[27]

J.M. Barrie later added gore: 'he wandered about the battlefield for
half-an-hour with his stomach hanging out, begging somebody to
finish him off',[28] but this is most likely the imaginative dramatist at
work. After his critical muttering about Guy's battalion, Burgoyne
was kinder to the commanding officer much admired and liked by
his men:

> Just heard over the telephone from Brigade Head Quarters that
> Colonel du Maurier ... was killed this morning by a shell which
> blew up Alston House, the old farm which is always used as
> Battalion Head Quarters ... I hear he had just ordered everyone
> out and into dugouts outside and was waiting in the house for his
> Sergeant-Major to report that everyone was in safety before he
> took cover himself.[29]

In London, Gerald was about to go on stage at the Wyndham's when
news of Guy's death arrived. A brief announcement told the hushed
audience that Lieutenant Colonel du Maurier had been killed; his
brother would not appear that night. Within a short week and a few
miles of entrenched wasteland, the du Maurier clan would suffer the
shattering of its next generation. It is not known if Sylvia's eldest
boy and Eton cricketer, Second Lieutenant George Davies of the
King's Royal Rifle Corps (KRRC), had heard of his uncle's death
before a letter arrived (dated 11 March) from J.M. Barrie describing
Guy fondly in the past tense:

> He had the du Maurier charm at its best – the light heart with the
> sad smile & it might be the sad heart with the bright smile ... He
> had lots of stern stuff in him, and yet always the mournful smile of
> one who could pretend that life was gay but knew it wasn't. One
> of the most attractive personalities I have ever known.[30]

George received this letter on 14 March. The next day he too was killed. His reply, written a few hours before his death, shows an astounding optimism and selfless empathy for others who themselves could scarcely fathom George's circumstances, whether they be his guardian 'uncle' in London or his commander, safely ensconced behind the front line:

Dear Uncle Jim,

I have just got your letter about Uncle Guy. You said it hasn't made you think any more about the danger I am in. But I know it has. Do not try to let it. I take every care of myself that can decently be taken. And if I am going to stop a bullet, why should it be with a vital place?

It is very bad about Uncle Guy. I wonder how he was killed. As he was a colonel, I imagine his battalion was doing an attack. Poor Aunt Gwen. This war is a dreadful show.

The ground is drying up fast now, and the weather far better … There have already been doings in various parts of the line, and I would rather be George Davies than Sir John French just now. He must have got some hard decisions in front of him. Well, let's hope for a good change in the next month.

Meanwhile dear Uncle Jim, you must carry on with your job of keeping up your courage. I will write every time I come out of action. We go up to the trenches in a few days again.

Yours affectionately, George[31]

Despite his breeziness, George had confided to a comrade his premonition of death. Sitting on a bank with the Rifle Brigade company to which he was attached, listening to his colonel, he was shot through the head. George was 21. From that first encounter in Kensington Gardens, the oldest of the 'lost boys' became the model for Peter Pan; many lines in the play were inspired by their childhood play with Barrie. George himself is credited with the most famous, 'To die would be an awfully big adventure', which was quietly dropped from the 1915 Christmas stage revival. The playwright was deeply fond of him and had funded him through Eton (*alma mater* to Captain Hook) and Cambridge since his parents' death. 'This dreadful war will get them all in the end,' cried Barrie when he heard the news. In July 1917, at great risk to himself, he spent a week searching behind the lines near Ypres before locating George's grave.

Guy Louis Busson du Maurier is buried in Kemmel Chateau Cemetery. His headstone, replacing the original temporary wooden cross, supplements Kipling's standard wording. After much fretting about uniformity, the Imperial (as it then was) War Graves Commission acceded to family pleas for personal inscriptions. The Latin tribute in 'whole-souled devotion' to Gwen must surely have been at Guy's request in a last will:

> Viva adhuc
> Et desiderio
> Pulcriora[32]

(Still alive/And in my missing her/More beautiful)

His mention in Sir John French's Despatch of 31 May for 'gallant and distinguished service in the field' would have been scant consolation. Guy's last letter to Gwen, written the night before his death, having heard from her of anti-submarine success and 'good news' from the Dardanelles, foretells the war's course but is sadly short on the body count:

> But none of these things is going to have anything but a very indirect effect on the war – what's going to do this thing is infantry soldiers, and more of them, and yet again more. We must make up our minds to the loss of another ¼ of a million of them – and then perhaps we will pull it off. No starvation, no blockade, no anything but hard pushing against their line is going to end this war. No talent wasted, no great men – thank goodness for our sakes – just men in masses – *and* equipment and ammunition for them.

The men in masses were falling fast. Mountaineer Geoffrey Winthrop Young visited the grave of Arnold Hosegood, one of three brothers to die within a year: 'a lovely spot and Guy du Maurier, his brother's colonel … was more than kind to us. We were hardly returned to Ypres when news of du Maurier's death also reached us.'[33] Guy donated his own copy of Hilaire Belloc's *The Battle of Tourcoing* to the Fusiliers' Officers' Mess in April 1913. The British lost this battle in 1794 due to poor staff work, little co-operation and a failure to bring all their troops into action. In 1915, history would repeat itself as both tragedy and farce.

ALEC TODD
LIONS LED BY A LION

The 'handsome English forward Mr Todd'. *(David Byass)*

Head south over London Bridge towards Borough High Street, the old coaching road to Kent. Southwark Cathedral crouches to the right and the clumsy bulk of the station's viaduct looms ahead. Look for a once-splendid, once-white façade: an elaborate blend of arch, balustrade and ornament, with carved swags of hops, grapes and even a stag's head. Now grey with soot, this, like Miss Havisham's wedding cake, is a ghost of a building.

The hands of its clock with black Roman numerals are fixed at 11.47, as they have been since the early 1960s [1]. Ragged shrubs sprout from crevices where no plant should grow, and the faience frontage offers a tempting canvas to the graffiti artist. This wan face among grimy walls and thrusting plate-glass neighbours like the Shard is a ghostly survivor from another era. It is a corner of the capital where time has indeed stopped.

For over a century, Findlater's Corner has been a familiar sight to the southbound City worker, 'passed or seen by more persons every day than any other spot in London'.[2] The current structure is shrunken from its Victorian original by the encroachments of railway and advertising hoardings. Peter Ackroyd's biography of London observes the lingering spirit of place that binds many capital landmarks to their past. Call this instead a 'place of spirit', for today it is a branch of an eccentric national wine-seller, evoking its first incarnation in 1856 as headquarters of Findlater, Mackie, Todd & Co. Ltd, Wine & Spirit Merchants.

In the cruellest month of April 1915, a boy brings a curt telegram from the War Office to these same premises, addressed to the chairman. Its formulaic words, by now dreaded in households across the country, regret a death in the family. A brother, husband and father are all fallen in one man. Since that day another spirit has haunted this corner: the gregarious wine merchant, soldier and international rugby player, Alec Todd.

Alexander Findlater Todd was born the son of Bruce Beveridge Todd, a man surely destined by his middle name for the booze trade. The first Alexander Findlater, a Scot from Greenock, founded a wine business in Dublin in 1827, opening the first Findlater's Corner on Sackville Street. The business generated more profit and charitable benevolence than the family produced heirs; the founder never married, his brother Adam fathered no children, and so they called in the Liverpool family of their deceased brother-in-law to run the firm. The second son Joseph ran the London office with Colonel John Findlater Corscaden. Neither had children, so in 1848 they took into partnership Bruce Todd of Forest Hill, to form Findlater, Mackie & Todd. As if by way of compensatory fecundity, Todd's wife Phoebe, his junior by twenty-four years, provided not just an heir, but two daughters and three more sons; the last, born in September 1873, was respectfully (and gratefully) named Alexander Findlater in honour of the grand old patriarch who died in August that same year while taking the waters in Harrogate.

Bruce Todd's descendants would run the firm until its ownership passed first to Bulmers, then Beechams. It now survives in corporate disguise as the mail-order arm of Waitrose Direct and supplier of kitchen sherry and brandy 'By Appointment to Buckingham Palace'. Bruce began as managing partner with a salary of £100 a year plus one-fifth of the profits. During the Crimean War, these amounted to £76 7s 5d, but within ten years his income was in excess of £2,000 – serious money in the 1860s. Number one son James entered the family business in 1884; on the death of his father nine years later he took control until his own death in 1956. His sixty-three years as chairman won a place in the *Guinness Book of Records*.

At its peak, Findlater's boasted fifty wine shops around London and the south. The firm's list of popular products included Dry Fly sherry, Vin de St Raphael, 'a tonic most suitable for therapeutic use supplied to Paris hospitals'[3] and mineral waters including Taunus (a favourite with Her late Majesty Queen Victoria) and Carabana, 'not unpleasant to take and free from constipating after-effects'. The list of medicinal compounds invokes another presiding spirit of place: Findlater's Corner stands on the site of old St Thomas' Hospital.

While James mastered the wine trade, youngest brother Alec was schooled at Mill Hill, where he captained both the XV and XI. He excelled in German – a prize volume of Schiller bears his name on an engraved bookplate. He also earned a certificate in phonography, or shorthand, signed (phonetically, of course) by 'Eyzak Pitman'. At the age of 15, the schoolboy rugby player was good enough to play with the grown men of Old Millhillians against Rosslyn Park. In June 1890 at the Guildhall Tavern, Alec – not yet 17 – agreed to join Park, then in leafy Acton; James would join him two seasons later. They graced the team photographs with the same good looks and splendid whiskers, and James was lauded as a 'tower of strength and reliability at [full]back'.[4] The pair later proposed and seconded brother William's membership to the club.

Alec went up to Gonville & Caius College in Cambridge in 1892, and became a serial collector of rugger Blues. Stearn's carefully posed Varsity Rugby XV photographs show the handsome Todd, taller by a head than most, chin cocked in jock-sure self-confidence, a real master of the univers(ity); he probably made little use of the last of three famous Caius gates headed Virtue, Honour and Humility. His talents extended beyond the sports field; a very clubbable and extrovert nature took him into Caius' Shakespeare Society. His Cambridge years are captured in a wealth of group social photographs, formal and informal, from freshers' cocktails and May Week balls to the Officer Training Corps.

When in London, he served for three seasons on the Rosslyn Park Committee, as Cambridge representative. Hoyer Millar's history betrays tight-lipped irritation at his next move: 'after playing for the Club for several seasons [he] ultimately went to Blackheath and got his international cap.' Blackheath had become the traditional opening fixture of Park's season and his defection to the South-east London rivals (after a disastrous Park season of only two victories) may have been a scandalous poaching. Or, less contentiously, it was simply closer to the family home, 'Taymount' in Forest Hill. Either way, 'The Club' was then more prestigious, a founder member of both Rugby Football Union and Football Association, boasting several capped players and past England skippers.[5]

Todd played in the same Blackheath side as the over-achieving C.B. Fry, the very model of the Corinthian all-rounder, who captained his country at cricket, played soccer for England and an FA Cup final for Southampton. For good measure he threw in the world long-jump record in 1893 as well. Fry was also author, diplomat, politician and teacher, and occasional nude model – to make impoverished student ends meet at Oxford. His party piece was a standing jump on to a mantelpiece – backwards – which he performed into his seventies. He later tried to interest the Nazi party in cricket and was one of the first television subjects of *This is Your Life* in 1955. Playing with such a teammate would be further education for the fresh Cambridge graduate.

Alec Todd captained Kent and travelled on several tours with the Barbarians Club, which numbered strictly sixty-five elected members every season. Its founder, W.P. (Percy) Carpmael, a Blackheath man, would have undoubtedly cast an admiring eye over the vigorous young forward, whom he had first spied in 1892 when Alec played for Park at Rectory Field. 'He had inches and physique, and not only did his share in the shoving but had great pace when the scrummage had broken; and his safe hands always meant a try at a pinch if the chance came in loose work near the line.'[6]

The family business may also have conferred some attractive fringe benefits on any club able to win his favour – scholars have discerned a natural affinity between rugby and purveyors of wines and spirits. It is hard, however, to visualise Findlater's Dry Fly sherry as shirt sponsor in the modern manner. But the Blackheath trump card was probably played by its captain, Johnnie Hammond, who invited the 22-year-old Blue to tour South Africa on the third British Isles tour in the summer of 1896.

Hammond, a British skipper who never played for England, had been one of ten Cambridge men on the 1891 tour, which spread the rugby gospel to the colony. Little could they know that it would prove a consuming religion to its people, inspiring worship at home and vilification abroad during the Apartheid era, and then a supreme moment of national unification at Ellis Park in the 1995 Rugby World Cup final. The opposition would perhaps not be testing – on the 1891 tour, the tourists' line was crossed just once – but who would not jump at time overseas playing rugby?

In 1896, Queen Victoria, shortly to surpass George III as long-est-reigning British monarch, saw her empire at its height: she was sovereign to one in four humans and a sixth of the world's land mass. The year signalled a new age of communications as Guglielmo Marconi patented his wireless telegraph. But an overseas tour to the southern colonies was still a full three months' undertaking, unpaid in the amateur era, which might explain the preponderance of Varsity men without annoying professional responsibilities to detain them. The young tourists were also off (not for the last time in rugby) to a political hotbed. South Africa was not yet a nation but a set of colonial states in some turmoil: war against the natives raged in Matabeleland (today's Zimbabwe), where Alec's brother William was fighting; in Durban an unknown young lawyer, Mohandas Gandhi, campaigned for the civil rights of Indians. The Prime Minster of Cape Colony, Cecil Rhodes, had failed to dislodge the Afrikaner govern-ment of Transvaal and annex it to the Crown; the 1895 Jameson raid by mounted pro-British forces had relied on an uprising of *uitlander* (foreign) prospectors which did not materialise, and so ended in dis-aster. The London trial of its ringleaders was head-line news as the rugby tour was being planned.

They were not yet 'Lions'; the touring side from the British Isles would not be known as such until 1930. Nor were they a select elite of internationals or even wholly representative of Britain; this tour was Anglo-Irish, as the invited Scots and Welsh unions declined to provide a single player. Throughout their African travels they were hailed as England, or 'the English footballers', which can hardly have thrilled the nine-strong Irish contingent, fresh from winning their first championship, let alone resentful Afrikaners. However, Tommy Crean of Dublin Wanderers had no problem and said so: 'he had been playing for England and would do so again with a heart and a half. He was an Irishman who would go hand in hand with England as long as he lived.' That he would.

So it came to be that, on Saturday 20 June 1896, twenty-one disciples of Saints George and Patrick (Andrew and David absent), eleven from universities and twelve uncapped by their country, congregated at Waterloo station under their guardian angel, RFU President Roger Walker, in a fervent spirit of missionary zeal. From halfback the Reverend Matthew Mullineux, later to be captain of the 1899 Australia tour and wearer of a Military Cross, would spur on his crusading forwards, including the Reverend Walter Carey, future Bishop of Bloemfontein.

Between the lines of decorous press reports, we glean that Alec Todd and the Dubliners, Crean and Robert Johnston, formed a breakaway trio who embraced their mission in a spirit entirely familiar to their respective Findlater's Corners. Todd and Crean were voted on to the Sports and Amusements Committee for the eighteen-day voyage. Alec became an honorary tenth Irishman on tour and Crean addressed him by his family nickname of 'Fin' throughout. This would become the closest of friendships, as the two men would play, drink, sing, fight and love together – until death did them part in 1915.

Modern rugby tourists will instantly recognise the antics reported in the *African Review*: Walker turned up 'all smiles, his genial features shaded by the broad brims of a brand new Leghorn straw hat, which at once excited the humorous risibilities of his protégés'.[7] Three rousing cheers from the platform were 'as heartily responded by those in the saloon' on the train.[8] The official party of blazer-clad dignitaries, former players and retired generals found themselves waving farewell with a 'gay crowd' – the rugby team shared the Union Line Special with a theatrical troupe bound for the Empire Palace of Varieties in the 'Golden City' of Johannesburg.

If there is a flavour of the American Wild West here, the rugby players were equally travelling entertainers. South Africa was frontier land, where fortunes were swiftly made in gold, diamonds and minerals. Rugby was growing in popularity over the 'civilising' game of cricket since 'rapidly ambitious men will not afford the time required to take part in the summer game. A couple of hours, instead of a couple of days, at the exhilarating pastime of "kicking the ball" is more to their liking.'[9]

They sailed from Southampton on the steamer *Tartar*, a 'very handsome boat with every modern convenience', in the 'most buoyant of spirits, determined to uphold the prestige of England in the football grounds of South Africa'. But not before the first of many long-winded speeches, delivered here by Sir Francis Evans, chairman of the Union Line, who set the tone when he said 'that he did not know of any greater good that was done to their great empire than that wrought by such teams as that who visited the various colonies and helped to cement that Imperial tie which they all trusted would last for many, many years'.[10] The tour was as much a diplomatic mission as an athletic adventure; sport and politics were already uneasy teammates. However, Evans, in referring to the bond that such a visit could create between 'two great English-speaking nations', showed blithe ignorance of local tensions with Afrikaans-speaking Boers, which would erupt in war only three years hence.

The *Athletic Review* persuaded 'one of the Party' to correspond under the 'Tartar' by-line. His first bulletin was from Madeira where, in 90°F heat, the party 'climbed a mountain in an hour and a quarter and descended in ten minutes' by toboggan, 'the recognized method of progression there, where all the streets are cobbles worn smooth as glass'.[11] Even before the custom of 'what goes on tour stays on tour' there was little need for discretion – Victoria was on the throne, morals were of the highest standard and players were educated as gentlemen, conscious of their role as ambassadors for their game, class and country. Unlike Alistair Campbell accompanying the 2005 Lions, 'Tartar' exerted complete control over the media from his ship's cabin.

The female company disappointed Alec:

I have always heard that being on ship-board for a long voyage tends to make one sentimental, but the Steamship Company didn't look after us in that respect, as I don't think there are more than two unmarried ladies in our part, and they seem pretty full up with acquaintances already.[12]

The model behaviour of virile young men seems too good to be true today: 'About nine of the team adjourned to drink the usual toast of "Sweethearts and Wives". Lights were put out at 10.30 but most of us had retired to our bunks before that hour.'[13]

Tommy and Fin busied themselves with 'Sports and Amusements', and ensured that the *craic* was good, with the help of the music-hall artistes who performed regular concerts. 'Amusements' went well, with some of the rugby men displaying their musical talents: Johnston, Crean and Todd showed an eagerness for song that would last the whole tour, and Mullineux and Carey proved fine accompanists on pianoforte and violin. What would they make of the 1997 Lions tour anthem, *Wonderwall*, by Oasis? 'Sports' brought a wake-up call: a tug-of-war contest ended in ignominious defeat for the players at the brawny hands of the ship's stokers – a sure sign that the long voyage had taken the edge off their fitness. Furious, they challenged the stokers to a rematch and this time 'the team regained their laurels, Mackie, Lee, Clinch, Walker, Crean, Johnston and Todd pulling the firemen over the line twice in succession'. In a ten-day tournament of deck quoits, Todd paired up with a Mrs Hacker to win the 'mixed double bull board'. Crean won the high jump and the half mile and, as the organisers became increasingly inventive, Dublin University winger Cecil Boyd won 'slinging the monkey' (no dwarfs available). Fin triumphed in cock fighting, and Robinson was the victor in ducking for coins.

Such was the excitement on arrival off Cape Town that the mayor could not wait for them to land and chartered a launch out to the liner. The first enquiry from the isolated voyagers was 'who won the Varsity cricket match?' The answer (Oxford), wrote Alec, 'caused much wailing and smashing of teeth, but we were recompensed by hearing that England beat Australia and Leander knocked Yale'. The Cape press gave a colonial sniff: 'such meagre information as Reuter condescends to send us was given and then the *Tartar* was boarded and the visitors welcomed to South Africa.'[14] Breakfast was washed down with toasts and 'a tremendous lot of speechifying'.

The press railed further at the lack of biographical detail or even names of the full party provided by English newspapers, complaining that 'the public always like to know something of the cast before studying the price of admission'. They inferred this might be because 'the Union's estate has diminished recently and players of the right sort [i.e., the Rugby Union sort] become scarcer'. The previous year had brought schism to English rugby when the Northern Union broke away in protest at the denial of payments for 'broken time' to working-class players. So began Rugby League and the dreaded professionalism. But this tour party was reassuringly the 'right sort' of gentleman amateurs. Nevertheless, column inches were devoted to decrying – politely of course – the quality of the present tourists versus their 1891 predecessors, in a precursor of the 'worst Lions ever' headlines that southern hemisphere journalists regularly trot out in the modern era.

If professionalism had not yet arrived, commercialism decidedly had, which may explain the lack of free information to journalists. An opportunistic souvenir book of the 'English Rugby Football Team', compiled by one 'HGC' used very modern promotional methods: 'each purchaser has the chance to win valuable prizes … being a silver keyless watch for the nearest guess of the result of next Wednesday's match at Newlands.' The book gave a necessarily 'short history of rugby in South Africa', every last detail on the players – tables of height, weight, age – and the full results from the last tour, plus the twenty-one matches of this new itinerary. This was a proper tour to every corner of the country with copious socialising and, of course, more speeches and toasts.

Hardly settled on dry land (or 'ground like a brick wall', in Alec's opinion), the tourists scraped home 14-9 in their first game against Cape Town Clubs, with Todd scoring: 'Your loving son managed to score the second try of the tour; hooray for Taymount.' The *Cape Times* had initially admired the 'lengthy specimens of manhood',[15] noting in particular that the 14-stone Todd and even heavier 'Baby' Froude Hancock were giants in stature, but now found them 'very disappointing. The forwards are by no means fit yet and they have not settled into united work.' To Alec this was hardly surprising: 'three weeks on board ship, lying on one's back, coming after a hot English summer (including items such as May Week festivities) is not conducive to good training. In the last ten minutes, I would gladly have changed places with a corpse.' The forwards would indeed unite, developing the art of wheeling and the snap shove on the put-in to counter their stronger opponents. Alec's great height of 6ft 2in would later be remarked upon in a much graver context.

The hard grounds left them bruised and raw. Alec complained that 'we've lost square yards of skin between us'. In the mining town of Kimberley, 'mostly built of very rusty, discoloured corrugated iron', Alec observed:

> ... the football ground has absolutely not one blade of grass on or near it; it is exceedingly flat, which is a good point (its only one). Before playing they have to put a sort of harrow on it which scrapes up the hard surface to a depth of about six inches and then they water it.[16]

In Johannesburg, 'the ground is just the road with most of the stones taken off'. The conditions took their toll by the end of the tour, as did 10,000 miles and twenty-one games: 'there are only ten able-bodied men, four crocks and one invalid playing for us.'[17]

As a restorative off the pitch, South African hospitality was royally extended and enthusiastically received, confirming the 'one fear entertained by Mr Roger Walker ... that the receptions would be more cordial than conducive in good condition and play'.[18] Before the third game, against Western Province, they took lunch with Rhodes' successor as prime minister, Sir Gordon Sprigg; the expert Alec noted appreciatively the Veuve Clicquot-Ponsardin '89. Despite Tommy Crean (acting captain for the injured Hammond) warning the players that their limit was four tumblers of champagne, somehow the message was garbled or his soft Irish brogue was misunderstood. 'It was a good job we had an hour or two to spare after lunch before playing,' wrote Fin. The result was a 0-0 draw and a true (and sober) 32-0 victory over Western Province had to await their return to the Cape and the penultimate match of the tour.

Alec Todd threw himself into the social round with relish. At a smoking concert in the Good Hope Hall, 'attended by a large crowd which was remarkably decorous he gave "Sally in our Alley" with great taste, and in reply to the encore gave "Lazily, Dreamily"'.[19] Alec felt somewhat ambushed:

> We thought there would only be forty or fifty people present and no formality. Judge of our horror when we were taken to a place larger that the Queen's Hall in Regent Street, with the best part of a thousand people there … the whole place rising and cheering like mad, and to think that we'd got to sing to them on a raised platform.

The 'accomplished vocalist' was rapidly becoming a public favourite; Mr Todd's fine features, steady gaze and waxed moustache had been noted from his tour photograph. The next night, bruised after a game, he was invited to the Masonic Hall to meet the author Mark Twain:

> … who has just completed a world tour. Then blow me, if they didn't make me sing again; my inside was all topsy-turvy and I never thought I should get through it, especially as it ended up on top A, but I managed it somehow and then went to bed and dreamt of fog-horns and steam whistles.[20]

Fin teases his mother about the female attractions: 'The ladies of Kimberley aren't much to look at, my first three introductions being ladies of distinctly mature age'; in Grahamstown the ladies 'were blessed with fairly healthy appetites and drink-itites'. In Cape Town:

> … quite unknowingly, I did a neat bit of gallery play, as I got a try and got winded at the same time … within about twenty yards of my favourite partner at a dance the night before. I think it was rather neat as I was unconscious of the fair lady's presence. I shan't forget that dance in a hurry …[21]

He kept score on and off the field: 'I had 26 dances down on my programme; that holds the record for the tour so far.'

Kimberley welcomed them with dancing Zulus and its diamond mine, the largest man-made hole in the world. They were taken to admire Rhodes' Arab stallions and a selection of de Beers' finest gems worth £500,000; each player received a gift of garnets. The toast that evening to 'The Ladies' was 'responded to by Mr Todd, the handsome English forward'. The charming Tommy Crean, whose life by his own admission was then made up of 'wine, women, song and rugby' also won friends after the first Test in Port Elizabeth by telling a drill-hall audience that '[we] were supposed to come to South Africa to teach the colonists to play good football but so far as he could see there was no necessity to do that (to loud cheers)'. The entertainment that night included the Guards' band and 'songs, step-dances and nigger sketches' – this in the year that the South African Coloured Rugby Board was formed.

A hunting trip on the Transvaal veldt provided unusual fitness training for the players. Not permitted to ride before a game, they followed the hounds on foot, while the mounted non-playing contingent bagged three buck antelopes. Doornkop, the site of Jameson's defeat, was a grisly picnic place: 'most of the party wandered over the battlefield and made the usual collections of bones and cartridges etc, before attacking the provisions.' The team continued its winning ways, but their punishing itinerary up country was anything but a triumphal procession. After beating Grahamstown, they rose at dawn on Sunday and covered 36 miles in carts on roads so rutted that the players often had to dismount and push. That night there was no hotel and 'we had to sleep where we could find a resting place and eat what we could get'. The journey from Queenstown to Johannesburg took thirty-seven hours. Sir Clive Woodward would have been apoplectic.

Despite the tense political climate in Johannesburg, conditions improved and the second Test was won 17-8, in front of large numbers of women who 'quite outnumbered the sterner sex … and emulated the latter in their enthusiasm'. The list of ladies at the Wanderers' Hall that evening ran to six column inches in the local paper and Tartar commented on 'a very delightful function [although] the room was perhaps a trifle too crowded'. The Tremendous Mr Todd, who had scored his first (and only) international try that afternoon, would surely not have objected.

The team remained unbeaten until the final Test at Newlands, Cape Town, when South Africa first wore the jersey of myrtle green. Five-year-old Charles Bayly was perhaps too young to watch the game. The referee, formerly halfback for the home side, repeatedly penalised English wheeling; after this tour only neutral referees would be used. The home try was controversial, not least because scorer Alf Larard had played professional rugby in England. The South Africans withstood huge pressure to win 5-0. They not only salvaged their pride, but started an irresistible march to world supremacy in the game. After this historic victory, the tour was declared a success by both sides and even returned a profit of £600 12s 2d.[22]

The *Cape Times* was complimentary: 'The team now about to return to the Mother Country has given exhibitions of the game which have been of the very best. Three months constant play together has enabled the members to develop a style of combination in the field which is worth watching.'[23] Future Bishop of Bloemfontein, Walter Carey, described the tour as 'a very happy one, as the play of our opponents was scrupulously fair'. He preached a fine sermon on rugby morality:

> I hope and pray that South African teams will always play like gentlemen. Rugby football is a game for gentlemen: it is so easy to cheat at it and so destructive for this wonderful game. If a man wants to do dirty tricks, let him do it at ninepins in his own back yard, but let him keep clear of rugby football.[24]

On 28 September, fifteen of the tourists were greeted on their return to Waterloo, 'their healthy and bronzed appearance testifying to the efficacy of the South African climate'.[25] Crean and Johnston had decided to stay in Africa, with Crean, a qualified doctor, taking up practice and Johnston, a former Royal Inniskilling Fusilier officer, scenting military adventure. The two Dubliners had no ties in Ireland and took advantage of the free passage, returning to Johannesburg after the final Test in search of riches. Both played for the Wanderers Club and Johnston captained Transvaal in the 1897 Currie Cup final.

Alec returned to England, where his father's will had left him comfortable with a capital sum to invest. Despite his admittance to the Worshipful Company of Vintners (and the quasi-masonic Royal Antediluvian Order of Buffaloes), he chose not to enter the family business with James and William, but went into partnership importing timber from Sweden. On a business trip he is photographed in furs, looking like Omar Sharif's Zhivago. Nor did he return to Rosslyn Park, but played his regular rugby for new club Blackheath and Christmas tours with the Barbarians.

Summers were filled with cricket. Wisden records that playing for Beckenham against Streatham in June 1899 he was bowled three times in two overs, twice by no-balls. A month later he played at Crystal Palace for London County Cricket Club, captained (and managed) by Dr W.G. Grace, then 51 years old but still able to take eight wickets. The following rugby season was his last: in September he played as a guest for Park against his old school, Mill Hill, and in early 1900 he won his two England caps against Ireland (victory at the Athletic Ground in Richmond) and Scotland (a pointless draw at Inverleith, Edinburgh). He was not reselected the following season, as a direct result of injury in service to his country on another field.

The siren call of Africa and the friendship of Tommy Crean would lure Fin south again, this time for war. Britain's imperial expansionism and greed could not tolerate Afrikaner desire for a self-governing republic. The strait-laced Afrikaners led by President Kruger feared both the moral decadence of the *uitlander* gold-diggers and the rapacious empire. In the summer of 1899, local representatives told the British government that its citizens in the Transvaal, denied any voting rights, were being treated as badly as the blacks. This was the excuse to dispatch 10,000 troops and by October they were massed on the border; the Boers, however, made the first move by invading Natal. The fighting Irishmen, Crean and Johnston, had enlisted at Pietermaritzburg in September into the Imperial Light Horse, an irregular unit drawn from the dominions. Johnston was commissioned, but Crean spurned a medical officer post and entered the ranks as a trooper.

Both would take part in the relief of Mafeking and Ladysmith and both, remarkably, would win the Victoria Cross. At Elandslaagte in

October 1899, Crean, now an officer, was wounded, while Johnston 'very gallantly rushed forward under heavy fire and rallied the men, this enabling the flanking movement which decided the day'.[26] Johnston's bravery earned him the highest military award, although, trapped in besieged and diseased Ladysmith, he was utterly unaware. Racked by fever, he was admitted with Boer permission to Intombi Hospital, outside Ladysmith, in January. The demand for trained medics took Dr Crean from his horse and into the hospital, and – to his great surprise – to the bedside of his old rugby chum. The 118-day siege was finally relieved by Sir Redvers Buller in February 1900 to scenes of national rejoicing.

Lieutenant A.F. Todd, having contested the Calcutta Cup in chilly Edinburgh, was then whisked off to the African heat as a squadron commander in Roberts' Horse, another mounted unit drawn from all nations. He was wounded at Diamond Hill in June 1900; 14,000 British soldiers squared up to 4,000 Boers and forced them from their positions on the hill. Conan Doyle wrote of that battle:

> The country was an impossible one for cavalry, and the troopers fought dismounted, with intervals of twenty or thirty paces between the men. Exposed all day to rifle and shell fire, unable to advance and unwilling to retreat, it was only owing to their open formation that they escaped with about thirty casualties.[27]

One such casualty was Alec who recovered, only to be wounded again at Goedgedacht in March 1901 – he would leave his bullet-holed badge to his son. Unable to fight on, he eventually returned to England on the *Custodian* in September. His wounds put paid to his international rugby career.

As with Mark Twain, whom he met in 1896, some greatly exaggerated rumours had reached London. His brother Jim wrote in April: 'we are all jolly glad to hear you are well again or sufficiently so to allow you to be on the active list once more … the *Sportsman* put up a sort of obituary notice about you & the *Mail* copied it. Still "all's well that ends well".'[28] Jim was not only minding the family wine business, but also managing his brother's financial affairs, acting as middleman in negotiations with Modin,

Alec's Swedish partner in the timber venture, who was somewhat discomfited by his prolonged absence (and rumoured death) in South Africa.

The prodigal son took Jim's advice on the timber trade to 'chuck it altogether', joined his brothers in the family firm and finally settled down. He retained a militia commission in the Norfolk Regiment. Surgeon Captain Tommy Crean won his own Victoria Cross in December 1901 at Tygerskloof, when 'he continued to attend to the wounded in the firing line under a heavy fire at only 150 yards range after he himself had been wounded and only desisted when he was hit a second time, and as it was first thought mortally wounded'.[29] Invalided home, he received his VC from King Edward at St James' Palace in March 1902, and an Honorary Fellowship from the Royal College of Surgeons in Dublin.

Back in London, Tommy was introduced by his sister Alice to her best friend from her Roehampton Convent schooldays, the beautiful Victoria Heredia, daughter of Don Tomas Heredia of Malaga. An outing was planned to Henley. As he could not see Victoria unchaperoned, Tommy asked Alice to make up a foursome with his old friend Alec Todd, whose charms he played down, describing him to his sister as short, without personality, a last resort in desperation, but 'you only have to put up with him for the afternoon'.[30]

At the station, the tall, handsome Fin stepped from the train and the afternoon was just the beginning. In December 1902, 'Alice Mary Crean, 24, and Captain A F Todd M.A., 29' were married by the Rev. Edmund English at the church of St Peter and St Edmund, Westminster, with Tommy and Victoria as best man and bridesmaid. The bride 'wore a gown of ivory satin, veiled in chiffon, embroidered with silver true-lovers' knots'.[31] Alec gave the bridesmaids 'gold and turquoise bangles' and the couple departed for a Riviera honeymoon. Tommy and Fin were now brothers-in-law, as well as -in-arms, bound together in both scrimmage and marriage.

The Edwardian era brought a golden age of prosperity and happiness for both couples, as it did for much of middle-class England. Constance Mary Todd was born in 1904 and Bruce Edward in 1907 (he would one day become chairman of Findlater's on the death of Uncle James in 1956 – no son and heir was born to either

James or William). Tommy Crean would marry Victoria in 1905 and have a son Patrick and daughter Carmen.

Both men finally retired from the army, Tommy to private practice in Harley Street and Alec to be company secretary at Findlater's and to his cricket. In his late thirties he would still play for Berkshire, as he was by then living at Sunninghill, near Ascot. He excelled as a 'capital wicket-keeper', making forty-three dismissals, but little else: batting at number eleven, he averaged just 6.36 runs over three seasons. Photographed in his striped county blazer, the old jutting chin and Blues cap had been replaced by a jovial and fatherly beam beneath a soft trilby. The moustache was still there, bushier but no longer waxed, and the cauliflower ears told of his years in the scrum. Alec Todd had become genial wine-merchant, team stalwart and family man.

Fin, however, like Tommy, was a born warrior and neither could resist the call to arms in 1914. Crean joined the RAMC on 12 August, was wounded several times and twice Mentioned in Dispatches. In June 1915 he was awarded the DSO. By then, however, his dear friend and brother-in-law had died in No. 3 Casualty Clearing Station, Poperinghe on 21 April 1915, at the age of 41 years and 213 days. Even under the later Military Service Act of 1916, Alec would not have been required to fight at his age, but he had chosen to rejoin the Special Reserve battalion of the Norfolks. He was commissioned into the 3rd Battalion once more as a lieutenant, and went to France in October 1914, joining the regular 1st Battalion, which had been badly mauled at Mons and in the subsequent retreat. By December he was in the trenches in the Wulverghem sector at Ypres. It is tempting to imagine Alec with his ready charm, good singing voice and proficient school German, honed on wine-buying trips to the Rhineland, as one of the first to thrust out a hand and cigar at the famous '*Heilige Nacht*' Christmas truce.

He was mentioned in General Sir John French's dispatches. The official notice card personally signed by Winston Churchill looks remarkably like an invitation to a party – one the gregarious Alec certainly would not miss, even in this harshest of winters. He had written to 10-year-old Constance in late November:

Dear Little Sunshine

I got such a nice letter from you which pleased me ever so much. Today I got a letter and <u>three</u> parcels from Mummy 1) Letter of 24th November 2) Air-pillow 3) 200 Quo Vadis Cigarettes 4) Parcel with warm underclothing, a pipe, a splendid muffler & a Balaclava helmet. I can't think where Mummy got the pipe from, as it certainly isn't one of mine, but it was just what I wanted as I lost my other pipe in the trenches a couple of days ago … It is much warmer now so we are having a much better time; sitting out in the snow for three days & nights wasn't at all pleasant, especially as shooting was going on all the time. Thank Bruce for his very nice & well written letter; I will write to him again soon.

Best love to you Mummy, Bruce and Granny from
    Your fond old Dad

He was gazetted captain in April 1915. On the 17th he returned to the Salient, fresh from leave at 'Firthorpe', the family home in Ascot. A snapshot taken by Alice of 'fond old Dad' in uniform with the children beams from the album. These last moments with his dearest would have been his first spell home from the front. Officers were permitted ten days' leave in every eight months, the uniformed stewards on the Channel steamers and leave trains shuttling them back to Victoria station and the unreality of metropolitan civilisation. Then back again, welcomed with the hearty breakfast of the condemned: 'Honour to serve you again, Sir.'

Had leave relaxed him and let the tall man's concentration slip? The morning after his return he was fatally wounded at the infamous Hill 60. This 'hill' was a man-made spoil heap from a 'cataclysmal railway cutting' (Edmund Blunden's phrase) dug between Ypres and Commines, starkly named on British maps after its height in metres above sea level. More romantically, its local name before the war was *Côte des Amants* or Lovers' Hill, as it was popular with courting couples. In the Flanders levels it was a priceless observation point from which German artillery fire could be precisely directed. The British assault on 17 April 1915 began at 7.05 p.m. with the explosion of three mines which blew off the top of Lovers' Hill.

During the infantry attacks that followed a German bullet would do much the same to the great charmer Alec Todd.

His file at Kew holds several witness statements to his death, usually only taken where there was some doubt or no corpse or, more prosaically, for life assurance affidavits and proof of tax deductibility to the Inland Revenue under the Death Duties (Killed in War) Act, passed by parliament in patriotic haste in September 1914. Accounts of his fatal wound differ – unsurprising in the fog of battle or a disordered mind on a hospital ward – but the charisma and leadership of Todd shine through them all. He fought as he played his rugby; standing tall and with no fear, and his men loved him for it. This Lion they willingly followed:

> Informant saw Capt Todd who was a very tall man, standing on Hill 60 in a very exposed position. He seemed perfectly regardless of his danger and two or three men remarked that if he stayed there he was bound to be hit, and suddenly they saw him fall. Informant was in a little shelter where they brought Capt Todd and gave him First Aid; he thinks that he was hit in the chest and he heard the CO say he thought there was every hope for him; he was then carried off to the nearest ambulance. It may be of interest to add that his men all liked him and were much concerned at his being wounded, and hope that he will recover.
>
> Pte Coleman, No. 12 Gen. Hospital, Rouen

> This Officer was hit in the trenches witness says that he knew no fear and that he was standing up watching the Germans through glasses. He habitually exposed himself to danger. He was hit in the shoulder and witness thought that he died of his wounds. He was very much regretted in the regiment and was regarded by everybody as a very fine officer.
>
> Sgt Halesworth, 6384 B Coy

> This officer was just made Capt and was shot through the head – on Hill 60 a week after the Hill was blown up. He was looking over the parapet being a very tall man and was shot by a rifle bullet. He was taken away and did not speak at all, so I fear that he

was unconscious. I do not know to which hospital he went but he died of wounds wherever it was. At least so I heard.

L/Cpl A. Valentine, 8657 Hospital Ship, Boulogne

Lt Todd was wounded at Hill 60 on Sunday 18th April by a bullet wound through the neck. He was very bad and I sent him back myself to the ambulance. They got him away from the ridge to the dressing station and he should have reached Poperinghe. The regimental doctor sent up a message that he was not in danger, but after such a wound I feel very anxious about him. He was conscious when I saw him and could talk, but could not bear to be touched and had no feeling in the legs.[32]

Capt. Stone, 1st Norfolks, Princess Hospital, Boulogne

Captain Stone asked for a volunteer to take him to an Advanced Dressing Station. Private Botwright (by now in Manton Grange Hospital, Oakham) got him safely to Transport Farm dressing station and stayed with him for three hours. Concern for his officer or understandable reluctance to hurry back to the cauldron? Alec spoke to other officers and asked Botwright for a cigarette, which he smoked. Captain Stone was right to be anxious: Todd fought on for three days in hospital before succumbing to his wounds on the 21st. The notice of his death was sent to his brother James, whom he had registered as next of kin so that Alice should not first hear the fateful knock at her Ascot door. The delivery address on the telegram was Findlater's Corner. This ghost of a building welcomed home Fin's spirit; was it 11.47 when that telegram arrived to stop all the clocks?

Praised by E.H.D. Sewell, former Harlequins captain and compiler of the Rugby Internationals Roll of Honour, as 'this great big delightful boy, merely to know whom was one of the pleasures of existence', Alec was much loved as a 'good straight Briton of the type that makes us proud to be of the same race'. One of Alec's last letters (sadly lost) from Ypres was to Frank Mitchell, his old Cambridge captain from 1895, regaling him with tales of the rugby fraternity at the front. Sewell had played cricket for Buckinghamshire against Todd in 1912 and was both fond friend and obituarist:

'Toddles' had no enemies. His friends could not be counted. He played both great games of Rugby football and cricket to the last ounce, for all they and he were worth. He was one of the very best of opponents to meet when you had made a duck at cricket, as he made you feel your trouble was his, and not as is so often the case, that your failure was fit subject for gloating or cynical joy.[33]

A century later another tall, charismatic Rosslyn Park Lion would be remembered with similar affection on his death in 2010. One journalist wrote in tribute: 'there are two distinct kinds of great man: the great man so great that he makes every other man feel small – and the great man so great that he makes every other man feel great. Andy Ripley's was the latter species of greatness.'[34] Is it pure coincidence that A.G. Ripley, also of England, the British Isles, Barbarians and Rosslyn Park, was remembered by his friends at a packed memorial service in Southwark Cathedral, opposite Findlater's Corner? Those friends then adjourned to the nearby wine vaults to celebrate his life – Fin and Rips would surely have hit it off big time.

The mystery of the witness statements deepens: Capt. A.F. Todd's name is found engraved on the cavernous hall of the Menin Gate, memorial to those with no known grave. His body was first lost, which is a testimony to the chaos of the casualty stations or perhaps a long-range shell, scattering medics and corpses alike – Poperinghe was within range of the German naval gun 'Little Willie'. Alec Todd was then finally buried at Poperinghe Old Military Cemetery, shoulder to shoulder with his teammates. On either side lie two 'Soldiers of the Great War Known Unto God', in Kipling's phrase. A red rose blooms against the English white of his grave. Carved into the Portland headstone is the Norfolks' cap badge of Britannia. In her service Fin has played the game of rugby, fought wars in Africa and Belgium and, finally, laid down a life lived to its fullest.

4

ERIC FAIRBAIRN
BODY BETWEEN YOUR KNEES

Australian-born G.E. Fairbairn, known as Eric.

The tall figure slumps forward, exhausted by his efforts, bent double, hands trailing in the water. A deafening roar thunders in his ears; his lungs burn as if hot sand pours through them; he feels the blood pump in his temples fit to burst the drum-taut skin. His whole body shrieks with pain. In front and behind him the other men groan, yet relief shows on their faces. It is over; victory is theirs. He rolls to one side and vomits.

George Eric Fairbairn came from a large family in Melbourne, Australia. Several senior Georges were already prominent, so he was known as Eric. The leather-bound octavo annals of Rosslyn Park show that G.E. Fairbairn played just a single game, away against Chatham Services in March 1913, the last of the season. Inscribed in the secretary's elegant copperplate, his name is shown amongst the forwards for this 'fairly even game in boisterous weather' which Park won 8-3. But he does not reappear in September for the last season before the war.

He may have laboured the season unreported in the second XV before being rewarded with a first start at the top level. Or, in true

Corinthian casual style, he may have simply picked up a game in the absence of the regular starters. As a double Cambridge Blue, his sporting and social credentials were beyond question by the Hon. Secretary; any lingering accent from his native Australia had been polished away by his years in England, including two years of remedial speech training at cut-glass Eton College. At 6ft tall with a 40in chest, he was without doubt up to the mark in the pack, as in the army, where the minimum chest size was 36in. Peacetime criteria were relaxed in time of need in 1914, when 44 per cent of recruits fell short.

More likely he was strong-armed into playing by his friend, John Brenchley Rosher, the pillar of the Park scrum. You did not argue with this friendly giant, who rowed in the six seat of the 1911 Cambridge Varsity eight: in the first hundred years of the Boat Race, Rosher at 93kg (14 stone 6lb) was the second heaviest oarsman to take to the Thames.[1] Today he would be dwarfed by modern behemoths: the 2009 Oxford crew was the heaviest ever at an average 99.7kg, while Thorsten Engelmann at 110.8kg in 2007 was hardly a light Blue.[2] But few modern oarsmen now go on to lead a battalion and win the MC, DSO and bar as did John Rosher. A request to play rugger, old boy, was not lightly refused.

Perhaps Eric also had the luxury of time on his hands with an allowance from his prosperous parents, at whose Westminster address he lived. On the day after war was declared in August 1914, he enthusiastically presented himself at the Dukes Road, Euston recruiting station to enlist in the 28th London Regiment (Artists' Rifles) as Private 1623, Fairbairn. His application declares his age as 25 years 11 months, but under trade or profession he states 'None'. In late season 1913, the sturdy Chatham sappers and subalterns may have decided to teach this indolent toff a lesson and given him a tough baptism on the field of play from which he never recovered. Or it may simply be that, despite his imposing stature, he was a fish out of water. For rugby was not his first love: like Rosher, Eric Fairbairn was decidedly a 'wet bob' – his domain was not the field but the river. Rowing was his reason for living and it would give him the cause for which he would soon die.

The Fairbairn dynasty in Australia had Scottish roots. Grandfather George had emigrated from Berwickshire on a free passage in 1839, built up large sheep stations in Victoria and started the first canning and meat-freezing works in the 1870s. This was lucrative business in a country whose main export trade was shipping meat on the long voyage back to Great Britain. It made him a very wealthy man, known for his tough constitution – in old age he had a damaged hand amputated without anaesthetic.[3]

He married Virginia Armytage and they raised 'my thirty-seven feet of sons', as he fondly called them. The six brothers were not only tall but great sportsmen and natural leaders. The eldest, George again, had Cambridge Varsity trials before returning to Australia, where he built an extensive business empire in livestock, farming and insurance, and became a notable public figure, being returned to the Legislative Assembly in 1903 and knighted in 1926. Brothers Charles and Stephen both won rowing Blues for Cambridge. To George's fifth son, Thomas, and Margaret Lena Fairbairn was born a son, George Eric, at Toorak, Melbourne, on 19 August 1888.

For scions of wealthy dominion dynasties, the destination of choice for a decent education was England. After early schooling in Folkestone and Dover, Eric arrived at Eton in January 1902, aged 13. Here he began a long acquaintance with various stretches of the River Thames, if rather a short one with the college, lasting only until July 1903. Fairbairn did not flourish at Eton: he was in Brinton's house but left little mark, and there are no records of 'sent-ups', when distinguished work would be sent up to the headmaster. Either Eton was not to his liking or he may have been 'incapacitated by illness' as he would later be at university; the house list for Michaelmas term 1903 shows his name but he is marked absent for the whole term. The *Times* obituary writer commented rather sniffily, 'as he only stayed at school for two years he cannot wholly be said to be an Etonian oarsman'.[4] We can safely assume the obituarist was an Old Etonian.

A spell under a private tutor was enough to earn him a place at Jesus College, Cambridge. When he went up in 1906 he was the latest in a distinguished line of rowing Fairbairns (and by no means the last):

    ... the most frequent name in Boat Race annals is that of Fairbairn, for their name has appeared in the Cambridge lists in no less than seven past contests: Mr AA Fairbairn rowed in 1858 and 1860; Mr C Fairbairn in 1879 and Mr S Fairbairn in 1882, 1883, 1886 and 1887.[5]

Young Eric Fairbairn was under greater pressure even than aviator Charles Bayly to live up to the family example; his over-achieving uncle was still very much alive, kicking and coaching him from the towpath. Eric's obituary would note his uncle's influence: 'His rowing achievements are rather connected with Jesus College, Cambridge, which owes no small part of its fame as a rowing college to that great oarsman of the eighties, Mr Stephen Fairbairn.'

Steve Fairbairn's own claim to fame lies less in rowing than in his successful coaching; such was his influence that his name applies adjectivally, as in 'Stevian' or 'Fairbairnist'. Like other charismatic coaches – say Bill Shankly or Vince Lombardi in gridiron football – he left a legacy of memorable aphorisms: 'If you can't do it easy, you can't do it at all'; 'Enjoy your rowing, win or lose'; 'Mileage makes champions'. In keeping with this last dictum, he also lent his name to the murderous Head of the River endurance races rowed from Mortlake to Putney and on the Cam in autumn; the author has personally suffered the mileage of this last ordeal, but it did not make him a champion. A memorial stone obelisk to Steve on the Surrey bank marks the mile post from the Putney start of the annual challenge race between Oxford and Cambridge; it also marks the last mile of the Head of the River championship rowed in the other direction.

Steve was called to the Bar in 1886, but never practised. To his four Blues he added the Grand Challenge Cup (the pinnacle of rowing), the Stewards' Cup, and the Wyfold at Henley, whilst – by his own casual claim – winning 'hundreds of Regatta races'[6] before returning to Australia in 1887. On a fleeting visit to England in 1898, he competed at Henley, 'to general astonishment', aged 36. From 1904 he lived again in England, dividing his time between his London directorship of Dalgety & Co. and his *alma mater*, Cambridge, where he pursued his greatest love. He passed this on to his son Ian, who rowed for Britain in the 1924 Olympics and then invented unit trust investment at M&G.

Steve coached Jesus College for a third of a century; invariably its boats went Head of the River, and never came lower than fourth. His so-called 'Fairbairnism' aimed to focus the mind on the oar and on moving the boat, rather than on the supposedly correct motions of the body. He experimented with long slides and swivel rowlocks. In his 1931 autobiography *Fairbairn of Jesus*, he described the best action for moving a boat as 'an exact imitation of the Heave Ho of eight sailors heaving at a rope, a perfect loose and easy elastic action' – elsewhere described as 'swan-like' and 'dreamy-looking'. The Jesus coaching revolution 'speedily began to attract the attention of the rowing world and gave rise to considerable controversy'.[7] The conservative rowing establishment derided the new style imported from a land peopled, as far as it knew, by kangaroos and convicts. But Jesus freshmen took to the water in hordes, which caused great envy and some student cynicism at rival colleges. Everest mountaineer George Mallory, then rowing at nearby Magdalene, wrote in ironic prose of deepest purple:

What great things are now expected of this Jesus method of rowing! The style of the captain, the style of the secretary, the style of stroke, all imaginable styles … all are to be blended in an homogeneous, ergocosmic device, the ingenious and possibly ingenuous Quintessence of a Facile, Indefatigable Compendulum. We are to have a Jesus coach. Goldsmith has said: 'God will provide. But alas, how fickle, how selfish the Theocracy'. A fortnight has passed, and still no god to coach us.[8]

Unsurprisingly it was the river and not academic study that was to preoccupy Eric at Cambridge. He spent five years there, winning Blues in 1908 and 1911. Despite passing preliminary exams and part one of the history tripos in December 1910, he did not do enough to proceed to a degree. He features as a 'Cock of the Roost' in the Jesus College magazine, *Chanticlere*,[9] which states that he had also started reading for the economics tripos but transferred to the 'General' – reading for an ordinary degree, not honours. On the river, however, 'his rowing career has been one unbroken chain of successes … Like all geniuses, he has his idiosyncrasies. He hates collars, takes no milk in his tea through fear of dead flies, and is a confirmed Peripatetic after bump-suppers.' In other words, he was given to wandering about in a drunken state after Boat Club dinners; this would not markedly distinguish him from thousands of lesser oarsmen since, as this author can testify.

His *annus mirabilis* was 1908, although it was not without controversy. Eric stroked the victorious coxless four in Michaelmas term. Jesus rowed over as Head of the River in the Lents. In the May Bumps, Jesus was unable to dislodge Trinity Hall as Head of the River (they would prevail in 1909), but won the Ladies' Plate at Henley Regatta for the first time in thirty years. Eric Fairbairn also won the Colquhoun single sculls by 40 yards from another Jesus man, H.E. Swanston. Eric is photographed 'come forward' in his racing shell, dark-eyed and intense. Greater challenges were to come.

At Putney Bridge on 4 April, at precisely 3.30 p.m., he sat in the two seat of the university eight for the annual Boat Race against Oxford. Cambridge was hot favourite, having won the two previous encounters. This was the year that a stadium was built on 'Billy Williams' cabbage patch' in rural Twickenham: two covered stands, east and west, for 3,000 spectators each, a south terrace for 7,000 and an open mound to the north, all at a total cost of £8,812 15s raised by debentures. The Empire Stadium Wembley was not yet an imaginary figment. Much has changed since in these two iconic stadia and their sports, but the Boat Race and Old Father Thames still look largely the same. The Tideway course is 4 miles 374 yards, rowed against the stream; it is one of the most gruelling sporting events in the world.

In the Edwardian era, rowers had the glamour of David Beckham with the added pedigree of impeccable breeding. *Vanity Fair* accorded them sporting profiles alongside cricketers, boxers, jockeys and Bisley sharpshooters (not one rugby player appeared and the only footballer was the aristocratic Lord Kinnaird, who kept goal for England attired in long white cricket trousers). With a bevy of Etonians and sprinkling of Hons in every Blue boat, oarsmen were the eligible pin-up boys of pre-war sporting society – they kept their looks better than bruised rugger players. Not that rowing girls could flirt with their idols – Oxford Women's Boat Club 1906 rules made strict stipulation:

Rule 1: Young ladies shall take their outings at such times that they do not encounter gentlemen's crews.

Rule 2: They shall have a draw string in their skirt hems so that no ankle is exposed.

Rule 3: If coaching by a gentleman is desired leave must be obtained from their moral tutors and a gentleman cox must act as a chaperone.

Cambridge stroke, D.C.R. Stuart, was controversial for a new unorthodox style – a fast, jabbing stoke with little swing – that had traditionalists harrumphing with almost 'theological fanaticism',[10] but which brought three successive victories for his Varsity. Stuart's portrait by 'Spy' (A.G. Hales) shows tousled blonde hair, scarf rakishly draped around his wide shoulders, hands casually in shorts pockets and an expanse of muscled arm and leg that would have had female readers all of a flutter. The adoration of 'Golden Oars' gushes faster than the ebb tide on the Thames:

> Mr. Douglas Stuart is a great athlete … An oarsman of demoniac swiftness and skill, who has led the Cambridge crews to victory over Oxford and Harvard. Originally of health so delicate that he was not expected to live, he has made himself an athlete by sheer determination of will. When racing, the passion and rapture of the contest possess him till he shouts aloud and his eyes flame with a sort of joyous anger. His presence infects his whole crew with the same combative high spirits. The river reeks with men who are good, but greatness comes to few, and Stuart is great; the old grey river has sung its song in his ears, and he has heard the song and held it.[11]

Both crews had trained over the course for three weeks. The *Centenary History* recounts a day of victory for the Light Blues on a course whose landmarks are enduringly familiar:

> There was a fairly strong headwind on the day, but a good tide. Oxford won the toss and took the Surrey station. In the first minute Cambridge rowing 39½ [strokes per minute] to Oxford's 38, began gradually to draw away. The water was very lumpy, and

the smoother easier style of Cambridge enabled them to gain rapidly. They were clear at the Mile Post and two lengths ahead at Harrod's. Here their superiority in pace came to an end, and hard though they rowed, they could not add materially to their lead. Oxford attacked again and again, and it took Cambridge all their time to ward off these attacks. It was not till after Barnes Bridge that Cambridge were able to draw away, and in the end they won by two and a half lengths, in 19 min 20 sec.[12]

The *New York Times* reported that 'the Oxford men who had gamely rowed a losing race were much distressed at the finish'. Triumph and despair at the finishing post at Chiswick Bridge come in equal measures for winner and loser; Eric would experience both, but at dinner on that triumphant night in 1908 he would have been as peripatetic as a newt in his duck-egg blue blazer.

Despite the win and acclaim for Stuart, the Cambridge victory was deemed a lacklustre performance from the eight nominated to represent Great Britain in the Olympic Games that summer. The selectors, fearful of losing at home, 'made a bold experiment' – they hedged their bets. The gentlemen of the committee, for whom a 1908 Will Carling would have coined a choice name, decided:

> … to invite some of the older men to try to get fit with a view to rowing in the Olympic Regatta. Several responded to the Committee's invitation, in a manner that deserved the highest praise. They began rowing at Putney early in April and took an infinite amount of trouble to get fit and regain old time form.[13]

They assembled a second crew of veteran Blues, including 40-year-old Guy Nickalls, long retired from the river, to row under the cerise flag of Leander, of which all were members. The Light Blue crew was reshuffled; the only man to lose his seat was Eric Fairbairn, replaced by fellow Jesus man and former Cambridge president, Henry Goldsmith. No explanation was given and he remained a substitute; was there some prejudice against an Antipodean in the Blue Riband event of the Olympic regatta? It did not stop him competing for Britain in another boat; Eric would have the last laugh.

The 1908 Olympic Games opened on 13 July at the White City Stadium, amidst the fairyland of gleaming stucco pavilions that was the Franco-British exhibition. It rained all day before the opening parade and there were large empty stretches in the 10 miles of seating – only 17,000 of 150,000 seats were under cover. Rowing took pride of place: the Great Britain team paraded past King Edward and Queen Alexandra, led by oarsmen of both hues of Varsity Blue. Photos show bare legs, baggy shorts, scarves and blazers buttoned against the unseasonal cold, and a casual stroll that betrays the lack of military conscription in Britain, in contrast to the regimented march of the Europeans. Shepherds Bush not being known for its watercourses (although an open swimming pool was built within the stadium), the rowing was held at Henley-on-Thames, spiritual home of the sport.

The regular Henley course of 1 mile 550 yards was lengthened by 330 yards to the presumed advantage of the heavyweight GB/ Leander crew. They first triumphed over the renowned Canadian Argonauts. Would imperial yards also prevail over those suspect European metres? In the second semi-final, the Cambridge student eight faced the mighty Belgians of the Royal Club Nautique de Gand (Ghent), twice winners of the Grand Challenge Cup at Henley. Despite Stuart's dashing looks and noble heroism, the Light Blues 'showed unmistakable signs of staleness … and when the strain came the crew disintegrated'.[14] This was the only rowing heat in which a British boat was defeated by a visiting nation. Cambridge had to be content with bronze but Leander saved the empire's blushes by pulling through for final gold over the Belgians 'in a triumph for the traditional style of University rowing' – and vindication for the committee. Huzzah!

Substitute Eric Fairbairn, watching from the bank, would see the red, yellow and black of Belgium again – and more than once. Meanwhile, he teamed up with Jesus colleague Philip Verdon in the coxless pairs and enjoyed that rare British experience of beating the Germans in a semi-final (no penalties in rowing). The all-British final saw Fenning and Thomson take gold over Verdon and Fairbairn. But Eric had his Olympic silver medal, one up on his erstwhile colleagues in the eight. Today's BBC stands on the White City Stadium site;

Fairbairn's name is etched into a silvered wall, just yards from the spot where Dorando Pietri was memorably helped across the marathon finishing line, unable to stagger the extra 385 yards added to 26 miles so that grateful athletes could finish at the Royal Box.

The following year Eric captained Jesus Boat Club, but missed a second Blue when he fell ill a week before the Boat Race (he would regain his seat but lose to Oxford in 1911). Jesus entered the Grand at Henley, beat London Rowing Club and Leander but lost the final to those pesky Men of Ghent. They would wait until 1911 for the rematch (losing the 1910 final to Magdalen, Oxford); in May they set out on what coxswain Conrad Skinner called the 'Belgian Expedition'. The future Reverend Skinner had no hesitation in comparing Jesus to Biblical underdogs:

> The enterprise of taking a crew drawn from a single college to race the Belgians on their own waters was greeted for the most part with the scorn ridicule and cynical indifference which David evoked in his hardy challenge to Goliath of Gath. *The Sportsman*, however, was kindly and cordially disposed; *The Field* most magnanimous and cheering; also there were some others among their contemporaries which did not carp or ignore.[15]

The Sportsman indeed managed down any expectations, but with a whiff of suspicion that the foreign opposition might be – whisper it – 'professional':

> Once more it is necessary to point out that the Eight which has just left to row the Belgians is not a representative English crew. It is just Jesus College that is going to race a combined Belgian crew, with the knowledge that the Belgians have won on three of the last four occasions they have visited Henley – and when they were beaten it took one of the finest amateur eights, the Leander crew at the Olympic regatta. It is difficult to think that the Jesus men will win, but they carry with them the good wishes of their countrymen.[16]

Much as the press portrayed this as a plucky 'Old Pals 3rd XV' against the All Blacks, the crew did not lack experience or motivation, with six of the crew beaten by the Belgians in the 1909 Grand Challenge. Coaches were Uncle Steve and Stanley Bruce, a Blue and 'enthusiastic student of "Stevian" methods'; he was another Toorak boy who would later become Prime Minister of Australia. Eric rowed at seven, having bulked up by 12lb; behind him sat Henry Goldsmith who had taken his place in the Olympic boat and suffered defeat by Belgian oars. Thanks to Bruce they 'came to the post in the pink of physical fitness … able to turn out 43, 45 and even 47 strokes a minute without the least discomfort'. The crew photograph shows them sporting a variety of blazers, caps and boaters. Eric, in full Blues regalia, looks relaxed, but there are no smiles; these were men on a mission.

To their astonishment, they were hailed as superstars 'from Antwerp to Ghent, and from Ghent to Brussels':

> The race became the primary topic in press and popular conversation. English ideals of sport were paramount and my cutting book is an almost unbelievable revelation of Belgian devotion to English sport and representative sportsmen. Not one invitation in ten that was lavished upon us could be accepted. If we entered the Opera the prima donna stopped in mid-aria and the orchestra struck up 'God save the King'.

Over 100,000 spectators lined the canal at Terdonck on 25 May, putting the genteel indifference of Henley to shame; in today's stewards' enclosure, the striped blazers, champagne flutes in hand, still have their backs turned to the river. Skinner recounted:

> Cheering broke out as the Belgian crew seized the lead on the first half-dozen strokes, but then having set the boat moving in four quick but gradually lengthening strokes, we settled into our stride, and speedily drew level … we gave a 'ten' which let daylight in between our rudder and their bows, and with steady confidence this was increased to a lead of a length and a half before the bridge was reached. This huge structure, marking the mile, witnessed the decisive struggle. Under cover of its shadow and hidden for perhaps a hundred feet from our opponents under

our respective arches, we raised our stroke slightly and gave such a 'ten' that we leaped ahead … we both battled on to the finish, amid an uproar that was little short of deafening.

The popular acclaim continued off the water. 'Our reception was magnificent. Sportsmanship we had expected, but of such enthusiasm for a foreign crew unexpectedly winning this eagerly anticipated race on home waters we had never dreamed.' A march composed in their honour was played at the gala dinner; 10,000 Belgians waited four hours outside the banquet hall to catch a glimpse of the Jesus crew; a set of race postcards sold 170,000 copies in one week.

The previously sceptical English press was now quick to hail the 'national' achievement by the unfancied college crew:

And these young fellows who had come down from Cambridge and lived together and quietly practised to meet a picked Belgian crew just for the honour of English rowing and to return a visit long since overdue. For, while the Belgians' eight had come here, even the wealth and numbers of Leander had not risen to the occasion and sent an Eight as courtesy required. It was a thoroughly sportsmanlike piece of work on the part of the Jesus men. Their College may well be proud of them.[17]

Back at the proud college, *Chanticlere* printed a mock-heroic saga of 'Briton v. Belgian',[18] with 'ample apologies to the late Poet Laureate', full of student in-jokes, paying tribute to:

Eric the mighty;
Red was his face
And blue was his raiment.
Kinsman was he
To Steve the great trainer

Conrad Skinner, in a mood of post-war and post-imperial humility, later admitted: 'no crew was ever feted as we were and many of us took shame at the poverty of England's welcome to Belgian crews at Henley in past times.' The experience clearly left an indelible mark in the minds of these young men, for whom, other than Eric, this was probably their first time outside the borders and attitudes of Little England. 'Never will any member of the crew forget the amazing generosity of the Gantois, in fact of the Belgians as a nation.'

Jesus College did not forget. Moved by the fate of tiny Belgium as Germany overran it in the first weeks of August 1914, the college started a Belgian relief fund and raised £800 (around £60,000 today). President of the Royal Club Nautique, Maurice Lippens, rowing legend and lavish host in 1911, 'was deported on account of his patriotic energy by the Huns, and only after four years of internment in Germany was able to render thanks to his Jesus friends'. For the outraged Jesus rowers, the Germans' cynical violation of Belgian neutrality was a personal affront.

Oarsman Eric Fairbairn joined the Artists' Rifles immediately the recruitment offices opened after the August Bank Holiday; his Belgian rivals were now allies in need. He was commissioned in October as second lieutenant into the 10th (Service) Battalion Durham Light Infantry (DLI), experienced men, many with service in the Boer War. Cambridge and Rosslyn Park comrade John Rosher joined the 14th Battalion. The northerners would be as strange to an Eton and Cambridge Aussie like Eric as they were to Ernest Parker, also of the 10th, who wrote: 'Around me was a sea of unfamiliar faces queerly different in type from any others I had known. Words like *yam*, *cracket*, *ganin* reached me and very little I heard could I understand. A queer army was Kitchener's.'[19] At Witley camp, without roads or drains, their huts were unfinished and leaking. It was February before they were issued with service rifles and new leather equipment.[20]

In Cambridge's first weeks of war, Arthur Gray, master of Jesus, entertained the troops marshalling on Midsummer Common:

… the officers of the Durhams messed in hall with the Fellows – the beginning of much good fellowship … Despite the tension of the time, the ill news of the Mons retreat, and rumoured Hun barbarities, it was a happy time – at least for us who were outside the penumbra of war. On four Sundays of glorious August sunshine there were great parade services on our Close – sights and sounds unforgettable.[21]

By December, wrote Gray, 'Belgian refugees flocked into the town – many of them university professors and students – and were hastily housed under any hospitable roof that offered. There was a big reception at Jesus Lodge on New Year's Day.' The Jesus Roll of Honour was lengthening daily: 150 college members, including fifty from the Boat Club, were to give their lives in the war.

The members of the 'Belgian Expedition' of 1911 were hardest hit. Like Eric, they rushed forward to volunteer for the defence of their gracious hosts, outraged by reports of German atrocities on civilians. The popular press carried lurid reports of bayoneted babies, mutilated children, raped nuns and British bodies boiled for their fat as tallow or grease. Lt Hugh Willoughby Shields, RAMC, who won the Lowe Double Sculls with Eric in 1910, was first to die in October 1914, tending a wounded Irish guardsman at Ypres; Lt Henry Goldsmith of the Devonshires was killed at Ploegsteert in May 1915; Thomas Crowe died at Gallipoli in June; and Gerald Hudson was killed in January 1916. All four vanished without trace: their names are found on memorials to those with no known grave.

The 10/DLI left Aldershot on 21 May 1915, crossing from Folkestone to Boulogne that same night. On the 25th, the fourth anniversary of the 'Triumph at Terdonck', they left by train for Cassel and marched to Volkerinkhove, destined for the Ypres Salient. They would spend the night billeted in barns. No band played, no crowds cheered and the banquet was plain bully beef and tea. From here they moved eastwards, closer to the front and were in Bailleul, still inside France, on the last day of May. Eric Fairbairn was ready to fight for what little remained of unoccupied Belgium.

He stood once more on Belgian soil on 12 June, when the DLI went into the trenches west of Wijtschate ('Whitesheet' in Tommy vernacular) around Kemmel, where Guy du Maurier died in March. Eric was a few miles from Ypres, and 50 miles from Ghent, where the reception had been so tumultuous on that far-off day. Unknown to him, Tom Crowe had died at Gallipoli the day before; the athlete's bodies of Shields and Goldsmith, honed to 'the pink of fitness' by Stanley Bruce (now in the khaki of the fusiliers), were now grey corpses lost and rotting in Flanders mud. On the night of 17 June, Eric moved into the front line with D Company.

There was no attack over the top, no offensive onslaught, just the sapping attrition of nightly shelling and mortar fire, and the ritual 'stand-to' at dusk and dawn. This was the inglorious warfare that accounted for more deaths than the famed set-piece battles. The War Diary for 20 June records: 'All companies returned from trenches early this morning ... D Coy reports 2/Lt Fairburn [sic] dangerously wounded ... by rifle grenade.' Like so many of the New Army's inexperienced junior officers, Eric's heroic defence of Belgium did not last long; he was fatally wounded in his first week at the front.

The first telegram arrives at Burton Court, Chelsea, on 22 June, informing Thomas and Margaret Fairbairn that their son 'is reported dangerously wounded nature or degree of wound not stated'. By this stage of the daily slaughter, the telegrams from the War Office were expediently pre-printed with the stark introductory words in their boxes:

Regret | to| inform | you | that |

The 26th brings the additional handwritten news that '2/Lt GE Fairbairn Durham LI died of wounds June 20th Lord Kitchener expresses his sympathy'. The sender has pencilled in the word 'Deeply', in some small attempt at regret beyond the dry brevity of the Secretary for War. His cause of death, the catchall 'GS [gunshot] Wound Head and Trunk' was reported by No. 3 Casualty Clearing Station at Bailleul, where he was then buried in the communal cemetery.

Two silk handkerchiefs were the only personal effects returned to his mother. In February 1919, she would receive his 'Death Penny' bronze plaque to place alongside his silver Olympic medal. The outer rim of the 12cm disc bears the words: 'He died for freedom and honour'. The accompanying scroll from the king reads:

He whom this scroll commemorates was numbered among those who, at the call of King and Country, left all that was dear to them, endured hardness, faced anger, and generally passed out of sight of men by the path of duty and sacrifice, giving up their own lives that others may live in freedom. Let those who come after see to it that his name be not forgotten.

Conrad Skinner, one Ghent victor who survived, remembered his friends from that glorious day of sporting battle in 1911: 'it is a melancholy coincidence that the whole stern four of the Jesus crew, and also Shields, lost their lives in the Great War. Yet there is a feeling of just pride that this should occur in aiding Belgium in her gallant defence.'

Regaining the freedom of Belgium took four more years of fighting and many thousands more deaths. As King George wished, the name of Eric Fairbairn – 'universally recognised as one of the finest oarsman who ever rowed'[22] – is no longer forgotten. Ten days after Eric's death, another Park player would set off by boat on his own crusading mission for King and Country, this time to a far-off fatal shore.

Nowell Oxland
A Green Hill Far Away

Lieutenant Nowell Oxland, Border Regiment, killed at Gallipoli, August 1915.

Aegean, July 16th 1915

Dearest Father,

I salute you from the decks of the Empress of Britain. She is a sturdy enough vessel, quite like her late namesake, although not like the fighting ships of your day. You should take pride – I have become quite the nautical character on our two weeks passage, & many of our chaps praise the scraps of seafaring knowledge I have gleaned from my paternal instruction. To hear them you would think me Admiral Jellicoe, & I know this will amuse you as I am a landlubber at heart but have got my 'sea-legs' working.

We have left Alexandria and now we near the isle of Lemnos – where we will put in at Mudros & I hope to send back this letter, since we cannot be sure what will be at our destination. You can imagine these last days have been a tumult. My fingers trembled even at the word 'Aegean' atop this paper – to find myself sailing as Odysseus did in antiquity through 'wine-dark' seas ('blue violet 'is closer to the truth). I hope you may see this as suitable adjunct to my education, at His Majesty's expense!

The years of study at dear Durham & Oxford have certainly paid off – I read the charts to my men, who are ignorant of the Hellenic Alphabet. I have explained that the very word is Greek & you should see their eyes open wide that they know 'some little Greek' already. Cuthbertson has asked that I give him a few more of 'them old words' & I am becoming quite the teacher. I know that the Third was a disappointment to you, & you feel I have wasted too many hours on the rugger field, & should be more like Hodgson in my studies. But it has proved useful in a way that neither of us foresaw, & I now have a renewed appetite to tackle Greats again, or History, when we have finished this little show. Our destiny lies across the straits from Troy, and I dream that we may finish our business in short order and cross the Hellespont to walk on her ancient stones.

I think of you often in Alston & upon dear Cumberland (& even the hideous Taffy – throw him a stick for me). You must not worry on my account, and pray tell Mother I am in good heart – please ask her to return the Lovelace book to Worcester – it was forgot in all the haste of summer, but I fancy they will have no need of it while this war lasts & not judge me harshly.

I shall write again once we are settled & have pushed the Turk back to Constantinople. I do not know how the postal service will fare – we are hardly as close by as 'somewhere in France' – but news from home is welcome. This poor missive brings with it my love.

Your affectionate son, Nowell

***

En route Lemnos July 17th 1915

My dear Amy,

We are now departed from Alexandria – we were hard at work & saw nothing of her charms. As we rounded Crete & into the Aegean, my spirits soared – to think that we are so close to Athens itself! Our vessel is hardly the Argo although she does well enough & every island that we pass has a magical name & full of legend. Karpathos has a volcano which blows off perfect rings of smoke.

Yesterday we passed Skyros, home of Achilles, where poor Brooke is buried – several fellows here carry his poetry. His words were a beacon in those early days & it seems most queer that he is now gone – such beastliness that he should die so young & of sickness too, before he was able to reach the fight. I read that they gave him a fine burial – he has gone to 'join Achilles & the Immortals'.

My men are little touched by echoes of Antiquity – the heat is too much for them & in truth it is a misery – many of them were laid out through exposing themselves to the sun too quickly. Some cut off their trousers at the knees with knives & are a ragged bunch. All true Borders men, more used to Cumberland chills and mists, & their schooling is of more of shepherding & tillage than of Troy – if not for the consolation of seeing my learning in its glory, I too should find it intolerable.

We rest as we can by day, the evenings are more pleasing for the setting sun & the moonlight on the waves – I marvel and drink deep its beauty. There is a sparkle in the crests which they say is phosphorescence, & – wonderful to see – a dolphin gambolled in the bow-wave. We were sorry to see him go, as he was a fine fellow & good companion for an hour. We keep fit & well although there is quite a crowd on deck & little space to drill & exercise or pass a ball.

There is little else to occupy us on this voyage – semaphore practice, machine-gun drill & Swedish exercises & we play cards – although we are in good cheer & eager for the fight. I should not pretend that we are not mindful of others' fate in France & poor Belgium & hope that I shall show one hundredth part of their courage. Since April the papers are brim full of names from the Dardanelles & we know we shall have a fight & no man wants to funk it. To let the side down would be unbearable. I hear that the Yorks & Jimmy Dingle are on their way too – what fortune if we were to meet by chance & I know he will be a fine fellow in any fray. How he will fly down the wing at the head of his men!

I enclose some new verses I have penned in our days at sea. I know that newspapers print such trifles & should you and an Editor find them worthy I should be very glad of their publication – I venture they are superior to my 'juvenilia' which you have; they are but poetry (of a poor sort). Worry not about the title – the poem is of fond remembrance, not adieu.

Be assured I think of you often & long to be in your company in the Cumberland I love.

Your friend Nowell

These letters are imagined; their originals written, but now lost. Nowell Oxland's poem, however, was saved by its publication in *The Times*, attributed only to 'An Officer who has recently fallen in Gallipoli'. His close friend, Amy Hawthorn, collected his eighteen poems and seven stories in a slim volume, bible-black and gold-blocked for 'Private Circulation' in 1917 as war grew stale at Passchendaele. The frontispiece sketches his brief life in stark lines:

Born December 21, 1890
Educated at Durham School & Worcester College Oxford
Granted commission in the 6th Batt Border Regiment August 1914
Sailed for the Dardanelles, June 30, 1915
Killed at Suvla Bay, Gallipoli, August 9, 1915

Nowell was born to William and Caroline Oxland in Plympton St Mary, Devon, close enough to Christmas Day to be christened Nowell by his father, a Royal Navy chaplain. On his retirement, William became vicar of Alston in Cumberland, where his son would grow up to roam the fells as a sturdy yet scholarly boy. He entered Durham school as a King's Scholar in September 1903 and rose to be Head of School. He excelled at sports, rowed in the crew and played for the XV for three seasons. But he left suddenly and mysteriously 'under a cloud' and completed his studies for Highers at Tengewick Rectory, Buckinghamshire.[1] On his team at Durham was Jimmy Dingle – known as 'Mud' – who succeeded him as Head of School and went up to Keble, Oxford, in the same year that Nowell went up to Worcester College.

Their lives were intertwined on the rugby field: Dingle played for the Varsity at centre three-quarter, for England on the wing and, at Nowell's urging, for Rosslyn Park in London. In February 1912, the two friends faced each other on the pitch as Nowell turned out for

Park against Jimmy's Blues in Oxford. Oxland had not played at Park for over a season and 'filled in' for this midweek away fixture; Dingle scored twice. They would both make final appearances on another field: Nowell was killed two weeks before Jimmy, a few hundred arid and bitterly fought yards away from each other at Gallipoli.

Nowell Oxland was ever present in the Park forwards of the 1910/11 season, showing talent as a place-kicker. He converted his own try into a goal against RMC Sandhurst, for once outshining the stellar Dingle; kicking duties for forwards were not uncommon then, as a sodden leather ball needed more 'welly' than the three-quarter gazelles could give it. Oxland spread his rugby favours wide, also donning the jerseys of Richmond, Middlesex and his beloved Cumberland. Rugby for county, London club and skippering Worcester College left him little time for study; he took third-class honours in classical moderations in 1913. He then switched from classics to pursue an interest in history; his published work conjures the Roman and Celtic past of the northland, summoning ghosts of legionnaires and centurions. When war intervened he had not sat final examinations and graduated, but planned to return for a fourth year at Oxford.

He somehow found time to indulge another passion: literature. He joined Worcester's Lovelace Club, a literary society at which guest speakers read papers. Gatherings rarely mustered more than a handful in college rooms. Named after Richard Lovelace, a seventeenth-century Cavalier poet who attended Gloucester Hall, an earlier college on the site, the society had a lengthy pedigree. Oxland was elected a member in September 1913 – at its 376th meeting.

Overcoming a shyness rarely encountered in rugger players, Oxland threw himself enthusiastically into its intellectual scrimmage, presenting papers on de Quincey (a college alumnus) and Swinburne. He seconded a motion deploring the refusal of the Poet Laureate (Robert Bridges) to send the society a paper; but there is no evidence that he openly declared his own poetry. In a discussion on the revered Wordsworth, he stridently asserted that 'imagination was all-important in poetry. Experience alone was useless.' His own best poem would flow from his imagination, before hard experience abruptly dammed the stream.

The Lovelace's last minuted business in June 1914 was to elect 'Mr Oxland as Secretary for the coming Michaelmas term'. He took the minute book home but would never take up his duties. Amongst the names carved on the college memorial are club members, Elmhirst, Farquharson, Cottrell and Oxland. In January 1916, his mother Caroline returned the book to Worcester. Like rugby clubs, the Lovelace Club did not meet during the war and was only revived in 1919.

Nowell's poetic enthusiasm was influenced by another Durham rugby teammate, Oxford friend and child of Yuletide, Noel Hodgson, who stuck to his books at Christ Church and took a first in Mods, before his Greats were curtailed by war. Known affectionately as 'Smiler', Hodgson also loved the Lake District, where his family roots and home lay. Together, he and Nowell strode the hills and passes from Rosthwaite to Buttermere in the last untroubled summer of 1913. At Oxford he wrote poetry and published in wartime under the pen name of Edward Melbourne; did Lieutenant W.N. Hodgson know his most famous poem was published just two days before the Battle of the Somme? In 'Before Action' this bishop's son and devout Christian anticipates his fate as 'sanguine sacrifice' and prays, 'Help me to die, O Lord'. His fellow Devonshires officer, Captain Martin, had accurately plotted the enemy firing lines on to their position and foresaw the inevitable slaughter under the rattle and spatter of machine-gun bullets. Oxland's friend took one clean through the neck and died instantly, his servant and over 160 comrades beside him. Their bodies were hastily buried in their own trench at Mansell Copse. Perhaps aware that the mass tomb held a classically educated poet, an unknown hand carved on the wooden grave-marker: 'The Devonshires held this trench; the Devonshires hold it still.' This legend marked Hodgson's grave; now carved in stone, it marks it still.

This was to be a war of poetry, not prose. Diaries were strictly forbidden, although officers wrote prolifically and other ranks kept paper scraps hidden inside wrapped puttees. Men were in a hurry to express their feelings. Novels are crafted from narrative, characterisation and description, for which there was neither time nor paper at the front; poems were often written in snatched moments on the march or waiting for an attack. Only the stark juxtapositions, fractured language and jagged dislocation of syntax of poetry would do for the heightened and unreal experience of the trenches. The Georgian poetic conventions – sunrise as hope and sunset as calming beauty – were the first to be undermined by the tense expectation at 'Stand-to' at dawn and twilight. This war indelibly linked those hours 'at the going down of the sun and in the morning' with grieving remembrance. Lyricism was supplanted by a 'deep cry' of sadness and disillusion. After the war's bloody midpoint at the Somme, the poetic voice spoke only in tones of savage irony.

On 17 August 1914, Nowell's medical examination at Oxford shows him to be solidly built: 5ft 9in, 162lb, with a 38½in chest. In September he joined the Border Regiment, as befitted an Alston boy, where he might expect the volunteers under his command to be similarly robust, hardened by the tough rural life and climate of the north; certainly they should have been in far better shape than the poorly nourished, slack-chested workers from the cities. This is the man who wrote passionately of 'Cumberland' in his poetry, with a jibe at 'soft southerners':

> The Wild for us! our sensuous palate tires
> With surfeit of insipid battening:
> Give us the North – and keep your level shires –
> The high wet North, lit by a gleam of Spring
> And all aglow with opalescent fires
> Great fells and leap of waters glittering[2]

Unfortunately for this lover of the fells, he found himself at training camp at Belton Park, near Grantham, in the very 'level shire' of Lincoln. The 6th Battalion, the first of the Borders' service battalions, raised under Army Order No. 324, was a mixed bunch, as Henry Johnson recounted on rejoining at its Carlisle depot:

> Here were old men, young men, men of varying degrees of fatness, ex-soldiers, ex-militia men, ex-volunteers, tramps and a sprinkling of sleek-looking individuals who looked like shopkeepers. However, they were all keen and attentive, and although

many of them had never been in the Army before, they were all the stuff of which soldiers were made.[3]

Nevertheless, the avuncular retired colour sergeant with twenty-one years' service continues:

Cumberland answered this first call splendidly, and we all felt like real comrades to each other … The training was intensive, and between drilling, taking men to the doctor, getting them to sign attestation papers, taking them to meals in relays, and finding a place where they might rest their weary heads at nightfall, we ex-soldiers who had returned to the fold worked very hard. However, the 1914 spirit was strong within us, and we soon learned to love these new-comers and to let them have the advantage of our experience …

'Colour' is clearly in his element and might, for vastly different reasons, echo the sentiment of the younger Rupert Brooke: 'Now, God be thanked/Who has matched us with His hour.'[4] He sounds like a proud scoutmaster on annual camp:

I shall always remember the day we arrived at Grantham … how hopeless it seemed. There was only a large field with neither tents, nor blankets, nor food, so we ate our haversack rations and rolled ourselves up in our overcoats and went to sleep, for we were all very tired, having had a long journey and a long march. We were awakened by the noise of a motor lorry which had arrived with a few tents, blankets, rations, some fuel and two 'dixies'.[5] Needless to say, we at once started a fire, cooked a meal for ourselves and pitched our tents …

This was a very makeshift New Army, but one with 'the stout 1914 heart', according to Johnson:

Gradually we got clothing and equipment of sorts, emergency blue suits, emergency equipment, long worn-out rifles, civilian boots and overcoats of various patterns, and, most grotesque of all, emergency water-bottles made of tin and tied on with string!

These men did their training in these strange garments and did it well, and however curious they looked at the time, later, when we managed to rig them up properly, they did indeed present a fine appearance …

They were good enough to impress Lord Kitchener who inspected them on 18 October.

While in training for Flanders, they had an ominous foretaste of trench life: 'The weather began to be dreadful after the middle of October and the camp became a sea of mud', so they transferred to huts. They remained in camp until Christmas, forming part of 33 Brigade, 11th (Northern) Division under Major General Hammersley. There was ample time for battalion photographs. Lt Oxland stands in the back row of thirty-seven officers, looking more the sensitive poet than county rugger forward. The seated senior officers, including the white-moustached Lt Col Broadrick, sport swagger-sticks and canes. Just eleven would return unscathed from their first active service.

The Western Front had ground to a halt in static trench warfare from the sand dunes to the mountains. The Eastern Front with Russia divided the imperial German forces and had to be sustained. The Ottoman Empire's entry into the war on the German side closed the supply route to Allied Russia from the Mediterranean, the most viable given the climatic and tactical obstacles of overland routes or the Baltic. First Lord of the Admiralty Churchill originally conceived a purely naval affair in the Dardanelles; unlike Berlin or Vienna, the Turkish capital of Constantinople was within gunnery range of His Majesty's Navy. However, the loss of British ships to mines in the narrow straits forced the most hazardous of military operations: a seaborne invasion of the Gallipoli peninsula. This in many ways presaged Normandy 1944, by which time Churchill had fortunately learned a few lessons.

At Aldershot on 30 June 1915, the order came 'out of the blue' to prepare for overseas duty. The Borders' destination was not across the Channel; they were to reinforce the original Mediterranean Expeditionary Force (MEF) at Gallipoli, which had suffered heavy losses since the first April landings. Kitchener had low regard for

Territorial battalions and felt that his New Army volunteers had more of the fighting stuff needed to overcome the dogged resistance of the Turks. As the new draft was leaving England, the War Office in its wisdom had published General Sir Ian Hamilton's first dispatch from the Turkish front; the Borders knew just what lay ahead. They were bound for the inferno of Helles:

> The Isthmus of Gallipoli
> Is Satan's own abode,
> Where there isn't any water
> And there isn't any road[6]

They marched to Farnham station that evening and entrained for Liverpool. Such was the shortness of notice and speed of movement that 200 NCOs and men on leave were unable to return in time and had to rejoin the battalion later. Escorted by torpedo-boat destroyers, the *Empress of Britain* sailed on 1 July, passed through the Straits of Gibraltar by night and reached Valletta, Malta. Three days were spent ashore under an emblem familiar to Oxland: the Knights Templar cross was sewn on to the first Rosslyn Park shirts in 1879, for reasons unknown. It remains there today. The island's history reinforced the sense of a just crusade that impassioned the better-read of the brigade. Hamilton had argued successfully against Kitchener's original denomination of his 'Constantinople Expeditionary Force'. But for young, classically educated men like Oxland, this war was a quest for the Holy Grail, Golden Fleece and the honour of Helen all intertwined – and no less powerful than those mythical prizes.

Aboard the *Empress*, the private poet Lt Oxland composed the sixty-four lines of verse that would preserve his name in future anthologies, although their first publication is anonymous. His opening lines echo the popular song by Stoddard King, a Yale American, doubtless sung by the departing men. As the strains of *There's a long, long trail a-winding* drifted from the decks on the night air, he wrote of Cumberland in nostalgic mood:

> There's a waterfall I'm leaving
> Running down the rocks in foam,

There's a pool for which I'm grieving
Near the water-ouzel's home

He was wrenched from his reverie into the present moment of their voyage to the 'fringes of the world' as they left behind the harbour lights of the Mersey (deleted from the first draft as less than mythical). A lost draft carries an epigram from Virgil's *Aeneid* (*O terque quaterque beati* – O thrice, four times happy).[7] Like many educated men on the same trajectory to a hard landing near ancient Troy, he invokes another fleet of heroes bound for the Hellespont:

Though the high gods smite and slay us,
Though we come not whence we go,
As the host of Menelaus
Came there many years ago[8]

There are echoes too of Rupert Brooke's sonnets, recently published in May and declaimed from the Easter pulpit of the Dean of St Paul's. On the same voyage three months earlier with the Royal Naval Division (RND), Lt Brooke was in a classical whirl of Rome, Carthage and Ilium, writing to the painter Jacques Raverat:

We've been gliding through a sapphire sea, swept by the ghosts of triremes and quinquiremes, Hannibal on poop, or Hanno … and soon – after Malta – we'll be among the Cyclades. There I shall recite Sappho and Homer. And the winds of history will follow me all the way.[9]

Brooke's ambition fell short of Lord Byron, who swam the Hellespont in homage to Leander's visits to Hero. Today by sponsoring the same swim for charity you can 'Help a Hero' – 'spirit of place' again? More exciting, as he told Prime Minister Asquith's daughter Violet (whose brother, Arthur, was with him), was the prospect of the Trojan battlefield: 'I've been looking at maps. Do you think that *perhaps* the fort on the Asiatic corner will need quelling, and we'll land and come at it from behind and they'll make a sortie and meet us on the plains of Troy?'

No hero's death in battle for Troy or Byzantium awaited Brooke, but septicaemia from an untreated mosquito bite in Egypt. His 'war poetry' was untested by combat, beyond a day in the evacuation of Antwerp. He unwittingly contrived a final romantic flourish by dying on St George's Day, as one of Housman's 'lads that will die in their glory and never be old'. His body was buried in an olive grove on the isle of Skyros, legendary home of Achilles and burial place of Theseus, secure in his own mythology. On a white-painted cross was pencilled: 'Here lies the servant of God, Sub Lieutenant in the English Navy, who died for the deliverance of Constantinople from the Turks.' Oxland read of his poetic death in prosaic Aldershot.

Frederick 'Cleg' Kelly, Eton and Oxford, 1908 Olympic oarsman (with Fairbairn) and composer, wrote of the funeral: 'One was transported back a couple of thousand years, and felt the old Greek divinities stirring from their long sleep.'[10] In his tent at Gallipoli (ironically, from the Greek for 'fair city') Kelly wrote his *Elegy for String Orchestra*: '*In Memoriam Rupert Brooke*'. Brooke's own notebook contained fragments of verse showing Homer's epic on his mind: 'They say Achilles in the darkness stirred/Priam and his fifty sons/Wake all amazed, and hear the guns/And shake for Troy again.' Perhaps he was less mindful of Menander's fragment, ὅν οἱ θεοὶ φιλοῦσίνά ῥοθνήῃσκεί νέος – 'he whom the gods love dies young'.

Mourning for the youthful celebrity poet was nationwide. Churchill paid tribute to the 'nobility of our youth in arms engaged in this present war … He expected to die; he was willing to die for the dear England whose beauty and majesty he knew'.[11] Brooke was the first notable casualty of the MEF sent under Churchill's grand plan, which turned to disaster. General Sir Ian Hamilton, who had fallen under Brooke's spell and offered him a post as aide-de-camp, was almost unmanned by grief in a bitter diary entry:

Rupert Brooke is dead. Straightaway he will be buried. The rest is silence … Death grins at my elbow. He is fed up with the old and sick – nothing but the pick of the basket will serve him now, for God has started a celestial spring-cleaning and our star is to be scrubbed bright with the blood of our bravest and best … War will smash, pulverize, sweep into the dustbins of eternity the whole fabric of the old world; therefore the firstborn in intellect must die.[12]

Charles Bean, the official Australian war historian, observed the humane Hamilton had 'a breadth of mind which the army does not in general possess'.[13] On the eve of battle, this broad mind was clearly under attack from Churchill's 'Black Dog'.

From Malta the flotilla steamed for Alexandria and more consequence of the hurried departure, 'where all the transport, except cookers and water-carts, had to be landed and left behind, and much labour was necessarily expended on this owing to the faulty loading of the ship'.[14] Finally on 18 July they reached the teeming Mudros Harbour on Lemnos. Here Agamemnon, King of Mycenae, once lit a chain of beacons to announce the taking of Troy to his queen, Clytemnestra, at Argos. Now it had become the main staging point and hospital base for the Gallipoli campaign, and the place that would launch a thousand ships and a thousand score men against the Turk.

Patrick Shaw-Stewart commanded the firing party at Brooke's graveside. Eton, Balliol and another at the 'Latin Table' of bright young intellects in RND uniform on the *Grantully Castle*, he carried Herodotus and Homer as guidebooks. (T.E. Lawrence shipped the *Odyssey* across the sea of sand; wounded Harold Macmillan read Aeschylus in a shell hole at Loos.) His only known poem, written in a copy of Housman's *Shropshire Lad*, wonders 'Was it so hard, Achilles/ So very hard to die?'[15] His 'flame-capped Achilles', screaming from the Achaean ramparts after the death of Patroclus, betrays a close bond with Brooke. Siegfried Sassoon, similarly stricken by the death of David Thomas, went on reckless night patrols; his alter ego 'George Sherston' sets out to avenge his beloved 'Kendle'. Sassoon was 'looking for Germans to kill', according to Robert Graves, but more urgently sought his own quietus; he was awarded instead the Military Cross for 'gallantry', the quaintly chivalric term for exceptional bravery.

Before leaving England, Shaw-Stewart had written of the Dardanelles as 'the real plum of this war: all the glory of a European campaign … without the wet, mud, misery, and certain death of Flanders'. There was little glory in Gallipoli and the last certainty lay in waiting in 1917. His solitary poem was written on Imbros in a brief respite from the heat of fighting in the peninsular furnace. The nearby mound of Hisarlik in Asia, which Heinrich Schliemann had excavated as the site of Troy in the 1870s, inspired the scholar fresh from the Radcliffe Library:

Fair broke the day this morning
Against the Dardanelles;
The breeze blew soft, the morn's cheeks
Were cold as cold sea-shells

But other shells are waiting
Across the Aegean sea,
Shrapnel and high explosive,
Shells and hells for me.

Nowell Oxland found the same murderous welcome of shells on the beach. After two days riding at anchor with the armada in Mudros, his battalion sailed to Imbros and transhipped to two smaller vessels, the SS *Whitby Castle* and SS *Partridge*, for the last hop to Cape Helles. They landed at night on 'V' beach next to the *River Clyde*, the collier that had been run aground as a landing stage in the first April invasion. Bernard (later Lord) Freyberg of the RND performed heroic deeds here, but would fancifully liken it to a new Trojan horse, his classicism undimmed fifty years on by the slaughter that turned it into a charnel house.

Divisional notes on 'the character of the Turk' had firmly asserted that he did not like night attacks because he hated the dark, and invariably slept with a night light. Now, as in April, the Turk had manfully conquered his fears. As one party came ashore at 1 a.m., heavy artillery fire rained down, and the rest of the battalion had to put to sea again, only returning later that afternoon. Turkish snipers were also afforded all possible assistance in overcoming any fear of the dark: the New Army troops, nervy before their first contact, were instructed to wear armlets of white calico and tin squares or triangles to aid identification by their own artillery. Some were even told to polish their mess tins and wear them on their backs so that they glinted in the sun or moonlight. All were easily visible from enemy high ground when they lay down under fire.

By 22 July, the novice Borders had suffered their first casualties. An officer described the first day on enemy soil for these newly minted soldiers:

> … as dawn broke, we looked about and found ourselves on a flat plain … in some very shallow dugouts very much exposed to view. Orders were at once issued to the men not to show themselves, but like so many rabbits, first one and then another kept bobbing up; they had not yet learned what fire was like. Even some of the officers, who had seen much service, failed to realise the power of modern artillery.[16]

They spent the day carrying ammunition and water to the front-line trenches, in full view of the accurate Turkish guns on the heights of Achi Baba: 'A shell caught our dugout and blew a Lance Corporal and a man of [Oxland's] D Company to bits.' After this baptism of fire they soon became inured to the Helles shells, as Lt Col Broadrick wrote to his mother: 'The Turks shell us at intervals, but do singularly little damage and don't disturb anyone very much; the lads scarcely look to see where the shells strike now.'[17] Forward they went, to improve trenches and sink telephone wiring, work which was squeezed between darkness falling and moonrise – about thirty-five minutes – with the Turkish lines just 150 yards away. The battalion's Wigan coalminers came into their own, their commanding officer describing them as 'A1, and as they can work sitting down, they do not get hit much'.

Oxland's company under Captain McAuley was thrust into the firing line in a gully slap bang against a Turkish sap head – a trench offshoot towards enemy lines, used to launch mortar or bomb attacks and as a listening post at night. One Lt James 'spent many days cheerfully bombing' with a catapult. Broadrick commented with satisfaction: 'He had the situation well in hand and must have accounted for a certain number of Turks.' James[18] was a resourceful chap; in the absence of proper grenades, his 'bombs' were improvised from jam tins stuffed with gun cotton, nails, wire barbs and stones. The original apricot content of the cans was far deadlier.

After a week the battalion retired to Imbros with 'only about 12 or 13 hit, 3 killed, no officer killed, only 2 slightly wounded'[19] (including James the cheerful bomber, whose leg wound 'should only take about a fortnight to heal up' – reason to be cheerful, indeed). But this was hardly a rest period: August heat brought new enemies to their unsanitary camp, as dysentery, gastritis and reactions to cholera injections swept through the Borders and made for little sleep. Weakened as they were, they practised hard on the new 'Beetles' – black-painted, flat-bottomed lighters with bow ramps, which were the forerunners of modern landing craft. A 'Big Push' was widely rumoured for Suvla Bay, to the north of the Australian and New Zealand Army Corps (ANZACs) pinned down and dug into the cliffs above the cove that would become a place of patriotic pilgrimage for later generations.

Such was the poor planning and communication that only at midday on 6 August were the troops told that the Suvla landing would take place that night. Hamilton trumpeted: 'you are privileged indeed to have the chance vouchsafed you of playing a decisive part in events which may herald the birth of a new and happier world. You stand for the great cause of Freedom. In the hour of trial remember this.'[20] Fine words, but operational messages were so tightly restricted that units had no idea who was to either side of them. The Borders embarked with the 6/Lincolns in haphazard fashion, Oxland's company on the destroyer *Scourge* and the rest of 11th Division in lighters towed by destroyers. Many officers had not seen a map of their destination.

Suvla Bay presented an open coastal plain, guarded first by the low mound of Lala Baba and a sun-dried salt lake, then by the twin humps of 'Green Hill' and 'Chocolate Hill', the latter named for the burnt scrub on its slopes. Beyond was a horseshoe of connected higher ridges. It was 'shells and hells' for the Borders again. Captain George Darwell recalled:

> At about 5.00pm, Chocolate Hill had not fallen so the Reserves were called out … we pressed on, the battalion being in eight lines on a frontage of two companies for about 2½ miles … We reached the ditch as it was getting dark and by then had lost about 60 men.[21]

Despite the losses and evident confusion, the objective was taken by a joint force of Lincolns and Borders, stiffened by Dublin and Royal Irish Fusiliers. Five exhausted battalions of men who had not slept for two days became hopelessly intermingled and most of that night was spent sorting out the chaos. However, the Borders seemed resilient and the order to retire after their hard-fought gain was not popular: 'the men were wonderfully fresh on the top of Chocolate Hill and were dreadfully depressed at being sent back to the beach.' Worse was to come.

Sunday at the beach was hardly relaxing, as their dugouts were within artillery range and the shortage of water in the 90°F heat became desperate. More troops came ashore and added to the confusion. Some men went swimming to cool down, raging thirsts unable to resist the temptation to drink salt water. Orders arrived that evening to attack Turkish positions at Ismail Oglu Tepe, or 'W' Hill (after a distinctive pattern of vegetation), with the Borders to the right of the South Staffords and Lincolns. The advance was timed to start at 5.15 a.m. at the foot of Chocolate Hill.

All went well for fifty-five minutes, until the brigade's left was enfiladed by fire from Scimitar Hill. Records show that the advancing line had been told that this hill was held by British troops. Unknown to Oxland (or anyone in command), his friend Jimmy Dingle's East Yorkshire Pioneers had indeed taken it, but were then ordered to abandon this key vantage in pursuit of a secondary attack that would fail. There was no clear plan of battle, just a deadly game of snakes and ladders amongst the hills and gullies.

Every officer bar one in A and B Company was killed, leaving two sergeant majors in command. As they moved forward, the inexperience of the 'Kitchener Crowd', compounded by lack of clear orders, ensured chaos. Captain Drury of the Royal Dublin Fusiliers criticised them as 'all over the place lying up in funk holes … a whole lot of them started running away like mad, shouting out that they were cut to ribbons'. Drury and fellow officers had to threaten them with revolvers to halt their flight, but they were still timorous and 'would not put their heads up and fire although I showed them good targets … Then a hare got up, and the whole party blazed away at it, although they were too afraid to shoot at the Turks'.[22]

The struggle lasted the whole day; the survivors dug in with Lt Col Broadrick until he gave the order to retire at 5 p.m. At dawn roll call on 10 August, the cost of the attack was counted: 12 officers and 26 men killed, including all four company commanders; 5 officers and 241 men wounded; 1 officer and 131 other ranks missing. George Darwell's brother was leading a platoon of D Company: 'I went with my brother up to the top of the rise, and never saw him again.' Major Caulfield DSO DCM, aged 57, was last seen 'walking off towards the Turkish trenches as if he were walking down Piccadilly'.[23]

This single day saw 416 casualties, nearly all between 6 a.m. and 9.30 a.m. of 9 August. One of the twelve officers killed was Nowell:

Lt Oxland with twelve men was far in advance of his regiment. He was ordered to take possession of a gully and attempted to do so, but finding it impossible without reinforcements, he retired & took up position on the crest of the gully. Lt CB May advanced to him with orders to retire further and in doing so he, Lt Oxland, was shot in the chest & died immediately.[24]

Nowell's 'close friend', Amy Hawthorn – a Newcastle teacher of 38, whose sisters lived in Alston – pursued all avenues to understand more of his death. She wrote to the Worcester College bursar, F.J. Lys, after seeing his first obituary:

I have been in communication with a private who was with Mr Oxland at the time ... This private (McCreedy) fell, wounded. Mr Oxland went over to him, dressed his wound with a field dressing and then went to attend to a Capt Cunningham who fell near. The order to retreat was sound [sic]. McCreedy called to Lt Oxland, who answered 'I am all right; look to yourself, lad' – and then immediately after, received a wound in the head and fell; death was instantaneous. McCreedy, wounded himself, could do nothing and was carried away after having lain some hours, by the stretcher-bearers. Mr Oxland's body was never found, nor do we know if he was buried. The Adjutant Captain Darwell went to look for his brother, killed at the same affair, and for Mr Oxland, but was unsuccessful. That is all I know and all, I suppose, that will ever be known.[25]

Not quite. While his friend Hodgson also believed in 1916 that Oxland was lost without trace,[26] and wrote of 'a noble heart whom I shall not meet again', his body was somehow later identified – by no means the norm at Gallipoli. Putrefying heat and the intensity of conflict until the evacuation of January 1916 meant that many remains were not recovered until 1919. Some burned to death or were blasted into fragments of bone and tissue:

> The shells from the Turks set light to the dried sage, and thistle and thorn, and soon the whole place was blazing. It was a fearful sight. Many wounded tried to crawl away, dragging their broken arms and legs out of the burning bushes and were cremated alive. It was impossible to rescue them. Boxes of ammunition caught fire and exploded with terrific noise in thick bunches of murky smoke. A bombing section tried to throw off their equipment before the explosives burst, but many were blown to pieces by their own bombs.[27]

Although the Turks were respectful in carrying out field burials, the wooden grave markers, tacked together from bully-beef cases, were later taken by needy peasants as firewood.

At Suvla there is a corner of a foreign field that forever bleeds the red and white of Rosslyn Park. In four August days, five young officers from the club lost their lives: Captain Harry Stevenson of the Rajput Rifles, attached to the 10th Ghurkhas; halfback Alec Geary-Smith, Captain 9/West Yorks at Lala Baba; fullback Lt Arnold Huckett of the 1/5 Wiltshires; and winger 2/Lt Bertram Silcock of the 7/Royal Welch Fusiliers, a former Royal Naval Volunteer Reserve (RNVR) surgeon. Second Lieutenant Cecil Crosley of the 5/Royal Irish Rifles and Capt. Jimmy Dingle would soon join them. The corpse of Royal Irish Fusiliers Captain Bertram Falle, recruited from freezing Petrograd, melted away in the August heat. Only Nowell Oxland's body was found; he now lies under a simple stone tablet in Green Hill Cemetery. The names of his vanished team-mates – their remains by now Brooke's 'richer dust' – are inscribed on the Helles Memorial at the southern cape of the peninsula, a Turkish Thiepval to those with no known grave.

The Borders were taken out of the line – they were so depleted they could only fight on when merged with the Lincolns – and the paternal Broadrick busied himself with their welfare and morale, writing again to his mother:

> … the men would like cigarettes in large quantities, Woodbines and others of the American sort. We mostly want things to eat in a portable form … Get anything you can in that line regardless of cost; I am spending no money at all here, and will pay for everything … Also will you try and interest the wealthy people of Westmorland in the widows and orphans of my men; we have lost a lot and 60 per cent of my men are married.[28]

Broadrick himself would last only another few weeks, before being forever lost to all but the Cape Helles stonemasons.

Back in Cumberland, Nowell's death was such a blow that his father William resigned his Alston living in grief. The Oxlands moved to Southsea and to the comforting presence of the ocean for an old navy chaplain whose son's 'precious blood' would never return from his 'Green Hill far away'. Amy Hawthorn told Lys that William 'has not heard everything, because his health is too frail to be told much, and his memory too bad to retain anything he might be told'.[29] Beside the altar at St Augustine's church, Alston, the grieving parents left two portraits of Nowell as Saints Michael and George, set against a Middle Eastern landscape. This artistic canonisation of their beloved child still glows with colour, but their sincere epitaph would be eternally twisted with irony by another poet: *Dulce et Decorum est pro Patria mori*. Surely they did not share the sentiment of the *Times*' tortuous editorial on the more celebrated soldier-poet, Brooke:

> … we might add the epitaph of Schubert, without complaining of the waste of war. *He died before he had fulfilled his own hopes or ours*; but either we believe in waste altogether or not at all. And if any seeming waste is not waste, there is none in a young life full of promise and joyfully laid down.[30]

Amy Hawthorn was immune to such nonsense and more perceptive about Nowell's death which, in plainer terms:

… seems all the sadder in that it has put an end to a career full of promise. And to me it seems all the harder that the Gallipoli affair, as it is told in Sir Ian Hamilton's dispatch seems to have been a series of terrible blunders & that all these gallant lives were sacrificed in a hopeless cause.[31]

She learned that 'Lt Oxland was exceedingly popular with the men on account of the interest he took in [rugby] football. At Oxford he played for his College and only narrowly missed his Blue.' Amy now busied herself with publishing Nowell's works, explaining to Lys:

Mr Oxland was extremely reticent about his work and never thought them worth publishing … I believe I was the only one who saw all his work & believed in his powers … he spent all his vacations at Alston where I saw a great deal of him and he gave me all his manuscripts … he gave me leave to publish anything I liked that he wrote after leaving England … he was intensely reserved and one or two of his College friends and myself were the only people who knew he wrote.

The poet's muse became his literary executor.

Enlightened by Amy, Lys, writing of Oxland's death in November's *Oxford Magazine*, swollen by a supplement of death notices, now observed that:

… he took a prominent part in the life of the College … His place in the Moderations list did not give the measure of his abilities, which were considerable. He had a facility of expression and a poetic gift which to those who had the opportunity of knowing them seemed rich in promise; and when he threw off the reserve he commonly wore, he discovered a sense of humour unsuspected by those who only knew him slightly.[32]

Nowell Oxland's poetry is at its most luminous when he writes of the northern fells and waters, and funniest in his fond contempt for the family mongrel, Taffy – 'unwieldy yard of canine hideousness' – and the dismal food of Putney boarding houses. His paeans to 'Phyllis', 'Daphne' and Oxford itself reveal universal student infatuations; there is an intriguing girl in the Radcliffe, about whom Amy may have raised a querulous eyebrow:

> Pale with a name and college
> I'd like to know (but how?)
> She sits absorbing knowledge
> With calm contracted brow

Thanks to his 'long and close friendship' with Amy, his poetic gift found public voice in *The Times* of 27 August 1915, when he was already eighteen days dead but not yet buried. She sent the editor his last poem. The playful whimsy, student pastiche and exuberance of his earlier works are distilled into a reflective, sombre tone. Halfway through, personal reverie gives way to an officer's compassion for his fellow Borders men. Oxland writes in the Lakeland tradition of Wordsworth, but this poet's intimations are of mortality and shared humanity with his countrymen of the north. The local Cumberland newspaper commented: 'a soul that gave expression to such fine passages must have had a wonderful vision of life.'[33] His mood is one of resignation and leave-taking, clutching to the consolation that while bodies 'mingled with mother clay' may not return to Cumberland, their spirits might.

The poem appeared in *The Times*, shoehorned between reports of '780 Officer Losses in eight days in Turkey' and the 'names of a number of officers killed, whose deaths have not yet been officially announced'. Also printed is an 'Enemy Report of a Repulse' from German wireless stations: 'The British troops landed here on August 6 and 7 have so far done little to improve the situation of the Allied forces on the Peninsula.'[34]

The editor of *The Times* clearly felt that the 'fallen Officer's' original title was too downbeat for his readers after two pages of casualty lists and a whole dispiriting year of war. No defeatist nonsense for the '*Thunderer*': he headed it 'Outward Bound'. Most anthologies follow his lead, but Amy restored its author's title in her published tribute. The poet Nowell Oxland, who at the age of 24 would 'go not forth again' and whose body would never return to Cumberland, had sent his own 'Farewell':

There's a waterfall I'm leaving
Running down the rocks in foam,
There's a pool for which I'm grieving
Near the water-ouzel's home,
And it's there that I'd be lying
With the heather close at hand
And the curlews faintly crying
'Mid the wastes of Cumberland.

While the midnight watch is winging
Thoughts of other days arise,
I can hear the river singing
Like the saints in Paradise;
I can see the water winking
Like the merry eyes of Pan,
And the slow half-pounder sinking
By the bridge's granite span.

Ah! to win them back and clamber
Braced anew with winds I love,
From the river's stainless amber
To the morning mist above,
See through cloud-rifts rent asunder,
Like a painted scroll unfurled,
Ridge and hollow rolling under
To the fringes of the world.

Now the weary guard are sleeping,
Now the great propellers churn,
Now the harbour lights are creeping
Into emptiness astern,
While the sentry wakes and watches
Plunging triangles of light
Where the water leaps and catches
At our escort in the night.

Great their happiness who seeing
Still with unbenighted eyes
Kin of theirs who gave them being,
Sun and earth that made them wise,
Die and feel their embers quicken
Year by year in summer time,
When the cotton grasses thicken
On the hills they used to climb.

Shall we also be as they be,
Mingled with our mother clay,
Or return no more, it may be?
Who has knowledge, who shall say?
Yet we hope that from the bosom
Of our shaggy father Pan,
When the earth breaks into blossom
Richer from the dust of man,

Though the high gods smite and slay us,
Though we come not whence we go,
As the host of Menelaus
Came there many years ago;
Yet the selfsame wind shall bear us
From the same departing place
Out across the Gulf of Saros
And the peaks of Samothrace:

We shall pass in summer weather,
We shall come at eventide,
Where the fells stand up together
And all quiet things abide;
Mixed with cloud and wind and river,
Sun-distilled in dew and rain,
One with Cumberland for ever
We shall go not forth again.

JIMMY DINGLE
'A GENTLEMAN, WHO MADE US TEA'

Captain Arthur James 'Mud' Dingle, 6/Yorkshire (Pioneer) Regiment, killed at Gallipoli.

There are ninety-eight steps to the chapel at Durham school, one for each Dunelmian who died in the Great War. The chapel over-looks the school and the Norman cathedral, resting place of Bede and Cuthbert – 'God's ancient house, over the windy uplands gazing out/Towards the sea'[1] – and the Holy Isle of Lindisfarne. A plaque tells us it was built by 'the inspiration and generosity of Richard Budworth, Canon of Durham, Headmaster from 1907–1932', who watched his boys pass through the school on their way to early deaths. He never married but, after the war, devoted his time and any money he had to this memorial to his lost generation of pupils.

Canon Budworth was every inch a rugby man. Capped for England, he was an original 1890 Barbarian, for whom he faced Corinthians at athletics, rugby and association football in a three-day charity festival at Queens' Club. Durham school matched his fervour: its football club, founded in 1850, is the third-oldest in England. The Old Boys' side, playing in school colours of green and white, became Gosforth and eventually hatched Newcastle Falcons. Old Dunelmians were honoured with a visit (a 5-18 defeat) by the touring Barbarians in 1897. Under Budworth, Durham rugby flourished and the school supplied four England internationals before the war. One was Arthur James Dingle, both pupil and teacher at Durham, and among the ninety-eight dead in a school which then counted only 90 pupils in total.

Dingle, known as James to distinguish him from his father, Reverend Arthur Trehane Dingle, then rector of Egglescliffe in County Durham, burst into the world at the vicarage at Hetton-le-Hole in October 1891. Brought up in relative privilege in a mining district where the local lads went down the pits at 12, young Jimmy was educated close to home at Bow, the preparatory school for Durham. He entered school in the second master's house in September 1904, was elected King's Scholar in 1906 and was head of school by 1910, succeeding Nowell Oxland.

He was an excellent gymnast and oarsman, rowing in the eight which won the Wharton Challenge Cup at Durham Regatta in his senior year. But on the rugby field he was exceptional: for three years he starred for the school XV at centre or wing. The pitches of the tempestuous north-east give him the nickname 'Mud'. Then came Oxford and theology, at architecturally controversial Keble College, with a view to following his father into Holy Orders. An advocate of muscular Christianity like Canon Budworth, he won his rugby Blue in his second year. That same season he first played for Durham County and received his North cap.

His Durham friend, Oxland, already a regular at Rosslyn Park, enticed him to spend his vacation Saturdays in Richmond. Jimmy travelled up regularly by train, also playing for Richmond and Surrey. His first Old Deer Park game against Harlequins was a daunting baptism, as he was thrust into an unfamiliar halfback role opposite England stars Stoop and Birkett; the Quins romped home by four tries to one 'placed goal', although the points system of the day only scored this as 12-5. After a happier 15-6 away victory over RMC Sandhurst at Camberley, when he was restored to the wing, the university pressed its claims and he discarded Park's hoops for the plain dark-blue jersey of Oxford.

The 1911 Varsity match, played at the Queen's Club, Kensington, on 12 December, was a resounding 19-0 victory for the experienced

Dark Blues. The young Cambridge side tried to stifle the Oxford backs rather than play their own game; their own defence had no answer to Oxford's attacks and 'AJ Dingle settled matters by scoring between the posts after a clever piece of combination'.[2] The Keble *Clocktower* chortled to Jimmy: 'you are, perhaps, the most popular Rugger man in the Varsity with the "townees" and equally popular with members of the fair sex.' He and centre partner Ronnie Poulton should have faced each other in an England versus North trial four days later, but for Poulton's injury in this match. For Jimmy this was to be his only Blue: selected again in 1912, the 'irreplaceable' Dingle withdrew with a strain and Oxford lost. It would also lose six of the 1911 team to the war.

After university, he was appointed junior master at his Durham *alma mater*. With fellow teacher Francis Steinthal (Ilkley and England), he maintained the school's prowess on the field while playing club rugby at Hartlepool Rovers. Its history praised him as 'a personality who took the eye and warmed the heart, while his play was resplendent with colour. He personified the dream of all young Rovers – unlimited energy, driving ambition and a conquering spirit.'[3] His 1913–14 season was prolific; he scored a record thirty-nine tries (thirty-two coming in just eight games) and captained the club. He scored in all seven county matches, notching sixteen tries, of which twelve were secured in three games (four in each), and took Durham to the county championship finals. He played in three national trials, but his inevitable tries are not recorded.

Durham county rugby's historian wistfully recalled him in terms that would make a modern backs coach salivate:

Jimmy Dingle was built on 'stocky' lines, he had a rare turn of speed allied to a most deceptive running action; though going very straight for the line, he gave the impression of progressing on a perpetual curve, somewhat like a skater. He was an exceptionally quick starter and possessed the gift of changing not only his action, but also his speed and direction in one and the same move, which, in conjunction with his tenacity and determination, made him a most difficult man to stop.[4]

It came as no surprise to his admirers in the north that while still at Oxford he was selected for his country against Ireland at Lansdowne Road in February 1913. This revived his earlier Oxford centre partnership with the 'genius' Ronnie Poulton (but displaced his friend and colleague Steinthal – some awkwardness in the common room, perhaps). Victory was England's by fifteen points to four, but it was not his best game. Dingle, described as 'strong in defence, but not altogether a success', was dropped for the rest of the international season. 'Time and again when he should obviously have passed out to CN Lowe, he neglected him.'[5] But he had still played his part in England's first Grand Slam.

A season later, his club form at Hartlepool made him irresistible to the selectors: he was recalled to play against Scotland at Inverleith in March 1914, upsetting his *Times* antagonist, who opined that he was no more than a good club player. The prevailing poor weather cleared on the morning of the match, although gusting winds made kicking difficult. To counter this England played a wide game, meaning more ball for Jimmy on the wing, but without initial success: 'At the opening of the game Dingle missed a pass with the goal line undefended 10 yards away.'[6]

England steadily drew ahead by ten points with twenty minutes to play. Scotland fought back but just failed to overcome the auld enemy who sneaked it by sixteen points to fifteen, claiming the Triple Crown as well as the Calcutta Cup. Many felt that Dingle was wasted on the left wing and should have stayed in 'his correct position', with 'RPP' in the centre. Both these outstanding players would be killed in the war, along with eight 'flowers of Scotland' and five more Englishmen. Another doomed Dunelmian, Alfred Maynard, stands alongside Jimmy in the official photograph taken at Edinburgh castle. He would die at Beaumont Hamel in 1916.

Despite the dropped pass, the selectors kept their faith in 'Mud'. His final game, England's last for five years, was against France in front of 20,000 at the Olympic Stade Les Colombes in Paris. England's backs outclassed their French opponents in an easy victory, but the match was marred by rough play from the French and a 'disorderly crowd' who barracked the players throughout and, in the view of the press, 'have learned very little by the lesson of playing Rugby football'.

Scotland refused to play France after similar Parisian antics when the referee and players were 'mobbed and assaulted'.[7]

England started slowly and Dingle again failed to reproduce his club form at national level. In the English back line, wrote his *Times* critic, 'AJ Dingle was the weakest of the four. He failed to take the passes and was very slow getting into his stride.' To be fair, he was alongside some of the greats: Poulton, scorer of four tries that day; James 'Bungy' Watson; and the small but coruscating Cyril Lowe, the Shane Williams of his day and winner of twenty-five consecutive caps. France, admitted to the Five Nations in 1910, was not then the power it is today, but a win in Paris is always acceptable and gave England back-to-back Grand Slams. Dingle's ball-handling reputation was shaky. Sewell later observed that the sturdy centre 'wanted a lot of stopping on the move, but was always rather apt to drop passes'.[8]

The English victory 39-13 is overwhelmed by another statistic: of the thirty players on the field, eleven lost their lives in the conflict that erupted fourteen weeks later. From a one-eyed Rosslyn Park perspective the Paris game is remarkable in that three players from the club wore jerseys, blue or white: Dingle and Arthur Harrison for England, and Frenchman Jean-Jacques Conilh de Beyssac.

Dingle had helped found the OTC at Durham and joined up immediately in August. As a schoolmaster, he was exempt from service (George Mallory at Charterhouse waited until late 1915), but such was the will to fight that he sought Budworth's permission to go. His application confirms his stocky build at 5ft 7in and 160lb; a century later, England winger Matt Banahan stretches a full 12in taller in his socks. Dingle joined the East Yorkshire Regiment in September and was commissioned to its 6th (Pioneer) Battalion, infantry trained in front-line engineering skills in advance of specialist support from Royal Engineers. There was little rest for Pioneers.

While training for 'the greater game' being played overseas, Jimmy still found time for rugby. On 10 April 1915 he made his only appearance for the Barbarians – Budworth would be proud. The match against the RAMC in aid of the Red Cross Fund was held at Old Deer Park, one of many organised by the indefatigable Burlinson. Played in front of a good crowd of 3,000, the traditional scratch team of Barbarians was captained by Edgar Mobbs.

The classy line up won 10-3, with Dingle scoring. These were charged-up Baa-Baas, glad to be playing competitive rugby. A week later a much-changed team, without Dingle, beat a representative Wales side 26-10 at Cardiff (although it is questionable how strong the Welsh team would have been in wartime).

In June, Lt Dingle embarked at Avonmouth for the Dardanelles, in the same Expeditionary Force as so many friends from Durham, Oxford and Rosslyn Park. He would not return, other than as one of Budworth's ninety-eight steps.[9] His body was never recovered, but we can piece together a remarkably full account of his brief and bloody three weeks of active service from four sources: the battalion's War Diary is an astonishing achievement by the relay of officers who kept it going as each lost his life; Dingle also wrote home with admirable frequency[10] and Kew records carry witness accounts of his death. Finally, and rarest of all, he is enshrined in the poem 'Ballad of Suvla Bay', written in a Turkish prison by brother officer Lt John Still.[11]

A land campaign against Turkey was seen as a new colonial skirmish where the victory of the fair European over the darker-skinned native was complacently assumed. As one bigoted and ill-informed staff officer opined, 'the Turk is an enemy who has never shown himself as good a fighter as the white man'. However, impassable terrain and fierce Turkish opposition bottled up the invasion force. The fighting was savage. On occasions, orders were given that Turkish rifles should not be loaded: 'Attack the enemy with the bayonet and utterly destroy him. We shall not retire one step; for if we do, our religion, our country and our nation will perish.' In an effort to break the deadlock some 60,000 more British troops were to land at Suvla Bay on 6 August 1915, to force a breakout and link up with the besieged Australians and New Zealanders 5 miles to the south.

Conducted largely at night and over the most confusing of battle grounds, the action degenerated into chaos. Dingle's battalion, like Oxland's, formed part of 11th Division. Rosslyn Park was strongly represented: in one of many interwoven strands in this tale, the East Yorks were shipped to Suvla on HMS *Theseus*, whose ship's surgeon John Rutherford, a doctor's son from Exeter trained at Bart's Hospital, was also a Park forward. Over 1,000 men were landed from *Theseus* and she anchored offshore in order to maintain steady covering fire on the hills encircling the invasion beaches. Rutherford would not have many quiet days: he would stay on in the hot, unsanitary Aegean for the Salonika campaign, cutting out gangrenous flesh and amputating shattered limbs, and would succumb to tuberculosis in 1917, aged 28.

From the start the Suvla Bay campaign was badly mismanaged: Lt Gen. Sir Francis Stopford, retired since 1909 with no prior wartime command, and Maj. Gen. Frederick Hammersley, recently recovered from a breakdown, were imprecise in their orders, requiring only that 'the high ground should be taken *if possible*'. The landings in darkness achieved little more than just getting ashore. Turkish numbers were not high, but the New Army troops and their hesitant commanders, conducting the campaign from the safety of ships in the bay, lost valuable momentum in the face of stubborn resistance by the outnumbered but well-positioned defenders. Familiar Western Front tactics applied as they 'advanced in two lines across rough & sandy rocky ground at slow pace'.[12] Medic John Hargrave watched, horrified, from offshore:

We could see lighters and small boats towing troops ashore. We saw men scramble out, only to be blown to pieces by land mines as they waded to the beach. On the Lala Baba side we watched platoons and companies form up and march along in fours, all in step, as if they were on parade ... a high explosive from the Turkish positions on the Sari Bair range came screaming over the Salt Lake: 'Z–z–z–e–e–e–o–o–o–p—Crash!' They lay there like a little group of dead beetles, and the wounded were crawling away like ants into the dead yellow grass and the sage bushes to die. A whole platoon was smashed. And so it went on hour after hour. Crackle, rattle and roar; scream, whistle and crash. There was no glory. Here was Death, sure enough – Mechanical Death run amok – but where was the glory? Here was organised murder – but it was steel-cold! There was no hand-to-hand glory. A mine dispersed you before you had set foot on dry land; or a high explosive removed your stomach, and left you a mangled heap of human flesh, instead of a medically certified, healthy human being.[13]

The first objective, the low hill of Lala Baba, was taken at some cost by the West Yorkshires. The East Yorkshires fared better, but the Pioneers' first duties were digging in and the hasty burial of the dead, including Captain Alec Geary-Smith of Uppingham, Sandhurst, Rosslyn Park and 9/West Yorkshires. The War Diary for 7 August records:

> LALA BABA. HQs with Lt Col Moore A & B Coys landed first C & D Coys followed under Major Cowper; the landing was unopposed; a few shots only being fired. The Battalion (strength 775) was landed at C Beach: After the hill was taken by the 32nd Brigade the Battalion occupied and entrenched S.E. slopes of Lala Baba where it received considerable attention from the Turkish Artillery. 12 casualties.[14]

Jimmy Dingle wrote breezily to his father of this first ordeal under fire:

> … one soon gets used to it. We landed at night and did not get hit, and early that morning we were ordered to entrench ourselves. About ten minutes after we had begun, the Turks started shelling us from all sides. We had no cover and had to continue digging. Luckily the shooting was bad and we only had about twenty casualties.

Hamilton had not considered the problems of attacks at night over strange and unfamiliar new ground. In his third Gallipoli dispatch he admits to Kitchener:[15]

> The enemy, knowing every inch of the ground, crept down in the very dark night on to the beach itself, mingling with our troops and getting between our firing line and its supports. Fortunately the number of these enterprising foes was but few, and an end was soon put to their activity on the actual beaches by the sudden storming of Lala Baba from the south.

Ominously, Hamilton also alludes to 'friendly fire' (surely one of the most unfortunate modern phrases), admitting to his Lordship, 'it is feared that some of the losses incurred here were due to mis-directed fire'. Maps were inadequate for this wild terrain broken by gullies and ravines running in all directions. This was decidedly not the facing lines of the European theatre, where the enemy could be precisely located as 'just over there' and communications followed established trench systems. Also there was then the water problem; the hindsight of his dispatch is a wonderful thing:

> The want of water had told on the new troops. The distribution from the beaches had not worked smoothly. In some cases the hose had been pierced by individuals wishing to fill their own bottles; in others lighters had grounded so far from the beach that men swam out to fill batches of water-bottles. All this had added to the disorganisation inevitable after a night landing, followed by fights here and there with an enemy scattered over a country to us unknown.[16]

The 8 August saw a fresh catalogue of confused orders and officers killed, as told bluntly by the War Diary author:

> Orders were received to join the 32nd Brigade with the West Yorkshire on our left; attack to hold a position running from Chocolate Hill to Sulajik, the records of these orders have been lost ... At first no opposition was met with but on occupying the ridge which joins up with Chocolate Hill and lies about W. by S. from Anafarta Sagar heavy firing was encountered. Capt Rogers was killed and shortly afterwards Major Eastridge was wounded in the arm. The Turks employed numerous snipers and shot par-ticularly at our men as they went for water from a well, parties were sent out but were unable to find them.

The ridge occupied by the East Yorkshires, unknown to them, was the key vantage of Scimitar Hill; its abandonment to the enemy would have fatal consequences for Jimmy's friend, Nowell Oxland of the 6/Borders. At the very moment 32 Brigade's order to retire was received from division ('because the regiments to left and right of you have not been able to get up'), another order was issued directly to them by Hamilton, impatient for action, to attack the hill at Tekke Tepe. This 800ft-high point was the key position to occupy before the Turks reinforced.

Hamilton's original order through division was issued at 6 p.m.; the brigade did not pass it to the men on Scimitar Hill. His direct order of 11.30 p.m. did not arrive at brigade HQ until 2.15 a.m.; finding fighting units in the dark caused further delay. Lt Still, acting adjutant and signalling officer, complained bitterly in a letter to Hamilton after the war: 'the Brigade Major was lost! Good God, why didn't they send a man who knew the country? He was lost, lost, lost and it drives me almost mad to think of it.' Still had sent a patrol to reconnoitre Tekke Tepe much earlier, found it empty and had signalled brigade. However, no order to attack came. Hamilton's order finally arrived just before dawn. His reputation in tatters after the war, he had been much criticised for diverting troops from Scimitar to Tekke Tepe; he was quick to forward Still's letter to *The Times*,[17] firmly shifting the blame to Stopford as division commander.

At 4 a.m., a mixed force led by Dingle's D Company, with Lt Col Moore in charge, marched north-east towards Tekke Tepe. The diary entry for 9 August is a familiar one of confusion, exhaustion and breakdown of command:

After some confusion in getting the men into the trench in the dark orders (lost) were received at 3.30am (Late in reaching us) to deliver an attack (orders lost) on Tekke Tepe … The men at this stage were in a state of extreme exhaustion and hunger … Lt Col Moore was with D coy; the other three coys owing to the extreme exhaustion of the men and the absence of explicit instructions failed to keep in touch with D coy who proceeded to advance up the lower slopes of the hill without waiting for B coy to come into position on their right or for the other two coys to get into place. D coy with Lt Col Moore, 2nd Lt Still (Acting Adjutant) and H.Q. party seem to have encountered no opposition at first: It was only when they were up the first shoulder that the strength of the enemy was disclosed. Fire was poured in from concealed Turkish trenches and our men were unable to hold their ground. There was considerable confusion due to the rapid advance of D coy and to the effect that the other coys had lost touch.

D coy suffered heavily: Capt Grant had been wounded in the hand early in the engagement:- Lt Col Moore, 2nd Lt Still, Capt Elliott, Lt Rawsthorne, 2nd Lt Wilson were all missing when what remained of the company fell back. A general retirement took place during which there was much mixing of units, due to the battalion failing to keep its formations … All orders and despatches relating to these are lost as the orderly who carried them is missing.

Lt Eric Halse in the following group was in no doubt where blame lay. In an angry (uncensored) letter, he described the superior position of the Turks, whose reinforcements had arrived under the command of Mustafa Kemal (one day Ataturk and father of modern Turkey), while Stopford and his staff dithered:

They also had a machine gun enfilading us on our left & a party of them enfilading us on our right. They had us in a trap pure & simple. The regiments that were supposed to be on our left & right flanks had gone somewhere else. We lost 15 officers and 30 men in ½ hour. Human nature could stand no more. One company was captured altogether and the rest turned & ran. I don't blame the men for it was their first time under fire & really men could not be expected to endure it. I collected a few & we made a bit of stand further back, but eventually had to retire back to the reserves who were a mile & a ¼ behind instead of 400 yards. The staff work was damned rotten & nearly all the S. Officers are incapable inefficient fools. There is no other word for them. They take no interest in anything at all. The only thing they care about is their own d__ skins if they are safe it doesn't matter about the rest of us.[18]

James Underhill, of the patrol which had found Tekke Tepe unoccupied, was also much aggrieved in a public letter of 1925: 'all of K's Army who took part in this landing and the following few days felt it intensely that they were blamed by the Staff for the failure on the grounds of being green troops.'[19] The battle was fought again in the letters page of the post-war *Times*.

The litany of casualties over the two days lists fifteen officers, including the commanding officer, and 343 other ranks. The battalion was halved from its strength at landing. Most are termed 'missing', which was not always a euphemism for 'dead', as darkness and hurried withdrawals simply made it impossible to assess the facts. For the missing Lt Still, taken prisoner by the Turks, the war was over; he would while away three years of captivity writing verse on paper hidden inside a hollow walking stick, to accompany a later account of his prisoner-of-war experiences. D Company (Moore, Dingle and Still) made it to the 'first shoulder' of Tekke Tepe with some thirty men, but withdrew when reduced to twenty. Still's prison ballad of December 1916 may not be great poetry, but it is a vivid personal account, with more colour and motion than any war diary:

> We marched across the twilit slopes.
> Eight officers and some seven score men;
> It looked the most forlorn of hopes,
> And in my heart I wondered then
> How many would ever come back again.
>
> Two officers fell in the first half mile
> To dropping shots from the eastern flank,
> And sadly thinned were the rank and file
> When we breathed in cover a little while
> And left our packs on a rocky bank.

He describes the retreat and his ultimate capture:

> So we drew away and turned to go,
> For we mustered about a score;
> And we looked right down a mile below.
> Where the fight, like a moving picture show,
> Sent up a distant roar.

Then down that dreadful mountain-side
The Colonel went with broken pride,
Finding a way with the handful left
Where a gully cut a winding cleft
That helped our path to hide.

The Turks fired down on the beaten men:
Half way down we had shrunk to ten;
And they claimed as prisoners only five;
These were all who came out alive
At the foot of that winding glen.

John Still, one of the 'prisoners only five', was interned in an Armenian church at Afion Kara Hissar concentration camp. Despite its sinister name – *Afion* (opium), from the local poppy crop, and *Kara Hissar* (black tower), from a rocky fortress – this was a safe and relatively healthy location. He appends epitaphs to three fellow officers, all Oxford men: Lt Stephen Jalland, a York surgeon's son and land agent; Captain Norman Pringle, a teacher; and another teacher and international rugby player, James Dingle:

Broad and simple, and great of heart,
Strenuous soul in a stalwart frame;
Whatever the work, he took his part
With energy strung from the very start
To learn the rules and play the game.

He played for an English side before;
And all unspoiled by the crowd's applause.
He took for his side their greeting roar:
And so in the greater game of war
He gave his life for the greater cause

This war made poets of many men – perhaps too many, as the *Wipers Times* drily noted in 1918[20] – fewer men were immortalised in the poetry itself. It is unclear if Still believed Dingle was killed in the attack or if he heard of his later death while incarcerated. In fact,

Jimmy survived this episode to tell his own tale of confusion to his father in a letter:

> I can't tell you the date because I don't know it. It is Tuesday, and I think about August 13th. We have been in the thick of it for some time now and until last night we had no sleep for about four days … after digging all night, we were ordered to make good a position taken the night before by some other regiments. It was on the top of a hill [Scimitar] and we remained there about twenty hours under heavy rifle fire.
>
> In the end we were ordered to go and attack another huge hill with another regiment. That was the most terrible day one could imagine … I got mixed up with another regiment part of the time and how I escaped is a marvel to me. There was a perfect hailstorm of bullets. I only got within forty yards of the Turks, but part of our line got quite close … About sixty of us got into a deserted farm house and there made up our minds to stick till we were done for. We were all pretty well exhausted and had no water, but we found a small spring. Reinforcements eventually came up and helped us retire gradually, though it was hot work the whole time … I am the only officer in the Company. We have to go and dig trenches all night, worse luck, so that means no sleep for me … I am fit as ever and got over my weariness with the aid of a bathe this morning … We are doing fairly well here.

The East Yorks stayed in reserve for the next ten days. After the disaster of Tekke Tepe, the remnants (now under command of Major Cowper) bivouacked on 'A' Beach by the inlet to the dry salt lake. Dingle, now commanding B Company, wrote, 'We have suffered very heavy casualties, only six officers left and about 280 men out of 700. I have not been touched yet, but had some extraordinary escapes. We are doing fairly well.'

They marched to Nibrunesi Point, to dig trenches across the low ground south-east of Lala Baba. An engineer officer suggested 'a safe place' to bivouac, but as the Pioneers moved off, a Turkish shell fell in their midst, killing one man and wounding six. The commanding officer 'thought it better to try another place'.

Eventually, the battalion dug itself into the face of the cliff, where it was comparatively safe from the attentions of a Turkish heavy gun nicknamed 'Billy Beach'.

Hard nights of Pioneer work ensued: trenches dug, wells sunk and revetted, redoubts put up. New officers and men arrived from Imbros – the first reinforcements since the battalion left England. Lt Dingle is in confident mood in a letter of the 15th:

> We have been living on the cliffs near our artillery for the last few days and have been digging trenches by night and doing odd jobs during the day. Our reinforcements have come up, so we are now ready for another go at the old Turks. I think we have just pulled ourselves together after our first experience of fighting. We got it badly as any other regiment, and as for casualties, we know of four officers killed for certain and four wounded. The nearest I had was a bullet which cut my puttee over my boot. At one time I thought I was done for when sixty of us were almost surrounded when defending a farm house, but help came just in time. We are still shelled where we are now but only a chance shot will touch us. Nobody minds the shrapnel much now, in fact we get a bit of it while bathing … I think most of us have got over our weariness now and personally I am as fit as a fiddle again. I expect we shall be off to the firing line again soon … Did I tell you I am now in command of 150 men, but with only one other officer? I hope I don't lead them to destruction!

Sea bathing, despite the attendant shrapnel, brought some respite from the gruelling work. More than one soldier stripping off to swim was touched by the exotic beauty of his surroundings:

> … the bay had changed to pale blue with green ripples, and the outline of Imbros Island, on the horizon, was a long jagged strip of mauve.
>
> Later, when the sunset sky turned lemon-yellow, orange, and deep crimson, the bay went into peacock blues and purples, with here and there a current of bottle-glass green, and Imbros Island stood clear cut against the sunset-colour a violet-black silhouette.

Queer creatures crept across the sands and into the old Turkish
snipers' trenches; long black centipedes, sand-birds – very much
resembling our martin, but with something of the canary in their
colour. Horned beetles, baby tortoises, mice, and green-grey liz-
ards all left their tiny footprints on the shore.[21]

However, the beauty on the beach rarely went undisturbed; Jimmy
writes of an 'exciting five minutes yesterday evening with a Taube
[German reconnaissance plane] dropping four bombs on us without
success and an outburst of shrapnel at the same time. Only one man
was wounded … I am quite fit.'

After dark on the 16th Lt Dingle and 100 men set off with a guide
to improve and deepen a communication trench at Chocolate Hill.
Stores had arrived, supplies of food and water were more regular,
but clothing and equipment were still scarce, as Major Cowper's
diary reveals:

Most of us by this time had managed to raise a blanket by hook
or by crook. Mine, I think, must have belonged to a rather dirty
Turk, but it was warm, and after washing it in the sea, it was more
or less disinfected. My breeches had suffered, and, to my joy, the
Sergeant-Major turned up one day with an almost brand-new
pair: 'I was wondering if these would be any good to you, Sir.'
I had not thought mine were quite so noticeable as all that, but I
suppose that he thought for the good of the Regiment he could
not allow the temporary Commanding Officer to walk about like
that. I was, however, profuse in my thanks, and asked no questions.
The worst of it was, Major Bray, now second-in-command, had a
pair worse than mine, and he begged that I should have my own
washed and mended, and I could wear them again, while he wore
the much-coveted pantaloons. So there was nothing for it, and I
had to part with them.

On Friday, the 6/East Yorkshires received orders to relieve the
trenches near Chocolate Hill, where Nowell Oxland had been
killed. The battalion, now under orders of 34 Brigade, was to attack

'W' Hill; the Pioneers were to dig in 400 yards behind the front-line troops, ready to support their advance. The Suvla attack, intended as a decisive swift strike, was now following the pattern of trench warfare it was hoped could be avoided. The regimental history relates:

Dusk had fallen on 20th when the 6th East Yorkshires, with 150 paces between companies, advanced from the shore of the Bay. The Battalion Padre, standing on the cliff edge, had given the Battalion a stirring address before companies moved off. As they approached their destination, a line South East of Chocolate Hill, sniping became more frequent, but they reached the position they were to occupy and set to work to dig themselves in, in four lines. It was difficult work for the ground was like iron, but all ranks did their best, though the Turks were busy most of the night and several casualties were suffered. The East Yorkshire men were also set to dig trenches for the Brigade Staff as well as their own, so that there was no rest for them that night and when dawn broke on 21st the whole Battalion was anything but fresh. With daylight came the inevitable shelling and it was necessary to keep well down in the trenches to avoid shrapnel and rifle bullets.

Nor had communications improved after the lessons of ten days ago:

Although it was understood that an attack was to be made, it is necessary to state that at 8am, on 21st, 11th Divisional Operation Orders had not reached the Brigades in the front line. These Operation Orders are timed 1am, 21st, and were sent out shortly afterwards, but apparently the orderly who carried them was either shot down or lost his way. Eventually, it was 10am before duplicate copies were received by H.Q. of the Brigades in the line, the orders were lengthy ones, and it took some time to master the details and to draft Brigade Orders. The result was that the COs of some of the units which were to attack were only able to inform their officers of the scheme of operations and the officers were unable to circulate orders to NCOs and men: this fact had a direct bearing on the day's operations.

At 2.45 p.m. artillery bombardment of the enemy began from ship and shore. At 3 p.m. the Dorsets and Lancashire Fusiliers climbed out of their trenches and went forward to the attack. The East Yorkshire men advanced to occupy the vacated trenches. Cowper wrote: 'We got it pretty hot … you could see the shells burst and feel bullets whistling through the air, could see the dust kicked up and the grass beaten down as though a severe hailstorm was going on.' As the troops ahead were in difficulty, the Pioneers pressed on, bayonets fixed. The Turks fled from their trench. But then a halt was called as Cowper had no orders to go on. He had been told that other troops were to pass through them and capture the next line of hostile trenches. Having sent back word that his battalion had occupied the Turkish trench, he set the men to widen the trench and adapt it for defence.

Yet again, lack of orders would bog down the attack. The 34th had done its job, but the other two brigades went in the wrong direction; most officers were dead and NCOs and men knew little or nothing of what was expected of them. The Turks trained heavy fire on their lost trench, but the East Yorks now had battle fever. One man stood up, waving his arms about like a madman and shouting incoherently at the Turks; a bullet dug a groove along his cheek, which only made him worse, until at last he was pulled down, still shouting, to the cover of the trench. Another man put his rifle on the parapet and pressed the trigger without taking aim.

On the right of the battalion was a *nullah*, or dry stream bed, leading back to the trench it had vacated, but forward to the second-line Turkish trenches. Major Bray had a sandbag wall built across it and they clung on to this position awaiting the arrival of new troops. They never came. A message was sent back asking for more ammunition, food and stretchers for the many wounded; only ammunition arrived and even that not until morning. In the meantime, stretchers were improvised for serious cases and the lame and slightly wounded had to get back as best they could.

Darkness brought no lull in the volume of rifle, machine-gun and shell fire. The ground in front of the trench sloped steeply downwards and was covered with thick scrub; the Turks crawled up and threw bombs over the barricade into the trench. They used eight-second fuses and these episodes could get frenetic, with bombs tossed back and forth three times before they exploded. A dropped pass by Dingle in this game would be fatal.

After a sleepless night, dawn broke on the final moments of newly gazetted Captain Dingle. Major Bray dutifully recounted to Reverend Arthur four days later:

> In the early morning of August 22nd he (A.J.D.) was holding part of a trench which we had captured the afternoon before. He was the only officer in about 200 yards of trench, so there are only the statements of a few private soldiers to go on. About 5o'c a.m. the Turks counter-attacked our trenches and threw a lot of bombs, to which we had nothing with which to reply. During this counter attack he was shot through the head and became insensible. Unfortunately we were driven out of the trench and he was left behind in it, as it was quite impossible to remove him … It seems impossible that anyone so full of life should be killed so suddenly.

In reply to the reverend's query of whether there was any possibility he might be a prisoner (like Still), Bray wrote again in October:

> I only wish I could hold out some hope of his surviving. There is no one of all those who have been killed whom I regret more. The men had all got to like him and followed him to a man when he led them in the advance into the Turkish trench on August 21st.

The American Embassy in Constantinople offered no more hope. Further heavy blows were to land on Egglescliffe Rectory: Jimmy's younger brother Hugh would die on HMS *Petard*, smashed by a shell at Jutland in 1916. He also played school rugby, studied medicine at Durham University and joined the RNVR as surgeon probationer. Arthur's wife had also died, leaving him to take care of two young daughters, Mary and Beatrice. Both sons' bodies, once so strong and fit, would never be recovered. Faced with such heartbreak, other men might lose the will to live, but not Arthur: at the age of 80, long retired from the Church, he took up factory work in the Second World War and only died at the age of 92. He applied for Jimmy's

1914-15 Star 'in respect of the service of his late son' but in 1920 returned the Victory medal he had not lived to wear.

The remaining 6th Battalion also showed a will to survive; fighting all the way, with Major Cowper wounded, the Pioneers retired in good order back to their original front-line trench. It was fourteen hours before they were relieved. Utterly worn out, the survivors trooped across the scrub to the beach. When the roll was called only four officers and 250 other ranks remained from the dozen officers and 500 men who had gone into action on the 21st. The battalion was reorganised and Major Bray assumed command. Work on dugouts was begun as they resumed their function as Pioneers. There was time now for writing letters to the families of those killed. Dingle's fellow subaltern, Lt Coultas, wrote:

> It was just before dawn on August 22nd. The Turks were making a counter attack in large numbers with bombs … Lieut Dingle had a lot of the battalion under him and made two lots of tea for them during the night. He was in the highest of spirits before going up … Before he was in 'B' Co'y, he was with us in 'D' Co'y and so you can tell how much I feel his death. In the Battalion he was always a restless spirit of energy. At the end of a long march he would suggest rugger or hockey, and we always played however tired we were. His good spirits seemed infectious. The men adored him and he could get anything out of them. One of his most admirable qualities was his extraordinary modesty. He would have been 2nd in command of 'B' Co'y long before, if he had not been so retiring and modest.

More touching still are the tributes from his men, who indeed adored their officer. Their letters are sincere, heartfelt and beyond the formulaic. Lance Corporal Baker wrote that he 'died in action trying to make good what looked like a forlorn hope; he went down showing no fear of danger, a gentleman in every sense of the word'.[22] From Pte Manners: 'Your son was very well liked among the men he had under him. We looked upon him as a gentleman and the last words I heard him say were that he was very proud of his men the way they stuck to him.' While many letters preferred to ease a parent's distress by describing instant (and painless) death, Pte Watson related that he 'continued to encourage his men while lying wounded and died game to the last. His servant Brown told me also that he tried to reach Lieut Dingle in order to get his papers but couldn't do so.'

He endeared himself to the Tommies in his command by making a brew under fire, wrote Pte Tucker:

> He was a brave man and even went to the charge with a pipe in his mouth. He was also a kind hearted gentleman and a good soldier and he died a brave hero also. After we took the first line of trenches he even made some tea for ten of us, and we felt his death very much.

Pte Petfield recalled the last words of his captain, whose natural authority earned their respect: 'when he heard the "cease fire", he said "Don't cease fire, I am commanding here."' Pte Wilkinson saw the last of A.J. Dingle when 'he raised his head above the parapet and was shot immediately'.

He was killed on 22 August 1915, exactly one year after Charles Bayly's fiery death in Belgium. In that single year of war, twenty of the club's doomed youth had already died as cattle. England's Jimmy Dingle was the twenty-first – a dismal coming of age for Rosslyn Park.

7

SYD BURDEKIN
FROM THE UTTERMOST
ENDS OF THE EARTH

Second Lieutenant Burdekin, Royal Field Artillery. *(TAS)*

A new century dawned and the city of Sydney awoke on New Year's Day 1901 to find herself in the new Commonwealth of Australia. *Terra australis incognita* had been known as Australia since the early 1800s, but the real birth of a nation happened in the early hours of a tumultuous twentieth century: six Crown colonies, largely self-governing, had formed a federation. At its inauguration, a choir of 10,000 – one-twentieth of Sydney's entire population – performed a song written by a Scotsman which urged *Advance, Australia Fair*.

Despite the death three weeks later of the maternal Queen Empress Victoria, the fair child advanced happily in the Edwardian sunshine. She sat at her imperial mother's knee, enjoying her warmth and nourishment. She tried hard to please her distant parent by setting before her mineral and agricultural riches and, increasingly, her manpower: Australian Light Horse and Imperial Bushmen fought for Britain's empire in South Africa, although their natural empathy was more for the hardy Boer farmers. In 1907 the well-behaved child was rewarded with dominion status, alongside her sisters in

Canada, New Zealand and Newfoundland, all pretty in pink in the imperial family portrait that was Mercator's projection.

The mother ship of Great Britain was at the hub, radiating beams of light to its satellites, as benign protector, administrative and spiritual provider, and vital economic market. While descendants of Australia's oldest families might harbour lingering resentment at their enforced 'resettlement' to Botany Bay, the relationship with the old country was positive. Young Australians of a certain class found it natural to spend their formative years there in education or employment (no change there, then). Aussie athletes like Eric Fairbairn competed under the flag and sovereignty of the Crown for a nation of which they were still officially citizens.

When war came in 1914, few hesitated to fight for distant Britain. Some did not wait for the Australian Imperial Force (AIF) to embark, but sailed promptly in eagerness to push to the front. With a six-week sea passage, this was no sudden whim after a few beers and a glimpse of a recruiting poster – this was a commitment to shared values and a common cause. Such a willing soldier was Sydney Burdekin, of Macquarie Street in the city whose name he bore. Having returned in 1912 to his native Australia after seven years away in England (and two seasons of rugby with Rosslyn Park) he chose to go back and fight with the British. He would die with them in France.

Burdekin was born into a notable Sydney family. Grandfather Thomas arrived in Australia in 1828, opened a branch of Burdekins & Hawley – 'Ironmongers and General Merchants of London' – and built the family fortune from finance and land deals in the former penal colony of New South Wales. As often with such wealth, the manner of its acquisition bred lasting resentment among the colonial landed gentry that would resurface generations later. The mansion on Macquarie Street that Thomas completed in 1841 in neo-Greek regency style was the finest private residence in the city. However, before he could move in, a stranger arrived from England with proof of original title to the land, and took possession. Thomas settled the legal battle by paying £600 per annum for the rest of his life. This was not long, as the oft-repeated whispers of 'Burdekin's folly' were mortifying to him – he died in 1844.

Thomas' widow and four sons were left wealthy. The grieving Mary Ann financed the 1845 expedition by Ludwig Leichhardt that 'discovered' the Queensland river gratefully named in her honour. From that first Burdekin River flow several eponymous landmarks and buildings (and even an Australian navy frigate) that ensure the survival of the family name to this day. Back in 1840s Sydney, Mary Ann perhaps did not foresee 'Speakeasy March Mardi Gras Love-in with DJs Magda and Risq' at the upmarket Burdekin Hotel in 2010.

After her death, youngest son Sydney and his wife Catherine took on the house. They hosted meetings for his political free trader allies and entertained lavishly; the magnificent Burdekins were the toast of Sydney society. Number 197 Macquarie Street, opposite the Legislative Assembly where Sydney Senior served prominently for fifteen years, was so associated with the family's civic and social exploits that it became known as Burdekin House.[1] It epitomised glamour and affluence, and stood as a symbol of the 'Australian dream' of material and social success. Into this privileged pile of Pyrmont sandstone in 1885 sprang Sydney Junior, known as Syd.

The silver spoon of his birth fed Syd some impressive connections from an early age. He was too young to attend his parents' society soirées, but would peer through the banisters as a procession of political grandees beat a path to his father's study. Among them were New South Wales State Premier Sir John Robertson, Sir Henry Parkes, the 'Father of Federation', and Lord Hopetoun, who would become the first Governor General of all Australia. His companion impressed the schoolboy more; Captain Edward Wallington was private secretary to Hopetoun and this dashing military officer and cricketing Blue would have dazzled young Syd. Years later, his 1915 application for the Special Reserve of Officers would be signed in London by Wallington, then private secretary to Her Majesty Queen Mary, certifying he had known Syd for 'over 20 years ... to be of good moral character'.[2]

Syd's father used his wealth liberally in his electioneering and was renowned for the picnics and other favours distributed to his constituents. After a succession of august offices, Burdekin Senior was elected Mayor of Sydney in January 1890. Despite (or possibly because of) a tendency to follow the political weathervane, 'tributes to his benevolence and affability'[3] abounded, although the Sydney *Bulletin* gently lampooned him:

> There is a rich party named Burdekin
> Who in the House is now heard agin:
> He posed democratic
> But he's – well – erratic
> And, perhaps, may go back on his word agin.

He and Catherine drew social reporters to council events and their parties featured in the women's pages. Perhaps not wishing to out-stay such welcome and rare political popularity, Burdekin abruptly resigned the mayoralty after a year and went 'walkabout' – as erratic as the *Bulletin* had predicted. On the eve of departure in April 1891, the Sydney Liedertafel singers serenaded their vice-president as the whole family of eight began the long voyage to England on the *Orotava*, with Catherine again pregnant. Brother Beaufort was born in Dorset in December after a family continental tour. In their absence, Burdekin House was extensively redecorated.

Like any child, the young country of Australia watched her parent carefully, mimicked her voice and movements and dreamed of growing up in her image. Twelve thousand miles of separation, however, can stimulate independent thought and action in the most obedient of offspring. New character traits began to form, many born directly from an isolated existence in an unforgiving climate. The parental example was modified to suit the emergent nation's growing desire for its own identity. Customs and traditions from the Old World were cherry picked to provide a social and moral frame-work for Australia's young, some of whom were giving concern, as the *Bulletin* fretted:

> Among young Australians there is, unhappily, a demoralised residuum whose antics give occasion for keen anxiety, and whose influence, if not checked and controlled, threatens to be burdensome and offensive to the community as it expands. The larrikin residuum is not peculiar to Australia. But in these colonies, where the struggle for mere subsistence is a condition

scarcely known, the idle and thriftless come more prominently into view than elsewhere.[4]

The answer was in schooling. In her aspiration to nationhood, well-to-do Australia now wished to educate her children on the English model, rather than send them away. These new schools, often staffed by teachers from the mother country, sought to take the best elements of that model, add their own and build a distinctive character for the sons and daughters of the new nation.

Syd Burdekin attended just such a novel enterprise: The Armidale School (TAS) on the New England tablelands of New South Wales. When he arrived in 1897, the school was just three years opened and he would stay until December 1903. Mr Wing, known as 'the Admiral', recalled its first day:

> … there were the school buildings (not yet, it is true, quite finished or completely furnished), and … a small muster of boys, all quite as much at sea as I was; in fact we were all starting from scratch in what I afterwards realised was a new experiment in Australia – a boys' boarding school 350 miles away from each of two capital cities, intended to be on the lines of an English Public School.[5]

The Rev. William Fisher, the first head, and 'his small band of teachers, products of British establishments and traditions, thus embarked upon their educational encounter with unbridled and unfettered Australian youth'. Fisher, a Preston Grammar boy, avoided the straitjacket of English public school conformity. Released from rigid formality, he and his teachers, all still in their twenties, revelled in a more relaxed relationship with their charges. They played alongside them in school teams at cricket and even rugby (today's governing bodies, look away now), and acted and sang in their plays. So relaxed was Mr Lawrance – second master, opening batsman and singer of Gilbert & Sullivan operetta – that he dared to be photographed tieless in an open-necked shirt, quite unthinkable at stiff-collared Eton or Harrow.

In these formative years, Armidale followed its English antecedents but always added a flavour of its own. The 1911 school song captures it perfectly:

We've a name to make and a place to take in our country's struggle and fight.

We must follow the rules of the ancient schools, which have done so much for the world.

A heraldic coat of arms features a slung lamb fleece to signify the chief local industry; 'after sending to England for designs, the [school] flag was made in Sydney at a cost of £5.17s.9d'. Above all, the school's magazine had a vibrancy, humour and directness which presaged the 'no worries' attitude which is modern Australia's most popular export – after a losing Ashes team. Through *The Armidalian's* pages,[6] we follow the lives of its young scholars, until some end brutally and prematurely in war. Its editors openly faced sensitive issues in a way that English politeness would scarcely permit. Take this solicitous entry on a boy whose academic progress had previously been unstoppable:

> We are sorry to hear of Concanon's misfortune in breaking down from over-work. He had won a history scholarship at King's College, Cambridge but had to take a rest. He is now, we believe, staying in Toowoomba, and we shall be glad to hear that he has recovered sufficiently to go back to Cambridge.

Concanon returned but, suffering again from stress, turned his back on university for the militia. Another illness led him to resign from the army for 'a wandering life for some years in Australia, North and South America and the Continent of Europe', thus pioneering another noble Australian tradition. He was killed in a bayonet charge at the first Gallipoli landings in April 1915.

The rural setting of Armidale would contribute to the independent character of TAS pupils (and the language of horse-breaking used above). *The Armidalian* reports in May 1903 that 'great excitement has been caused of late by the riding of stray horses which wander into the school grounds'. One pupil, Arthur Cooper, rode his pony to school every day for five years; when Syd later declares on his officer's application that he can ride, it is not through the horsemanship of the aristocratic English yeomanry, but the bareback instinct of the outback.

Bush wildlife added bite to the eternal schoolboy fascination with creepy crawlies; picnics netted a fine haul of 'scorpion abominations and a "snake" with legs fore and aft'. In vivid contrast to English counterparts who rarely confronted nature red in tooth and claw, a TAS Easter excursion was determined to hunt possum and bandicoot to supplement an already exotic Sunday breakfast of bacon, sardines, sheep's tongues and anchovy paste (try feeding that to the youth of today). The day's bag amounted to no more than a small bush rat, which was gleefully roasted and eaten.

The bustling township of Wollomombi ('four wooden buildings, viz. two Hotels a Store and Post Office') was also explored – presumably, not at great length. The next day, in the gorge of the Chandler River, larger prey escaped the eager hunters: 'This was very vexatious, as we had been assured that the wallaroo about the Gorge are as large as bullocks and bite pieces wholesale out of you if you get near them unawares.' They had to be content with a hare 'and should have got another if the gun had not been dawdling behind with the photographer', but made up for the disappointment (and some unpalatable hare) by 'boiling him and frying him twice with bacon and half a pound of butter'.

The school had its tribal initiation rite: the Singing of the Lambs – as terrifying for new boys as Hannibal Lecter's later *Silence* – was held in 'Big School'. The lambs' offerings varied greatly in quality and entertainment value; parodies of *Mary had a Little Lamb* were regularly sung (one year 'White startled us with the real thing') and *The Boy Stood on the Burning Deck* was recited so often that one attempt was drowned out with cries of 'something else!' But the evenings ended in good spirits and 'having shown their best smiles and embraced each other, the lambs went away happy'.

Sport played its part in making boys into men. As in the distant motherland, 'compulsory attendance at games was an excellent preventative of loafing'. The exuberance of the school 'experiment' shines through in reports of the cricket trip to the Federal Club: 'the bus was a bit crowded but from the vocal efforts that proceeded from the interior, they certainly had plenty of room to breathe, which after all is the first necessity.' Pragmatism was balanced by a yearning for better facilities: summer swimming in the reservoir was cancelled in 1903 due to the low levels of water, which 'shows that a school swimming bath is very desirable'; in 1900 the tennis courts were 'more than usually cracked' and play was delayed for some months. Every coach will surely recognise the plea made in 'Rugby Prospects':

> At last we have a supply of white jerseys for practice games, and we are free from the great muddle that formerly existed when all wore coloured ones … These games are very important and we would conclude by asking everybody to look upon them as such; always let all change and turn up punctually, and let the talking be done by captains only.

This is a small, intimate school. Family names trickle down in cascading numerals like Roman football scores: White III, Anderson II. When Syd enters in 1897, the inaugural *Armidalian* records him as one of just seventy-six boys. Mr Lawrance and Mr Skuse regularly bolstered the cricket XI, although their opponents must have protested the teachers' regular hatful of wickets. Hardiness was essential, even in genteel cricket, when the lush squares of Lawrance's Dulwich College were a distant memory. How about this for character building in a young country:

> … we rose at 5am and travelled by train to Guyra to play the Ollera Club. A new concrete wicket has just been completed there and played rather queerly at one end. This fact coupled with the wet black soil, which effectively prevented hits from travelling to the boundary, made runs difficult to get.

Why be surprised by the obduracy of modern Australian cricket when forged from such early adversity? Syd scored ten runs in this victory and Mr Skuse used this most unyielding of surfaces to good effect, taking nine wickets.

Cricket was undoubtedly Syd Burdekin's game of choice. The *Armidalian's* 'Cricket Characters' deems him 'a stylish bat with great power on the leg side. A keen and good field.' He topped the batting averages in 1902, even with a modest 13.55 (must have been the concrete and black soil), although this slipped to 11.75 the follow-ing season. He finally blossomed with unbeaten centuries against Tamworth and Reform CC, sending his average soaring to 34.07 and leaving the journal to deliver its verdict on his first XI career: 'very successful with the bat this year. A bad starter but scores well all round the wicket when set; especially powerful on the legside. Improved much during the season as a wicket-keep. Left at Christmas.'

As Australia moved towards nationhood, it was an overseas war in Africa that made TAS conscious of its place in empire. An *Armidalian* editorial of May 1900 must have deeply impressed the 14-year-old Syd, and presaged attitudes to the greater conflict of 1914:

England, formerly more or less of a name to younger Australians, now stands before us as a power whose world-wide interests over-shadow the smaller ones of our Australian life … And it may be that this taste of war that Australians have voluntarily taken may have something to do in moulding our as yet unformed national character, and giving it a bend in higher directions than it might otherwise have followed.

To us, able only to look on at the stirring events in Africa, this war has brought a sense of the greatness and unity of the Empire to which we belong, with, perhaps, some clearer perceptions of England's mission in the world, as we see our cousins from Canada, New Zealand, the West Indies and elsewhere, eager to respond to her call for men, eager to fight in a cause which has no direct concern with any of them …

The editor plays the recruiting sergeant with conviction, invok-ing the patriotic spirit of a Briton, 'whether a British, Australian, or Canadian Briton':

Patriotism in its truest sense is self-denial, readiness to devote life, time, money, everything if need be, to one's country. But greater than country is the Empire … Perhaps one good result of this Boer war will be to make the younger citizens of the Australian Commonwealth adopt as their political life motto not 'for Australia' but 'for Australia and the Empire'.

British soldiers playing
rugby in Afghanistan,
1879; 59th Regiment at
Khelat-i-Gilzai. Try or no
try? *(Author's collection)*

The original source.
Rosslyn Park minute
book 3, 1898–1919.
(Club archive)

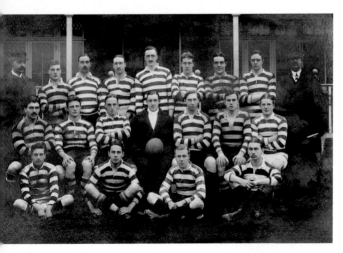

3 Six players in this Rosslyn Park 1909–1[0] team would be killed in the Great War. *(Club archive)*

4 'Big Side' (seen here in the 1950s), where Bayly played for the St Paul's school XV. *(St Paul's school)*

5 Charles Bayly (left) with half-back partne[r] Wilfred Jesson (right) H.E.V. Farrell (centre) survived. *(Club archive)*

22 The Bodenham family at Ivy Lodge. Jack, the youngest, is at the front. *(Floris Archive)*

3 Jack Bodenham, in the garden at vy Lodge, with brothers Jim, Frank nd Charles. *(Floris Archive)*

24 Rifleman J.E.C. Bodenham, Queen's Westminster Rifles in Richmond Park (left). *(Flori Archive)*

COUNTY CRICKETERS.

MR. R. W. JESSON,
HAMPSHIRE.

25 Wilfred Jesson, Hampshire County cricketer, o a 1908 cigarette card. *(Hampshire CCC)*

26 Royal Victoria Hospital, Netley, where Jesson arrived in 1916 suffering from 'neurasthenia'.
(Author's collection)

27 Soldiers of 5/Wiltshire Regiment in tropical kit in northern Mesopotamia. *(Author's collection)*

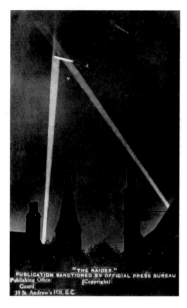

28 Zeppelins caught the public imagination. This propaganda postcard shows a search-lit attack by planes; the reality was far different. *(Author's collection)*

29 Harman's restored gravestone in Gainsborough churchyard, Lincolnshire. *(Peter Bradshaw)*

EASTER TOUR, 1911

Back Row: J. R. McGregor, L. Haigh, W. P. Geen, A. R. Ross, G. H. D'O. Lyon, L. G. Brown, S. S. L. Steyn. Middle Row: G. H. Dodds, A. D. Roberts, D. L. Monaghan, J. A. S. Ritson, C. H. Pillman, K. C. Hands, S. N. Cronje, L. B. Stringer, G. D. Campbell, E. G. Ede, F. le S. Stone, R. H. M. Hands. Front Row: C. F. Constantine, H. C. Harrison, W. P. Carpmael, T. Smyth, E. de Lissa, G. D. Roberts, J. M. B. Scott, H. Whitehead, F. G. Handford. On Ground: L. R. Broster, B. B. Bennetts.

30 Denis Monaghan with the 1911 Barbarians touring side. *(Author's collection)*

The Tank Corps Christmas card from 1917 which Denis Monaghan would never send. *(Author's collection)*

2 'Spotting in a kite balloon car': the precarious life of a 'balloonatic' observer, Robert Hale. *(Author's collection)*

33 Arthur Leyland Harrison (back left) with Rosslyn Park, 1913. *(Club archive)*

34 Harrison aboard HMS *Vindictive* before the raid (second from right). A few hours later he and Hawkings (right) would be dead. *(Rosemary Fitch)*

35 *Vindictive* at the Mole in a painting carefully briefed by Captain Carpenter (apart from the apparent daylight). *(Author's collection)*

36 *Vindictive* after the Zeebrugge raid, battered but unbeaten. She would soon end her days at Ostende. *(Author's collection)*

37 Charles Sargeant Jagger's artillery memorial in a 1925 postcard. *(Author's collection)*

38 Charles Sutton (centre with ours) with his brother John and family, on leave in Leyland. *(Jimmy Button)*

39 'The Last Stand of the 5th (Gibraltar) Battery, 1918', by Terence Cuneo. *(Carole Cuneo)*

40 A New Zealand 'trench team' playing the Army Service Corps at Richmond in 1917. The ASC shirts look familiar. *(F. Humbert)*

"This is not the time to play Games" *(Lord Roberts)*

RUGBY·UNION·FOOTBALLERS
are
DOING·THEIR·DUTY
over 90% have enlisted

"Every player who represented England in Rugby international matches last year has joined the colours."—Extract from *The Times*, November 30, 1914.

BRITISH ATHLETES!
Will you follow this
GLORIOUS EXAMPLE ?

41 'Over 90% have enlisted.' Recruiting posters held rugby players up as a glorious example. *(Library of Congress)*

Subsequent issues of the *Armidalian* carry letters from patriotic Old Boys. Lt F.L. Donkin writes from Beira, a 'wretched little place … about as unhealthy a place as there is on a very unhealthy coast' but whose 'acquaintance I first made in Mr Wing's classroom, form iv, Geography, 10 till 11, on Mondays and Thursdays':

> I hope perhaps some fellows may take my tip when I tell them there's no life like a soldier's especially a British soldier's. I can vouch for its being a very jolly life, the pay is excellent and if a fellow is so inclined he can (just now!) get into the Imperial Army without any exam at all.

It is no coincidence that Henry Newbolt's poem '*Vitaï Lampada*' ('There's a breathless hush in the close to-night …') now appears in the *Armidalian*. Its mantra, born out of Clifton College (Douglas Haig's school), was adopted by schools across the empire, but its sentiment is made for far-flung Armidale. The tale of a schoolboy cricketer would shine a torch for Syd, the new corps cadet:

> The river of death has brimmed his banks,
> And England's far, and Honour a name;
> But the voice of a school boy rallies the ranks;
> 'Play up! play up! and play the game'[7]

The opportunity for military adventure in the bloodless *Boy's Own Paper* style was tantalisingly out of reach for those under volunteering age; this did not stop them from dreaming of soldierly heroism. Burdekin features in a dramatic report of Cadet Corps exercises:

> Lt Burdekin, with three sections, left the school to clear Lion's Hill and the North-West of the town of some snipers under the command of Lt Garland, who were suspected to be threatening the Glen Innes Road. The snipers betrayed their presence by firing at a scout, and were quickly surrounded and annihilated by Lt Burdekin's force.

Notwithstanding his cadet officer prowess, Syd Burdekin would scarcely see action before his death in the real show. In May 1915, his cadet adversary Charles Garland, 'an idealist with a high sense of honour, strengthened by the traditions of his School', enlisted in the AIF as a private, having heard of the deaths of friends like Concanon at Gallipoli. He rose to sergeant by the time he was killed by machine-gun fire in no-man's-land at the Battle of Fromelles on the Somme in 1916. Like Syd, he did not see out thirty years.

Burdekin was prominent in all fields of school life: starring in the duel scene from Sheridan's *The Rivals* and as Fabian in *Twelfth Night*; winner of a chemistry prize; colours in athletics, rugby and cricket (although unable to dislodge one J. White from team captaincy and the Senior Champions Cup); a senior prefect; and on the *Armidalian* committee. But it is the corps that most laments his departure, and foreshadows a future in uniform:

> From such a good set of fellows it would seem invidious to select any for special mention; yet a few words will not be out of place in respect of one, a share of whose praise the rest may claim for themselves. Lieutenant S Burdekin joined the cadets in Feb 1899. After passing through the ranks, he became Colour Sergeant in Feb 1902 and Second Lieutenant in October. When Lt HF White left, Lt Burdekin took up his place. From first to last he was devoted to the best interest of the Cadet Corps as well as to all the sports of the school, and by his unselfishness, enthusiasm and example, he did more perhaps than anyone to raise the Company to its present state of efficiency.

His next step may show the influence of Wallington, the cricketing Oxford Blue, or even a 'splendid lantern entertainment of views of Oxford and Cambridge which caused great admiration'. His father had died in 1899, predeceased by three children; as the eldest son and heir, Syd was not short of money. While many of his contemporaries went to St Paul's College, Sydney, he left Australia to further his education at Merton College, Oxford. Catherine, Florence and Beaufort moved to England with him. His passage from possum hunts to dreaming spires carries with it the aspirations of a whole school.

The *Armidalian* of May 1904 reports that he 'has reached Colombo, travelling to the old country', and exhorts: 'May he uphold the honour of Armidale at Oxford where we shall eagerly watch for news of him.'

News came, predictably enough, from the cricket field. In the Old Boys section of August 1905, 'S. Burdekin writes very brightly of his life at Oxford. He played in the University Freshmen's Match at cricket, scoring 32 and 11. His fielding was singled out for special mention by one of the London daily papers.' *The Times* indeed commented that 'Mr Burdekin was the most conspicuous of the fieldsmen … several of whom tired towards the end of the day'.[8] But he did not win his Blue. Nor did he complete his degree, as he left Merton in June 1906, after only two years.

London had a more powerful pull for this young Australian and he found employment there as a mercantile clerk, albeit one who could afford to lodge in swanky Jermyn Street. He and his fellow lodger at 113, forward Herbert Hodson, joined Rosslyn Park in October 1909. The imperial heart certainly held an attraction for the socialite Catherine Burdekin, who presented her daughter Florence at court in June 1909, then sailed for Sydney in January 1910 on the *Otranto*, her life's ambitions fulfilled. Syd stayed in England as guardian to Beaufort, now boarding at Cheltenham College, and as rugby three-quarter at Old Deer Park.

At TAS, Syd had played halfback for the XV for three years and was 'one of the most useful members of the team; fast and clever; tackles well'. As might be expected of a boy who won the 100 yards in ten and two-fifths seconds, he now found himself on the wing for Park; being 'Winner Senior Obstacle Race' also helped when faced with opposing prop forwards. His fellow southern hemisphere expatriates were as refreshingly direct in their opinions of English rugby as they are today. The 'Full Back' column in the esteemed *Otago Witness* carried this letter from New Zealander Alan Adams, a London Hospital student doctor and Park centre three-quarter:

I have been here for a few months now and have seen a fair amount of English football, but have not been greatly impressed. Things are very slack in the Rugby world, and the best matches get very few spectators. Matches are generally fixed to start at 3pm, but the majority of players turn up late, with the result that you very seldom get a start before 3.30 and then play spells of about 30 minutes each. Very little practice is indulged in and a scrum is never formed from one week's end to another, so that a player unaccustomed to the formation here has to spend weeks trying to find a place to pack into. The club football is very poor, and I have not seen a team here yet, county or club, which the Otago and Sydney Universities of 1906 or 1907 would not have beat quite easily.[9]

Whatever their opinions, their rugby talent was undeniable and a boon to London clubs then, as now. Against Blackheath in 1909, five itinerant hospital Kiwis all turned out for Rosslyn Park – Adams, Mehaffey, Macpherson, Macfarlane and Moore. The following season Adams played centre in the same fixture, and gave a scoring pass to his Aussie winger, Syd Burdekin; he also won his only international cap, playing for England against France.

The term 'lost generation' has been overused in regard to the Great War. However, if Rosslyn Park lost one, then it was Syd's 1909/10 vintage: six friends in that season's team photograph were killed, including halfbacks Bayly and Jesson, and wing Denis Monaghan. Indiscriminate death reached beyond the stars of the first XV: Henry Townsend-Green, captain and honorary secretary of the second XV, also captained the Queen's Westminster Rifles to his death in March 1915; Conway John Hart, who skippered the 'A' XV for three seasons died on the Somme in October 1916; and Neil Shoobert, lieutenant of the 23rd Middlesex (Second Football) Battalion, died at the third spasm of Ypres.

After his walkabout years, Syd returned to Australia in 1912. Did he see his brother Beaufort win a silver rowing medal for Great Britain at the 1912 Stockholm Olympics? He certainly missed his 1914 Boat Race Blue. But he took the opportunity to see more of the world by travelling overland across the United States and crossing the Pacific, rather than his imperial route via Suez and Ceylon of 1904. In Sydney he took a post as freight manager for the McIlwraith & McEachern Shipping Company. Perhaps the dwindling family fortune no longer allowed him to lead a gentleman's life. His mother died in 1913. By the time of his wartime passage back to England he had become a 'grazier', or livestock farmer.

As war arrived like a new term, the Armidale School and its Old Boys were vocal in their pro-British support, and considered it their duty to serve the empire. The eager desire of the young federation to prove itself by marching with its parent to the South African war had been subsumed by a new adolescent yearning for cleansing from staleness. War, thought the *Armidalian* editor in December 1914, would stimulate growth, national strengthening and purification and 'our young men and boys will one day rejoice merely to have been alive at such a privileged epoch of the world's slow tedious development'. This echoes the Englishman Brooke's 'swimmers into cleanness leaping/Glad from a world grown old and cold and weary'.[10] But the aspiration to nation-building – or the editor's 'dignity of racial pride' – is wholly Australian.

The school hailed its heroic Christian alumni marching to war as if its own reputation would be judged by their bearing. As the butcher's bill mounted, Bishop Cooper could still say at speech day in 1916: 'Two things are necessary for the conduct of war, munitions and men – TAS cannot make munitions, but it is responsible for the manufacture of men; yea, and the best sort of men too.' The bishop did not live to see his own pony-riding son Arthur, a third-year Sydney arts student, manufactured into the best sort of AIF subaltern and killed by a shell fragment at Ypres in July 1917, aged 21.

Newbolt was again pressed into service on posters to recruit sporting Australians: 'Enlist in the Sportsmen's 1000: Join Together, Train Together, Embark Together, Fight Together. Play Up, Play Up and Play the Game!' Letters from the front in the *Armidalian* again played their part, despite the black-edged obituaries, lengthening Roll of Honour and even a stained-glass window in memory of Anderson I who died from wounds at Gallipoli. One S.B. (not our man, but clearly a propagandist in the making) exposed the flaw in German education and sportsmanship that had caused the war:

Directly the German boy is old enough, a military cap is put on his little square head, and large leather satchel of books is

strapped behind his shoulders. He does not become very enthusiastic about cricket, which he terms strike-ball, and he knows
very little about football, which he plays in a lady-like manner
that would bring tears of compassion to the eyes of his prototype
in an Australian school ... The Australian school-boy sometimes
displays his mechanical ingenuity in the form of paper boats
and aeroplanes: little Fritz will surreptitiously tear leaves from
his exercise-book to make Zeppelins, Parsevals [a lesser-known
airship] and other baby-killing implements.

Historians have unaccountably overlooked the German indifference
to cricket as a causal factor in the conflict.

In 1914 Syd Burdekin made his own decision and set off quickly
from the crease. The P&O steamer *Malwa* docked in London in late
January 1915 and he booked into the Sports Club, St James Square.
A swift visit to Buckingham Palace saw Wallington sign his application for the Special Reserve of Officers. OTC service permitted such
officers to be commissioned after a shorter training period – the regular army was crying out for leaders to replace those massacred in 1914.
Application to acceptance took Syd just one week – surely a sign of
fast-track influence even in the dire need of the day. He did not wait
long in the reserve and the *London Gazette* reported his commission
as second lieutenant (on probation) the day before it came into force
on 20 February. Despite his leading role in the corps, he never made
the school shooting team (too many Andersons), so was not destined
for the infantry. He joined the Royal Field Artillery (RFA) and was
quick to spend part of his £50 uniform allowance on an engraved
ceremonial sword from Henry Wilkinson's of Pall Mall[11] – not much
use 'overseas', but allowed him to cut a dash at Beaufort's wedding to
Catherine Cade (sister to Rowena of Minack Theatre fame and later
feminist novelist) before leaving for France.

This was to be overwhelmingly an artillery war, but in 1915 the
British Army in France had neither guns enough nor shells. Most of
the latter were shrapnel, effective against cavalry, but not the high-
explosive (HE) type needed to destroy barbed wire. A shortage of
fuses meant that many 'duds' simply failed to explode, and there was
talk of American-made shells filled with sawdust. Howitzers and

mortars that could plunge projectiles into deep trenches were at a premium. German industry meanwhile was pumping out 250,000 artillery rounds each day, compared to 22,000 in Britain.

Syd's 10th Trench Mortar Battery (TMB) was attached to 22 Brigade, 7th Division, under command of Maj. Gen. Sir Thompson Capper. Its regular battalions had taken crushing losses at Ypres and were being rebuilt with hastily trained new officers and men. Trench mortars were unknown at the outbreak; the British had to borrow ancient French 'Coehorn' mortars dating back to Louis Philippe's 1830s. With the arrival of the Stokes mortar in late 1915 they became vital to every division's armoury.

Unlike the Field, Garrison and Siege artillerymen, whose big guns were widely believed to protect the infantry, these highly mobile trench mortar men were not popular. They would arrive with their lightweight weapons, fire off a few high-trajectory rounds from a saphead close to the enemy line and decamp before the return fire lobbed in, much to the botheration of the Poor Bloody Infantry. The enemy's 'mortal terrors … like huge toffee apples sailing over rather slowly in the air' caused even more problems:

> They have been brought to a fine art by the Germans – they send one over to the left of a section one moment, we all scoot to the right and by the time we arrive panting, another one has been sent and is about to drop among us – we run back and almost fall into one another – terrific explosion. It's impossible to describe how much damage, death and destruction they're capable of.[12]

In September 1915, the brigade found itself on a 600-yard frontage at Loos, between the Vermelles-Hulluch road and the Hohenzollern Redoubt. Field Marshal Sir John French had by now spent several months demonstrating to doubtful French allies that his men were made of stern fighting stuff, a quality which the French, with their policy of *offensive à outrance* (all-out assault), appeared only to measure in six-figure casualty counts – 360,000 in 1914 alone, against 27,000 British.

The BEF, badly depleted by 1914's battles, now bolstered by Territorial troops and the peacetime reserve, was not yet at critical mass of either manpower or *matériel* to mount major offensives on a long front where sheer weight of numbers was a key factor. The French, however, were stubbornly insistent and Kitchener did not know how to say no to his ally. His paradoxical directive to his field marshal instructed him to support the French but reminded him 'that the numerical strength of the British force … is strictly limited and … it will be obvious that the greatest care must be exercised towards a minimum of losses and wastage'.[13]

The battles of Neuve Chapelle and Aubers Ridge in spring 1915 promptly wasted thousands of British lives – including many valuable trained regulars and Territorials – to prove a point to the French. As a final irony, after battalions of hapless infantry had been laid waste, both battles were 'closed down', not through loss of men but lack of artillery ammunition.

By September, the mobile slaughterhouse had moved to the industrial coal-mining area around Lens and Loos. Kitchener changed his tune and issued a new direct order to Sir John French to 'do our utmost to help France in their offensive [in Champagne] even though by so doing we may suffer very heavy losses'.[14] Loos was a forbidding landscape of 'dark satanic mills', dotted with fosse pitheads and massive steel winding towers. The German front line incorporated huge *crassiers*, or slagheaps, and clusters of miners' cottages (known grandly as *cités*), poorly built of red brick, which exploded like puffballs under artillery fire but whose cellars hid protected emplacements for German machine guns. Over terrain already viewed as highly unfavourable for an attack, the British decided to unleash for the first time the suitably industrial weapon of chlorine gas – 150 tons of it. Germany had first used gas at Ypres on 22 April; the British, embarrassed in following their 'barbaric' lead, primly referred to it as 'the accessory', released from cylinders, not the projectile shells prohibited by the Hague Convention.

There were not enough guns to soften up the German trenches and wire. The dud problem continued: the 35th TMB reported that of sixteen rounds fired in the pre-attack bombardment, nine were blinds (did not go off) and one was air high (exploded early).[15] At dawn on 25 September, Syd's mortars fired smoke bombs which mixed with the yellowish-green gas to provide a deadly screen for the infantry advance. The law of unintended consequences applied and variable wind direction blew the gas cloud anywhere but over the German lines. Almost suffocated in their primitive gas hoods (barely preferable to the cotton pads soaked with urine improvised at Ypres), the British troops removed them to breathe and were overwhelmed by the fumes. Furthermore, the enemy attempted to clear the gas cloud by sending in HE shells, which caused devastation amongst the foot troops, who had hoped that this new and sinister 'fog of war' would conceal them.

Just where it was needed most, the cloud lifted; some 30 yards of no-man's-land had to be crossed in full view of the Germans. The wire barricades were uncut and swathes of Staffordshires and Warwickshires were scythed down by machine-gun fire as they tried to scramble across them. Somehow, the German front line and second line were taken. Just a few hundred yards to the north, 2/Lt Charles Vaughan, Rosslyn Park winger, was killed leading his Seaforth Highlander platoon's attack on the Hohenzollern Redoubt:

> Revolver in one hand, rifle and bayonet [picked up on the way] in the other, he was first into the German trenches – 'it did give us a hearting', said his servant – but was wounded and knocked over in the second trench. He picked himself up, ran at two Germans and bayoneted them, then turned to attack two more on his right, when a second bullet killed him. [16]

The British failed to capitalise on the costly success of the first day as their reserves were too far to the rear – Sir John French would take the blame and lose his job to Haig. German counterattacks with superior 'potato masher' stick grenades halted further advance. By the time the battle finally ended on 16 October, some 50,000 casualties had been suffered, including 2,013 officers. 'Such,' said the Official History, with rare bitterness, 'was the tremendous sacrifice made by all ranks to support fully and loyally our French Ally, and the price paid in flesh and blood for unpreparedness for war.' [17] The Germans, stunned by the facile slaughter, named Loos *Der Leichenfeld* or 'corpse-field'; as the British retreated, a German officer recalled, 'no shot was fired at them from the German

trenches for the rest of the day, so great was the feeling of compassion and mercy for the enemy after such a victory'.[18] Of the
total casualty list, some 800 officers and 15,000 men were killed or
missing or never heard of again, including Maj. Gen. Capper, shot
by a sniper. The derided 'donkeys' did sometimes venture forward
into danger after all: 232 generals were wounded in the war and
78 killed (compared to 20 in the Second World War).

Syd Burdekin was reported missing on 27 September, the same
day as Rudyard Kipling's son, John. His body was never recovered;
but nor was it the object of frantic searches like Kipling's. We are
reminded how distant Australia is: the first report of him at the front
appears in the *Armidalian* in April 1916, when he was already some
seven months missing. The first mention of his death is not until
December, fifteen months after the fact. Or is it simply that Syd had
no living parent to pass on sad news to the school?

The dwindling Burdekin family did not give up hope. In November
1916, his sister Florence received letters from Lt Cmdr Eardley
Wilmott RN, writing from HMAS *Encounter*, and a friend, Charles
Waters, who reported tantalisingly that 'I saw in a paper that was sent
to me from Switzerland some 3 months ago the name of S. Burdekin
as a prisoner in Germany'. She asked that 'the Army Council post-
pone considering whether my brother is dead until I can get some
definite reply'. But none came.

Death was finally 'accepted on lapse of time' by the War Office in
May 1919. The following year, the British Military Mission in Berlin
confirmed to Captain Beaufort Burdekin, also RFA, that there was
'no record that he had been in German hands as a Prisoner of War'.
Syd's name is engraved on the Loos Memorial Wall at Dud Corner
Cemetery, named after the high number of unexploded shells found
there on the site of a German redoubt. British soldiers were not so
lucky under devastating German artillery: the wall commemorates
over 20,000 men whose bodies were vaporised, shattered and lost.

Beaufort returned to Sydney as a barrister in 1920, with his wife
and two daughters, but the marriage had broken down by 1922.
Florence had married the politician Alexander Hay and lived at
Macquarie Street. The family would shortly vacate the property
and Burdekin House was threatened with demolition. The Royal

Australian Historical Society lobbied government to acquire the house for preservation, but it was haunted by the usurious reputation of Grandfather Thomas, who did not pass the requisite 'Great Man' test. It was privately purchased, used as a community space for working artists and finally demolished in 1933. The dynasty had disappeared: Beaufort's lack of a male heir and Syd's demise saw Thomas' line die out. The rise and fall of the house of Burdekin was complete.

Much has been written about Australian national identity being forged in the crucible of Anzac cove: in the official histories by Charles Bean; in the unofficial and less scrupulous accounts by Keith Murdoch, who briefly visited what he was already calling 'the sacred shores of Gallipoli'[19] on his way to make his name in London; and in many subsequent books and the 1981 film by Peter Weir. Some 332,000 Australians fought for the empire, all volunteers, with conscription twice defeated by referendum. Almost 62,000 died among 214,000 casualties, the highest casualty rate (64 percent) of any combatant country. It is said they came from six federated states and returned as soldiers of one nation. This war also bred the opposing of rough-edged, straight-talking Aussies to class-ridden Pommie bastardry (especially of the General Staff officer class). Australia had been disconcerted by the ungentlemanly violence meted out by touring British Isles rugby players in 1899 and 1904. The sense of injury was inflamed by Murdoch's wartime journalism and the permanent smoulder has flared up in the press at every sporting confrontation since, from Douglas Jardine's 'Bodyline' tour onwards.

The 'larrikin residuum' – finely upheld by the latter-day likes of Shane Warne – contributed some wonderfully funny confrontations between disrespectful Diggers and pompous Red Tabs at Gallipoli. It also produced moments of modest, devil-may-care heroism. Two Australians saved the life of a wounded RAMC orderly, picking off four Turkish snipers in the process, and carried him to the beach at Lala Baba. They asked that no mention be made, because:

> ... we're not supposed to be up here sharp-shootin' – we jist done it fer a bit of sport. Rightly we don't carry a rifle; we belong to the bridge-buildin' section. We've only borrowed these rifles from the Cycle Corps, an' we shall be charged with

bein' out o' bounds without leave, an' all that sort o' thing if it gits known down at our headquarters.[20]

Charles Bean, who was best positioned to observe it in action, traced the origins of Aussie character:

Like colonists of all ages, the Australian came of a race whose tradition was one of independence and enterprise ... Bred of such stock, and left to develop themselves freely in their own way, Australians came to exhibit a peculiar independence of character ... If there was in them something of aggressiveness, there was also a vigorous and unfettered initiative. In them the characteristic resourcefulness of the British was perforce developed further. They had lived much in lonely places, where it was necessary to solve each difficulty without help, and in the process they learned to hold no practical problem insoluble.

The grown man was unaccustomed to commands untempered by the suggestion of a request. The only restraint he recognised before the war was self-imposed. This characteristic gave him a reputation for indiscipline, but it endowed him with a power of swift individual decision and, in critical moments, of self-control, which became conspicuous during the war ... These qualities of independence, originality, the faculty of rising to an occasion, and loyalty to a 'mate', conspicuous in the individual Australian, became recognisable as parts of the national character.[21]

In summary, your Australian in wartime was a nightmare to command, but a bloody good fighter to have on your side; he proved it from Lone Pine, Gallipoli, to Pozières at the Somme. A British officer at Lone Pine recalled later that:

... some of the Australians who were to be kept on reserve had offered up to five pounds to be allowed to take part in the attack. I had seen some of the Anzac troops in the peninsula; they were of magnificent physique, and often wore only shorts and entrenching tool carriers on their feet. They had no military discipline in the British sense but were as fine soldiers as had ever taken the field.[22]

In 2001 the pugnacious Steve Waugh took his Ashes team to Gallipoli to hone their psychological motivation. He came up with the idea over dinner with Australian General Peter Cosgrove, when the two men discussed the importance of 'camaraderie, discipline, commitment and the importance of following a plan'.[23] Captain Ponting, less profitably, took his 2005 side to the Australian memorial at Villers-Bretonneux. Not to be outdone, English skipper Andrew Strauss (b. Johannesburg) visited Ypres in 2009, with coach Andy Flower (b. Capetown) appreciating 'a greater understanding of what it really means to stand shoulder to shoulder and fight for your country'.[24] It is good to see sporting rivalry once again bring together these sons of the old Commonwealth, but some perspective has surely been lost here in the confusion of Waugh. Phil Vickery's England rugby squad laid wreaths at Thiepval in 2007 before the Rugby World Cup, not for team bonding or unity but to gain a 'sense of perspective'[25] – coach Brian Ashton's grandfather had survived the Somme.

Perhaps nationhood and sport both thrive on mythologies and stereotyped enmities. However, is it just possible that this is driven more by the commercial media of both countries? The author has stood shoulder to shoulder with Aussies in pubs and clubhouses from New York City to London, through two contested Rugby World Cup finals and many Ashes tests, and enjoyed only the warmest of rivalries and the coldest of beers. No worries, mate.

On the granite Australian War Memorial at London's Hyde Park Corner are engraved the names of 24,000 towns and villages (mostly Australian but many British) from which the Australian forces soldiers enlisted in both world wars. Inscribed on the plaques unveiled by the Queen on Remembrance Day 2003 are these words:

Whatever burden you are to carry
We also will shoulder that burden

On that very day, 2,000 Australians once again shared that burden with 45,000 British soldiers in Iraq, committed to another war by Prime Ministers Blair and Howard just eight months previously. In the first 'Great War for Freedom' there fought 268 boys and masters from the Armidale School. They came from the 'uttermost ends of the earth' (to borrow the ringing legend of the New Zealand memorials) to fight in Belgium, France, Egypt and Turkey on the side of an empire and values which, far from being obsolete, gave a framework to fashion a distinctive new character.

Syd Burdekin and forty-five more from TAS never returned to Australia fair, but through their sacrifice a new nation advanced. The bishop's post-war speech day address in 1920 had no doubt that 'the War was urged because a false view of human society strove to assert itself as supreme' and that the school represented 'a true ideal at once Christian and efficient' that might face continuing threats closer to home:

> To Prussia, society was a machine for the survival of the human race. This view has its counterpart in the Prussian ideal of education, whose aim was to train every individual to play his part in the State-machine, and in particular to pick out the individuals fit to direct it. The aim was not to improve the society as a whole, but to fit everybody into a given niche in the social mechanism. It is not so long ago that one of the chief officers of the Department of Education of NS Wales went on his travels and arrived back with the dogma that England could teach us little in the matter of education, compared with Prussia.

TAS was determined to foster individuality in its students, rather than the assembly-line conformity of any 'system', Prussian or English.

The living proof is found a century later. In the pages of *Binghi*, the school magazine that succeeded the *Armidalian*, news of a visit by George Smith, the great Australian flanker, packs down with the ANZAC day address of Lt Col Cox, Hunter River Lancers. His words echo Charles Bean's:

> Every generation of ANZACs has given us the example of courage, discipline, commitment, teamwork, tenacity and hard work. This has been tempered with humanity, compassion, a sense of humour and larrikinism and the importance of a fair go – these have become trademarks of the Australian character, and if we are

not applying these to our daily lives then our commemoration of the ANZAC tradition becomes cheap.

In this still young democracy where fair play is revered, the nation's war memorials are unusual in recording the names not just of those who died, but of all who served. At TAS in 1919, 'the School Board of Directors passed a resolution authorising the inclusion of the names of all those who enlisted whether they reached the front or not. The Honour Board is to be unveiled on Sports Day.'

In Australia, what other day could it be?

GUY PINFIELD
AN IRISH TRAGEDY

Second Lieutenant Guy Vickery Pinfield, 8th Hussars, in a locket commissioned by his mother. *(Sworder & Co.)*

In a quiet corner of this story is a door. Set in shadow away from the bright windows that frame Flanders and Gallipoli, it bears the name of Guy Vickery Pinfield.

Through the door is the small anteroom of his brief life, before his death aged 21 as an officer of the King's Army. The light flickers on a silver-framed photograph of his parents, Frank and Gertrude, and sister Nora in Assam, India, where Guy was born in 1895. His Liverpudlian father, a tea planter, died when Guy was an infant of 2 years, forcing the family into genteel poverty and rented lodgings in Hove. Gertrude next emerges from St George's Church, Hanover Square, on the arm of Guy's stepfather Patrick Russel, an East India merchant, in 1901; the new family home was the well-appointed Dane House, Bishop's Stortford, in the old county of Huntingdonshire.

The walls carry prints of Marlborough College, which he attended from 1908 to Easter 1913. His captain of house rugby described him as a 'small player at left wing three-quarters, runs very well being fairly fast and possessing a good swerve which he knows how to use. He is generally a sound collar and saves well.' There is no photograph of him at Rosslyn Park, with which Marlborough merged its 'Nomads' London Old Boys team in 1911[1], and which Guy joined with nine schoolmates from the sixth form. Perhaps he was too small a player to make the first XV.

Like Siegfried Sassoon before him, he exchanged the red brick of Marlborough for the golden limestone of Clare College, Cambridge. Another photograph shows Nora's wedding to Vincent Routledge, also of the Bishop's Stortford squirearchy, in the dazzling June of 1914. Soon after, khaki battledress replaced rugby jersey and morning suit: Guy stood proudly in the officer's uniform of the 8th (Kings Royal Irish) Hussars. He was commissioned two weeks after the outbreak of war in August, before he could begin his second year at Cambridge. Perhaps he shared the confidence of Private Godfrey Buxton, RAMC, who later recalled: 'I'd had one year up at Cambridge and then volunteered for the Army. We were quite clear that Germany would be defeated by the 7th of October when we would go back to Cambridge.'[2]

Across the room another door opens: we enter a maze, plunging ever deeper inside the tangled history of the British in Ireland and a remorseless chain of events on one April day. Guy Pinfield's death, tucked away on the back doorstep of a nation gazing fixedly at the Western Front, may be a perfect example of a footnote in history. But it leads us to a new theatre where a complex tragedy unfolds.

In pre-war Ireland, centuries-old hatred of England began again to show a violent side. The founding of the republican political party Sinn Féin (Ourselves Alone) in 1905 rallied growing anti-English sentiment. Ulster Protestants, however, worrying about losing their privileged position in British society, feared an independent Ireland, preferring union to Home Rule. While the unionist Ulster Volunteer Force imported arms illegally, the nationalist Irish Volunteers were harassed by the law; the cauldron simmered with the 1913 General Strike and lock-out in Dublin. Home Rule was planned for 1914 but war intervened. Young Irish Volunteers went off to the trenches to fight, misled by John Redmond, the Irish leader at Westminster, into the belief that Home Rule would be peacefully granted. Over 30,000 would die in the trenches.

In August 1915 Pádraig Pearse's graveside oration at the burial of veteran Fenian Jeremiah O'Donovan Rossa fanned the flames of revolt: 'Ireland unfree shall never be at peace.' Plans were made by the radical nationalist Irish Republican Brotherhood (IRB) for a rebellion that would have maximum effect while war raged on the continent. Germany, happy to ferment unrest in the enemy's rear, had no military force to spare but sent 20,000 rifles in April 1916 in a ship disguised as a Norwegian merchantman. Bound for the Kerry coast, the *Aud* put in at the wrong port and was captured at gunpoint in Tralee Bay by the British Navy on Good Friday. When she reached Cork Harbour under escort, the German skipper – still in command – scuttled her and the arms were lost.

An article in *The Irish Volunteer* had called for 'manoeuvres' on 23 April, Easter Sunday. Eoin MacNeill, head of the Irish Volunteers and not a member of the IRB, was in the dark about the planned uprising; a forged document had told him that his Volunteers were to be disarmed, the leaders arrested and Dublin occupied by the British Army. He ordered a 'defensive war' using the guns landed from the *Aud*, unaware that it had been sunk. On Saturday he discovered the forgery and issued a countermanding order. In the seat of government at Dublin Castle, the authorities were equally confused by the storm of wild rumours. The IRB leaders spent Sunday deliberating; without arms it was obviously hopeless, but Pearse issued an order at 8 p.m. – the rebellion was to go ahead.

Around noon on Easter Monday, Irish Volunteers began to assemble, but MacNeill's countermanding order meant that only 1,600 of 10,000 showed up. The plan was to seize a crescent of defensive strongpoints in the city, with headquarters at the General Post Office (GPO); all Ireland was expected to rise to support the rebellion. In Catholic Dublin, bells rang out in celebration of the son of God; this holiday celebrates the miraculous resurrection of one life. Guy Pinfield, however, would lose his at the gates of Dublin Castle on the first day of the Easter Rising.

This Easter holiday, most British troops were at the Fairyhouse races, leaving only 500 men in their various barracks. When they reported back in the emergency, it was to the nearest barracks, not always their own; confusion spread between officers and men who did not know each other. Guy Pinfield was one of the few officers in Dublin on duty. His 8th Hussars, part of the 10th Reserve Cavalry Regiment, were stationed at the Curragh Camp. A reserve cavalry brigade was primarily a training unit. Unlike its infantry counterpart, which trained men for a battalion within the same regiment, reserve cavalry incorporated squadrons from several units, rotated through basic training before returning to their parent formation. The 10th Reserve would jumble up lancers, hussars and yeomanry; regimental strength fluctuated wildly and command was in a constant state of change.

For the Hussars, their war so far had been one long wait. The regiment had a glamorous history to match its parade uniforms: the 8th charged the Russian guns with the Light Brigade at the Crimea, won four Victoria Crosses in the 1857 Indian Rebellion and earned battle honours in Afghanistan. It served with distinction in South Africa under Colonel Clowes, now temporary brigadier in Dublin, where St Patrick's Cathedral houses their ornate marble and bronze Boer War memorial. But this was no war for proud horse soldiers and the prospects for magnificent charges, reckless or otherwise, were nil. Recalled from India in August 1914, they landed at Marseilles in November and entered the trenches on 9 December 1914. As the terrain bogged down and stagnant trench warfare set in, mounted cavalry became redundant, held forever in reserve waiting for the 'gap' that was never blown in the German line. Dismounted, the Hussars moved up to Givenchy, but if they went forward it was to dig trenches, not to fight from them. Modern warfare had passed them by; their casualties came mainly from unsanitary trench conditions. There was painful irony in the Hussars' motto: *Pristinae Virtutis Memores* (the memory of former valour). The reserve posting to Ireland would only have added to the frustration of the Western Front: they were on what was then home soil, and the front line was hundreds of miles and two sea crossings away.

Another army spoiling for a fight in Dublin that Easter weekend was the *Arm Cathartha na hÉireann* (Citizen Army). Originally formed by James Larkin and former British Army captain Jack White DSO as a trade union group trained to defend worker's demonstrations against the brutal Dublin Metropolitan Police, it was later described as the 'first Red Army'. The playwright Sean O'Casey stated its credo in 1914: 'the ownership of Ireland, moral and material, is vested of right in the people of Ireland.' It vowed to 'sink all difference of birth property and creed under the common name of the Irish people', but never numbered more than 250 citizen soldiers, 211 of whom took part in the Rising.

Larkin and White departed for the Irish Volunteers and America respectively, leaving the Citizen Army under the command of James Connolly, a Marxist and Irish republican. He saw it as a revolutionary organisation, dedicated to creating an Irish socialist republic; political change through physical force, in the Fenian tradition, was legitimate for Connolly. Having served in the British Army in his youth, he knew something of military tactics and discipline. Appalled by the participation of Irishmen in the war, which he regarded as an imperialist, capitalist conflict, he openly called for insurrection in his newspaper, the *Irish Worker*. When they realised he was moving towards the radical IRB, many active members of the *Arm* left; these included O'Casey and a very singular individual by the name of Francis Sheehy-Skeffington.

Francis Joseph Christopher Skeffington was born in 1878 in Bailieborough, Co. Cavan. His father Dr Joseph Skeffington, 'a widely-read man of great intellectual curiosity, a hot temper, rigid principles and a kind heart',[3] was an inspector of schools and educated his son at home. Raised a Catholic Ulsterman with a marked Northern Irish accent, Francis entered University College Dublin (UCD) where a close friendship grew with the writer James Joyce. When in 1901 the Jesuits who ran the college magazine rejected both Joyce's *Day of the Rabblement* and Skeffington's essay on the admission of women, they published them privately as the pamphlet 'Two Essays'. Francis was a figure mocked by many, including his friend Joyce, who made him the knicker-bockered crank McCann in *Ulysses*. Small and wiry, a non-smoker and strict teetotaller, he was a vegetarian and pacifist. He wore a 'Votes for Women' badge and a long red beard – he had never shaved. He was Dublin's greatest eccentric, but he had spirit and wit. To those who called him a crank he replied: 'Yes … a crank is a small instrument that makes revolutions.'

Skeffington was college registrar for two years, during which he married Hanna Sheehy, from a notable Co. Cork nationalist family. As a token of his commitment to the equality of the sexes, he adopted her surname, thereafter calling himself Sheehy-Skeffington. (Friends referred fondly to him as 'Skeffy', and thankful for this example of brevity, so shall I.) The couple worked together in a number of socialist and radical causes, including women's suffrage. He resigned from UCD after refusing to stop campaigning for the admission of women. He then worked as a freelance journalist and edited the *Irish Citizen*. During the 1913 lock-out he was on the peace committee established to reconcile the two sides.

For a small man, he was certainly brave enough. After the August 1914 arrest of Jim Larkin on O'Connell Street and the subsequent police riot against a peaceful crowd he testified as witness. He was with a group of women tending to a victim of police assault; another policeman charged them with his baton raised. Skeffy halted him by calling out his police number. Later, he was abused by a gang of drunken policemen at College Green police station where he went to complain.

Skeffy's campaign against recruitment at the outbreak of war saw him sentenced to six months in Mountjoy prison under the Defence of the Realm Act. He went on hunger and thirst strike and was released under the 'Cat and Mouse Act', which permitted re-arrest without retrial; public indignation in Britain and Ireland, including protests from George Bernard Shaw, prevented this. While supporting Home Rule, Skeffy tried to impress upon Pádraig Pearse and Connolly that civil disobedience could be a more powerful weapon than rebellion, urging them to establish a force 'armed and equipped with the weapons of the intellect and the will'. If many thought Skeffy a crackpot, Pearse and Connolly considered him a man of high principle and intelligence.

He was soon to find himself torn between his horror of violence and his sympathy for the nationalist cause; Skeffy would stay doggedly faithful to his principles at the cost of his life. The IRB conspirators had asked James Connolly to co-ordinate preparations for the armed rebellion due to start at noon on Bank Holiday Monday. In Holy Week before Easter, Sean Connolly (no relation), a promising young actor at the Abbey Theatre, played the lead in James Connolly's new play in its first performance at Liberty Hall, headquarters of the Citizen Army. This Gaelic sportsman won an All-Ireland Junior Football medal and was remembered as a 'stone-wall goalkeeper'; in another age, he and Guy Pinfield might have argued the merits of rugby and Gaelic football over a pint or two of the black stuff. The play, *Under Which Flag*, is a deeply felt drama of an Irishman torn between serving in the Irish or the British Army. At its finale, Connolly raised a green flag and uttered the words: 'Under this flag only will I serve. Under this flag, if need be, will I die.'

On Easter Monday, he changed his stage costume for the real thing. As Captain Sean Connolly of the Irish Citizen Army he led out his 2nd Company (sixteen men and nine women) from Liberty Hall, his three brothers and sister Kathleen all under his command. They crossed the Liffey and headed for their objective, Dublin Castle, the seat of 'British tyranny', where it was symbolically important for the first shots to be fired. One section rushed the gates with German Mausers, smuggled into the country at Howth in 1914; Connolly fired the first shot that killed an unarmed police-man, James O'Brien. They captured the guardroom and tied up the three guards, but did not press home the attack, assuming that the castle had more than the twenty-five defenders actually present. Connolly's group then moved to City Hall, where he was shot while attempting to hoist the same green flag used in the play. In his dying moments, as life imitates art, did his stage lines run through his head? The first to kill, he became the first rebel to be killed in the Easter Rising.

With the troops away, the rebels were quick to gain the upper hand. Pearse proclaimed the Irish Republic from the steps of the GPO and declared a provisional government: 'We declare the right of the people of Ireland to the ownership of Ireland, and to the unfettered control of Irish destinies, to be sovereign and indefeasible.' Ireland, he told the crowd, 'summons her children to her flag and strikes for her freedom … supported by her exiled children in America and by gallant allies in Europe … she strikes in full confidence of victory'. Invoking the protection and blessing of 'the Most High God', he prayed that:

... no one who serves the cause will dishonour it by cowardice, inhumanity or rapine. In this supreme hour the Irish nation must, by its valour and discipline and by the readiness of its children to sacrifice themselves for the common good, prove itself worthy of the august destiny to which it is called.[4]

Those of the Irish nation who heard him seemed less than enthusiastic; they simply listened, shrugged their shoulders and glanced around to see if the police were coming. Some idly read the proclamation weighted to the ground by stones at the foot of Nelson's Pillar or stared at the unfamiliar green and tricolour flags. Others turned away in boredom and wandered off.

There were early moments of chaos and farce: the raid for gelignite in the Magazine Fort in Phoenix Park was abandoned when it was found that the storeroom key was in the pocket of the officer in charge – who was at the Fairyhouse races. Having cut the Dublin Castle lines with explosives, the small force dispatched to take over the Central Telephone Exchange was turned back by an old woman who screamed at them: 'Go back, boys, go back, the place is crammed with military.' Only five hours later did British soldiers occupy the undefended exchange. Via the open telephone lines, frantic calls were made to the barracks at Portobello, Richmond, Marlborough and the Royal Barracks, as well as to the main camp at The Curragh. The empire was about to strike back against the rebels.

The castle guards, recovering from the surprise attack, closed the gates. By 1.40 p.m., 180 men of the Royal Irish Rifles and Dublin Fusiliers arrived to reinforce them. As 2/Lt Guy Pinfield and his men moved towards the sound of gunfire at the castle, one story tells that they were accosted by an ancient and harmless nationalist who was exactly five times Guy's age of 21. The banter was good-humoured but a nervous private – younger even than Guy – loosed off a shot, which ricocheted and hit the old man. Rebellion turned to tragedy. In the early ragged exchanges of gunfire, heard all over Dublin and heartening to those who believed the castle impregnable, another soldier in Upper Castle Yard took a bullet from a German gun in Irish hands. He led a group of hussars who tried to enter the castle by another entrance, only to be trapped in a dead end of houses occupied by armed Volunteers.[5] He was shot from a window and fell to the ground crying, 'For god's sake, get the men back'. His bleeding wound was to prove fatal to Guy Vickery Pinfield and added another doleful distinction for Rosslyn Park. He was the first British soldier to die in the Rising.

Francis Sheehy-Skeffington, a horrified onlooker, now showed his courage and instinctive humanity in stepping forward to aid Guy where others feared to tread. Unable to staunch the blood himself, he dodged the gunfire and raced across Dame Street into a chemist's shop, shouting in his high-pitched voice, 'Come, we can't leave a man to bleed to death!'[6] Desmond Ryan, who took part in the GPO occupation, described the scene:

> … while the Citizen Army attack on the Castle approaches was in progress and volleys and counter volleys swept Cork Hill, Skeffington was amongst the spectators. A British officer, Captain [sic] Pinfield, fell dangerously wounded near the Castle gate and lay there apparently bleeding to death. Skeffington, in spite of the heavy fire which hindered the bystanders from helping the injured officer, persuaded a chemist to come with him, and they went through the hail of bullets up to the castle gate. As they arrived some British soldiers had succeeded in dragging the captain into the Castle, and there was only a great pool of blood. When Mrs Skeffington later reproached her husband for taking such a grave risk, he replied quietly: 'I could not let anyone bleed to death while I could help'.[7]

He could not help himself; it was in his nature to help his fellow man, regardless of personal risk or the colours under which his 'enemy' served. He could only speak his mind and stay true to his ideals. The Sheehy-Skeffingtons had planned a holiday during Easter; they were aware that some protest would occur but the Rising took them by surprise. As our story gathers pace and careers downhill, Skeffy's openness and idealism would be the death of him.

By late afternoon, Lord Wimborne, Governor General of Ireland, issued his own proclamation, warning 'His Majesty's subjects that the sternest measures will be taken for the prompt suppression of the existing disturbances and the restoration of order … and in particular we warn all citizens of the danger of unnecessarily frequenting the streets or public places, and of assembling in crowds'.[8] British reinforcements poured in from all over Ireland and many more were ordered from England. General Lowe took charge and martial law was declared. However, some citizens ignored not just Wimborne, but also Pearse's appeal to be worthy of their august destiny. They had a mind to go looting instead.

Plate glass shattered as the poor saw an opportunity for some profitable plunder while the authorities were distracted: Noblett's confectioners, Dunn's hatters and Saxone, the shoe shop, were all ransacked. Sean O'Casey saw a woman strip naked to try on looted camisoles. James Connolly ordered a rifle volley over their heads, but even this was ignored by the mob. Skeffy mounted the steps of Nelson's Pillar and told the crowd to go home. They jeered him and set about McDowell's the jewellers and Clery's, the Selfridges of Dublin.

Concerned about this collapse of law and order, Skeffy urged Connolly to start a citizens' militia to prevent looting. Hanna, who had brought food to the rebels occupying the GPO, returned home out of concern for their son, Owen. On his own way home after his militia meeting, Skeffy crossed Portobello Bridge, guarded by Royal Irish Riflemen, jittery after a day under fire from the Jacob's biscuit factory. He kept to the centre of the empty bridge, in full view of the soldiers, who did not hinder him. When he was heckled by passers-by who recognised the unmistakable figure from his reproaches at Nelson's Pillar, he was arrested and taken to Portobello Barracks. There the adjutant, Lt Samuel Morgan, asked him, 'Are you in sympathy with the Sinn-Feiners?' His honesty made him reply: 'Yes, but I am not in favour of militarism.' At a loss, Morgan reported to HQ that he had questioned this friend of the rebel leaders, but found no grounds for a formal charge. What should he do? The brusque order was to detain him, but no charge was entered on the sheet.

In the darkness of night, a new figure enters the story: Captain John Bowen-Colthurst, Royal Irish Rifles, from an Anglo-Irish landed gentry family from County Cork. Born thirty-five years previously, he was a product of Haileybury and Sandhurst, commissioned into the regiment in 1899. At 6ft 4in, this 'man of exceptional stature'[9] was 'a tall, gaunt captain with the light of battle in his eye. A very religious man he was too, always talking about duty and a great Bible reader.'[10] He was captured by the Boers at Reddersburg and freed when Lord Roberts took Pretoria; he was awarded the Queen's Medal with four clasps. Seven years in India included an expedition to Sikkim-Tibet, for which he was also decorated, and promoted to captain. He was a devout member of the Church of Ireland and had three children by his wife Rosalinda. Generally well regarded by his peers, if considered a little eccentric, he was highly intelligent and spoke ten languages; throughout his life he would act impulsively and write very strange and insulting letters to those who offended him.[11]

Prior to the war he had blotted his record by an argument with his commanding officer over rumours of a posting to Belfast to put down any possible revolt by the Ulster Volunteers – he was as much against Home Rule as they were. The new war went wrong for him very early: his only brother Robert was killed at Ypres and his commanding officer reported him in September 1914 for attacking without orders. Impatient with retreat, he had marched his men back to the fight; no matter that several witness statements swore that orders had been received. This insubordination ended his advancement in the army. That same month he was badly wounded. In addition to severe physical injury, his Medical Board reported he was suffering from 'nervous exhaustion as result of active service'. Veiled in the official language of ignorance, it seems that Bowen-Colthurst was an early victim of shell shock.

Psychiatrists today understand better this condition now known as Combat Stress Reaction (CSR), whose effects can last for years with damaging results for the sufferer and those around him. The pioneering work of doctors like W.H.R. Rivers at Edinburgh's Craiglockhart Hospital had then hardly begun; there was little official understanding and even less sympathy. Senior officers, who stayed safely to the rear, took a harsh view of 'unmanly' behaviour under fire and feared for its effects on military discipline.

It was eight months before Bowen-Colthurst was again declared fit for service, but the War Office had already decided that he could not be promoted or return to the front. He was sent to Dublin to recuperate on recruiting duties; this was considered a safe posting where he could stay out of trouble. But this is a man who declared, 'in any other country except Ireland it would be recognised as right to kill rebels'. For this damaged and thwarted soldier, a religious and empire fundamentalist on the verge of breakdown, this ungrateful act of rebellion by a people he was there to defend pushed him over the edge.

Arriving at Portobello, Bowen-Colthurst ordered 18-year-old Lt Dobbin, less than a year out of school, to hand over the prisoner Sheehy-Skeffington – an illegal act without written authority from his commanding officer. Skeffy was hauled from the guard-room and ordered to say his prayers. Bowen-Colthurst joined him, praying, 'O Lord God, if it should please Thee to take away the life of this man, forgive him for Our Lord Jesus Christ's sake'.[12]

For now, however, all he wanted was a human shield for a raid-ing party – another highly illegal act. Ordering his deputy to shoot Skeffy immediately if the Sinn Feiners fired on him or his party, he headed up the Rathmines Road, firing his revolver wildly. He roared at two boys leaving church, 'Don't you know that Martial Law has been proclaimed and I could shoot you like dogs?' Seventeen-year-old Coade turned away to avoid trouble, but too late: Bowen-Colthurst cried 'Bash him!' to a soldier who smashed his rifle butt across his face, breaking his jaw. As Coade fell to the ground, the captain shot him dead. It was the first of six murders he would commit in twelve hours.

The rampage continued to Kelly's Corner tobacconists, in the belief that it was Sinn Fein's Thomas Kelly; in fact it belonged to James Kelly, alderman, justice of the peace and former high sheriff. The raiding party bombed the shop and seized four men who sur-vived the blast, including two newspapermen, the disabled Thomas Dickson and Patrick MacIntyre, ironically both editors of fiercely loyalist papers which had backed John Redmond's Irish recruiting campaign. Their protests went unheard. They were dragged back to Portobello and locked up with Skeffy.

Bowen-Colthurst retired to his quarters at 3 a.m. and read his Bible all night. A passage in St Luke preyed on his disordered mind:

'And these mine enemies which will not have me to rule over them, bring them forth and slay them before me.' By dawn, God had told him what he had to do: he would be judge, jury and executioner.

Lt Dobbin, giving evidence at the subsequent court martial, testified that he announced, 'I am taking these prisoners out and I am going to shoot them because I think it is the right thing to do'. Bowen-Colthurst told the prisoners to stand against the far wall of the tiny yard, and the guard fired before the three realised what was happening. Skeffy's leg moved, Colthurst ordered the firing squad 'Shoot again'. The bodies were buried in a quick-lime grave.

Fifteen minutes later, the captain reported the shootings to Lt Morgan, mumbling about 'having lost a brother in this war' and that 'I'm as good an Irishman as they are'. On his way to the mess, he bumped into Major James Rosborough, commanding officer at the barracks, and told him of the executions and added, 'I suppose I'll be hanged for it'. Rosborough stared back at him, dumbfounded.

For good measure, he continued his personal killing spree: Richard O'Carroll, a city councillor, was shot point blank in the chest for declaring his Sinn Fein allegiance and left to die in the street. His last victim was a young teenager from whom he demanded information. When the boy refused, Bowen-Colthurst ordered him to kneel and summarily shot him in the back of the head as he raised his hand to cross himself. Captain Edward Kelly later found his fellow officer sprawled across a mess table and warned Captain MacTurk, 'For goodness' sake, keep an eye on Colthurst … I think he's off his head'. MacTurk found him rational enough, brooding over his actions that morning: 'It's a terrible thing to shoot one's own countrymen, isn't it?'[13]

Hanna Sheehy-Skeffington was never told of either her husband's detention or death. She only discovered what happened four days later when she met the chaplain who had performed the Catholic burial rites. An attempted cover-up began immediately, led by Major Rosborough, who explained to army HQ that the shooting was in response to 'fears that the prisoners might be rescued or escape'. Bowen-Colthurst had been aide-de-camp to Wimborne's predecessor and seemed untouchable. As rebellion was ruthlessly suppressed that week, he ransacked Skeffy's home in a spurious search for incriminating evidence; Owen, then 6 years old, recalled 'windows smashed, British soldiers pouring in from front and back ... a young Belfast soldier who soon revealed that he was thoroughly ashamed of what he was doing; but military discipline is military discipline'.[14] On 7 May, the bricks damaged by the bullets of the execution squad were replaced by Royal Engineers.

The cover-up might have succeeded had it not been for Major Sir Francis Fletcher Vane, a Dublin-born Munster Fusiliers officer. He was on leave but rushed to Portobello Barracks to help its defence, earning a Mention in Dispatches. Vane was a man of contradictions: a democratic aristocrat with socialist and republican sympathies, who lived for a time at the social reform centre, Toynbee Hall in East London, and founded the Italian boy scouts; a career soldier who challenged generals and spoke on anti-war platforms; an empire loyalist who hated jingoism. During the Boer War, he strongly objected to the atrocities arising from the policies of two Irish-born generals, Roberts and Kitchener. Roberts gave the world the concentration camp; Kitchener refined the horror by incarcerating Boer women and children – without proper food or medicine, 26,000 would die. Vane's views attracted the enmity of Bowen-Colthurst who, after the murders, was overheard denouncing him as pro-Boer and pro-Irish.

To the establishment, Vane had an 'attitude problem' which, like his peerage, was probably hereditary. He was not the first Vane to champion human liberties and upset powerful people. His ancestor, Sir Henry, was the civilian leader of the Commonwealth bloc in parliament during the English Civil War; he retired from politics rather than acknowledge Cromwell as Lord Protector. After the restoration of the Stuart monarchy he was executed for treason in 1662. Francis himself was removed from the magistracy in 1902 for being 'pro-Boer'; his critical pamphlets on the Boer War saw him 'retired' from the army in 1903 to become a crusading journalist campaigning anti-war and pro-suffrage. He was dismissed by Baden Powell from the Boy Scouts Association after objecting to its militarism and set up a rival body (which bankrupted him). Had they but world enough and time, Vane and Skeffy would have been the best of friends.

Vane was incensed when Bowen-Colthurst was allowed to get away with murder. He tried his utmost to have him charged, but when the other officers present refused to assist, he acted in true Vane style. He travelled on leave to London and forced a meeting with Prime Minister Asquith and Kitchener, Secretary of State for War. This took some nerve as he had 'previous' from South Africa with 'The Butcher of Khartoum'. Perhaps he threatened to go public using his journalist's connections, for Kitchener sent a telegram ordering Bowen-Colthurst's arrest. Sir John Maxwell, commander-in-chief in Ireland, demurred, but eventually obeyed. The mad, bad captain was found guilty by a private court martial.[15] Two doctors declared him insane on account of his shell shock; curiously, he was not under restraint during his trial but stayed in comfort at the Hibernian Hotel.

The government offered Hanna £10,000 'compensation' to forego an inquiry; she refused and demanded the full facts be made public. The sustained political furore culminated in a Royal Commission of Inquiry into the murders, led by Sir John Simon. This was widely reported, not least in the *New York Times*; even former US President Theodore Roosevelt became interested in the case. The commission noted 'that Captain Bowen-Colthurst added to the documents found on Skeffington's body, in an endeavour to excuse his action, a document entitled "Secret Orders to the Military" which was a forgery from beginning to end … There can be no excuse or palliation for his conduct from first to last'. The failure of other officers to stop him was attributed to 'the lateness of the hour or the strain of anxiety caused by events outside the barracks'.[16] The public in Ireland, Britain and America was deeply shocked by the facts as they slowly emerged, along with other allegations of atrocity by British troops.

Hanna travelled to the United States to publicise the Irish situation. 'Dead editors tell no tales,' she later wrote, 'though sometimes their wives may.'[17] There she published *British Militarism as I Have Known It*, which was banned in Britain until after the war. Thirty years later she wrote that what shocked her most in retrospect was:

> … not the brutality of the British Army in action against a people in revolt (we learned to take this for granted, and indeed it is part

of war everywhere) but the automatic and tireless efforts on the part of the entire official machinery, both military and political, to prevent the truth being made public.[18]

Sir Francis Vane may have won his battle, but the establishment had the last belligerent laugh: his action in reporting a fellow officer was rewarded with dismissal from the army. Or in official speak: 'This officer was relegated to unemployment owing to his action in the Skeffington murder case.' For years he campaigned for reinstatement, even appealing to the king. With time on his hands, he wrote a book on the Rising and a second book, *War Stories*, of incidents from Africa, the Great War and Dublin. Both were suppressed by the army censor, and the manuscripts conveniently disappeared.

Bowen-Colthurst 'conveniently became insane'[19] and was imprisoned at Broadmoor Criminal Mental Asylum, but was released in 1918 and was at liberty to conceive a fourth child. Psychiatric reports indicated that he would 'lose the run of himself when extreme exhaustion or anxiety set in'. One implied that he had obsessive compulsive disorder. He was moved involuntarily to a private asylum which he left in 1921 – as Irish independence was finally being won – and settled quietly in British Columbia, Canada, where he died in 1965, before the IRA could track him down.

For Bowen-Colthurst in 1916, insanity due to shell shock was a defence convenient to the authorities. However, later that same year, it was not to be so for 2/Lt Eric Skeffington Poole, of the West Yorkshire Regiment. He is drawn into our story not by the coincidence of his name, but by his contrasting fate.

On 7 July 1916, Poole was hit by debris from an artillery blast at the Somme; he was hospitalised with shell shock and only declared fit for duty on 1 September. Poole later stated that his injury meant that he would 'at times get confused and ... have great difficulty in making up my mind'.[20] This may explain how, on 5 October 1916, as his platoon moved up to front-line trenches at Flers, he wandered off without anyone noticing. Two days later he was stopped west of Albert, unaccountably far from Flers.

Poole's medical examination suggested that his mental state prevented any conscious desertion. Despite this, Lt Gen. Sir Henry

Rawlinson ordered a court martial for desertion at Poperinghe on 24 November. The five-strong panel sentenced him to death, despite evidence that Poole was unaware of the seriousness of his offence. After the verdict, he was again medically examined by a board headed by the same RAMC colonel who had passed him fit for duty after his shell shock injury. It found that Poole 'was of sound mind and capable of appreciating the nature and quality of his action in absenting himself without leave … and that such act was wrong … that his mental powers are less than average. He appears dull under cross examination and his perception is slow.'

General Haig confirmed the sentence, arguing that it was 'more serious in the case of an officer than a man, and it is also highly important that all ranks should realise the law is the same for an officer as a private'.[21] The 'insanity defence' was clearly not open to all officers, as it was to Bowen-Colthurst. At 7.25 a.m. on 10 December 1916 in Poperinghe Town Hall, Eric Skeffington Poole, aged 31, became the first officer to be shot at dawn, one of only three in the war.

Guy Pinfield's death in the Easter Rising is no more than a first knot in the tangled thread of its story. His affairs were quietly tidied: his stepfather 'settled all accounts due to the officers' Mess and to Regimental tradesmen', although there is clerical dismay at an over-payment of £2 17s, due to a misreported date of death.[22] Strangely, for a home front death, his body was then 'lost'. He was wrapped in a winding sheet and hastily buried in a garden in the Dublin Castle grounds during the Rising. Most bodies were claimed in May; Guy's never was. The reason remains a mystery. A year later Gertrude could place a memorial notice to his 'proud and dear memory',[23] but she would not bring his body home. He was only rediscovered (with four others) under granite slabs in the overgrown and disused garden during building works in 1963; his remains were reburied in Grangegorman Military Cemetery.[24]

Guy is remembered at Marlborough and on the war memorial in Bishop's Stortford. It would please him that the town's rugby club is now established on grounds facing his former home, Dane House. His cigarette case, with one unsmoked, was returned to the family. A gold locket, sold at auction in 2011, bears his initials, date of death and the 8th Hussar crest and motto.[25] It holds a portrait commissioned by his mother: his auburn hair and startlingly blue eyes rescue him from the bleak monochrome of war. At the time, Guy's death aroused strong feelings of anger and sorrow for Ireland itself. A fellow officer wrote: 'Poor Guy was my best pal. His murder is a crime which I for one will not forgive Ireland for. It has left my blood boiling with indignation.'

A nurse at the British Military Hospital in the castle was shocked to see his body and wrote in her diary:

I met Mr P. at a dance in the Curragh in January. He was so full of life. He enjoyed that evening thoroughly & seemed to like Ireland. Then to hear he was lying dead in a house here, killed by our people just outside our gates. It seemed too awful to be true. I thought so often that week of his people, of the shock to them & what they must think of Ireland.[26]

In St Patrick's Cathedral is a polished brass plate on black marble, set apart from the main regimental memorial with its 103 names. Elaborately engraved with a shamrock border and the Irish harp, British lion and royal crown of the 8th Hussars, it was dedicated by his fellow reserve officers:

To the Glory of God and in memory of Guy Vickery Pinfield
2nd Lieut 8th Hussars (Special Res)
Killed in action during the Irish rebellion on 24th April 1916

It is the only memorial to a combatant of the Easter Rising in the cathedral – a lasting reminder of Guy's bit part in a momentous Irish tragedy.

John Bodenham
'Your Affectionate Son Jack'

Jack Bodenham. *(Floris Archive)*

The seven pals were in high spirits as they walked towards St Pol. The town, some 4 miles from the barn where they were billeted comfortably enough, promised finer fare than the local hamlets. They would feast on the best an *estaminet* could offer in this time of war – egg and fried potatoes – and celebrate Jack's twenty-sixth birthday in proper fashion. To top it all, the slap-up meal would be his treat, courtesy of 30 francs sent by his parents.

He thanked them by letter: 'you may be sure that the cash will come in handy in order to give a realistic touch to 4 April'. Celebrations had been muted on the day, with passes hard to come by. Nonetheless 'all the letters & parcels which came for my birthday made this year's April 4th a day to be remembered. I had a very good time, & we finished up with a little "Cham" just before going to sleep last night to put a fitting ending to a jolly day.' But this was now Sunday, they had passes and were determined to enjoy 'a little dinner in honour of last Tuesday'.

They were in the habit of marching everywhere, so the pace was brisk. They were eager to reach their destination: Jack's money would see them all right, with champagne and some very quaffable bottles of port for 2 francs 20 centimes each. He talked the 'inky-pinky parlay-voo' as good as the locals, so he was a handy fellow to be with.

The weather had turned warm after a cold spell. The afternoon sun threw long shadows and spring flowers nestled in hedgerows. 'Snowdrops were in bloom weeks ago,' he told his father. The breeze carried the waft of primrose and violets to Jack Bodenham's finely trained nose. It thrilled him to catch a fragrance and know that his sense was not dulled by the stench of Lyddite, rotting corpses and the foetid straw of farm billets. His memory swirled with *White Rose*: top notes of rose, violet and carnation, middle notes with violet, jasmine, spicy rose and iris, and the base of orris-root, musk and amber. He wondered if Empress Alexandra still took her regular order, with all the troubles they were having in Russia.

These happy riflemen from the 1/16th London Battalion, Queen's Westminster Rifles (QWR) were William Butler, from Plaistow, Harold Jarrett, Frederick Cooper from Isleworth, Arthur West, Lee and Hughes. Their host, John Edward Cyril Bodenham, known to them as Jack, was now 26; he would live another ten Sundays. All but one of this 'merry gang' would die on 1 July 1916, the first day of the Battle of the Somme.

John Bodenham was born in 1890, the last of sixteen children of James Radford Dutton Bodenham and Mary Ann Femenias Bodenham. His mother was descended from a Menorcan, Juan Femenias Floris, who came to London in 1730. He founded the firm of perfumers which still bears his name and sells its fragrances worldwide from its original shop on Jermyn Street, once a residence of the Duke of Marlborough, in fashionable St James. By 1908, when the business was handed over to the two eldest sons, Charles and James, Floris numbered amongst its clients 'not only members of the British royal family, but also of all the royal families of Europe, Indian and foreign princes, a dozen dukes and marquesses, over fifty earls and many more from the ranks of the lesser nobility and gentry'.[1] Today Floris holds royal warrants as 'Perfumers to HM The Queen Elizabeth II and Manufacturers of Toilet Preparations to HRH The Prince of Wales'. Oscar Wilde, Winston Churchill, Errol Flynn, Noel Coward and James Bond have all been customers.

On a cold January day, Jermyn Street glows with warmth. Past mahogany fittings from the 1851 Great Exhibition is the office of the chairman, John's namesake and great-great nephew. On the table there are a small bundle of letters, tied with faded ribbon of the type that lawyers use, and a slim booklet in burgundy, like a battered passport. This diary, kept against regulations, and the letters from 3892 Bodenham A Company, 3 Platoon to his 'dearest father' cover ten months of active service in Flanders fields and France, up to 29 June, two days before his death on the most notorious day in British military history. Together they tell the story of a rifleman on the Western Front in 1916.[2]

Jack was born and raised in the substantial Ivy Lodge in Acton, West London. Photographs show how it earned its name: the mansion is swallowed by ivy up to the castellated roofline; windows fight their way through the foliage. Potted palms line the pathway and only a dog kennel escapes the greenery. The verdant garden is the setting for snapshots of his childhood and youth. Sister Dorothy (Dora) smiles knowingly at the camera; Jack, two years younger, dressed in his sailor suit, has dozed off on her shoulder as she reads to him. In a later portent of the soldier-to-be, he stands to attention with a military rifle as tall as he is, and clearly about to topple the 12-year-old. Scroll forward to a boy of 15, sitting proudly at the foot of a tower of handsome elder brothers, Charlie, Jim and Frank. As Ivy Lodge garden grows, so Jack matures; he would enquire of it to the last. In this green space, bright tennis whites are exchanged for drab khaki, as he poses shyly for the camera in his ill-fitting new uniform in early 1915.

The House of Floris at 89 Jermyn Street was another family, with sons and daughters entering the firm. Jack would write with genuine affection for the staff; he was one of them, working in the shop, not yet in senior management:

One of the lads who used to be at 89, & who is now in the Royal Engineers called in to see me today. His battalion is stationed about five miles from here and, as he was over this way & had heard that I was in the Westminsters, he looked me up.

Like his brothers, Jack attended the Catholic boarding school at
Ratcliffe College, Leicestershire. Two years followed at Ampleforth
College, the 'Catholic Eton' in North Yorkshire. Along with his parents' example and encouragement, this instilled in him a deep faith.
Catholics in Edwardian Britain were a minority – still viewed with
suspicion – of some 1.5 million souls, spanning rich landed gentry
and poverty-stricken Irish immigrants. Every coin reminded them
that although the king might be *Britt. Omn. Rex.* and also *Fid. Def.*,
as head of the Church of England, the royal job description did not
guarantee defence of the Roman Faith. So they looked after themselves: a burgeoning Catholic middle class asserted itself through
associations like The Catenians, founded to defend Liberal government threats to voluntary (including Catholic) schools. This was a
tight-knit and close group of Britons.

Ampleforth would give Jack a love of religion, but not yet of
rugby football; the game was not adopted until 1911, but is now
almost devotional at the school. A later alumnus, Lawrence Dallaglio,
described his first visit:

> We stood looking down this Yorkshire valley and it seemed to be
> full of rugby pitches, as far as the eye could see … I started to count
> and got to 27 … Many of the boys at Ampleforth didn't particularly
> care for rugby but what you couldn't do was ignore it … anywhere
> around the grounds, you were surrounded by the game.[3]

Not until 1925, however, did a Catholic play rugby for England.

On returning to London, Jack entered training as a perfumer
at Floris and as a rugby player at Rosslyn Park. The ground was
just two short Underground railway stops from South Acton to
Kew Gardens, under the eye of the Pagoda. In the firm's tradition
he was sent to France with the dual aims of learning the language
and the art of perfumery at the House of Roure Bertrand et Fils,
with which Floris had done business since the 1880s. The tradition
continues today. At its premises on rue Miromesnil, Paris, and the
distillery in Grasse, Provence, he would steep himself in knowledge
of *lavandula angustifolia, jasminum grandiflorum* and *thymus vulgaris*.

Brothers Charles, Frank and James all preceded him (they stayed in Cannes with a Mrs Atkins, whose son Herbert, another Rosslyn Park teammate, died of wounds at Loos in October 1915). Jack's mastery of French later came in useful for less refined requests than pomades, essential oils and orange blossom water.

When war came, he volunteered with the 1/16th London Regiment, Queen's Westminster Rifles. The Territorial atmosphere would be familiar, if slightly less sweet-smelling than Floris: before the war, these units were like family firms. Many soldiers were employees of officers like Lt Colonel Shoolbred who ran a furniture repository and whose delivery-van horses provided much of the transport. For men in the ranks, the annual camp was their only chance of a holiday; field days and trips to Bisley were highly prized days out from work. In April 1915, Jack went into his first battalion encampment in Richmond Park, where today over 600 junior rugby players ruck and maul every Sunday in the same red-and-white hooped shirts that he once wore. Jack will crawl through the ferns on night exercises, learn sentry duties and dig the first of many trenches.

In feverish August 1914 a high proportion had volunteered for service overseas – the QWR was the second Territorial unit into France. A year later it was Jack's turn. His battalion had been in the Armentieres sector since November and needed regular replenishment from England; Captain Henry Townsend-Green, late skipper of Rosslyn Park second XV, had already perished of wounds in March. On Tuesday 31 August 1915, his six months' training completed, Jack and a draft of 180 comrades left Richmond Park for the boat from Southampton which would take him over to a very different France.

They march the straight mile of Priory Lane, past the stately houses and parkland villas, the private lunatic asylum and the kite balloon depot at the Roehampton Club. The column wheels left at the new Railway Hotel (later the Red Rover pub, now flats) towards neo-Tudor red-brick Barnes station, nestling in scrubby common land. Here the men board their transport. Today, livestock no longer graze so the treeline is higher, but the same station sees Rosslyn Park players trudging from City, Wharf and West End offices to train on Tuesdays and Thursdays. They play on the former Roehampton polo field, a ground the club has occupied since 1956, just yards from the station where Jack Bodenham said farewell to his London home town. On the way to France, his battalion stopped overnight in Southampton where 'after tea [I] went to see Florrie & William & stayed to supper'. Two days later he sees the last of his family: 'Capt Evans told us first thing we were to leave camp at 1.30. Had short bayonet drill in morning then I ran over to say good-bye at Freemantle House.'

This was no distant colonial war: the battlefields were little more than a daytrip away, just as they are today. The *Atalanta* took the Queen's men across the Channel to Le Havre in a violent thunderstorm. Rumours of a U-boat in the vicinity prompted the order to don lifebelts at 10 p.m. and Jack found little sleep. France emerged from ominous summer weather that would do credit to Thomas Hardy:

> Raining all morning as we steamed up the Seine. Pretty scenery. Arrived at Rouen at 3pm. Marched to rest camp three miles out … had thunderstorm & heavy rain on way & got soaked. Glad to get to bed on our new tent at 9.30pm. Slept well. Heavy rain during night.

The dutiful son had time for a first letter home of optimism, reassurance – and weather:

> Dear Mother & Father,
>
> Now that we have arrived at our destination 'somewhere in France', I am sending you a line as promised. They have brought us to Rouen, & have given us permission to disclose the fact. We had a good journey from Southampton & were all very merry in spite of fair amount of rain & a thunderstorm thrown in. It took us 19 hours all the way by boat. Had lot of rain on arrival, but it has cleared up now, and is nice and sunny. Hope you are all well. I am absolutely fit and full of beans,
>
> Best of love to all from Jack.
> Sorry so short a note, but am in a great hurry, more later.

Life on the edge of Rouen forest with its 'hundreds of beautiful pine trees' was pleasant: glorious September sun dispelled the rain, and 'we have plenty of games & sports to occupy our spare time'. Drills took place on the mile-square sandy parade ground – 'more like desert than anything else ... pretty tiring to walk as the sand is quite loose as on a sea-shore'. Twice-daily parades were leavened with excursions into Rouen, cricket matches against the Queen's Victoria Rifles (QVR), night-training ops and concert parties by Lena Ashwell's troop.

Letters were written and received through a postal system processing 11 million letters a week and 60,000 parcels a day by 1916. Food parcels from home start to arrive and 'the contents are much appreciated in the tent'. His comrades must have rejoiced at Jack's eleven sisters, who sent regular parcels to supplement the bully beef, biscuits or 'bread and mustard pickles for breakfast' that provided the army's theoretical 4,193 daily calories for front-line troops. He greets each treat with lip-smacking appreciation: 'Mother, the pineapple was excellent, also the jam from Gertrude, the chutney from Nell & the sweets from May ... The cake was very good, Dora, so was everything else.' The sisters weigh in with reading matter too: 'many thanks to Agnes for the two editions of Punch which have fairly gone the round & caused much amusement.' These hampers for the dorm were much mocked by the *Wipers Times*, the satirical *Private Eye* of the Western Front, in spoof ads for 'Herod's, Universal Provider' and 'Messrs Shortone and Pastum'.

Amidst the school-camp atmosphere, there were more sinister reminders of war. Drafts of men left regularly for the trenches at night – always under cover of darkness. 'All this week there were rumours of big British advance about to take place.' This was Loos, where 8,251 of 10,000 British troops in the second day's attack were casualties, Syd Burdekin was declared 'missing' and Herbert Atkins wounded, later to die in hospital near Dieppe. The *Daily Mail* cheered 'real victories at last'. There was no 'big British advance'.

Apprehension prompted a change of routine, as the devout Catholic prepared his soul for the worst. The diary entries are terse:

Thu.30: Rumours that we might be going up to the line tomorrow. Went to confession.
Wed. 6 October: Draft of 50 of our chaps went up to the line &

left 30 here. I just missed going & was not sorry as all the rest of our tent are remaining.

Wed 13: All available of the Queens ordered to stand by to go up to the Front today. Went to Holy Communion before breakfast.

But a long, chatty letter responds to snippets of home news, clearly drawing comfort in the imagined life of his family in England, and taking refuge from his fears in the quotidian and mundane. He thanks his father for the cardigan and waistbands which 'I shall find most useful as the weather gets colder … I am told that warm garments are essential in the trenches in the winter'. He writes of Ampleforth friends suffering from dysentery in the Dardanelles, Chancellor McKenna's Budget and concern for his senior brother: 'I wonder whether Charlie is to be sent abroad shortly. If he goes to the Dardanelles he will, at least, have missed the most trying weather of the year there.'[4] Charles, aged 40, joined the Hampshire Yeomanry at the outbreak and would die on the Marne in August 1918, months short of the Armistice. Only in signing off does Jack address his own circumstances:

> We are still doing very well out here, and are told by those who ought to know that we are very lucky to have stopped at Rouen for so long. However that may be, I think we will all be glad to get up to the regiment, as here it is a real jumble of troops of all sorts & conditions continually coming and going.

When they move up to Poperinghe, 8 miles west of Ypres, the routine of drill and 'musketry' practice continues, punctuated by occasional passes to the village, where they stock up on 'several little things for the trenches, including a 'Tommies' cooker' – a small solid-fuel stove which barely heated food. Here the enemy is nearer, with the town taking 'a heavy bombardment last night and the night before'. Finally, on 20 October they move up to the trenches. The infamous road to Ypres was arrow-straight. Charles Carrington recalled that 'to find the way in the dark up this road was a task worthy of Bunyan's Pilgrim';[5] for hundreds of thousands of men this was the Valley of the Shadow of Death. Jack wrote simply:

Passed through Vlamertinghe, which is badly suffering from German shell fire, especially the beautiful old church, which has only the outer walls standing, & no roof left … We all managed to get into the same section – no.12 Section (I mean all our little circle of fellows) West, Hammond & self got a dug-out together where there is just room enough for us to lie side by side. It measures about 6 foot square & 3 foot high. I was on guard in the fire-trench from midnight till 2am with another fellow – Jones – in the same traverse. Things pretty quiet. Got quite a decent bit of sleep.

All ranks were peculiarly saddened by the destruction of churches in France and Belgium. While not always observant or even God-fearing men, they respected the church in their home parish as a symbol of authority and rectitude. To find these holy places reduced to ashes and dust was visible proof that God was not in his heaven, and all was certainly not right in this world war. QWR riflemen helped build the attic chapel at Reverend Philip 'Tubby' Clayton's Talbot House in Poperinghe. For men took consolation where they could: 'a massive crucifix … still standing intact among a sea of debris; all around shattered and yet this untouched – miraculous.'[6] For the devout Catholic Jack Bodenham, the offence against God and nature was a deeper wrong than the war itself. Nor did it make it easy for him to attend Mass, take communion or confess his sins, but he persevered.

While his letters show concern for the domestic tribulations of Chiswick, the diary captures the alternating trials and tedium of trench life. The blithe face he wears in correspondence is exchanged for emotionless stoicism. His precise recording of time goes beyond regulated military efficiency; it is as if he is trying to impose order on the disrupted hours of a world turned inside out, as night becomes day, and any semblance of routine is shelled into incoherence:

Fri 22 Oct.
I was on guard from 4am to 6am in the fire trench. Lieut. Adams, a Corporal & one rifleman went out as a listening post. They encountered a working party of Germans & laid them out with bombs & rifle fire at about 9pm last night & got back over the parapet in safety. This made the Germans mad, & they retaliated

with vigorous machine-gun and rifle fire for some hours. L/Cpl Smee was killed – shot thro' the head by machine-gun – while on guard in the fire trench at about 4am. Had breakfast at about 9am. Things fairly quiet till 4pm when the Germans sent us over 5 aerial torpedoes which fell about 300 yards behind us, but we felt quite enough of the explosives for our liking. Ration fatigues to St Jean & back as usual after dusk.

Sat 23

Misty morning. I was on guard in back trench from 3am to 5am. Things pretty quiet all day. Ration fatigue from 4.30pm to 6.30pm, taking empties to St. Jean. We moved out of the trenches at 7pm. Had a long & tiring march back to Poperinghe & passed thro' outskirts of Ypres, where everything is smashed to pieces by shell fire. Arrived at Pop. at midnight, & got to bed in a large disused garage. Found a fine parcel from Gertrude & Nell awaiting me. At 1am, after I had been asleep about ten minutes, we all had to turn out as the Germans started shelling the town. In fact the second shell fell very near our billet, & broke a good deal of the glass. We crossed the railway line & remained in a ploughed field for half an hour while about a dozen shells fell in the town (all quite close to the square). We had just got back to our billet when the shelling began again, & we had to turn out once more while about 8 more shells fell in much the same place as before. Two of our men in D company were wounded in the leg (one pretty badly). Finally, we got to bed again at 2.30am and managed to get a good sleep at last.

Jack returns to routine: Sunday Mass (in Flemish), drill, marches and manual labour, which he finds surprisingly satisfying. 'Several of us were detailed to load & unload coal in Poperinghe. Not hard work & rather good fun.' Entertainment was provided by a tented cinema and the 'Fancies' concert party: 'Very good show composed of five privates, three officers and two Belgian girls. House packed.'

After the filthy trench conditions, there was welcome relief for his perfumer's nose: 'Bath parade in morning. We all marched down to old brewery in Poperinghe where large iron vats were filled with hot water, thick with disinfectant, into which about 25 men at a time plunged & scrubbed.' Clothes were washed and deloused. The exercise was pointless: the lice would return once a soldier's body heat incubated the eggs lying dormant in the seams. But the reminder of civilised humanity would have done much for morale. A shave, however scratchy, does the same job for soldiers today.

That night he sent a Standard Field Service postcard, Official Form A. 2042. These pre-printed cards carried standard messages to be underlined as applicable with a simple pencil scrawl. The first print run of a million was ordered in November 1914, when it became evident that war would not, after all, be over by Christmas. With no room for added information that could trouble the censors and delay the post, this was the 'instant messaging' of wartime, known as the 'Whizz bang' or 'Quick Firer'. To Jack's mind 'they come in most useful to let the home folk know you are alright'. They also spared the soldier the ordeal of putting into words what he had seen or packing his own troubles into a homebound kitbag that could only alarm. Soldiers about to set out on hazardous missions such as occupying mine craters deleted in advance all but the line 'I am quite well'. On this occasion, Jack sends: 'All is well & letter following.'

This 'letter following', with spirits refreshed by the hot bath, but mindful of imminent return to the front, is typically 'cheerio-chin-chin'. This is a young man with humour and a zest for life – and no intimation that he may lose it just yet. The long arm of Rosslyn Park Secretary Burlinson reaches out; today's players will recognise the insistent call for 'subs' which prevails through wind and rain, earthquake, war and act of God:

... to answer May's question from you about the football club. Thank you very much for sending the photograph. I don't know what they can want with it, & hope it is not for the police. I should be grateful if you would pay the subscription of £1.1s which I should like to go forward with this, but money orders are difficult to get here, & I am afraid I must ask you to trust me for it till I can return it later on. We are having a rest, & see a good deal of town life for a change. You will be interested to know that the

Belgian girls are A1. They are far more English in appearance than the French, & often have fine complexions & a free teasiness after the Irish style – 'Nough said'!

The mud is inches deep, but we keep fit & merry.

He recounts news of his Ampleforth friend, Lieutenant Joe Buckley, 9/Rifle Brigade, who 'seems to be getting on very well, but has plenty of work to do'. There is a hint of Raleigh's worship of Stanhope in *Journey's End*: 'he looks tired but that's because he works so frightfully hard, and because of the responsibility.'[7] There is more than one reference to officers' responsibilities. Do we detect Jack's reluctance to take a commission which, with his education and background, would have been his for the asking? Guy du Maurier's workload weighed more heavily than the uncomplicated labour in which Jack took express pleasure. Buckley, promoted to captain, would earn the mauve-and-white ribbon of the Military Cross for conspicuous gallantry and devotion to duty, capturing sixty prisoners and two machine guns in April 1917.[8] He outlived Jack, only to die aged 27 when coming out of the line at Gravenstafel, days before Christmas. He is buried at St Jean-les-Ypres, where his friend Jack Bodenham had earlier lugged cases of thigh-boots and taken Holy Communion.

The first week of November is a losing battle against rain and quagmire. Jack departs again for the trenches:

Fairly long march of about seven miles through Ypres, past Cloth hall, which is a series of piles of bricks after all the shelling it has gone through. Arrived at front line trenches at 7pm, just in front of the Potege [Potijze] crossroads. Had to go over the top as the communications trench could not be used owing to recent heavy rains. West, Hammond & self in snug little dig-out to ourselves. Cold at night for sentry work. Four hours on & two off, so very little sleep. All merry & fit.

The enemy bombardment and its fatal toll punctuate the primary struggle against the weather gods, vengeful for the insults blasted on the terrain by the human combatants:

Tues. 2: Had to abandon dug-out as the wall opposite fell in against the door. The trenches are getting very muddy, & the water is inches deep in places. We managed to get a sleep at night in friendly dug-outs which were still habitable.

Wed. 3: Afternoon devoted mainly to pumping & bailing water out of the trenches. We are still without a dug-out & very wet.

Thu. 4: Trenches are falling in on all sides and are in a shocking condition. Capt Makin killed at 5pm. He was our O.C and a fine man.

Fri. 5: Day & night spend digging out the fallen-in trenches & trying to get the water away. Weather finer, but still a few showers now & again. Thick hoar frost during night – the first this winter.

Sat. 6: Dull but dry day. We managed to fix up our dug-out again & go back to it. Still a lot of water in the trenches & the mud is inches deep. Walls still falling in many places.

Sun. 7: Beautiful day. Lieut. Woods (of the Middx regiment but attached to the QWR) was killed at 7am. He was most charming man. Things fairly quiet all day.

Small luxuries helped alleviate the misery. His letter from 'Trenches, Belgium' is grateful for 'the gorgeous parcel which arrived last night'. Jack's platoon was getting vittles that would do justice to the officers' table:

> The cake which we have just put to the test is excellent & the ginger snaps were greatly appreciated in our traverse last night on guard. The chocolate is fine & will be most useful as also the tobacco & pipe. As for the soup squares & bivouac cocoa & tea tablets, they will be very serviceable, & will help to vary our cookery which of course plays a very important part in trench life as we have to prepare all our own meals. Jim sent me a small primus stove which is the very thing, of course, & I am the envy of the company on its account.

He retells the diary account of sleepless nights, forty-eight incessant hours of rain and collapsing dugouts:

> Some of the old men who were out here last winter say they have never had such a time in the trenches &, of course, none of us are

keen on a second helping just yet. We all managed to keep merry
& fit in spite of the conditions, I am glad to say, & are hoping to
go out for a rest shortly.

He politely enquires of domestic matters, of colds and gardeners,
of Elizabeth's new work as a nurse. Nowhere does he trouble his
'Dearest Father' with reports of the deaths noted in his diary.

A wintry Sunday 14 November is a day of observance and comforting nostalgia for school:

Beautiful day. Frosty morning & 1/8" ice on water. No RC service at huts, so got pass to Poperinghe for Mass 9am to 1pm.
Walked down & found convent where English chaplain says Mass
every Sunday at 11am for troops. Arranged with nuns to be back at
10.45 to go to Con[fession] as I had purposely had nothing to eat.
Went to Con. & Holy Communion & also served Mass. Chaplain
– Father Macauley, formerly at Ushaw College [Catholic semi-
nary in Durham] & latterly on mission in Liverpool – very nice.
Knew a good deal about Ampleforth & several of the fellows who
were there with me. After Mass, he asked me to have breakfast
with him. The nuns gave us an excellent meal in the convent, &
we had a long chat & a smoke afterwards …

Jack's father arranged for *The Ampleforth Journal* to be sent to France.
After the war, editor Reverend Marshall, commented on Jack's diary:
'If we knew no more of him than could be learnt from its pages it
would be impossible to doubt the uprightness of his character and
that love of his religion which was one of his marked characteristics
at school.' He further noted that 'Father Edmund was very much
struck by the frequent Communions and Masses. It certainly was a
mercy that he was able to get to Mass so regularly.'

Jack's letter is expansive on those perennial themes of soldierly
life – tobacco and undergarments. Tobacco supplies were abundant:
'the Lawrence's A2 mixture is very good, but a bit too strong for my
liking. I have plenty of tobacco now to last me some weeks as Paul
& Lou sent me a large tin of Murray's mixture recently, so I am well
supplied.' Clothing was more problematic:

I am afraid the vests would not be of use to me. The trouble is that you have to carry all your belongings on your back out here & so of course, the less the better as far as possible. Our underclothing is the regulation stuff – thick shirt & pants. These we change when we have a bath. Vests are not worn, but we make up with cardigans, wearing two of these if necessary.

Apologetically he requests instead 'an electric pocket lamp. They are a boon out here & are made great use of.' He signs off on one of his few low notes: 'Please excuse such a miserable letter, but I am very tired tonight & writing by the light of a candle is not ideal.'

As winter deepens, Jack becomes a nocturnal animal. Fatigues are carried out under cover of darkness, as daylight visibility constrains all movement:

Hard frost at night. At 3am, nine of A company (self included) had to take cart down from St Jean to canal bank full of thigh boots. Too light to get back to trench & we were told to go to drying room at St Jean & stop till evening. Had a good sleep from 7am until 3pm. Then got a fire going & fried a steak we got from stretcher-bearers & also made some tea.

On Thursday 18 November, the QWR were relieved, although not before two comrades, Jackson and Bennett, were killed in the trench after stand-down. Their tired march back through Ypres was 'very slow & straggly', but their resourceful (and now popular) Major Cohen arranged buses to take them back to billets at Houtkerque. These 'Old Bill' buses, still in their commercial livery and carrying advertisements for Pears' soap and Crosse & Blackwell, must have seemed a mirage to men thirsty for the familiar sights of London. Jack emerged from front-line darkness to a daylight round of inspection parades, morning runs, regular meals and village visits for coffees, boiled eggs and a good wash.

His devotional routine also revives his spirits: 'High mass in very nice church (in Houtkerque) at 10.30 with sermon in English by Belgian Priest for benefit of several of us English Tommies present. Quite a good sermon. "God Save the King" sung by the choir in English at finish.' A week's attachment to the Royal Engineers follows, billeted in the brewery in Vlamertinghe, to learn trench reclaiming – a very handy skill. Sir John French had predicted as early as September 1914 that the spade would be as great a necessity as the rifle. After four days, however, Jack wryly concludes: 'we have learnt nothing so far from the REs.'

By 9 December, the QWR boys were back at the front, this time in the reserve trenches: 'we have good dug-outs, & are allowed to make fires which are not allowed in the front line.' News arrives from home that Charles has his commission, and that under the Zeppelin threat London now shares the blackouts of the front:

> Sorry to hear you are getting so dark in Chiswick, but, as you say, it is much the same all over London. Out here, of course, lights are quite the exception (except under cover) and even the motors & wagons have to get along in the dark. How they manage it beats me. I think they must develop owls' eyes.

December was spent digging trenches on the Yser Canal bank, under shrapnel fire which forced them to work while kneeling and crouching in the trench. Jack experiences a new weapon: 'Gas attack & heavy bombardment from 5am to 730am. On our left the 14th Durhams got the gas & further on our left an attack is said to have been made on a three-mile front against the Shropshires.' The 25th is celebrated with nine glum words: 'On guard till 4pm. Weather fair. Some Christmas Day.' But there are festive fireworks at least for the enemy: 'Our big guns gave the Germans a hearty welcome as the New Year came in & I fancy we started it pretty satisfactorily.'

Jack's diary is now studded with short, desiccated entries, as he shuttles between front-line and reserve trenches, living under constant fire. He has a lucky escape: 'Addison was hit in the head by whizz-bang which dropped just outside entrance to our dug-out on parados. Hayes, Addison & self were all lying in the dug-out at 1pm when it happened.' There is no inkling of this in his letters, which he keeps resolutely cheerful, with humorous anecdotes and scenes of trench life:

The great sport here for the officers in their spare time is ratting, & they have plenty of material to practise on as there are thousands of the beggars about. They have one or two small dogs to assist them, & they have a great time. I think the gas killed a lot of the rats, but there are plenty left still.

As to his own well-being: 'I am in perfect health – was never better in my life – in fact only this morning one of the fellows who came out on a draft, & whom I hadn't seen for some time, remarked how extremely fit I looked & I feel like it too.'

February brought relief from the drudgery. Inspection by General Sir Herbert Plumer signalled the battalion's departure from Flanders. Jack notes 'the entrainment for our unknown destination – in cattle trucks'. He was about to exchange the frying pan of the defensive lines at Ypres for the firestorm of the biggest offensive yet. At midday on the 10th, their train stopped at Pont Remy, south-east of Abbeville. On a small island perches a chateau which once held out against the English in the Hundred Years War and where Cardinal Richelieu was held prisoner. The island sits midstream a serpentine river which meanders and slithers through the undulating chalk landscape, sloughing off small lakes and pools, known locally as *étangs*. This river, yet to become synonymous with mud and slaughter, was the Somme.

The QWR sat out the snowy months at Huppy, and later Ailly-le-haut-Clocher, with 56th Division, formed of London battalions with common allegiance to their home city and healthy rivalry. They were brigaded with 2/London Regiment, the London Rifle Brigade and the QVR. Jack conscientiously attended Mass and Communion at each new billet. Away now from the cramped dugouts, gas and shrapnel of the Ypres Salient, he threw himself into the new life afforded by the rolling countryside and fresh air free of chlorine and jagged splinters. There was even the chance to play rugby again:

We have managed to get hold of a very decent pitch & I am on the Committee. We play each afternoon, & had a very good game today. Later on, we will no doubt play against the other regiments stationed in the neighbourhood & we ought to get some good fun out of it. There are talks of cross-country running, paper chases & other forms of sport, so we should be able to hold a kind of Olympic Games before very long.

With spring came another change: Jack's diary entries again become briefer, noting only the weather and Sunday Mass, as if he has lost enthusiasm for recording the details of his daily life. In May constant fatigues even disrupt his Sunday observance. Occasional flashes reveal football games, village outings (his birthday feast) and brigade sports day at Frévent – a day of triumph for Bodenham and the Westminsters:

> There were nine events, and in the trials of speed and strength the Westminsters excelled … the same two men L/Cpl McMillan and 2nd Lt. Thurston, came first and second in the 100 and 200 yard sprints. In a one sided relay race the Westminsters four-man team finished some 200 yards ahead of their rivals in the LRB. The hurdle race was another one-two for the Westminsters with Rifleman Radcliffe getting his nose in front of Rifleman Bodenham on the finishing line … To round off their points scoring, the Westminsters won through to the final of the tug of war, beating the LRB by two pulls to one in the first round. In the final they met their close rivals the QVRs beating them 2-0, and thus assuring themselves of the overall title …[9]

Jack's verdict is contented, if succinct: 'Good day.'

In contrast, his letters to his father grow fuller and more thoughtful. There is much news: Jim and Ethel have 'a new arrival at Weybridge Cottage'; Joe Buckley is 'up to his eyes in work as Engineering Officer of his company' and then down with Trench Fever ('I don't know exactly what it is, but it seems to be a fairly common thing among the troops'). The problems of the garden have spread to the business at Floris. He comments wryly (and prophetically): 'the war certainly has made an effect on business & male labour. I can see the tables turned when we get back – the men living at home, while the women earn the money. I know you have always considered this the correct state of affairs.'

Conscription finally arrived in January 1916 (along with steel shrapnel helmets) and Jim's position in running the firm was cause for concern. Jack is reassuring and light:

> It will be rough luck for him if he has to join up. I should think the authorities will take circumstances into consideration & leave him alone. I don't fancy the age limit will be raised to seventy-two yet awhile &, in any case, you have done your bit for the country in the way of 'kid' management, haven't you? The married men seem to be giving the Government a good deal of trouble and it seems to me that they have cause for complaint, though the general opinion over here is that if compulsion all round had been enforced months ago, it would have saved a lot of time & discussions.

LeBlanc and Everett at Floris were called up and the 72-year-old patriarch Mr James stepped into the breach after seven years of retirement, much to his son's delight: 'I can quite believe that customers are surprised to see you back again & are full of admiration for your pluck. I am sure the girls will help you and keep things going till the Germans see fit to give their little game up.'

Information at the front was patchy, propagandist and economical with the facts. For Jack, the *Weekly Times* and other papers sent from home:

> … certainly don't give away too much news of the war, do they? I fancy the Verdun affair is going quite alright for us, nevertheless … the French have apparently given the Germans a great deal more than they bargained for, & everybody over here seems confident of success down there.

Rumour abounded, but was discounted: 'that the Kaiser is agitating for peace is nothing new, of course. I saw something to that effect in the *Daily Mail* weeks ago. Of course nobody believes it, like many other of their thrills.' Proof here that the journal's reputation has not been won without a century of consistent hard work. French papers told of Zeppelin attacks on East Anglia, and 'I am glad to see that one of the beggars was brought down'. As to his own lot: 'all kinds of rumour fill the air with regard to our future, but I don't put much faith in them.'

A stream of tobacco, dates, cocoa, marmalade, coal tar soap, Mexican chocolate and Fuller's Peppermint Lumps did much to lift morale. He praises a 'very decent swimming bath in town (rather extraordinary for France isn't it) & it is a great attraction these hot days … we get on well with the villagers & they are very kind to us. Rather different to the same class of people we came across in Belgium.' Diet, route marches and sports had made him lean and he was 'greatly amused to hear the new calf has been christened after me. If it resembles me in build however, it will be more like a grey-hound than a cow.'

June brought nightly digging of a new front line at Hebuterne, 150 yards from German positions at Gommecourt, at the northern end of the 18-mile Somme front. Exhaustion and apprehension at the 'Big Push' reduced him to monosyllables in his diary, but he carefully notes the celebrant at each Mass. On 28 June the attack was postponed due to bad weather. The next day he made his final entry: 'weather fine but cloudy. Had quiet time at St Amand.' He wrote a letter, which would also be his last:

> We have been pretty busy the last month & are likely to continue so … the ground is in a bad state, and the trenches are a mass of water & liquid mud … Glad to hear the gardener is a success & that the garden is looking so well under his care … Please excuse a short letter, but news is very scarce. All goes well with me. Trusting everybody keeps well & with very best love.
>
> Your Affectionate Son, Jack.

A few miles south, Noel Hodgson of the 9/Devonshires, Durham friend of Oxland and Dingle, may not have known that his poem 'Before Action' had been published that same day,[10] but was well aware that his God may shortly grant his final request:

I, that on my familiar hill
Saw with uncomprehending eyes
A hundred of thy sunsets spill

> Their fresh and sanguine sacrifice,
> Ere the sun swings his noonday sword
> Must say good-bye to all of this;
> By all delights that I shall miss,
> Help me to die, O Lord.

Perhaps Jack made the same humble plea in his own prayers that night. He wrote no more in his diary. The unexpected reprieve had silenced him; there was nothing more to be said. But battalion morale was high and the mood optimistic: 'in the week preceding the attack only seven men 'went sick' ... a record rarely beaten in peacetime'.[11]

Before battle, wills in army pay books were signed, cumbersome greatcoats handed in and personal effects left for forwarding to next of kin. At zero hour, 7.30 a.m. on Saturday 1 July (weather fine and hot, with an early mist that clears) the whistle blew. Jack and pals climbed their ladders and went over the top. In the London morning air the rumble of the massive mines that heralded the attack was distinctly heard. Windowpanes trembled in the peaceful shires of Sussex and Kent. That Saturday evening, the audience at a performance of Brahms' Requiem in Southwark Cathedral could not know how many Englishmen now rested in peace in French soil; nor could they hear the maimed and torn screaming in no-man's-land.

During this 'diversionary' attack on Gommecourt, the QWR would lose all twenty-eight officers and 475 out of 661 riflemen – over 73 per cent casualties in one day: 'All hell was let loose ... I remember feeling that there was not enough air to breathe – so many shells were bursting. Small bodies of men simply disappeared when a shell burst near them.'[12] Another rifleman was only able to recall the detached unreality in the third person:

> Horden stumbled blindly forwards across no man's land. It seemed to him that he was alone in a pelting storm of machine gun bullets, shell fragments and clods of earth. Alone, because the other men were like figures on a cinematograph screen – an old film that flickered violently – everybody in a desperate hurry – the air full of black rain. He could recognize some of the figures in

an uninterested way. Some of them stopped and fell down slowly. The fact that they had been killed did not penetrate his intelligence ... They were unreal to him. His mind was numbed by noise, the smoke, the dust.[13]

Jack Bodenham was one who 'simply disappeared'. Like so many that day, his body was never knowingly recovered. After July, soldiers were issued with a second name tag to aid identification in death. The battles of 1918 raged again over this landscape of mass graves and hasty burials, and pounded the decomposed remains to dust. In 1920, the War Office wrote to his father from Brussels regretting 'that the task of finding and identifying the bodies will in many cases prove impossible, owing to the terrible state of the ground'. In all likelihood, his bodily shell is just as badly churned as the clay and chalk; his devout Catholic soul has surely ascended. Jack's father would send a generous sum to Ampleforth for its War Memorial subscription, in memory of his youngest child and 'affectionate son'. At the thirty-seventh Park AGM on 9 October 1916, as the Somme battle drags on, Secretary Burlinson notes: 'since the beginning of the War, 32 Members have been killed, 46 wounded, 3 missing.'

On that single July day at the Somme, the British Army lost more men than it did in the Crimean, Korean and Boer Wars combined. *The Times* nevertheless saw fit to announce: 'Good Progress. All counter-attacks repulsed.' Jack Bodenham is one of 19,240 who lost their lives, mostly in an opening ninety minutes of frenzied slaughter by machine-gun fire. The morning sunshine in France now falls upon his name chiselled on the vast bulk of the Thiepval Memorial. His official CWGC details are scanter than most and only through the kindness of strangers have I learned so much of his life.

WILFRED JESSON
'BOWLED OUT, MIDDLE PEG'

Captain R.W.F. Jesson, Wiltshire Regiment, from a newspaper reporting his wounding, August 1915. *(Richard Ga...)*

In his stockinged feet, Wilfred Jesson stood just 5ft 6in tall; from its southern boundary, the cricket ground at Lord's rises some 2ft above his head. The slope still runs visibly uphill left to right across the famous terracotta pavilion towering over the green outfield. On a June day in 1908, Jesson achieved a schoolboy's dream to play at Thomas Lord's ground in St John's Wood, the high temple of the cricketing religion.

His pride was swelled by representing his University of Oxford against the Marylebone Cricket Club (MCC) – a fixture which conjures a lost world but survives today. At Oxford's University Parks the walk from Sir Thomas Jackson's Pavilion to the wicket is the same distance as Lord's. But at Jesson's Merton College ground a hefty slog might reach the island strip between the upper and lower River Cherwell, known to scholarly wits as Mesopotamia. Nine years hence, Jesson's feet will walk upon the ancient soil of the original 'land between the rivers', far from England's green and pleasant land.

On a day of disappointment, Oxford lost by six wickets; Wilfred, batting at seven, was bowled out for three and run out for four in his two innings. His leg-break bowling was scarcely called upon and he had no wickets to his name. For a young man just turned 22, the occasion and the opposition at Lord's were nonetheless memorable. MCC was more than an invitation club side: often indistinguishable from England's national team, it was also the governing body of the sport, a bastion of the values that had civilised the empire – the 'Colonial Office in gloves and pads'. It remains independent of national bodies and still owns the copyright on the Laws of Cricket.

Facing Jesson that day for the MCC were the Australian Francis Tarrant, a 1908 Wisden cricketer of the year, and Albert Trott, who represented both Australia and England. Trott remains the only man to have clouted a ball over the Lord's Pavilion, a feat he achieved in 1899 (Kieron Pollard came close in 2010 on his Somerset debut). Opening bat for MCC was the Maharaja Jam of Nawanagar, otherwise known as Ranjitsinhji, Ranji, or just plain Smith. Described by Neville Cardus as the 'Midsummer's Night dream of cricket', he was India's first Test cricketer when he played for England in 1896, scoring a century against Australia on his debut. The mother country was quite happy to plunder its empire for its best sportsmen, as well as fighting men and natural resources. The outposts in their turn were honoured to serve.

Ranji's opening partner was also Indian-born but as English as they come. Captain Teddy Wynyard scored the first goal for Old Carthusians in their 3-0 FA Cup win over the Old Etonians in 1881. He also played Test cricket for England, albeit without the distinction of the maharaja. He would treat young Jesson with respect, having witnessed his successful debut for his former county, Hampshire. That first game at Southampton in July 1907 against Warwickshire in the County Championship was everything Lord's was not: 'Mr Jesson who is in residence at Oxford, made a promising first appearance for the county by scoring 23 not out in good style and taking five wickets for just over eight runs each.'[1]

In an era where teams would mix gentlemen amateurs with professional players, the scorecard carefully notes him as *Mister* Jesson (the same distinction would be used for officers in the army, with privates known by plain surnames). With the Midlands opponents thriving at 260-4, Mr Jesson came on to bowl and 'met with remarkable success'; he claimed five victims, reducing them to 312 all out. This was his maiden and only five-wicket haul in first-class cricket, with figures of 5/42 for the innings. The next day was less successful with only four runs on the board, a single wicket and a catch. Hampshire made a 'very moderate display' all round and Warwickshire had no difficulty polishing off the sixty runs needed for victory. But bowling figures of 6/59 signalled an auspicious start for the young all-rounder.

Born in Southampton in 1887 to solicitor Robert Jesson and wife Annie (*née* Fairey), Robert Wilfred Fairey Jesson was a true son of Hampshire. His county ground debut in his home town would be quite the celebration for his family, who were all there to applaud his fine performance. The cricket ground (now redeveloped) was only a few hundred yards from the Jesson home in Archers Road. Wilfred had played three seasons for the XI at Sherborne School, with impressive figures in his last season of forty wickets and a batting average of thirty. He had the 'Indian sign' over St Paul's school in particular, demolishing them in 1904 with eight wickets and taking five in 1905.

On going up to Merton College, Oxford, in 1906, this fine all-round prospect played rugby and hockey in winter, but cricket remained his first love. He played in the Varsity freshmen's match in his first summer, but the coveted Blue never came. Once Trinity term was over, Mr R.W.F. Jesson was free to play for his county and commenced a grand tour by railway around the cricketing shires. Hampshire did not travel well and suffered a heavy defeat at Leicester by an innings and seventy-two runs. The return match against Warwickshire in Birmingham a day later saw him promoted up the batting order, without signal success, but another couple of wickets contributed to revenge for the home defeat. Indifferent games against Middlesex and Derbyshire were followed by England star Gilbert Jessop's Gloucestershire at Cheltenham, when the start was delayed by an accident on the railway.

Back on his home square at Southampton, he took four wickets against Surrey. Most satisfyingly he had the great Jack Hobbs caught off his bowling – unfortunately, not before he had made 135. His own 'hard-hitting' batting won his highest county score of thirty-eight in this game, but he then lost form: by the last innings in early September at Bournemouth's Dean Park, he had slipped down the order to number eleven. The tail end clearly suited him as he was unbeaten on twenty-nine, as Hampshire chalked up their season's highest score of 351 against Yorkshire. But the match ended in a tame draw, with Lord Hawke, the former England captain, playing out a cautious game until stumps were drawn: 'There was some little opposition by the crowd to the defensive methods employed and this Lord Hawke resented by refusing to continue the innings unless it ceased.'[2] There's a better class of crowd control for you.

In just under two months, Wilfred completed eleven first-class matches for Hampshire before returning to his jurisprudence studies at Merton. The promise of that first game at Southampton was not fulfilled and his batting average for the season ended on 10.76 from an aggregate of 183 runs. He took only 12 more wickets to finish with 17 at an average of 26.88.[3] Perhaps as a result, Hampshire only called on him twice in 1908; he had just ten runs and four wickets to show for it. That summer he had represented Oxford in his cherished game at Lords. He also played for the Etceteras versus the Perambulators (a side chosen exclusively from Charterhouse, Eton, Harrow, Westminster and Winchester boys) but the longed-for Blue remained elusive. In truth, his performances for his Varsity did not merit it.

Whilst he would play in the seniors' game in 1909, the final chance of a Blue slipped away. Perhaps he also spent too much time with the Myrmidons dining club, as he took only a third-class honours degree. No Hampshire flannels that summer for Wilfred, but a West Country tour with the Old Shirburnians and then to London. By September he was lodging at 23 Vincent Square and under articles with the legal firm of Barlow, Barlow & Hyde. Winter Saturdays were spent playing rugby for Rosslyn Park. The season opener against Blackheath saw him at halfback in a team that featured an international contingent of five London Hospital Kiwis as well as his Merton friend, Donald Grant Herring, Rhodes scholar and Princeton 'Yank at Oxford'. Herring, an American gridiron footballer, wrestling champion and hammer-thrower, became the first American to win his rugger Blue and would play for the United States against New Zealand in 1913. He tried in vain to persuade his compatriots that 'the English game of rugby be taken into serious consideration with a view to either substituting it for American football or improving the American game with the best features of the English game'.[4] A voice crying in the wilderness.

The Bedford game in October saw another exotic addition to Jesson's cosmopolitan Park team – one Carl Rudolf Baltzar von Braun. Rudi (to his friends), a Swedish student doctor at St Bartholomew's Hospital, lived in Mayfair with his aristocratic physiotherapist uncle Detlof and six staff to keep the household struggling along. Rudi played a dozen games for the club over three seasons. He also refereed the 1912 game between Park and Bart's, when his impartiality was sorely tested: 'Had a dropped goal by Richards been allowed the students would have won, but the Referee, much to the disappointment of the large crowd of spectators present, refused to allow the points.'[5]

Captain von Braun served in the RAMC at Gallipoli and France and survived the war. Perhaps sensibly – with a name like von Braun, and feeling the wind of war blowing – Rudi became a naturalised Englishman in 1914. How many times did he have to explain that as he bent over a wounded patient in an advanced aid post? But unlike the more celebrated Swede and local Barnes resident Gustav (formerly von) Holst, he did not change his name.

Jesson had just missed his rugby colours at Sherborne, but was evidently a late developer. In November 1909, the selectors deemed him good enough to partner Adrian Stoop (of Harlequins and England) for Surrey against Kent. It was Stoop who revolutionised halfback play in England, introducing an idea that had already been adopted by the Welsh and New Zealanders. Previously the two halfbacks had played 'left' and 'right', with one 'standing off' slightly. Now he championed the specialist 'scrum-half' and 'outside-half' roles familiar today.

Jesson's lack of experience of this system may have been exposed inside his innovative and stellar captain, who would lead England that season in the first international at Twickenham. According to

The Times: 'A. D. Stoop stood out conspicuously on many occasions, but was badly supported by Jesson and by the two centre three-quarters.'[6] Kent carried the day.

Despite this county setback, Jesson was ever-present for his Park club during the first half of the season, playing with a succession of partners including Aussie Syd Burdekin, before St Paul's school-leaver Charles Bayly joined him after Christmas to form a settled, if compact, halfback pairing. They sit in the front of the season's photograph. Wilfred, fair-haired and upright, looks serious, as if his thoughts lie elsewhere. A 1907 cigarette card of 'County Cricketer RW Jesson' again shows him brooding, troubled for a young man of 20.

His swansong for Hampshire – a single match against Sussex in May 1910 – quietly ends his first-class cricketing career on a low note (he is not even called upon to take the cherry). Nor does he reappear on the rugby field at Rosslyn Park, as more serious matters demand his attention on Saturdays. Guy du Maurier's play (a critical hit in Wilfred's home town as well as in London) had fanned national invasion fears and boosted the Territorial recruitment drive. In November the former Sherborne cadet joined the Inns of Court OTC; his weekends were now occupied with training and field exercises. King Edward had died in May; Wilfred's attestation was thriftily amended by hand in red ink to demand fealty to the new monarch, George V. In peaceful 1910, defending the homeland seemed the most likely call to arms. He could not have guessed that His Majesty would eventually require his services as far as 3,000 miles away.

By 1911, he has returned to the family bosom in Southampton (or at least he was there on the night of Sunday 2 April when the census taker called at Archers Road). *The Times* announced in July 1912 that R.W.F. Jesson BA Oxon. had passed his final law exam and he took up employment in 1913 as managing clerk of Hepherd & Winstanley. Living in Hampshire he turned out for the historic Trojans Rugby Club at Eastleigh, founded four years before Rosslyn Park and still playing today. He played cricket there and captained the rugby XV in the last pre-war season.

The OTC had given him his Certificate A, the first step to a commission, and in August 1914 it was an immediate advance for him from the Territorial Reserve to second lieutenant with 5/Wiltshires.[7] His experience led to rapid promotion: a photograph of the battalion's officers at Inkerman Barracks, near Woking,[8] in early 1915 shows his captain's stripes on his cuff (these obvious signs of rank were quickly dropped at the front as snipers drew an easy bead on their wearers). In the mess he swapped rugby yarns with Lieutenant Arnold Huckett, a missionary's son born in Madagascar who had also played for Rosslyn Park. The Wiltshire's cap badge was the familiar Maltese Cross of their old rugby jerseys. Like Wilfred, Huckett was a keen school cricketer (at St George's, Harpenden), but distinguished himself as a forward on the rugby field, being a 'really speedy player with a good shove off'.[9] At Wadham, Oxford, he just missed his Blue – Jesson would surely commiserate. The younger man would die before Wilfred in a blaze of Turkish sunshine and rifle fire, on one of the bloodiest days of the war for the Wiltshire Regiment.

The 5th (Service) Battalion Duke of Edinburgh's Wiltshire Regiment, under the command of Lt Col Carden, left its barracks for Avonmouth on 30 June 1915. Captain Jesson with his B Company set off first at 6.30 a.m. to the local station at Brookwood. C and D Companies were waved off later by local schoolchildren, and all troops were aboard the SS *Franconia* by 3.15 p.m. 'And so we sailed into the gathering night with all lights extinguished':[10] they were bound for Gallipoli. The jingoistic Jessie Pope (to whom Wilfred Owen would sarcastically dedicate his first draft of '*Dulce et Decorum*') wrote in the *Daily Mail*:

> Our cricketers have gone 'on tour'
> To make their country's triumph sure
> They'll take the Kaiser's middle wicket
> And smash it by clean British Cricket.[11]

Many Wiltshire men never returned. For those who did, it would not be for several years, as they remained on active service in the Middle East. After the Turkish fiasco, they were evacuated to Egypt and then sent to the Persian Gulf and into remote Mesopotamia. There were few comforts here to entice newspaper reporters, and boats carrying mail were slow or sunk by submarines – the *Franconia* herself would be torpedoed off Malta in October 1916. In that neglected Eastern theatre, the 5th became the 'Forgotten Battalion'. Wilfred Jesson would make a brief return to England, but he would be in no condition to play rugby or cricket.

Delayed by the late arrival of their destroyer escort, the Wiltshires sailed the next day in convoy with Nowell Oxland's *Empress of Britain* to Malta, where Wilfred shows a talent for vivid travel-writing:

> … there in the harbour countless pedlar boats with awnings rigged up to keep off the sun, lazily sculled by their owners. Suddenly the pedlars seem to spring to life and a battle ensued. Scurrying hither and thither they bombarded one another with tomatoes. The red fruit soon lay thick on the dark blue waters to be collected again later by the more thrifty and sold to the ignorant. Here and there naked boys invited us to throw money overboard for which they dived with great success.

Onwards they sailed to Alexandria and Lemnos, finally transhipping through rough seas to Cape Helles as night fell: 'a strange and faint yet perfectly beastly smell was wafted off the land, I remember it quite well and not liking it, I smoked a pipe until all lights had to be extinguished.' On this exposed headland overlooking the Dardanelles, the 30m obelisk of the Helles Memorial has stood for ninety years since. Scorched in summer, scoured by wind and frost in bitter winter, the panels have eroded and seismic activity has rattled the memorial's foundations and made it unstable. Wilfred Jesson will undergo a pretty similar experience in his short time on the peninsula. Men, however, are not made of stone; the destructive effect on the human mind and body is observed in days not years.

A five-year restoration programme at Helles began in 2010. The names of Rosslyn Park's Jimmy Dingle, Bertram Falle, Harry Stevenson, Cecil Crosley, Alec Geary-Smith, Bertram Silcock and 21,000 others will be made good and whole again in Italian Nebrasina limestone. The original British Hopton Wood limestone, quarried in Derbyshire by the suitably grim-sounding Killer Brothers, is no longer available in the copious quantities required for so many names.

Another scarred name at Helles is Huckett, now machine-gun officer, who landed with Wilfred that night:

> Like many another young Oxford man, he seemed to have found his vocation; a position of authority brought out in him a resourcefulness and a quickness which he had not developed as an undergraduate. He went out to the Dardanelles full of keen confidence; it is only too probable for him, as for many others, that his military promise found its sudden fulfilment there. [12]

They passed in darkness through the improvised landing stage of the River Clyde at 'V' Beach and marched to Gully Beach to bivouac on the Cliffside: 'It was difficult to realise the close proximity of war … that we were engaged in anything but a pic-nic with a host of good fellows.' Jesson's main hardship had been dealing with an 'intensely drunk soldier' under arrest. As the sun rose they were greeted by baking heat and swarms of flies: 'they were worst things on the Peninsula, never have I hated any animal so much, they were absolutely nauseating and from 7 am till night fall their presence was an abomination.' Bullets buzzed their heads as they moved up into trenches through dense, thorny scrub. Latrines and wells during water expeditions were magnets for Turkish snipers, although the first deaths came from rockfalls during nightly trench digging. Shelling accounted for more. They repelled their first enemy attack with rifle fire: 'it was quite exciting and I felt as one used to in a closely contested game of rugger when the opposing side were scrumming near one's own line.'

After twelve days in the trenches under bombardment and sniper fire, the Wiltshire men, exhausted by sleeplessness and dysentery, sailed back to the filthy villages and disease-ridden camps on Lemnos – and a pat on the back from the brigadier at Sunday's church parade. 'And so,' wrote Wilfred:

> ended the first phase of our operations. It had been a great experience and I may describe it as a period of novelty and interest. There was nearly always an amusing side to most things and two or three trivial incidents afforded me much amusement.

For instance whenever we passed something which had a more than usually disagreeable smell, the men used to hold their noses and exclaim 'Pooh! Pooh! Dead Turk'. It was always 'dead Turk', a remark which I think evinced their patriotism.

On 3 August, the 13th Division of New Army men again crossed 60 miles of the wine-dark Aegean to Anzac Cove, landing at night to bolster the tenacious Australian and New Zealand troops who had built there a beachhead and the foundations of national myth. The mid-section of the Gallipoli peninsula is a Gordian knot of ridges, spurs, gorges and ravines, spinning off the high point of Chunuk Bair. Slopes choked with scrub oak fall into deep gullies that lead nowhere. Compared to the tangled geography here, the horseshoe of burnt scrub hills to the north (where Dingle and Oxland would die) is like a cricket stand encircling the sunburnt pitch of the Suvla plain – without the ripples of polite applause. Jesson had an unexpected reunion with:

> Pte Gronow ... a huge Welsh miner with whom I had come in contact on the rugger field more than once, and such meetings one does not forget. I asked him whether he felt like rugger and he grunted there would be some dirty rugger work if he got amongst them and I knew he spoke true. [13]

B Company received orders for a night advance and attack:

> There was to be no firing at all, everything was to be done with the bayonet. The password and countersign were to be 'Godley' [the ANZAC commander] and 'success' (which it was fondly hoped we should achieve). Of the four days operations which followed perhaps 'ungodly failure' would have been more appropriate.

The division fought its way through the hostile terrain with units intermingling and casualties mounting 'in the inky blackness ... on a march which may best be likened to a nightmare'. They faced Turkish counter-attacks: 'Bayonets were fixed and we crawled up in close formation beneath the crest. And now you could not hear yourself speak, the roar of the guns, the crack of the rifles, the rattle of machine guns, the whiz and screeching of bullets and shells created an absolute inferno.' Jesson suffered a 'gunshot' wound to the thigh:

> Heavy fighting was in progress in front, and the Battalion was shelled. Capt R.W.F Jesson (wounded). Rations were drawn at 5.30pm and rumours were of 24 hours rest. It should be noted that the men had had no rest, and very little water and food since Friday evening and were consequently in a very exhausted condition.[14]

He was helped down the gully 'hanging on to my servant, Neeves' and evacuated to one of the hospital ships riding in the bay with green lights strung stern to bow and an illuminated red cross. Patriotism took his mind off the pain:

> I shall never forget the walk down that Gulley, one thing that struck me more than most was a unique example of the great- ness and unity of the British Empire. Here lay side by side an Englishman, a New Zealander, an Australian, a Maori, a Gurkha! England had not called across the sea in vain, the young manhood of the colonies had heard the call and answered it with amazing devotion, her subjects in far off India had been called and gladly gave of their best.

Deep thigh wounds and consequent blood loss from femoral arteries commonly caused fatal shock and he was lucky to escape with his life; doubly lucky as the coming days brought disaster for the Wiltshires.

That night, three columns advancing blindly with little recon- naissance were lost in pitch-black confusion. They failed to arrive on time at the planned starting point for the combined assault. Shrapnel rained down from enemy guns unseen in the darkness. Lt Col Carden's men were tasked to relieve the beleaguered New Zealanders who had taken the heights. But 'led wrong by the guide who ... must have been a spy', they found the forward trenches full, leaving them exposed, only an hour before dawn. They retreated down a steep slope and at 3 a.m. scraped hollows in the rocky ground, 'to make themselves comfortable as the position was quite safe'.

Exhausted after four days with no rest and little food or water, they removed their equipment, piled their rifles into stacks in this enclosed bowl with its landmark 'farm' (a tumbledown shack) and sunk down to snatch some sleep.

Some of the Wiltshires never fired a shot or woke again. Without warning at first light, six battalions of shrieking Turks cascaded down the slopes from the Sari Bair ridge. Like a human flash flood, they washed over the forward-lying Loyal North Lancashires, who lost half their number. Below them the Wiltshires – or at least those not bayoneted or butchered with scimitars as they lay in the open – had no time to grab guns or equipment. Their only escape was down the gully, which they found blocked by Turkish machine guns. Unarmed and desperate, some tried to rush past the guns, others attempted to scale the northern side of the ravine; waves of gunfire fell on them. Wounded men scrambling to escape over a barricade of bodies simply added another layer to the blood-soaked mound of flesh: 'The Farm was a sheepfold that became an abattoir.'[15]

Survivors cowering in the thick undergrowth were picked off by snipers in daylight. After dark they crept or dragged themselves towards the beach. Corporal Scott's group, trapped in a ravine for fourteen days, drank from rock pools and fed from the haversack rations of the dead, hearing the corpses being ransacked by the Turks. They were even accidentally strafed by their own side as they tried to return to the lines. Some of the 'friendly fire' was more deliberate: when some 300 to 400 men from panicked New Army battalions ran towards the Turks, hands up in apparent surrender, New Zealand Brigade Major Arthur Temperley, Jesson's fellow Shirburnian, indignantly ordered their slaughter. He later wrote: 'To save a disaster of the first magnitude and to prevent our whole front line collapsing I gave the orders to the machine guns of our Brigade to open fire upon them and at some cost in life the movement was checked and they ran back to their lines.'[16] While this was first recounted with 'deep regret', a later 1938 revision airbrushes the episode from his personal recollection.

The wounded Jesson was spared this dire August day. Neither Arnold Huckett nor Carden, his CO, was among the 150 who reached the safety of the beach. A total of 143 officers and men[17]

from the 5/Wiltshires died on the slopes below Sari Bair under fire
from Turks or Temperley; only two have known graves, with the
remainder remembered at Cape Helles. So depleted were the officers that a Captain Greany, returning from a wound suffered on the
8th, had to take command (and lead a heroic rescue of Scott's party).
The parent 13th Division fared as badly: it lost ten of thirteen COs
and 6,000 out of 10,500 other ranks. Its Major General Shaw retired
from command due to serious illness.

Wilfred Jesson heard news of so many comrades killed from the
sanctuary of a hospital bed in far-off Alexandria: his thigh wound
had been serious enough to move him from the unsanitary field
hospitals of Mudros to Egypt. While he was recuperating, the battalion moved north to Lala Baba by the beach at Suvla Bay. The
Aegean at their backs meant little respite from front-line fire: there
was no falling back outside the range of enemy guns and snipers,
as they could on the Western Front. Even sea bathing could end in
a churning stain of reddened froth as shells or bullets found their
mark in the turquoise water. Reinforcements trickled in from other
battalions of the regiment, and officers returned from sickbeds in
'Alex'. No sooner had some returned than they were invalided
directly out again with malaria or dysentery. Up to a thousand cases
a day were logged during September. Many of those evacuated by
ship to Malta or Alexandria did not make it as far as a hospital bed
and were buried at sea. The Wiltshire battalion – a weak and listless
ghost of its former self – struggled to maintain a muster of just 380
officers and men.

Having retired hurt from his first innings, Wilfred Jesson returned
to the peninsula on 16 October for his second knock, as the seasons
began to turn. A much stickier wicket awaited him. He was 'appointed
to command "B" my old company and was delighted at the prospect but "quantum mutatus ab illo" (how changed from what it was)'.
Changes to his chain of command brought more unhappiness:

> We had a new CO and somehow or other we did not see eye to
> eye. It was most unfortunate as I can faithfully say I enjoyed the
> life before he came; there was much to entertain and amuse but
> for the last three weeks or so there was constant friction. I will say

no more in this score and only mention it as an introduction to stating my mental frame of mind whilst on the Peninsula.

After the torrid heat of August, he was also about to experience another side of Gallipoli's hostile climate.

As the trees shed their leaves, Sir Ian Hamilton's fortunes fell with his recall to England. Freshly dug trenches, no longer shielded by foliage, were in full view of the enemy and took regular showers of shrapnel. November ushered in gales, thunderstorms and bitter cold at night. Just four braziers were issued to those in the fire trenches. The sapping losses to enemy artillery and disease weakened the whole Expeditionary Force to a state where another suicidal Turkish attack like that of 10 August would have driven it into the sea. A renewed offensive with 'fresh' divisions from France was considered, but the winter weather would make it impossible to land them. In an uncharacteristic moment of humane common sense, the General Staff acknowledged that the inevitable casualties from any such attack could not be safely taken off the beaches to hospital. Thoughts turned instead to a wholesale evacuation of the Expeditionary Force.

If there was doubt, the night of 26 November would dispel it. Thunderstorms that raged all night turned the dry gullies and trenches into rivers engorged by the floods pouring down from the heights. Cookhouses could not light fires so there was no hot food. Parapets were washed away on both sides by a torrent which carried everything in its path: men, mules, carts, stores, blankets and clothing. Jesson wrote: 'A man gave me a blanket to wrap round me as I had abandoned my great coat as it was wet through and was a nuisance as the skirts floated on the water as I walked.' Flimsy tarpaulins over dug-outs were swept away or shredded by the vicious gale. The hollows beneath – the only shelter for the shivering soldiers – turned from muddy pools into watery graves as men drowned in the darkness.

As the mercury dropped, the rain turned to snow and the wounded died of exposure in the blizzard. In the trenches, the Wiltshires stood in water which turned to solid ice around them; in three days at Suvla, 5,000 cases of frostbite were treated. Already weakened by illness, many exhausted men froze to death:

A Man in my particular Section had not returned off his Watch, so we went up to look for Him and there He was FROZEN Stiff against the Parapet like a Marble Statue. The poor chap had got so wet the previous day he decided to dry his Greatcoat, had taken it off, and there it was alongside him just as stiff as He was.[18]

The storm blew itself out by the 30th. An unexpected bonus of the cold was that the swarms of flies had also dropped like men – they could eat bully beef again without a seething black mouthful. But with no supplies, kit or blankets there were precious few other consolations from the improved weather. Their new divisional commander, General Stanley Maude, conveyed his admiration for 'their splendid courage, grit and determination in facing so resolutely vile weather' to men 'animated as of old by the bulldog character of our race'. More welcome to these bulldogs would have been his closing words: 'am trying to send more coal and coke and am authorising issue of rum tonight.'[19]

Wilfred was one of those evacuated with exposure, first to the Casualty Clearing Station on Mudros and then to Egypt again. In Alexandria he was passed from the Ras-el-Tin Military Hospital to No. 1 Red Cross Hospital in the suburb of Bolkly. Two months of medical care suggest that this was more than exposure. The stress of being under constant fire, allied to the appalling winter trench conditions and an incomplete recovery from his earlier wound could easily destroy a man's mind as well as his body. At the end of January 1916, he was sent back to England for three months' further treatment. Inauspiciously, his hospital transport was the liner *Britannic*, sister to the ill-fated *Titanic* and soon to suffer a similar fate off the Greek coast in November. The Hampshire native returned for the first time in almost two years, no longer the triumphant cricketer, but the damaged soldier. And it was not to the family home.

On 9 February, Wilfred was admitted on arrival to the Royal Victoria Military Hospital at Netley; its own purpose-built 170m landing pier on Southampton Water allowed ships to disembark patients directly into its care. The hospital was built by Queen Victoria after the Crimean War exposed the poor provision for wounded English soldiers. Army doctor John Watson, friend of

Sherlock Holmes, trained there. It stood on land between the rivers Itchen and Hamble, known locally as Spike Island. One thousand original beds had by now been doubled in hutted and tented extensions. The main building was so vast that the American Navy in 1944 would use jeeps to travel its corridors. Netley's D Block was a military psychiatric asylum; despite having capacity for only 3 officers and 121 other ranks, it treated 15,000 patients during the war (and Rudolf Hess in the next). It was here in 1917 that shell shock was first diagnosed in the poet Wilfred Owen. Our own Wilfred's state of mind would have deeply alarmed the Jesson family visiting from their nearby home.

Shell shock was little understood and was veiled in a variety of medical euphemisms, the most laughable being NYD(N), or Not Yet Diagnosed (Nervous). More commonly, its symptoms of chronic fatigue and listlessness were termed 'neurasthenia'. Early in the war, it was believed to be the result of physical trauma to the nerves, referred to as 'organic'. This could be from wounds, or from a battering or burial under heavy shelling (Skeffington Poole was hit by a clump of earth). Breakdown from 'paralysis of the nerves' was treated by massage, rest, dietary regimes and electric-shock treatment. Charles Myers, the medical officer who first coined the term 'shell shock' in 1917, was uneasy with it, observing that many men suffered its symptoms without having ever been in the front lines. Psychological factors were increasingly identified as the cause of breakdown – remember Wilfred's guarded references to his disliked new CO. New treatments included the 'talking cure', hypnosis and more rest.

Treatment of any sort, however, was designed to return men to the front as quickly as possible. Pathé Brothers' 1917 film of Netley's shell shock wards gives a glimpse, if little insight, into the complex condition and its therapies.[20] The chosen subjects are successfully treated, some supposedly in a matter of hours. In reality, four-fifths of those admitted with shell shock were never able to return to military duty and became permanent 'ineffectives'. To reduce these levels, occupational training and 'masculine' behaviour were highly recommended. One superintendent at a York military hospital asserted that, although the medical officer must show sympathy,

the patient 'must be induced to face his illness in a manly way'.
Some, like New Zealander Captain Chrystall, found their therapy
in playing rugby, 'when the doctors had given me up for dead', and
returned to the front. Others could not face it: Rosslyn Park's John
Beamish, an admiral's son, wounded at Bellewarde in May 1915, was
found dead on the Harrow Road with a revolver and suicide note.

In the first Medical Board report on Jesson, dated 12 February,
at the wooden-hutted Welsh Hospital, Netley, Captain Sydney
Rowland RAMC notes:

> From Alexandria where he complained of muscular pain. His cer-
> ebration was noticed to be somewhat slow and speech distinctly
> hesitating though not staccato. He had also slight drawing of feet.
> Babinski nil but normal plantar reflex not elicited. Nothing sug-
> gestive of organic disease.[21]

In checking for the Babinski reflex (big toe curls back, other toes
fan out; normal in an infant but abnormal in adults), the doctor was
evidently concerned about spinal cord nerve damage. He recommended two months off on account of 'physical & mental stress in
Military Service'. Jesson spent his time writing down his Gallipoli
memories. Captain Rowland saw him again in April and noted that
he 'appears to have improved but his speech has not quite recovered.
He is unable to sustain prolonged physical exertion'. A Medical
Board in mid-May specifically diagnosed neurasthenia and granted
a further month's leave. It is clear that, although improving, his mind
was more damaged than his sportsman's body: 'Condition much
improved but still complains of considerable exhaustion in exertion and he is at times very depressed. This condition of depression
which was so marked is growing less and he is gradually regaining
his confidence. His physical condition is good.'

By July, he was considered healthy enough to re-join his battalion.
There is no evidence on his record that he was officially passed fit
by a Medical Board. Perhaps six months out of the line was deemed
sufficient to recover his 'manliness'. Or did the massive influx of
casualties from the Somme to the landing stage at Netley simply
make his case less of a priority? It is likely that the popular officer

and team player wanted to get back to his men and asked to return to his unit. Wilfred Owen would later describe the overwhelming guilt at being away from the front and the paternalistic compulsion to return to look after his soldiers and be their voice. Such guilt at the 'evasion' of duty could only deepen Wilfred Jesson's depression, and the enforced inactivity on leave must have grated. Whatever his fitness of mind, in the full knowledge of the hardships of the trenches and the horror of wounding, he elected to return to 'face his illness in a manly way'.

In his absence the Allied troops were evacuated from Gallipoli in a brilliantly managed operation during December and January. The Turks were utterly hoodwinked by a series of elaborate subterfuges, as thousands of men were taken off by night: soldiers muffled boots and wheels with rags, empty cases of new 'supplies' were conspicuously moved about in full view of the enemy, unmanned rifles were rigged to fire by dripping water mechanisms. The Wiltshires would put such deception techniques to good use in their next theatre. The success of the evacuation far surpassed the rest of the peninsular campaign. It was a very British triumph and the improvisatory talent for beach evacuations would prove itself again a generation later at Dunkirk.

Christmas on Mudros brought some cheer, as they were at least under cover and briefly out of harm's way. The Wiltshires sailed for Egypt but could not escape the attentions of the weather: on their first night at Port Said, their tents on the beach were blown flat by a gale. Egypt offered many recreational pleasures, including musketry competitions, shopping and camel rides around the pyramids for the officers. Wilfred, meanwhile, was on his way to England for specialist treatment.

After a mere month's rest, the 5th was ordered to embark on the HMT *Oriana* in February to join the Mesopotamian Relief Force, charged with raising the siege of Kut al Amara, where General Charles Townshend and 10,500 troops of the 6th (Poona) Division were trapped. In a war of precious few long straws, the Wiltshires had again drawn one of the shortest. Mesopotamia – the land 'between the rivers' that is modern-day Iraq – is ancient, the home of Ur and Babylon and the original Cradle of Civilisation. It was 'the site of the Garden of Eden, of the Great Flood and the birthplace of Abraham'; Colonel Tim Collins would memorably remind his Royal Irish Regiment to 'tread lightly there' on the eve of another Iraq war in 2003. However fine his oratory, an Arab proverb knew better: 'when Allah made Hell, it was not bad enough, so he created Mesopotamia – and added flies.'

Private Henry Woolley commented drily on his journey up the Tigris in 1916: 'I did not see Adam and Eve there. They must have run away with the Turks.'[22] The desert combat kit of the day was issued, each man receiving a Wolseley sun helmet and two khaki suits. The battered 13th Division from Gallipoli was the only fully British outfit to fight the Mesopotamian campaign; eight other divisions came from India, some via France, as troops from the subcontinent were judged by the General Staff to be more attuned to the hardships of the local climate and terrain. Storms, mosquitoes, flies and cholera made little distinction between Englishman and Indian.

The 5th had been tipped out of the pan into a fire fuelled by oil. For centuries, this territory had been part of the Ottoman Empire. German expansionism eyed the oil supplies in the Gulf, and cultivated a friendship with Turkey. The Berlin–Baghdad railway was under construction, latterly using prisoners of war from Gallipoli like Lt John Still. Britain's fleet also craved oil, which was drilled mainly in neighbouring pro-British Persia (the Anglo-Persian Oil Company later became BP). Swift moves were made in 1914 to protect the oilfields in the south, but Turkish pressure from the north warranted further reinforcement. The Gallipoli campaign, Churchill's brainchild, was the first failed venture by politicians convinced that German defeat would come by flanking blows at her allies, Austria-Hungary and Turkey. The 'Easterners' were now led by David Lloyd George, who hated what he saw as Haig's Western Front obsession; the newspaper casualty lists and streams of wounded across the Channel were hardly palatable to any politician. At least Mesopotamia was conveniently distant: bad news and limbless men travelled slowly, if at all.

This land is mostly flat desert, a dry parody of its lush Oxford namesake. The rivers Tigris and Euphrates join at Qrna to form

the Shatt al Arab which flows into the Persian Gulf. These rivers
are swollen by snows thawing in the mountains of Asia and the
Caucasus. Spring sees the Tigris flood to a mile wide in places;
the small towns and villages along its banks in 1916 were generally
built on tall stilts. Apart from the rivers, there is virtually no rainfall,
although most of the annual 6in seemed to fall on the Wiltshires.
Nor were there any roads, so all travel was by boat, harder in
summer, as river levels fell.

With their appalling luck, the men disembarked at Basra during
a violent thunderstorm, through which they marched 5 miles to
camp. A strange assortment of river boats, barges and Thames steamers (many more floundered en route from England) ferried them
north on the Tigris towards Kut. Beyond it lay the ultimate prize of
Baghdad, 570 miles upstream from the Gulf. They arrived at dawn in
yet another storm to occupy front-line trenches just 150 yards from
the enemy. Bitter fighting at El Hannah, Fallahiya and Sannaiyat
drove the Turks back, but attacks repeatedly bogged down under
fierce bombardment. The Wiltshires took hundreds of casualties
throughout April, lost another CO and found themselves under a
major from the King's (Liverpool) Regiment. Flooding slowed communications and supplies of ammunition, rations and equipment.
For all their efforts, they could not save Kut: with his men dying of
starvation and sickness, Townshend surrendered on 29 April 1916.
The single wireless transmitter that had sent out 6,313 forlorn messages in 144 days of siege was finally silent. After Gallipoli, British
military humiliation was complete at Kut.

The damaged battalion withdrew to lick its wounds at Shaikh
Sa'ad, still within range of gunfire. They endured intense 50°C heat,
plagues of sandflies and mosquitoes, and storms of dust and sand.
The tortures were verily biblical, as Woolley described:

There were 1000 of frogs there, we could not sleep at night for
them they were making such an awful noise, the most of our
chaps was up just at the first night killing them and the boys that
was not out in the night was as soon as day light next morning
killing them. We had to rest the next night, there were very few
frogs left to tell the tale.[23]

Disease was rife, with dysentery and jaundice compounded by infected sores from sunburn and serious cases of sunstroke. Sick men in their tens of thousands were shipped out to Basra or India. Many never made the distant hospitals. Most vulnerable were the fresh reinforcements, who would arrive and immediately succumb to illnesses of which their immune systems had no knowledge. Other hazards included looting attacks by marauding Arabs; the 5th resorted to burying their rifles inside their tents and sleeping on top of them.

For a soldier suffering from serious mental and physical damage, there could be no worse posting than Mesopotamia. Yet this was Jesson's destination when he re-embarked at Devonport on 21 July for the five weeks' passage to Basra. He exchanged Spike Island, between two Hampshire waterways, for the land between the rivers of Babylon. A two-day-old newspaper on board reported the death on the Somme of 2/Lt Frederick Key; 'A Cricketers Last Message' to his parents reads: 'If you receive this you will know that I have been bowled out, middle peg. You can be sure however that I batted well.'[24]

Wilfred travelled upriver by steamer and re-joined his battalion on 4 September, at Abu Shitaib Camp, Amara, the day after it had returned to the rear camp from Shaikh Sa'ad. He assumed command of B Company, and was appointed acting major, second-in-command of a much-reduced battalion. The 1,100 men who had originally arrived at Basra had dwindled to 16 officers and 274 other ranks. No wonder they were the Forgotten Battalion in this 'Neglected War'.[25]

Their divisional commander, General Maude, was now given overall command of the army in Mesopotamia. The highly popular Maude was rare amongst his officer class in sharing the dangers at the front and talking to all ranks. His priority was to restore fighting strength and morale with improved care for health, including sanitising water, better communications and supply systems. He instituted sweeping reforms of the command structure and saw to it that units were fully occupied in training.

On 20 October, as cooler weather arrived, the tempo rose in readiness for a major offensive – a new assault on Kut. Jesson took out a reconnaissance party of 100 men from Amara to the

Musharrah canal, his mission to try different methods of getting men, transport and supplies across water. In late November, they marched back to Shaikh Sa'ad, 20 miles from Kut. Marching east in the almost proprietary Wiltshire wet weather, they forded the River Hai, a tributary of the Tigris. Christmas Day 1916 was dry and fine, enlivened by occasional shelling, and by festive dinner in the trenches, featuring Christmas pudding courtesy of the *Daily Mail* and a generous rum ration.

January and February brought further advances on Kut. Trench systems were dug and named with the usual reminders of home (Swindon Street) and English wit ('Hai Street'). Continual enemy sniping added tension to their labour and the ground was tangled with liquorice root and difficult to work. Turkish resistance and counter-attacks were costly to both sides. One night, the Wiltshires heard the Turks digging until the small hours. Day broke to reveal that they had been burying their dead and filling in trenches to cover their withdrawal across the Tigris in boats. Those trenches unfilled were found to be sturdy and well made with baked brick, sandbags packed with hardened mud and timber-beamed roofing – shades of the 'ritzy' German entrenchments at the Somme. To their greater amazement, the deep latrines were extraordinarily clean – only the medical dressing stations were found to be filthy.

In late February, Maude decided to cross the Tigris at the Shumran Bend, some 5 miles upstream from Kut. A force would create a diversion near a liquorice factory on the bank opposite the town. By day Jesson's men were on river patrol duty, harassed by sniping from the direction of Kut. At night, they used some of the ruses employed when evacuating Gallipoli; burgees, or small mounds topped with flags, were placed as if a new road was about to be built:

Made demonstration at Licorice [sic] Factory in order to make enemy believe that a crossing would be attempted from there ... empty A.T. [Ammunition Transport] Carts were led up and down under cover of darkness and planks, bridging material and etc's unloaded and reloaded, a little bridging material being partially hidden just sufficiently to be observed by an enemy aeroplane during daylight. On the night of the 22nd splashing noises were made at the water's edge. From information received from Corps, the enemy was entirely deceived and brought down 1 battn, several machine guns, wire, Field Guns etc to repel any attack that may have been launched from the Licorice Factory.[26]

The Turks were taken in; they lobbed over shells to deter any further activity and smash the stocks of bridge-building materials. No casualties that night, but during the afternoon of 22 February Major Jesson was visiting positions with two of his men when he was caught out, picked off by a sniper. The spin bowler never saw the googly. Wilfred's death at 30 was genuinely 'felt by all ranks' as he had been with the battalion since its formation and had repeatedly bounced back to his men from wounds, frostbite and shell shock. A fellow officer wrote later:

> His company particularly mourned him as he had been father, mother and sister to them. We buried him next day about 1½ miles West of Kut. There were no flowers in that part of the country but a very touching scene was enacted when a group of Headquarters signallers brought a wreath along made from message pads and other papers which they had cut to represent small white flowers and wired into a very neat design, with a simple message 'from sigs W.K.E' (our code word).[27]

The crossing at Shumran succeeded and Kut was captured within four days. Townshend's surrender was symbolically avenged and the road to Baghdad was open. The city of minarets, blue domes and orange groves was abandoned in flames by the Turks to the unchallenged British on 11 March. General Maude issued a proclamation, famously stating that 'our armies do not come into your cities and lands as conquerors or enemies, but as liberators'.[28] The Wiltshires found new duties as firemen and police, as Arabs and Kurds looted the burning buildings with gusto. Maude was to carry all before him in Mesopotamia and was widely acclaimed in Britain, until he was suddenly carried off by cholera in November. He had refused inoculation in the belief that a man of his age was immune, but had typically insisted that all others be immunised.

Word from this forgotten army was slow: Wilfred's promotion to acting major in September 1916 was not gazetted in London for five months and appeared a month after his death. He was mentioned in Maude's dispatches of April 1917, for gallant and distinguished service in the field. Colonel Graham, Assistant Military Secretary, wrote to his parents in Southampton as late as August, when the cricket season might ordinarily be in full swing: 'I am to express to you the King's high appreciation of these services and to add that His Majesty trusts that their public acknowledgement may be of some consolation in your bereavement.'[29]

Major R.W.F. Jesson is commemorated on the slate panels of the Basra Memorial. Originally at the naval dockyard on the Shatt-al-Arab just north of Basra, the memorial was moved in 1997 by Iraqi president Saddam Hussein to the site of a major battleground in the first Gulf War of 1991. It carries 40,658 names of Commonwealth soldiers who died in Mesopotamia from 1914 to 1921 and whose graves are unknown. While the country remains politically unstable, the memorial is not presently maintained. Some names, like that of Captain Greany, leader of the rescue party at Chunuk Bair, were broken off when the panels were moved. Wilfred Jesson's mortal remains have long since mixed with the soil of the Garden of Eden.

The game was over for the sportsman of the Forgotten Battalion. On his own death in 1932, Wilfred's father bequeathed his shares and debentures to Hampshire Cricket Club in memory of his only son of seven children. The Jesson line was cut short at Kut. In Southampton's Victorian cemetery a vacant plot, next to his parents and two sisters, remains empty of the boy who never returned from between the rivers.

JOHN AUGUSTUS HARMAN
THE MAN WHO HUNTED ZEPPELINS

John Augustus 'Jack' Harman, Royal Flying Corps. *(Charles Harman)*

The November night is chill and clear. From the east across the Lincolnshire plain, the pilot feels a light breeze – a bellows to stoke the flames from two lines of burning rags in oilcans that mark the strip. Tonight he will fly alone, with only his thoughts and his Lewis gun. Far better this way. No worry that his observer, standing in the gaping forward nacelle with only the pillar-mounted gun to cling on to, will plunge to his death in the black depths below. He will fly without night instruments, at the limit of his abilities and his machine's performance. He looks over the nose to the point where the flare path gives up its fight against the darkness. He is ready.

He waves to his aircraftman. The pusher propeller swings behind him. Once, twice, it catches with a rattle, then a roar. He listens with practised ear, feeling for any hesitant tremor, for any distress in the Beardmore engine which has given trouble before. The sound is good; he signals again and opens the throttle.

Our lone flier, John Augustus Harman, entered the world on 15 June 1893 at 29 Marloes Road, Kensington. His parents were John Eustace Harman, barrister at Lincoln's Inn, and Ethel Frances, whose father, Reverend Augustus Birch, tutored Prince Edward. The cries of their firstborn filled the white-stuccoed house in this well-to-do London enclave; there was great happiness in the Harman household. John was christened at St Mary's, Northchurch, in Hertfordshire, where his parents married and where his grandpa was rector. In his beginning is his end, as his baptismal name remains at the church, engraved on its war memorial. John would grow up to become Flight Lieutenant Harman of the Royal Flying Corps, killed in a 'flying accident over Lincolnshire' in 1917. A second son, Charles Eustace, arrived in November 1894 to be playmate and friend. He survived the war to have a distinguished legal career and a son who told me an intriguing family story of the 'Uncle Jack' he never knew.

The fate of our English airman was first foretold some thirty years before his birth, on the prairies of North America. In 1863, 4,000 flying miles west of London, a young German lieutenant of 24 stood outside the town of St Paul, Minnesota. This was Count Ferdinand von Zeppelin, former student of engineering and chemistry and now an ambitious officer in the Württemberg Army.

The American Civil War was at its bloody height, with General Meade turning the tide in July against Lee's Confederacy at Gettysburg, at the cost of 50,000 casualties. Northerly Minnesota was far removed from the conflict; in 1863 it was still frontier country where the US Army had recently ended the Dakota Wars by hanging thirty-eight Indian rebels. In this vast land, Ferdinand travelled hard: by railroad from New York to Ohio, steamship over the Great Lakes to Michigan and by portage to Minnesota. He followed the Mississippi from Crow Wing to St Cloud by stagecoach, and finally arrived at the International Hotel, St Paul's on 17 August.

He was greeted by 'Professor' John H. Steiner, a German-born aeronaut preparing for a series of public balloon ascents. The *St Paul Pioneer* published 'The Fearful Adventure of Professor Steiner: Ballooning in a Thunder Storm: the Scene as Witnessed above the Clouds':

> I could not see the balloon that bore me, save when the whole scene was illuminated with flashes of lightning, which occurred

every few moments; so powerful was the light of those flashes that I became totally blind; the concussion of air was so terrible that blood commenced to flow out of my ears and nose; my balloon reeled and staggered like a drunken man; the car was thrown from side to side, and I was obliged to hold fast to keep myself from being thrown out. I expected every moment that the gas would take fire and that I would be precipitated to the earth.[1]

His account was more likely to chill the good burghers of Minnesota than to thrill. But it would not deter the young count on his mission of discovery.

Von Zeppelin's American adventure was as much fired by ambition as by early frustration in his military career. Fascinated by the American use of militia to provide a wartime surge to a small professional army, he requested assignment as military observer. Ferdinand wrote to his influential cousin, Baron von Maucler, Cabinet chief to Kaiser Friedrich Wilhelm:

I believe it is my duty to use this opportunity through travel to gain information that I may be able to use for my father land at some time. Despite a totally chaotic situation, North America still offers the richest rewards at the present ... The Americans are especially inventive in the adaptation of technical development for military purposes. I do not need to mention the benefits which such a journey promises to have for the general enlightenment.[2]

Two years of civil war had stimulated a young nation to murderous ingenuity more than enlightenment. This conflict foreshadowed the morass of the Western Front, not least in the hideous mismatch of man and machine gun.

Granted twelve months' leave, the young officer set out promptly on his warlike 'gap year'; such was his impatience to reach America that he declined to act as best man at a friend's wedding. After a brief stay in London, he boarded a Cunard steamer in Liverpool and arrived in New York in early May. The young man in a hurry to reach the front spent little time seeing the sights. Bearing documents that designated him, in the international language of diplomacy, the 'Comte Zeppelin, Chargé d'Affaires de son Majesté le Roi de Württemberg', he sailed for Baltimore on a French warship.

Ferdinand found the Union Army of the Potomac, where Professor Thaddeus S.C. Lowe – with the blessing of President Lincoln himself – gloried in the grandiose title 'Chief Aeronaut of the Union Army Balloon Corps'. Lowe used balloons for aerial observation in the First Battle of Bull Run and had also directed artillery fire from an unseen location on to a Confederate encampment. Von Zeppelin begged to be taken on as an aerial observer, but the Union military command had no desire to risk an international incident with a titled civilian diplomat from Europe. So he was dispatched to the relative safety of Minnesota and the tutelage of Steiner – who at least spoke his language. There, he first rose above the plains in a device invented by man. He wrote to his father in Württemberg:

> Just now I ascended with Prof. Steiner, the famous aeronaut, to an altitude of six or seven hundred feet … Should one want to harass with artillery fire [opposing] troops … the battery could be informed by telegraphic signals where their projectiles hit. The above technique has at times been used with great success by this country's armies. No method is better suited to viewing quickly the terrain of an unknown, enemy-occupied region.[3]

The experience had a dramatic impact: 'While I was above St. Paul I had my first idea of aerial navigation … and it was there that the first idea of my Zeppelins came to me.'[4]

Back in Europe, cavalryman Ferdinand saw little action in the Franco-Prussian War. But he renewed his admiration for the balloon, which the French used to send countless messages and 164 people out of besieged Paris over Prussian heads – when the wind was in the right direction. What success, thought Ferdinand, might be achieved with a steerable or 'dirigible' balloon?

The French not only lost the war in 1871 but Alsace and Lorraine too; a united German Empire was proclaimed under Wilhelm of Prussia. Von Zeppelin meanwhile turned his scientific mind to the airship. His 1887 report to the King of Württemberg declared it should be elongated (not spherical) and rigid for control and steering.

Enough lifting gas would be needed for twenty-four hours aloft with a payload of crewmen, supplies and weapons – a cubic yard of gas would lift about 2lb in weight. To close his sale, he hinted that the defeated French, through a Colonel Renard, were ahead in their work. Like many irksome visionaries he was ignored by the orthodox high command. The sudden end of his military career in his prime at 52 – probably for insubordination – returned him to his family estate on Lake Constanz and full-time pursuit of his vision of lighter-than-air craft.

In 1893, the year of John Harman's birth, von Zeppelin submitted his design to the Prussian airship service. It would be five years before he finally received a patent for a 'steerable air vehicle': a rigid aluminium frame covered by fabric, Daimler engines and gondola rigidly attached, with multiple internal gas cells, each free to expand and contract. His invention was termed an 'airship-train', or in the succinctness for which the German language is renowned, *Lenkbarer Luftfahrzug mit mehreren hintereinanderen angeordneten Tragkörpern*. To everyone's relief, the first airship was known more snappily as Zeppelin *LZ1*. Her maiden flight over the Bodensee in July 1900 came three years before two American brothers would fly their heavier-than-air machine at Kittyhawk, North Carolina. Harman, now almost 7 years old, was under early instruction from his governess, prior to boarding at Edgeborough School, Guildford.

A new century gave greater import to new technologies, especially for the newly unified peoples of Germany. Public response to the new wonder was euphoric, allowing the count to pursue development of a second airship wholly financed through donations and a lottery. His *LZ4* embarked on a twelve-hour promotional tour over Germany and, ominously, for the first time over the photogenic but undeniably sovereign mountains of Switzerland, flying at 40mph as high as 2,400ft. German national pride also soared: Zeppelin souvenir sales rocketed, squares and parks were renamed in the count's honour and addresses on many new Zeppelinstrasse were highly coveted.

Such enthusiasm meant that when *LZ4* crashed at Echterdingen in 1908 it caused little alarm but set off renewed airship mania: public subscription raised 6.5 million marks to create a new company

Luftschiffbau-Zeppelin GmbH. From 1909 to the outbreak of war, DELAG (*Deutsche Luftschiffahrtsgesellschaft*, or German Aviation Association) carried 37,250 passengers without mishap on over 1,600 flights. Pleasure cruises in this German engineering marvel were a highly visible focus for ardent patriotism. Von Zeppelin had created both a new age of air transportation and a national icon.

In Britain, however, the Zeppelin cast a gloomy shadow in people's minds, if not yet over their homes. The supremacy of the Royal Navy and British industrial might were both directly challenged: island Britain suddenly seemed less secure. As Germany forged ahead with the Zeppelin programme (the military bought *LZ3*), committees in London debated who should be responsible for British aircraft development. They compromised by giving airships to the navy and airplanes to the army. Scaremongers in parliament and the press had a field day with this lack of direction; they manipulated public paranoia to urge the building of a substantial aerial force to counter the sinister Zeppelin threat.

War was very much in the air in 1909: H.G. Wells' prophetic novel was serialised in London newspapers. His fictional war erupts when Germany attempts to wrest control of the skies before America can build a fleet of its own. German airships and the sinister *Drachenflieger* bomb New York to destruction with young hero Bert Smallways watching in horror as the city becomes a 'furnace of crimson flames'. *The War in the Air*, Wells' self-confessed 'fantasia of possibility', may have been dismissed as science fiction, but events would soon prove his case.

In May, the Wright brothers visited the War Office, fuelling speculation over new airborne weapons. Sir George Doughty MP told parliament on 12 May that Germany had already carried out a secret naval exercise using airships over the North Sea, designed to test British coastal defences. His claimed source was a 'German military officer'.[5] 'Scareship' hysteria filled more newspaper pages than airship technology could fill English skies. Constable Kettle of Peterborough stated, in true policeman style:

> I was on duty in Cromwell-road at 5.15 a.m. when I heard what
> I took to be a motorcar some 400 yards distant. It was quite dark

at the time, and I looked along Cromwell-road expecting to see the lights of an approaching car. Nothing appeared, but I could still hear the steady buzz of a high-powered engine. Suddenly it struck me that the sound was coming from above, and I looked up. My eye was at once attracted by a powerful light, which I should judge to have been some 1,200 feet above the ground. I also saw a dark body, oblong and narrow in shape, outlined against the stars. It was travelling at a tremendous pace, and as I watched, the rattle of the engines gradually grew fainter and fainter, until it disappeared in the northwest.[6]

This was the first sighting to be picked up by the London *Daily Mail*; the press sniffed sensation and hacks were swiftly dispatched to East Anglia, the *London Evening News* and the *Daily Express* to the fore. Engine drivers and Norfolk farm labourers were quick to provide eyewitness accounts and, on 14 May, the *Express* correspondent in Berlin filed by telegram:

> … it is admitted by German experts that the mysterious airship which has been seen hovering over the eastern coast of England may be a German airship. England possesses no such airship, and no French airship has hitherto sailed so far as the distance from Calais to Peterborough. On the other hand, the performance of several German airships, including the Gross airship, which has made one voyage of thirteen hours, would render it possible for them to reach the English coast. At the same time it is improbable that the German airship seen above England ascended from German soil. An aerial voyage to the English coast would still be a dangerous and formidable undertaking even for the newest airships.[7]

Then came the real shocker: 'German expert opinion,' he announced, 'is unanimous in believing that the mysterious airship ascended from some German warship in the North Sea, on which it lands after each of its flights.' Britain's hegemony of the waves was now as threatened as its airspace.

That same night two men appeared at the office of the *London Evening Star* with their own tale. Messrs Graham and Bond stated with 'every evidence of conviction' that, when returning from Teddington to Richmond late the previous night, they saw a landed aircraft on Ham Common and approached the two pilots:

> The German spoke first. He said: 'I am – sorry – have – you – any – tobacco?' I just happened to have an ounce or so in my pouch, and I gave it to him, saying: 'Help yourself, here is the pouch.' He said: 'Will you accept payment for it?' I said 'Certainly not'. He said: 'Will you accept a pipe for it?' and I said I would. He gave me the pipe and here it is.[8]

The pipe was Austrian. To his credit, the reporter did establish that the pipe was available in any tobacconists on the Strand, but the implication was clear. To a sceptic, the late hour might suggest a long evening in a public house with a copy of that day's *Express*, but the clearly authentic voice of Gentleman Johnny Foreigner was enough to swing the *Evening Star* on to the scareship bandwagon.

That month, from Devon to Berwick-upon-Tweed, hundreds claimed to have seen sausage- or cigar-shaped craft moving across the night sky, with whirring engines and dazzling searchlights. Jack Harman and his schoolfellows at Uppingham in Leicestershire were willingly distracted from summer examinations by late night vigils in the dorms; the phantoms considerately avoided daytime missions and any annoying disruption to the cricket season. Not to be outdone, the distant dominion of New Zealand, some 12,000 improbable flying miles from Germany, had a phantom frenzy of its own – perhaps Zeppelins might frighten the sheep.

The bubble was pricked on 21 May when *Daily Mail* proprietor Lord Northcliffe wired an editorial from Berlin, warning of the harm done to Anglo-German relations by the panic and of 'the real danger' – the advanced building programme of the German Navy. 'Germans who have so long been accustomed to regard Great Britain as a model of deportment, poise and cool-headedness,' he snorted, 'are beginning to believe that England is becoming the home of mere nervous degenerates.'[9] Events suggest that Northcliffe was merely clearing the front page for more circulation-building headlines.

On 25 July 1909, Louis Bleriot's fragile monoplane flew from the Sangatte cliffs near Calais to Dover in thirty-seven minutes; the Frenchman won Northcliffe's £1,000 prize for the first man to cross the Channel by powered flight. H.G. Wells commented that, from a military standpoint, Britain was no longer 'an inaccessible island'. Northcliffe, echoing Wells, screamed from the front page of the *Mail*: 'England is no longer an island.' Just six years later the first Zeppelin raids launched against East Anglia would make the fictional terror of aerial bombardment a fact of war.

In the summer of 1914, the men of the Harman family took a holiday: John from the Chancery Bar, Charles on the Long Vacation from King's College, Cambridge, and Jack from the tea-trading business he had joined after school. Like so many young men keen to defend their country against invasion, he had also joined the Inns of Court OTC back in 1911, at the same time as he joined Rosslyn Park. Jack would shortly leave to work on the plantation in Ceylon and was discharged in May as he prepared to go overseas. This was a good chance to spend some time together; they decided to go salmon-fishing north of Trondheim in Norway.

The far north was wild and isolated, but the fishing was grand. The summer days were long as the sun shone well past midnight; further south, unknown to the Harman party, darkness was descending over the Continent. The Kaiser, also in Norway, cruising the fjords, steamed the imperial yacht back to the fatherland. In the days before wireless, there was no news, but local whispers of war somewhere in Europe gradually became a rumble. After the Balkan upheavals of the previous decade, however, this would hardly be remarkable. On 3 September, they came south to Bergen to catch the packet back to England. There they found that the Great War for Freedom with British, French and Russian empires ranged against Germany and Austria-Hungary was already a month old. Many of Jack's fellow Uppinghamians and Park-ites had volunteered in the first weeks of August; airman Charles Bayly had already been shot down behind enemy lines in Belgium.

As the Harmans re-crossed the North Sea, U-boats patrolled unseen below. Charles would not return for his second year at Cambridge but would go straight to the recruiting station and join the Middlesex Regiment. Jack felt he could not break his promise and was honour bound to sail for Ceylon. Surely this war would be over by Christmas and all would be right again? The two brothers parted. They would never see each other again.

When hostilities were declared, the Imperial German Army moved swiftly to impress the three DELAG commercial airships into its fleet. It stripped out the wicker seating to allow space for bombs and a primitive aiming device. Their first military missions supported the infantry, dropped bombs on strategic bridges and observed enemy movements. But low cruising altitudes and speeds made them easy targets for ground troops and artillery: three ships were quickly downed by the French and one by the Russians at Tannenberg on the Eastern Front. New ships raised their ceiling to 10,000ft and top speed to 63mph. Crew protection and safety improved, with the first fully enclosed gondola cabins slung from the hull. The navy expanded its fleet from a single airship and built its first base, at the remote northern coastal spot of Nordholz. Gigantic revolving sheds allowed take-off whatever the wind direction. More bases followed at Hamburg, Tondern and Hage and by late 1914 the navy's intention was clear: their Zeppelins would be used to cross the North Sea in daring raids on England.

Kaiser Wilhelm initially blocked all such plans. This was less about observing the 1899 Hague Convention, which had banned the 'dropping of projectiles or explosives from flying machines', than maintaining his standing within the royal family tree which spread its boughs from St Petersburg to Windsor. 'Oma' (grandma and queen) Victoria had died in his arms in 1901: he could condone the slaughter of Tommies by the thousand in France and Belgium but shuddered at the thought of bombing cousin George in Buckingham Palace, where he had so often stayed. Churchill, First Lord of the Admiralty, helped to change his mind by getting British retaliation in first; Royal Naval Air Service (RNAS) aircraft raids on the airship shed at Düsseldorf in October 1914 incinerated ZIX. November saw a daring strike on Friedrichshafen, the home of the Zeppelin Company. On Christmas Day seaplanes delivered incendiary gifts to the sheds near completion at Nordholz.

Home-front Britain braced itself for the onslaught with black-outs and mounting nervous excitement. Vera Brittain recorded in her December diary: 'It was just dark, and all the streets were dim, as London ever since the war began had been lighted as faintly as possible, for fear of Zeppelin raids. It was thrilling, intoxicating to walk down Regent Street amid the hurrying crowd.'[10]

On 9 January 1915, the Kaiser finally gave in to navy pressure and sanctioned attacks on the Thames estuary and east coast; by imperial edict, however, London was to stay untouched.

Bad weather was England's greatest ally in January. Airships were highly vulnerable: heavy rain and snow would saturate the outer envelope, adding tons of extra weight; ice on the propellers could fly off and puncture the bag and gas cells inside; strong headwinds halted progress and crosswinds could hurl airships way off their plotted path. But on 19/20 January, two Zeppelins crossed the North Sea with no opposition from intercepting aircraft. Blown off course from their Humberside target, they hastily unloaded their bombs over Great Yarmouth, Snettisham and King's Lynn in Norfolk, killing four civilians. The fears of H.G. Wells had been realised: destruction rained from the darkened skies and 'this island race' became the first in history to endure aerial attack. Germany was triumphant. The *Kölnische Zeitung* exulted:

> ... now the first Zeppelin has appeared in England and has extended its fiery greetings to our enemy. It has come to pass, that which the English have long feared and repeatedly have contemplated with terror. The most modern air weapon, a triumph of German inventiveness and the sole possession of the German military has shown itself capable of crossing the sea and carrying the war right to the sod of old England! ... This is the best way to shorten the war, and thereby in the end the most humane. Today we congratulate Count Zeppelin that he has lived to see this triumph, and we offer him thanks as a nation for having placed us in possession of so wonderful a weapon.[11]

Hysteria immediately resurfaced in the British press. This time the airships were indisputably real, so the press embellished its outrage with stories of German infiltrators and spies – mysterious 'men in black' – and invasion conspiracies. Reports from Snettisham told of two automobiles pacing the airship intruder, one to the right and one to the left, flashing their lights upwards or on to a significant landmark, such as the medieval church which indeed suffered some bomb damage.[12]

Britain's airborne defence was risible: at the outbreak of war the RFC had five squadrons, all sent to France with the BEF. The RNAS had more aircraft but its early role was fleet reconnaissance, patrolling coasts for enemy ships and submarines, attacking German coastal territory and (in theory) defending England from air raids. But no British aircraft was equipped for night fighting or capable of reaching a Zeppelin flying at 10,000ft.

There is nothing like a crisis for bringing out the worst in British military politics. The air defence of the realm was dogged by inter-service rivalry between RFC and RNAS. Competition for aircraft and engines, and the critical problem of wartime production was addressed by the creation of an Air Board; successive versions under different chairmen (the last being Northcliffe's brother, Lord Rothermere) failed to solve the worsening problem of supplying both RFC and RNAS. So much so that cab drivers nicknamed its Hotel Cecil headquarters 'Bolo House', after a conman executed as a traitor by the French. 'Everybody there was either actively inter-fering with the progress of the war, or doing little to help while championing their own cause.'[13]

It was not until 17 May 1915 that a searchlight first picked out a raider and an RNAS pilot actually saw a Zeppelin, *LZ38*, which easily out-climbed him. Top-secret reports to the Admiralty, stolen and smuggled to Berlin, must have delighted the German command. The hard-pressed Kaiser now reluctantly sanctioned raids on East London – but only as far as the Tower.

On 31 May *LZ38*, captained by Hauptmann Erich Linnarz, again reached London on a moonless night. Twelve anti-aircraft guns and twelve searchlights defended the whole capital; not one of them located the invader. Fifteen RNAS planes took off; only one saw *LZ38*, but was forced to land with engine trouble. Shortly after 11 p.m. Linnarz dropped 3,000lb of bombs over twenty minutes on a meandering line from Stoke Newington to Stepney; the lack of precise navigation meant that the Zeppelin bombing was almost random. It was not military or industrial targets that took the brunt, but unsuspecting civilians; London had no public or private shelters. The charred bodies of Henry and Caroline Good of 187 Balls Pond Road were found kneeling next to the bed in prayer.

Once again, newspapers revelled in the circulation boost provided by the menace from the skies; this was more gripping than dreary casualty lists from Gallipoli and Ypres. Both the *Daily News* and the *Chronicle* seized the moment by offering new subscribers free insurance cover 'against the risks of bombardment by Zeppelin or aeroplane'. Sir Edward Henry, Metropolitan Police Commissioner, helpfully advised in a subscription leaflet that an air raid 'will take place at a time when most people are in bed' and, with patrician insight into how the other half lived, gave some practical advice: '... in many houses there are no facilities for procuring water on the upper floors. It is suggested therefore that a supply of water and sand might be kept there, so that any fire breaking out on a small scale can at once be dealt with.'[14]

The Zeppelins had truly brought the war to the home front with incendiary effect. William Shepherd, a visiting American, reported: 'suddenly you realise that the biggest city in the world has become the night battlefield on which seven million harmless men, women and children live.'[15] Linnarz had enjoyed free passage over London: he had killed seven civilians, dropped 121 bombs and departed without a shot fired in return; East Londoners reacted angrily, with violent attacks on storefronts carrying German names. A June raid on Hull left twenty-four dead; there was 'pandemonium and panic'[16] and more fury directed at German shops. Many poorer people refused to stay in the defenceless town at night and slept in the fields; others vented their anger by stoning RFC vehicles in Hull and mobbing a flying office in nearby Beverly.

Public outrage at ineffectual defence mingled with private fascination at the spectacle. Shepherd, standing on Fleet Street, waxed poetically:

Traffic is at a standstill. A million quiet cries make a subdued roar. People stand gazing into the sky from the darkened streets. Among the autumn stars floats a long, gaunt Zeppelin. It is dull yellow – the colour of the harvest moon. The long fingers of searchlights, reaching up from the roofs of the city are touching all sides of the death messenger with their white tips.[17]

For the villages of the eastern counties a Zeppelin was, quite literally, the biggest thing ever to hit town. The church of St John the Evangelist in Washingborough, Lincolnshire, has an incongruous stained-glass window recalling the visit of a Zeppelin, which dropped its bombs harmlessly in a field. The only casualties came the next day when hundreds of sightseers walked from Lincoln and overloaded the small river ferry which overturned, drowning a man and a small boy.

By September, raiders over London flew low enough to be seen at Vera Brittain's hospital: 'All the patients sat in their windows watching one of the Zeppelins, which looked like a great silver cigar in a luminous cloud … the streets were full of excited semi-dressed people whom a policeman was vainly trying to keep quiet.'[18]

Lady Cynthia, daughter-in-law of Prime Minister Asquith, wrote in her diary: 'Zeppelin attack on London occurred in the night. Mamma came up and told me. I was horrified at the idea of having slept through it.'[19] On another occasion: 'some men there said they saw the Zeppelin, Alas I didn't! But our guns were popping away and shells bursting in the air. I felt pleasurably, but not the faintest tremor and I longed and longed for more to happen.'[20] Lady Cynthia would presumably have been first in line for one of the special 'Zepp nighties' offered by one London store.

This taste of war proved a vicarious thrill for those insulated from the horrors of the trenches, although the sensible kept it in perspective. Marjorie Secretan wrote to her fiancé at the front on 9 September:

Talk of you running into danger in the trenches. Read this evening's paper and see how a Zep visited Waltham and dropped bombs. Think of two maidens returning by a late train, hearing a noise, and looking out of the window and there, like the Ghost Ship 'sailing comfortably over the stars' was a fine fat Zeppelin. Soon – Crash! Crash! and we caught a glimpse of falling bombs, our heads thrust out of the window. Then, splash! one fell into the river quite close at hand as well. The [River] Lea water does not improve coats and skirts and Olive says we shall send in the bill to the Kaiser! The damages were – so they say – two men killed and two poor old women died of fright.[21]

She wrote the next day with heavier irony, 'WHY GO TO WAR? Stay in beautiful London: AIR RAIDS DAILY. Fine views of Zeps in action. Bombs dropped in all quarters. Numberless casualties and all without crossing the Channel!' With an unwavering ability to find a silver lining in this dark cloud over England, recruiting posters urged: 'It is far better to face the bullets than to be killed at home by a bomb. Join the Army at once and help to stop an Air Raid. God save the King.'

That summer, John Harman returned from Ceylon to the family home, now in Onslow Square, with the intention of volunteering. He found London in a state of alarm at the raids, but needed no recruitment poster to convince him. He had peacetime military training in the OTCs at Uppingham and the Inns of Court; in wartime Ceylon he had trained with the Planters Rifle Corps. The rugby forward was ready for the scrum. In July he applied for a commission in the Army Service Corps (ASC), the transport arm, and his good moral character (if not glowing academic record) was attested by Henry McKenzie, headmaster of Uppingham, who certified: '[He] has attained a good standard of education by the time he left Uppingham School in subjects necessary for an Army exam. He was in our 2nd Army Class.'[22] Harman reported for duty at Aldershot on 16 August 1915.

In September he boarded the ill-named HMS *Terrible* at Portsmouth, bound for Gallipoli. By the time he arrived in October, brother Charles had been captured at Loos and would remain a prisoner of war until 1918. (He occupied himself by learning French, Italian and Russian). John's service record shows him leaving Gallipoli in February 1916 – the very last of the orderly evacuation – for Egypt and Abbassia Barracks, a large training centre on the outskirts of Cairo. In May he drove 100 miles to Kantara (*al Qantarah*), site of repeated battles for control of the Suez Canal.

A massive distribution warehouse and hospital centre was located in the town. The ASC's role – now called logistics – was vital.

By June, Harman was off to Salonika, where he spent seven months before returning to Egypt 'for transfer to the Royal Flying Corps'. He began his instruction in 1 March 1917, seven days before Ferdinand von Zeppelin died – condemned as a 'perverted genius' by one English newspaper obituary. Shuttling between Abbassia, Suez and Aboukir for his three months' training, Harman won his wings and 'passage was applied for to return to the Home Establishment'.[23] In June he boarded the HT *Saxon* at Alexandria bound for Marseilles.

He stopped briefly in London to see his parents and hear news of Charles in captivity. After his privations overseas, he packed more than the average soldier's kitbag; the list of personal effects returned after his death runs to a page and includes '12 shirts, 41 collars, 4 pipes, 13 pairs socks ... one tin–opener, one tin & contents ... one double-barreled shotgun and one Webley & Scott revolver'.[24] Then he took a cab from Onslow Square to King's Cross, pausing only at Maull & Fox Photographers, Piccadilly, for his formal portrait in uniform, before boarding the train to Lincolnshire to join his new RFC Home Defence Squadron.

The pressing need for well-equipped home defence had been prompted by growing public anger and the plunging national morale that German Navy chiefs had anticipated. Air raids were relatively infrequent but now diverted men, planes and guns from the Western Front; by the close of 1916, 17,341 officers and men and 12 squadrons (110 planes) were retained for home defence. But the legacy of pre-war indecision and continued inter-service disputes meant that the tools for defence were not combat-ready. A lingering British disdain for machines over the valour of men also played its part, just as Captain Scott spurned the use of dogs, preferring 'the height of that fine conception which is realised when a party of men go forth to face hardships, dangers and difficulties with their own unaided efforts ... the conquest is more nobly and splendidly won'.[25] This had contributed to the slow introduction of the machine gun to the trenches: while perfectly acceptable for slaughtering wild-eyed natives in colonial insurgencies, it was deemed that the machine gun was inappropriate for 'civilised' European warfare. Mr Gatling's invention, it seemed, was not for gentlemen, although it was devastatingly good enough for Germany. As was the super weapon created by Count von Zeppelin.

Failure by the RNAS to prevent bombing raids led to the RFC taking responsibility for home air defence in February 1916. No. 33 Squadron was the first of three to be formed in Lincolnshire to counter the Zeppelins which, like the later Luftwaffe, would cross the coast between the landmarks of the Humber and the Wash. As well as its strategic location, Lincolnshire had its Edge, a high limestone escarpment running along the line of the Trent Valley. The sudden rise from 20ft to 200ft above sea level gave extra lift for aircraft; the RFC built its airfields along the Edge, stationing 33 Squadron at Elsham Wolds, Kirton-in-Lindsey and Brattleby (now RAF Scampton), with its HQ and workshops at Gainsborough.

Before 1916 home defence squadrons were equipped with obsolete and cast-off aircraft types which were not wanted at the Western Front. These were gradually replaced by the modern BE2c, designed and built by the government-owned Royal Aircraft Factory at Farnborough and produced in large numbers. Produced to a specification for a stable airplane free of difficult handling characteristics, the BE2c was indeed so stable it could not manoeuvre rapidly in front-line dogfights. This hardly mattered in Lincolnshire and the stability was ideal for night flying and training. But it was not fit for its air-defence purpose: the combination of a low-performance engine and high-drag airframe meant the aircraft was incapable of reaching Zeppelin cruising altitude. Even if it did, the raider usually had enough time to deliver its payload and depart before being sighted.

British inventors had at least been working on a better bullet. The Zeppelin's internal gas cells inside a larger envelope confounded the munitions men: anti-aircraft shells and Lewis gun bullets might puncture the gasbags, but did not ignite the highly flammable hydrogen. New explosive bullets were designed by John Pomeroy and Royal Navy Commander Frank Brock (of the firework family), whom we shall meet later at Zeebrugge. It was these, fired from the machine gun of 19-year-old 2/Lt William Leefe Robinson, that made him a hero overnight on 3 September, when he shot down the first airship (not strictly a Zeppelin, but a Schutte-Lanz) at Cuffley, Hertfordshire. Thousands watched as one of King George's men finally slew a flaming dragon and earned the adoration of a nation – and a Victoria Cross from the grateful monarch. Nine-year-old H.G. Castle witnessed the death throes of *SL11* and the wild celebrations: 'The spontaneous barrage of cheering and shouting made the roar of a hundred thousand people at a pre-war cup final sound like an undertone. People danced, kissed, hugged and sang ... The crowd reaction everywhere was described as being greater than that which celebrated the relief of Mafeking.'[26]

The loss of life and dull stalemate on the Somme and Jellicoe's failure to make Jutland a new Trafalgar no longer mattered: England was winning the war where it mattered to the baying crowd – with a home victory on London's back doorstep. Come on, England!

Three more Zeppelin kills were swiftly notched. Such was the anxiety of Britain under the aerial bombs that even George Bernard Shaw was cheered (not without guilt) by the fiery death of *L31*:

> ... after seeing the Zepp fall like a burning newspaper, with its human contents roasting for some minutes ... I went to bed and was comfortably asleep in ten minutes. One is so pleased at having seen the show that the destruction of a dozen people or so in hideous terror and torment does not count.[27]

At the front they were less impressed: Philip Dodgson, a Royal Fleet Auxiliary (RFA) officer, wrote to his sweetheart:

> The British Nation seems to be quite unbalanced as far as Zeppelins are concerned. To a casual reader of the papers it would seem that the destruction of one Zeppelin was of more importance than everything else put together. I suppose it is natural as it is only by reason of the Zeppelins that large numbers realize there is a war at all. When it comes to spending hundreds of pounds on a memorial of the spot where the Zeppelin was brought down it is getting rather absurd. It is bad enough giving the man who brings the thing down money, especially as he also got the VC.

What about the airmen out here who run greater risks almost every day?[28]

The Zeppelin builders redoubled efforts to stay ahead of the chasing pack. The new British bullets and higher-performance aircraft meant that the only defence was to climb where they could not follow. A new generation of Super Zeppelins, known as Height Climbers, could routinely fly at 15,000ft and even reached 21,000ft. This made life for the crews even less pleasant: two dozen deaths were caused by heart attacks brought on by cold and oxygen starvation. Altitude sickness would render crews unfit for duty for a week after a mission; gunners and navigators were often found unconscious, with oxygen masks that either failed or poisoned them. The Maybachs required constant attention: a stopped engine would freeze solid in minutes. Even the consolation of a cigarette, which sustained the ground troops through the terrors of the trench, was denied to Zeppelin crews in their combustible clouds of hydrogen – on penalty of death.

In September 1917, the BE2 was replaced by the FE2 – the 'Flying Experimental' or more fondly, the 'Fee'. Also produced by Farnborough at a cost of £1,521 13s 4d (cost of airframe, less engine, guns and instruments), 1,939 were built of which 213 were allocated to home defence units.[29] The FE2 was underpowered by the otherwise reliable 120hp Beardmore engine and a more powerful 160hp version was fitted to later machines. This proved somewhat recalcitrant and engine trouble caused many forced landings.

On the night of 19 October 1917, Lieutenant John Harman would be cruelly frustrated by the failings of his 'Fee'. It was the night of the biggest raid that year with eleven Zeppelins seeking targets in the industrial cities of the north and midlands. As he patted his gun drums, loaded with alternate Pomeroys and Brocks, and taxied for take-off, he felt on his cheek the brief kiss of heat from the flares that marked the airstrip. The 24-year-old shivered with excitement: this was his chance for glory, just like Leefe Robinson VC.

He took off from Kirton-in-Lindsey at 8 p.m., as pilot of FE2d *A6375* with First Airman Booth as his observer. Just forty minutes later he had to return with engine trouble. Of four planes from

B Flight that took off that evening, three had the same problem. The
fourth searched the skies for over two hours but had to land at Elsham
due to fuel shortage. An FE2b crashed at Gainsborough, killing the
New Zealand pilot Harry Solomon: one theory had it that his bulky
thigh-length boots had fouled the controls. The energetic Squadron
Commander Thomson flew three sorties in his single-seater and
visited all three flights. Inspired by his example and determined to
see some action against the Zepps, Harman went out again later that
same night with Lieutenant Stevenson in *B1884*, taking off at 1 a.m.
for a fruitless fifty-minute patrol.[30] By that time it was too late: high-
altitude gales had swept the Zeppelins helplessly southwards towards
London, which experienced its first airship attack in more than a year.

The huge raid was disastrous for both sides: headwinds scattered the attackers and five airships were destroyed over France
and beyond on their run for home. As the Zeppelins had flown so
high, only two home defence night-fighters managed to climb high
enough to engage them despite seventy-eight sorties flown. The
great height and windy conditions so muffled the droning engines
that this was later christened the 'silent raid'. Ground mist blanketed
the defenders. Unable to hear any noise, they covered searchlights in
the suburbs and halted AA gun barrages to avoid attracting the raiders to the capital. The deadly 660lb blockbuster that hit Piccadilly
Circus squarely at 11.30 p.m. dropped from the moonless night
entirely without warning; twenty-five people in the crowd milling
around the 'heart of empire' were cut down by flying shrapnel and
glass. Seven died, including three soldiers on leave, and a woman
who could only later be identified by her clothes and jewellery.[31]
Rosslyn Park's AGM the next evening decamped from Carr's to the
relative safety of the Richmond clubhouse. Total casualties of the
raid were thirty-six deaths and fifty-five injuries.

Public outcry was immediate. Where were the home defence
squadrons? It emerged that of 229 aircraft available, 110 were inadequate older models and only seventy-two efficient machines
were serviceable. Further modifications were made to the 'Flying
Experimental' in a desperate attempt to raise its operating ceiling.
The gaping forward cockpit, which created huge drag, was covered
with fabric or a plywood fairing. Without a gunner, a solo pilot

also made for a lighter plane; trials were made with dual-mounted Lewis guns to maintain firepower. But despite this tinkering, the FE2b could still only reach a ceiling of 17,000ft after a considerable time – little use against Height Climbers. October saw the last of the big airship raids, but Jack Harman and the RFC were not to know that. The 'silent raid' had shown that engine noise would not always advertise the Zeppelins' presence: 33 Squadron crews at Brattleby, who had been standing by awaiting orders, were amazed when two bombs from the silent and unseen *L41* suddenly exploded just a few hundred yards away from their twinkling flare path.

On the night of 17 November, Harman took off again on patrol in one of the troubled FE2bs, *B416*. He flew alone in this newly modified single-seater: an experienced pilot, he would hardly need night-flying training and he carried no observer for instruction. To have any chance of intercepting the inaudible high-flying airships, he would need to start his own climb early, so he circled steadily into the towering darkness.

At night a pilot relied on his sense of balance, which could often mislead. A slight banking turn, for example, could cause sufficient G-force to give the impression that he was flying straight and level. Under those circumstances, it was dangerously easy to stall the aircraft, which often led to an uncontrollable spin with little chance of recovery. Jack Harman was never to return to base that night: he crashed at Hibaldstow, a few miles to the north-east.

A terse telegram from Gainsborough addressed to 'Adastral One London' – RFC HQ at the requisitioned Hotel De Keyser by Blackfriars Bridge – was received at West Strand at 11.50 a.m. on 18 November. Machine and engine specification seem of greater concern than an expendable human pilot: 'CC2 18/11/1917 FE2B B416 with 160 HW Beardmore 9604 pilot Lt J A Harman killed – observer nil – next of kin father JE Harman – caused while night flying at 630pm last night – investigation by accident committee not necessary – Aeronautics 33 Gainsboro.'[32]

Strangely, despite the recommendation, a Court of Inquiry was nonetheless held nine days after his death, and found that the aircraft and engine were in satisfactory condition and that, without evidence of failure in either, pilot error was the most likely cause of the accident. *Flight* magazine reported the funeral (and the official verdict of 'flying accident') on 13 December:

> Amidst every token of sympathy the funeral took place at Gainsborough Cemetery, Lincolnshire, of Lieutenant JOHN AUGUSTUS HARMAN, R.F.C., who was accidentally killed whilst flying in Lincolnshire (where he was stationed and had a host of friends), at the early age of 24 … The funeral was fully military, and started from the headquarters of the 33rd Squadron R.F.C., Lincoln.[33]

Harman's family attended as the 'coffin, draped with the Union Jack, was borne to the grave by six officers of the R.F.C., and a large contingent of the R.F.C. followed in the funeral train. The firing party was furnished by the North Staffords, and the customary three volleys were fired over the grave, the buglers sounding the Last Post.'[34]

The funeral expense of 10 guineas was added to his unpaid mess bill and his bereaved father was requested to certify that he would 'pay all outstanding debts incurred by the deceased'. In the same churchyard, 33 Squadron buried its own international brigade of three Canadians, two New Zealanders, one South African and one Argentine. Other Englishmen returned in death to their home towns; Jack stayed with his comrades, where he fell to earth.

The salmon-hunting trio of summer 1914 would never land another fish. The story handed down in the Harman family is that 'Uncle Jack's plane broke up in the air before he could reach the Zeppelin'. We know now there was no Zeppelin that night. At the time, could Harman and the home defence fliers of 33 Squadron on patrol have been sure? For a War Office under severe public pressure over its repeated inability to repel raiders, a 'flying accident' was an expedient explanation. It was unpalatable to admit that military aircraft, produced at a government-owned factory, were simply not good enough, that young pilots were being sent up to almost certain death and that, as a result, England's citizens were effectively defenceless. The official record is as silent as the pilot: John Harman, 'eldest and dearly loved son', lies under a Celtic cross in Gainsborough General Cemetery and keeps his own counsel.

London survived the Zeppelin threat, as it later did the Blitz, battered but with morale intact. A love-hate relationship had developed with the majestic silver airships, which would find a curious echo some ninety years later: a German company, DZR GmbH, announced in 2008 that it would offer 'London Zeppelin Experience' flights over the capital from Upminster. The new Zeppelin *NT07* would be sponsored by a reassuringly expensive Belgian beer.

DENIS MONAGHAN &
J.J. CONILH DE BEYSSAC
TIN CAN ALLIES

Left: Captain Denis Laurence Monaghan, in the uniform of the Heavy Machine Gun Corps.
Right: De Beyssac (right) smiling with the ANZAC team pack. *(BNF)*

On earth as in heaven, both sides worshipped technology to gain advantage. German airships had carried destruction from the battlefield to civilians at home. Gotha bombers followed, their outstretched wings foreshadowing future raids on London and Berlin. Another new machine, which would indelibly mark the next war, was born directly from the Western Front: after the airship came the 'landship'.

Legions of men, few of them wholly intact, lay in mass graves as proof (far from living) that fragile bone and flesh are no match for high explosives, bullets and barbed wire. One man observed from a unique position: Lt Colonel Ernest Dunlop Swinton DSO, a Royal Engineer decorated in the Boer War, had been appointed by Kitchener as the army's official war reporter in 1914. On the strength of his history of the Russo-Japanese War and a novel, *The Defence of Duffer's Drift* (published under the pseudonym Backsight Forethought), his military writing skills were preferred to the reportage of Fleet Street's finest, who were banned from the front line.

Firmly within the chain of command, not the Fourth Estate, Swinton was given strict orders: no mention of place names or units and to write about 'what he thought was true, not what he knew to be true'. No article would be published if it indicated that he had actually seen what he had written about. His reports were first censored at GHQ in France and then personally vetted by Kitchener before their release under the laughable byline, 'Eyewitness'. In his later book, he wrote:

> The principle which guided me in my work was above all to avoid helping the enemy. They appeared to me even more important than the purveyance of news to our own people. For home consumption – that is for those who were carrying the burden and footing the bill – I essayed to tell as much of the truth as was compatible with safety, to guard against depression and pessimism, and to check unjustified optimism which might lead to a relaxation of effort.[1]

Whatever the principles behind his propaganda, he was honest enough about the 'formidable enemy, well trained, long prepared and brave' and supported his Lordship's assertion to Cabinet that Britain must be prepared to put millions in the field for several years. Swinton saw the devastating effect of machine-gun fire on infantrymen advancing across open ground – he first coined the telling phrase 'no-man's-land'. Constrained in his ability to report the awful mismatch of Churchill's 'bare chests versus machine guns', he pondered instead devices to protect man and counteract Maxim and *Maschinengewehr*.

Inspiration struck while he was driving in France. He noticed artillery tractors lugging heavy ordnance slowly but surely across broken roads. He had a vision of new 'petrol tractors on the caterpillar principle and armoured with hardened steel plates'. They would be both protective shield for foot soldiers and mobile gun platform. His idea was initially rejected: Sir John French exhibited similar Luddite tendencies towards aeroplanes before his Damascene conversion to aerial reconnaissance.

On Boxing Day 1914, Colonel Maurice Hankey, Secretary for the Committee for Imperial Defence, cheered Swinton with a supportive memorandum headed 'Special Devices'. First Sea Lord Churchill was even more enthusiastic. His navy had already used armoured cars in Belgium to protect airstrips from attack, so he set up the 'Landships Committee' in February 1915. After the Gallipoli debacle, neither his influence nor the 'landship' name would last. Development of these metal boxes on tracks was nevertheless encouraged by the Army, perhaps most surprisingly by Haig, a man vilified for anything from needless waste of lives to nostalgia for obsolete cavalry warfare. But the idea needed populist branding, akin to the 'Zep' which so fired the public imagination despite its 'baby-killing' notoriety. Swinton later wrote, 'we rejected in turn – container – receptacle – reservoir – cistern. The monosyllable Tank appealed to us as being likely to catch on and be remembered.' Likely indeed.

The Admiralty and the Army again did their best not to collaborate. But in a rare British moment, two military committees – Landships and the newly formed Inventions Committee – agreed with each other on specifications for Swinton's new beast. This should, they declared, have a top speed of 4mph on level ground and be able to turn sharply, as well as reverse. It must also climb a 5ft earth parapet and cross an 8ft trench with ten crew, two machine guns, a 2lb gun and everything they would need for a day's fighting. The brief was entrusted to Lieutenant Walter Wilson RNAS, a successful automobile engineer before the war, and William Tritton of William Foster & Co. Ltd of Lincoln. On 11 September 1915, they demonstrated the first prototype, nicknamed *Little Willie* (no surprise, coming from two Williams and a Wilson), to Swinton's committee.

Little Willie did not quite make the specified grade: he could only carry three crewmen at 3mph (or just 2mph over rough terrain) and could not cross trenches. But on 2 February 1916, the second prototype, *Mother*, soon to become a rhomboid sibling known as *Big Willie*, was presented as the first combat tank in a secret trial on the Duke of Salisbury's golf course at Hatfield Park. He was watched over the bunkers and greens by the big guns of government: Lord Kitchener, Chancellor McKenna and Lloyd George, then Minister for Munitions. He recalled the 'feeling of delight with which I saw for the first time the ungainly monster plough through thick entanglements, wallow through deep mud and heave its huge bulk over parapets and across trenches. At last, I thought, we have the answer to the German machine-guns and wire'.[2] Kitchener provocatively described the tank as a 'pretty mechanical toy but without serious military value', but *Big Willie* passed his audition and Lloyd George ordered 100 of the Mark 1 model into production.

The French had their own Swinton – artillery colonel Jean-Baptiste Estienne. He had visited Peoria, Illinois, to study the American Holt Company's 'Baby Holt' that utilised a distinct tractor and chassis assembly. The resulting French design was termed a *tracteur blindé et armé* (armoured and armed). Understandably keen to sell his idea, the Frenchman naturally chose a name with more *élan* – invoking war chariots rather than water-carriers – and urged his *char d'assault* on Joffre. Orders were placed for 400 each from the Schneider and St Chamond factories, at a cost of 56,000 francs apiece. They would not be the best investment.

The British, with hardware in production, began writing the software. Swinton started work on the manuals and doctrine for fighting with his new machine. No simple task, 'as the tactics had to be decided upon with no realistic experimentation as ground work; and moreover, with the very difficult task of working in concert with other arms of the Service that had had two years of fighting'.[3] Special crews needed to be recruited and trained for the mystery weapon. A 'Strictly Secret and Confidential' War Office Order stated: 'Volunteers are required for an exceedingly dangerous and hazardous duty of secret nature. Officers who have been awarded decorations for bravery, and are experienced in the handling of men and with an engineering background, should have their names submitted to this office.'

They reported to 'Siberia Farm' (the eastern end of Bisley Camp) for duty with the Heavy Section Machine Gun Corps (MGC). This unit name drew a veil of secrecy over the mystery weapon.

The adjacent training school of the Motor Machine Gun Service provided officers and men, as did the RNAS, Army Service Corps drivers and fresh recruits drawn from the civilian motor trade. The stipulated 'mechanical experience' attracted a motley crew including agricultural workers and men with interesting crime sheets. Such a polyglot crew spurned regimental trappings for the spirit of specialists, drawn together for fighting purposes not parade-ground pomp. They were multi-disciplined; each man trained to perform 'every duty which he might be called upon to carry out'. They could hardly, however, be termed an elite. One unofficial flag flew the skull and crossbones until they were granted corps status by the king in 1917, and a later commander would refer to them as a 'band of brigands'.

Briefing was patchy: one man recalled 'all officers and some 300 men underwent a machine-gun course, but no one was shown a tank'. They finally encountered the real thing in June, at Lord Iveagh's Elveden estate near Thetford, where the locals had been evacuated. They trained inside a perimeter guarded by cavalry and Indian units. The black cloak of censorship descended, leave passes from the 'Elveden Explosives Area' were unknown, and even his Lordship was in the dark in his own house. A Royal Academician was commissioned to disguise the 'gigantic cubist steel slug' (Swinton's words) with camouflage dazzle patterns of pink and green. The visiting Estienne was accorded a glimpse; he urged that the Allies' programmes be synchronised for the greatest impact on launch.

Conditions inside were daunting for the trainees. The six-cylinder Daimler engine, open for easier lubrication and revving at 1,000rpm took up much of the interior. The cramped space was occupied by eight men: the commander and gearsman at the front; four loading and firing the guns; and two brakemen at the rear. Vibration was bone-jarring and the lurching motion carried the danger of being hurled against the engine's exposed moving parts. Prototypes were too precious to risk against real bullets in Norfolk; under fire in battle the noise was 'like fifty hailstorms on one corrugated iron shed'. The heat and fumes were overpowering: carbon monoxide caused vomiting, collapse and convulsion.

Summer temperatures inside the closed cauldron reached 125°F. Clothing was not designed for comfort. They wore leather jerkins over their uniforms, but abandoned padded leather 'anti-bruise' helmets like scrumcaps in favour of goggles and chain-mail masks. These shielded the face and eyes against the 'splash' of molten lead and the flaking of tiny metal fragments from the inner hull (known as spalling) when bullets struck the outer plating – a lethal echo of the oak splinters that speared sailors in men-o'-war.

These dangers lay in wait for 28-year-old Lieutenant Denis Laurence Monaghan. Born in Stroud where his father ran a high-street outfitters and yet another Uppingham boy, Monaghan was a flying three-quarter for Rosslyn Park from 1909 to 1912, scoring at will through interceptions against Blackheath or from the halfway line against Old Leysians (Nowell Oxland threaded the white needle with the kick). He was good enough to represent Middlesex on the wing, and enjoyed two Easter tours to Wales with the Barbarians, in the exalted company of internationals. At the outbreak, he dashed to join the Artists' Rifles as Private 2233, before commissioning as a second lieutenant in the Royal Irish Rifles in October.

He went into theatre in France as a lieutenant seven days before Christmas 1915 and endured the bitterest winter. In the culling of subalterns on the first day of the Somme he was wounded at Thiepval. The Irish Rifles' Service battalions fought in the independently minded 36th (Ulster) Division of Protestant volunteers. On the anniversary of the Battle of the Boyne,[4] they set off without waiting for the barrage to lift, ignored General Rawlinson's standing orders to walk line abreast and rushed the Schwaben Redoubt. It was the only division to take its objectives that day, but in so doing lost half its strength, including the wounded Monaghan. It was back to Blighty for him, for repairs and rehabilitation.

The British 'hush-hushes' were now in France, but no tank had yet faced the enemy. They were instead occupied with endless show demonstrations for curious brass hats, dignitaries and the Prince of Wales, who witnessed the 'land submarines' near Amiens and judged them 'nice toys worth trying'. The specialist crews succumbed to the ceremonial spit and polish of a peacetime infantry regiment.

The Somme campaign thrashed on relentlessly in offensive spasms. Some ten weeks after Denis Monaghan's wounding, the new wonder weapon was deployed prematurely in an attempt to break the stalemate. Despite Swinton's entreaty not to use tanks in 'driblets', staff brass insisted that the secret could not be contained and was best launched before enemy spies and German inventors conspired with counter-measures. The ungainly toddler took its first steps into battle at Flers-Courcelette on 15 September 1916, the midpoint of the war.

The first tank into action, Captain Harold Mortimore's D.1 *Daredevil*, cleared an enemy trench, but was then disabled by a shell. The manicured fairways and greens of Elveden were no preparation for the moonscape of craters between Albert and Bapaume. Of the next six tanks, three were bogged down, one had engine seizure, but two moved ahead supporting the infantry advance. Shortly afterwards thirty-six tanks attacked Flers, 'frightening the Jerries out of their wits and making them scuttle like frightened rabbits'. Rifle rounds bounced off the steel hulls.

Tanks were unpopular with the infantry. They had not trained with them and quickly realised they were a magnet for artillery fire and the last place to seek cover. But the immediate effect on enemy morale was just as Haig had hoped. One German infantry-man recalled:

Panic spread like an electric current passing from man to man along the trench. As the churning tracks reared overhead, the bravest men clambered above ground to launch suicidal coun-ter-attacks, hurling grenades onto the tanks' roofs or shooting and stabbing at any vision slots within reach. They were shot down or crushed while others threw up their hands in terrified surrender or bolted down the communication trenches towards the second line.[5]

The panic was short lived and the resilient Germans soon treated tanks as a target like any other. Their use of armour-piercing bul-lets, designed to penetrate sniper shields, was proof to some that the 'hushes' had been betrayed. Tank commander Basil Henriques railed later: 'If we only had a little more sleep and a little less showing off, what a marvellous story this Somme battle might have been. As it was this precious secret was out, and our own infantry hated us ...'[6] But once again it was less down to military intelligence and more to German flair for effective counter-attack. There was no breakthrough: yet again, the cavalry were stood down and the battle was called off.

Although impact at Flers was fleeting, the newly unveiled weapon had an electrifying effect on the British public at home, which now lauded an invention to rival the Zeppelin overhead. Tanks were hailed in the press as Leviathan and Behemoth and – in a single *Times* paragraph – portrayed as a 'buffalo ringed with wolves' and a 'bear worried by terriers'.[7] Politicians fought to take the credit: Churchill was championed by the *Daily Sketch* as 'The man who made the tanks' and then lambasted by the Haig-ophantic *Mail* for his self-publicising. The first photograph of a 'galumphant' tank appeared in the *Daily Mirror* in November. By Christmas a clockwork toy was on sale at Selfridges and tank teapots to piggybanks were much in demand.

Geoffrey Malins' film of the first days on the Somme, released in August, had drawn moving-picture-goers in their millions (including American-born Sir Hiram Maxim and his good lady wife, brazenly admiring the handiwork which had brought him riches and a knighthood from the English). Houses were packed for the sequel, with audiences cheering their first sight of the 'land Dreadnoughts'. King George visited a Tankodrome (hi-tech jargon for the new age) and accepted a painting of a tank – like a prize racehorse – from his loyal subject, Mr Alfred Pearse. The morale-boosting effect at home was inversely proportional to the mood of the fighting troops who had to live with the unwieldy, temperamental and downright dangerous technology.

Nevertheless, the tank's biggest fan was General Haig, keen to salvage any positives from the Somme abattoir. He ordered a thousand more for 1917 (1,277 were eventually produced with new factories in Glasgow and Newcastle coming on stream). The 28-ton Mark IV had two variants: a 'male' armed with 6-pounder cannon; and a 'female' with Lewis or Hotchkiss machine guns to protect the male from infantry attack. Armour plating was thickened to counter the piercing bullets. The production ratio was two female to one male (lucky *Willie*), but the landship, like her maritime forebears, was always a 'she'. Crews fondly named their tanks: Monaghan's I Battalion had rugged names like *Indomitable* or *Invincible*, while dry soldierly wit triumphed in F Battalion's bully-beef can *Fray Bentos*. C Battalion ran through the *carte des boissons* from Chartreuse to

Crème de Menthe; the ' Cocktail Boys' fielded their own 'Tanks' rugby XV against 'France' in February 1918, losing narrowly to a team led by French international skipper and air ace Maurice Boyau.

After its early haphazard recruiting, the Heavy Section cleaned up its act. A new cap badge was designed. It left the borrowed Norfolk estate and set up camp near Wool in Dorset, where crews were trained before transferring to the tank depot at Bermicourt in France. Its specialist crews were bolstered by men with experience from the front. An active interest in combative sports was encouraged to build fitness and the necessary 'offensiveness'. Richard Haigh was honest about its appeal after life in the infantry:

> … not that death is less likely in a tank, but there seems to be a more sporting chance with a shell than with a bullet. The enemy infantryman looks along his sight and he has you for a certainty, but the gunner cannot be so accurate and twenty yards may mean a world of difference. Above all, the new monster had our imaginations in thrall. Here were novelty and wonderful developments.[8]

Recovered from his wound, Monaghan saw the call for men of 'an engineering background' for hazardous duty. He had graduated in engineering from University College London and was a civil engineer before the war. In the eyes of the tank recruiters, he had put his body on the line as a Barbarian in Wales and with the BEF in France – this rugby-playing officer, with his wound stripe on his sleeve, ticked every box. Most of his former Royal Irish comrades were mouldering in the Schwaben Redoubt, so there were few voices to call him back to the infantry.

Monaghan, promoted to captain in January 1917 (as Haig was to field marshal), is photographed in his new uniform with its crossed Vickers guns and crown. After his clean-shaven playing days at Rosslyn Park he now sports a trim moustache. Soldiers of all ranks were originally required to have moustaches, but were forbidden beards. In April 1915, a Routine Order noted – in an impressive wartime display of missing the point – that King's Regulations regarding shaving of the upper lip were being disregarded and that future offenders would be severely punished. Some were simply too young to sprout facial hair – he who drafts a regulation that stimulates male hair growth will be a magician of incalculable wealth. Some pointed out that this was a rum do when the king had a beard and the Prince of Wales was clean shaven. Shortly afterwards the regulation was withdrawn.

Another Rosslyn Park rugby player in France took a shine to tin-can fighting. Jean Jacques Conilh de Beyssac, born in Caudéran, Gironde, in 1890 into a family descended from one of Napoleon's generals, was no engineering graduate but a philosophy student at Bordeaux. He played lock and prop for Stade Bordelais, the university club that broke the Parisian hegemony in French rugby, starring in its championship-winning side of 1911. He was 'reputed to be the most complete French forward before the war. A skilful dribbler, he was a good line-out technician and a sound scrummager.'[9] Having made his debut as a three-quarter, he was 'fast, skilled with ball in hand or at his feet, both untiring worker and "sprinter" with lightning thrusts that often carried him over the opposition try line'.[10] Winningly, 'he always smiled, even in the scrum'.

The attractions of his Bordeaux home region are liquid and overflowing; Stade Bordelais and Park exchanged tours. Over Easter 1909, Stade enjoyed English ale at the Old Deer Park. The secretary was quick to sign up the impressively built visitor to turn out for Park when he returned to study in London in 1910, when he lived in Richmond. It is not recorded if he paid his subs in francs, but pay and play he did, alongside the fleet-footed Monaghan. To his time in England one French writer attributed his 'respect to the letter [for] the rules of fairplay', in an era when French rugby was notoriously brutal.[11] When Park visited Bordeaux and quaffed Grand Cru claret at Christmas 1913, de Beyssac was noted by the home side as 'the most brilliant player on the field'.[12] He won the first of his five French caps against Ireland on New Year's Day, 1912. J.J.'s international career would end, like so many others, against England in Paris on 13 April 1914; opposite him in the forwards was Arthur Harrison, whom we shall meet at Zeebrugge.

De Beyssac began the war in the Transport Corps but then joined the Artilleries Lourdes (Heavy Artillery). By October 1917 he was inside a very different kettle of fish, as lieutenant, 500ème

Régiment Artillerie Spéciale (RAS). This, like the MGC, was a thin disguise for the new armoured *chars*. The French Schneider had a boxy hull with a sharp prow, and protruding beam for cutting barbed wire. It sat over short tracks that left the fore and aft hull sections hovering. The family likeness was more to the rhinoceros than the Roman chariot. Armament was the ubiquitous French *soixante-quinze* (75mm) gun, with two machine guns on either side of the upper hull. The six crewmen lay flat on their bellies in less than a metre between the roof and the 60hp engine. How Jean Jacques squeezed his 1.85m, 90kg frame into this crawl-space is hard to imagine.

Denis Monaghan returned to France on 22 July 1917. Five days later the British Tank Corps received its formal charter from its new colonel-in-chief, King George. Tanks were being thrown into action piecemeal, over terrain where they were hardly suited, at Arras, Bullecourt, Messines and Ypres. This was calamitous for the tanks and the infantry's faith in them; after Bullecourt the Australians refused to have anything to do with them, although their anger was directed more at the 'chicken-hearted' officers and crews than the machines.

Nor was Passchendaele's swamp the ideal proving ground: most machines were left ditched, sunk in the ooze or stranded by blasted tree stumps under their bellies. This would certainly justify one newspaper evocation of 'blind creatures emerging from the primeval slime', but did little to build their case. One driver complained:

> If these officers had been to see the salient, and if they had the brains of a child, they surely would never have committed the tank crews to practically certain death. Every member of the Tank Corps even those of the lowest rank, knew that they should not be there.

The element of surprise had been squandered by generals greedy for offensive glory. Swinton's irksome objections had also been dispensed with, as the tank was now the Big Boys' toy. But 'there was very strong feeling among the tank units, we'd made a world beater and it was being frittered away'.[13]

The French too were furious that British tanks had been deployed before theirs were ready; this may have been simple national rivalry or genuine conviction that they should only be used en masse, as Swinton and Estienne had argued. The Schneider was used for the first time on 16 April 1917 at Berry-au-Bac during the Second Battle of the Aisne. It proved disastrous as the short tractors were useless over anything but flat roads. The overhanging prow, intended to crush down wire, caused the tank to ditch easily. Of 132 French tanks, 128 were disabled or became sitting ducks for artillery fire and fifty-seven were destroyed. Fuel tanks next to the machine-gun positions caught sparks and exploded. Inadequate armour, poor ventilation and vision, and no escape hatch on the left side made these chariots of fire into death traps: 180 tank crewmen died that day, many burnt alive.

The French eventually abandoned the Schneider in favour of a new Renault design and even swallowed their Gallic pride to order the British Mark V. Forty Renault engagements compared to nine for the Schneiders tell the tale: after their unhappy start, they were relegated to a defensive role or to stop counter-attacks. As late as June 1918, Jean Jacques Conilh de Beyssac would still command one of these mobile crematoria, with all too predictable results.

As a tank captain, Denis Monaghan would normally command a section of four tanks, in a company of four sections. Months of shell-pocked terrain and oozing slime had highlighted the value of human judgement on choice of ground. Swinton's manual had recommended: 'Preparatory to action, it is essential that routes to be traversed by these animals should be carefully reconnoitred by their keepers, their sense of direction being somewhat inaccurate.'

Monaghan became Battalion Reconnaissance Officer (RO): he went forward on foot with a stick to test the best routes to the jumping off point, and marked them with tape – all under cover of night. Several memoirs tell of the tank man's particular terror of stumbling in the darkness and being crushed by his own iron beast. During the advance the RO would also place small flags where fascines – 4ft-diameter chained bundles of brushwood made by Chinese labourers and weighing 2 tons – had been laid to assist trench crossing, directing other tanks to follow. In the open, Denis Monaghan, captain of tanks, was as fatally exposed as any infantry officer.

In early November, his I Battalion trekked to new quarters at Bray-sur-Somme. C Battalion had already taken the best huts and most of the furniture but there was little time for rest during ten intensive days of preparation, again under conditions of elaborate secrecy. Senior tank officers disguised themselves in Burberries, blue-tinted glasses and private's uniforms; according to RO Clough Williams-Ellis (later architect of Portmeirion) they stopped short of false beards.[14] Engines were tuned, minor repairs made and fascines fitted to the tanks. They also trained with the troops they would support; the infantrymen were nonplussed by the mechanical beasts, but appreciated the joyrides offered. On the 10th, Monaghan and the company ROs attempted to leave camp unobtrusively to recce the forward area; their departure was noticed and it was clear that the battalion would soon be in action. The real giveaway was ammunition in meaningful quantities, as one tank man complained:

> It was really staggering the amount of essentials that each tank took on board. We had trebled up for this attack. It struck us as being too much by a long chalk. The extra .303 ammunition was left in their original boxes. The extra 6-pounder ammunition was loose. Petrol in 2 gallon cans was stacked anywhere it could be stacked. There was precious little room for the gunners to operate their guns when it was finally arranged in some kind of makeshift order.[15]

The next step was to get the cumbersome machines to their kicking-off points. Captain Weaver Price, supervising the loading of over 300 tanks on creaking rail trucks (which gradually collapsed under the strain), recalled 'the scene of a night when company after company of tanks would creep out of cover and crawl to their respective ramps'.[16] I Battalion entrained its machines and crews over three nights at a plateau siding near Albert, a considerable feat as torches and Helleson lamps were only sparingly allowed. By the time they were safe again under cover of woodland and camouflage netting, all ranks had been without sleep for several nights. With battle imminent, it was adrenaline that kept them going. The corps history asserts that 'once all ranks realised that they were preparing for battle, the longest hours and most strenuous work failed to elicit a grouch'.[17]

They laid up to rest – if they could – and final preparations were made. Maps were distributed and Special Order of the Day No.V from corps commander General Hugh Elles, who had risen spectacularly from major in 1915, called for its best efforts:

> Tomorrow the Tank Corps will have the chance for which they have been waiting for many months – to operate on good going in the van of the fight. All that hard work can achieve has been done in the way of preparation. It remains for unit commanders and tank crews to complete the work by judgement and pluck in the battle itself. In the light of past experiences, I leave the good name of the Corps with great confidence in their hands. I propose heading the attack of the centre division.[18]

He made a brown, red and green flag from the only silks left at the local draper's shop; he later glorified its colours with the post-rationalised motto: 'Through mud and blood to the green fields beyond.' As soon as darkness fell on the 19th, Monaghan and his ROs marked the approach march with luminous tape and set each tank's position at the jumping-off point.

The night was quiet. For once there was no long preliminary bombardment to 'soften up' the enemy lines (or crater the ground to impassibility). This was to be a genuine surprise attack. The tanks moved out of their hiding places at 9 p.m. and were in position with their supporting infantry by 3 a.m. An hour before zero, the rum ration was issued to fend off bitter cold and nerves; the habitual calmer of cigarettes had been forbidden (on penalty of being shot) as had cooking fires. Light would give them away. Company commanders did their rounds, wishing their men luck, and assuring them it would be a walkover. Engines were fired and at 6.10 a.m. they rumbled forward to the front line. At dawn on 20 November, the entire corps of 476 tanks, led by Elles, head and shoulders out of the hatch of his flag tank *Hilda*, finally got to show its paces along a 6-mile front at Cambrai.

A section commander wrote of this first mechanised cavalry charge: 'On either side of us, as far as the eye could see, monstrous tanks like prehistoric animals, each carrying an enormous bundle on its head, were advanced relentlessly.'[19] The smoke barrage to hide the infantry added to the primordial sight. Heinz Guderian witnessed it from the German side:

> Suddenly indistinct black forms could be discerned. They were spitting fire and under their weight the deep and strong obstacle line was cracking like matchwood. Alarm! … the troops rushed to their machine guns; it was all in vain! The tanks appeared not one at a time but in whole lines kilometres in length.[20]

Not all the 'tankasaurs' roared into battle. Captain J.K. (Jake) Wilson in Denis' I Battalion wrote:

> When filling up with petrol before the start, one driver came to me in trouble. One petrol tin containing water (the petrol having been flogged) had been poured into the tank. In reply to my question 'How do you know?' he answered that he was 'suspicious of the sound' and, tasting the last few drops, was sure it was water. Having got to the enemy front line the engine conked out with water in the jets. This was the pivot tank in which I was travelling. I had to make a quick decision and ran the gauntlet to the left rear tank commanded by Lt Parsons, which became the pivot.[21]

Parsons' own I.35 had suffered a similar 'mishap'. Clearly not every crew was keen on taking fire in these hot, noisy and stinking artillery targets, and sabotage was rife:

> I started off almost midway between Villiers Plouich and La Vacquerie, after my driver accidentally put a can of water in the gas tank. We only got into No man's land when we stopped and had to disconnect the gas lines and suck out as much of the water as we could, before we were able to go again. We spent nearly 40 minutes in the middle of the German barrage and instead of leading the attack we became part of the second wave.[22]

Wilson and Parsons nevertheless met with success in their attack:

> We successfully silenced any enemy machine guns that were plas-
> tering our lookout slits, paving the way for the infantry following
> in our wake to mop up and take La Vacquerie on our right flank
> almost without cost. Having flattened out the wire of the two
> front line trenches, which enabled the infantry to amble peace-
> fully along, some of them enjoying a 'gasper' [the night cigarette
> ban now over] we made for what was considered by the enemy
> the impregnable Hindenburg line. The isolated machine-gun
> nests that were left behind to impede our progress were easily
> disposed of by our six-pounders. I remember thinking to myself
> that these men were much too brave to die like that.[23]

In an exhilarating start to the battle, 12 miles of German line were
breached, with the capture of 10,000 prisoners, 123 guns and 281
machine guns. As so often, however, initial success was cancelled
by swift German counter-attacks, because there were insufficient
infantry to exploit the gaps created by the tanks and first wave. On
the brink of breakthrough, the attack fell victim to the failing that
had consistently dogged the British since Loos – the inability to
reinforce success with ready reserves. But in the first few triumphant
days, the pace of advance took them by surprise; on the 22nd a halt
was called for rest and reorganisation.

The next morning (Denis' twenty-ninth birthday) I Battalion was
tasked to support the Seaforth Highlanders' advance on Fontaine-
Notre-Dame, east of Bourlon Wood. The infantry could not be
found, so the tanks attacked the village alone; resistance was fero-
cious, with Germans swinging on the tanks' hot gun barrels to
misdirect their fire. They groped their way from the village when
dusk made it hard to tell friend from foe, unsure if they had gained
possession or not – the village was in fact untaken. While the men
later rolled out nets to camouflage their tanks, a German spotter
plane circling overhead gave the position to their artillery which
opened fire, killing several men.

The next day they were to assist 121 Brigade in attacking the village of Bourlon. At 6.30 a.m. the tanks trekked up to the lying-up

point in Orival Wood and awaited instructions. Brigade HQ had set zero hour at noon, but since tank commander Major Vandervell was not briefed until 10.00 a.m., this would not allow them time to reach the front line. Tanks were deemed indispensable, so the attack was postponed and orders dispatched through Denis Monaghan to section commanders. The tanks left Orival and at 2 p.m. received word that the attack was set for 3.30 p.m.; they sped up immediately, covering the 2,700m in an hour and twenty minutes, and arrived just on time. As they arrived, 2/Lt Parsons, now in I.28 *Incomparable* (his third tank of the battle), saw 'Major Vandervell and Captain Keane staggering back down the road, white as sheets'.[24] They had been on reconnaissance at the edge of Bourlon Wood when a shell had passed through their group and neatly taken off the head of Captain Denis Laurence Monaghan, now late of Rosslyn Park, Surrey and the Barbarians.

The War Diary, avoiding the graphic horrors of the incident, simply states that:

Capt Monaghan, the Battalion RO, was struck by a piece of shell and killed in Bourlon Wood, just as the attack started. He was an extremely keen and competent officer, and was very popular in the Battalion, his death being felt as a personal loss by all ranks. The Battalion Rugby XV suffered greatly by his untimely demise.

He was buried where his headless body fell and is named on the Louverval Memorial to those at the Battle of Cambrai with no known grave.

At home the name of Cambrai had signalled a great victory, with the first two defensive works of the Hindenburg Line (Siegfried Line to the Germans) initially overrun. But the only tank that reached the actual town was one captured by an enterprising German, Hauptmann Leu. The new salient could not be held and the enemy counter-attack negated all the gains. The Germans employed new infiltration tactics using elite storm troopers: fit, fast-moving marauders tore through the British lines with light machine guns and grenades. Bourlon Wood, won at such high cost, was evacuated and derelict tanks blown up.

Undaunted, *The Times* printed 'Tales of the "Tanks"' – always inverted commas for this strange novelty – and a lengthy account of derring-do from 'His Majesty's Land Ship Hotstuff'.[25] General Elles, whose wife and daughters would feature in the Christmas *Tatler*, sent a gracious telegram to Swinton saying, 'All ranks salute you. Your show.' The chairman of a Birmingham factory sent Elles a seasonal message, which became Special Order VIII: 'A resolution has been passed unanimously by the works people of the Metropolitan Carriage Co to forego any holidays and do their utmost to expedite delivery of tanks, to assist their comrades in the field.'[26] But the press (and Lloyd George) sniffed defeat being snatched from the jaws of victory and launched a blame hunt, which Haig just survived.

The Tank Corps, brimming with new confidence in its winter quarters at Bray, issued its first festive greetings cards for Christmas 1917, proudly showing off its cap badge and battle honours from the Somme, Ancre, Arras, Messines, Third Ypres and Cambrai. A crewman cheerily waves his cap from the hatch of his ironclad. The sender's name is handwritten under 'All best wishes from'; Denis' parents, Thomas and Mercy Monaghan, at Kent Avenue, Ealing, received only a bleak telegram of regret from the Army Council.

Denis' fellow tanker, Conilh de Beyssac, a year younger, survived seven months more. In April 1918 he was cited in Army Orders (French equivalent of a Mention in Dispatches) and played his last 'international' rugby match for a French military XV against a combined ANZAC team at the Olympic velodrome in Bois de Vincennes. Once more the celebrated smile is on display, contrasting the intimidating scowls of the All Blacks pack. The close game was lost 8-11, but the French had improved since the 1917 'Coupe de la Somme' when the ANZACs thrashed them 40-0. De Beyssac played both games.

He commanded the First Section of the 1st Batterie of Groupe AS15 (501ème RAS) based at Champlieu. His Schneider 61256 was designated '*As de Pique*', or 'Ace of Spades', the inauspicious 'Death Card'; the French expression *fichu (foutu) comme l'as de pique* means (in the polite version) badly deformed or mangled. In General Mangin's counter-attack at Méry in June, it took three direct hits to its left flank – the side with no escape hatch. Jean Jacques and two gunners, Julien and Bouchet, were severely *fichu*. The smiling French international died of his wounds at St Rémy l'Eau on 13 June, in an ambulance heading to hospital in Compiègne, where Germany would sign the Armistice five months too late for him.

The British Tank Corps men were copiously decorated: 446 MCs and 73 DSOs for the officers, 604 Military Medals for other ranks. The tank itself had a controversial war. Despite playing its part in the final advance to victory, with Australian General John Monash employing it particularly well in 'all arms' warfare, it was not deemed a total success by Britain or France. After the Armistice, tank development coughed and spluttered like an early Mark 1 engine.

It was Germany that took the greatest notice, despite producing only twenty of its own lumbering A7V machines (and far more wooden dummies). The Fatherland would fête Swinton as a pioneering genius on his visits after the war. Twenty years later his very British invention would spearhead the Wehrmacht's blitzkrieg on Europe.

ROBERT DALE
'THEY GO DOWN, TIDDLY, DOWN, DOWN'[1]

Robert Dale at home in Wimbledon with father Bernard. *(Eileen Laird)*

The great stage tragedies contain moments of humour – black, satirical or just plain farce – that briefly lighten the mood on the way to the inexorable end. Think Hamlet's gravediggers or Macbeth's porter. The dramatist's intent, however, is that these glimmers of light deepen the shadows of the final events.

In a war that was not exactly full of laughs, one part of the army produced more unintentional comedy than any other. Men in kite balloon sections could perhaps see the innate humour in being suspended helplessly beneath a giant inflated sausage. Unlike high-flying Zeppelins, however, these lumpy tethered gasbags became easy targets for an aeroplane's machine guns. Life expectancy at the front was short: observers suffered appalling fates in airborne fireballs or in broken heaps of mangled limbs. But, as with the spoof advertisement in *The Wipers Times* (overleaf), it is difficult to read of their exploits without a smile.

The Montgolfier brothers' linen globe of 1783 quickly found military admirers; the first observation balloon was used by France in

1794 at Maubeuge (Charles Bayly's 1914 rendezvous with the BEF). America's Civil War proved the value of captive balloons for map-making, directing artillery fire and even ascents from 'aircraft-carrier' ships. The French and Prussians, experienced after their 1870 war, were swift to deploy these floating observation platforms in 1914. On 28 August at Epinal on the Lorraine front, Capitaine Saconnay launched his antique hot-air balloon, its ground crew travelling by omnibus. The spherical shape proved less than ideal for observation, as it revolved uncontrollably around its axis. A more efficient design (soon copied by the French) was the ellipsoidal German *drachen*: 65ft long, hydrogen filled and stabilised by a primitive rudder.

Two hundred and eighty officers and men and thirty-five horses were needed to man and move a launch site but, despite this vast entourage, balloons had given the German artillery an edge in their early advance. Once the war settled into static confrontation between shallow trenches dredged from the sodden Flanders plain, a view from above was critical. If an Ypres hillock of 60m could give tactical advantage, a stable eyrie at 2,000ft easily commanded any battlefield; in fine weather, observers could see 40 miles or more with binoculars. Sir John French was soon demanding his own balloons – his BEF did not possess a single one. The first kite balloon section arrived in the Aubers Ridge sector in May 1915.

Once again, the fault lines of British air command gaped wide. The RFC was busy promoting aeroplanes as flying cavalry scouts and captive balloons did not fit their strategy. The RNAS inherited control of lighter-than-air craft from the Engineers, but coastal breezes made them less than ideal for naval support. The kite balloon 'department' (a Major Maitland and one NCO), tucked away in Room 1005 over Admiralty Arch, ordered a French design by Lt Albert Caquot for delivery to its embryo Balloon Training Depot at the Roehampton Club, where the former polo pitch – a suitably level launch pad – now sports slender white rugby posts.

Recruitment drew not only Royal Engineers but police and post office workers with mechanical and electrical experience. Less explicably, Roehampton also attracted enthusiastic volunteers from music hall and theatre. The polo ground troupe included minstrel artist George Henry Elliott, known as the 'Chocolate Coloured

DO YOU LIKE BALLOONING?

—o—o—o—

IF SO WRITE TO

"SAUSAGE," FRANCE,

AND ALL ARRANGEMENTS WILL BE MADE.

—o—o—o—

THIS FIRM IS FAMOUS FOR THE RAPIDITY OF ITS DESCENTS.

—o—o—o—

PARACHUTING A SPECIALITY.

—o—o—o—

SPLENDID SCENERY AND VIEW OF WAR TAKING PLACE IN THE DISTRICT.

o—o—o—

MOTOR TRIPS ARRANGED.

—o—o—o —

"In this awful pitch and toss age,
Don't omit to try a sausage."

—o—o—o—

Charges   Moderate.

Coon' (how the world has changed), and a young Tommy Handley, later of ITMA wireless fame in the next war. They wore the upswept half-wing silver emblem of the Kite Balloon Corps, now under the RFC. Ballooning has always attracted colourful extroverts but these larger-than-life characters are somehow punctured by their inflatable associations: from the exclamatory American publisher (James) Gordon Bennett, whose 1906 Coupe Aéronautique is still awarded annually for an eponymous Gas Balloon race, to the fictional Phileas Fogg and factual Richard Branson. Members of this new military fraternity wryly christened themselves 'Balloonatics'.

Training at Roehampton mixed comedy with tragedy. Near-crash landings on to the British Museum roof and the electrified railway on Barnes Bridge, or parachuting into parading troops at Baron Rothschild's mansion, contrasted with a McEwan-esque horror in Richmond Park. Air Mechanic James clung too long to the trailing rope of a runaway balloon and fell to his death from 1,000ft; a second mechanic Pegge climbed into the rigging but fell from a greater height over Croydon. Nearby Roehampton House became a hospital in 1915 (later Queen Mary's) and a renowned centre for limb fitting and amputee rehabilitation. Most patients arrived from 'Overseas', but a steady stream came from just down Roehampton Lane.

The lives of balloonists hung on slender threads. Kites flew at an angle, like the child's toy on a string. The winch cable was no thicker than a pencil, easily cut by shell fragments. Observers shivered in waist-high open 'cars' whose wicker floors occasionally gave way. Hauling down a balloon from 2,000ft took forty-five minutes, so the only escape under attack was by parachute, a comfort not vouched to RFC pilots. Nonetheless, some fifty years later, Godric Hodges fondly recalled his training at Roehampton as:

> ... a romantic link with the unknown world, with infinity, an expression of our childhood's yearnings ... feeling scared, but hoping I was succeeding in concealing the fact, I looked out over Barnes Common towards Hammersmith and to the left away towards Richmond Park, the great curves of the Thames and the rows of suburban roofs. In those days there were no civilian air services. To be in the air was an adventure.[2]

Flight Sergeant W.S. Lewis also recommended the experience, albeit with one important proviso:

> For people with jaded nerves who are perplexed with the cease-less hurry, bustle, and noise of modern life, I recommend a few hours up aloft in a kite balloon as a tonic and respite from its cares and worries. There is a charming and attractive calm and quietness about the experience that is recuperative and restful. Of course this is not recommended whilst there is a war on ...[3]

Even with a war most emphatically on at Vimy Ridge, while locating a troublesome German gun known as 'Ginger', Lewis could still find time for reverie:

> ... for a long time Lieutenant H. and I did not trouble much about guns. We were too enraptured with the glorious sunrise. It was wonderful, marvellous – words fail me to express what I felt. I felt very near to what some people call the infinite, whatever they may mean, or, as some may say, near to God, but whatever it was I was thinking and feeling, I began to realize in some dim way that to be absorbed in a vision of unutterable beauty is a fine experience.

While the view from above may have been inspiring, the ground troops' view of the bulbous cylinders invited earthy ridicule. 'Sausage' was one British nickname, *Nulle* or 'testicle' the German choice; the comic potential was as vast as the balloon itself in its drab yellow or grey. Even the solemn Field Service Manual contributed unwittingly: 'Officers of Field rank on entering balloons are not expected to wear spurs.'[4] As for the crew, Heath Robinson's eccentric 'Aeronaut' drawings were only mildly exaggerated. The English language even gained a new expression: filling the envelopes with hydrogen on the ground required great care, lest too much gas rush to one end and it go 'pear-shaped'.

For all their cumbersome wallowing in the air, balloons initially proved hard to shoot down. They were usually some 3 miles behind the front-line trenches and roughly 12 to 15 miles apart. Small arms fire could not reach them and early aircraft weaponry, such as small bombs, house-bricks and *fléchettes* (5in darts harking back to medieval times) were ineffective. Machine-gun bullets passed through the hydrogen bag, causing damage but no immediate collapse. Not until 1917, when the incendiary bullets of Brock, Pomeroy and Buckingham – designed to fry Zeppelins – became available, did airplanes have the edge over balloons. Sadly, fragile humans in flimsy baskets made an easier target for their guns.

The most celebrated balloon casualty was Captain Basil Hallam Radford, better known to theatregoers as Basil Hallam. He trod the boards in the Bard before overnight success at the Palace Theatre in April 1914 established 'his position in the first rank of light comedians',[5] playing a 'typical pre-war nut'. His song *Gilbert the Filbert* brought him both fame and stage name. An old leg injury requiring a steel plate defeated his wish to join the infantry, so the Balloon Corps it was. At the Somme, his balloon broke away from its mooring: 'having thrown all the papers overboard, he tried to descend by parachute. It failed to open, and he received fatal injuries.' He shares the billing with Guy du Maurier on the Theatre Royal's memorial.

The life of a balloon could be as little as half a day. Germany lost 250, an average of five a month during the war. As scout fighters began to relish the duck shoot against captive heffalumps, balloon sections employed their own bodyguards of flying escorts and 'Archie' guns. Elevation was reduced to 1,000ft, forcing attackers to risk ground fire. One German 'balloon-buster' ace in Bulgaria, Rudolf von Eschwege, was even lured to attack a kite loaded with a dummy observer and 500lb of ammonal detonated from the ground. He was buried by the British with full honours – and no little satisfaction.

Motorised winches now meant descent in minutes, but the hazards of parachuting made for hair-raising stories, if only from survivors. Parachutes were attached to the outside of the basket, and observers snapped their harness on with a spring hook, like a dog lead. When W.S. Lewis' musings on eternity are rudely interrupted, his account is pure Buster Keaton:

Bang! Like a big drum being struck. Swish-rip – a sighing whistle, a noise, or rather a shriek like the tearing of some gigantic piece of canvas. Christ! What's happened? Gee! The balloon has burst.

It had collapsed about us, and we were coming down. I desperately struggled to push away the fabric of the balloon from the basket, and suddenly from underneath the mountain of fabric, I glimpsed the white face of Lieutenant H.

'We must jump,' he said. I agreed with him, and immediately dived over head – first, and nearly dived through my harness. It had no shoulder straps, only a waistband and loops for one's legs. Never shall I forget that sickening horrible sensation when, in my first rush through the air, I felt my leg loops at the knees, and my waistband round my buttocks. I managed, however, to grab hold of the thick rope which is toggled on from the waistband to the parachute. Meanwhile, everything else seemed to go wrong; the cords of the parachute somehow in the struggle got entangled round my neck, so that as the parachute began to open with a deadly pull on my body, I was literally being strangled in mid-air. The sensation was horrible and unforgettable; my face seemed to swell to twice its size, and my eyeballs to become too big for their sockets.[6]

Fortuitously released from strangulation, he plummets on down. His parachute then coils itself around the mooring cable, trapping him again as his lieutenant floats to earth with some implausible Bigglesworthy aerial dialogue:

Then I slowly began to unwind – round and round I went like a cork, and broke away with a rush, the silk of my parachute being torn almost across, and I began hurtling down at a great speed, with my damaged and useless parachute flap, flap, flapping above me.

I thought it was all up with me. I had seen a couple of parachute accidents, and I knew what to expect. I could do nothing but curse at the damned bad luck I was having. Crash! I had shut my eyes. I thought I had struck the ground. No; in a slanting, rushing dive, I had struck poor old H.'s parachute, and the force of my fall had caused his parachute to collapse.

'Sorry,' I shouted. One had to shout I remember, for the wind seemed to be blowing a gale, although actually it was a calm, sunny day. 'Sorry, but I couldn't help it.'

'It's all right, old man,' he shouted, 'but couldn't you find some other bloody patch to fall on? Millions of bloody acres about you, yet you must pick me to fall on.' 'It looks like finish,' he continued. It did.

Suddenly his parachute began to bellow out with a flapping roar, tumbling me off like a feather, but I was too inextricably bound up with his cords to shoot away altogether; incidentally, I was hanging like grim death to something or other. What it was I don't know, but I imagine it was about half a dozen of his parachute cords. And so we landed, two on one parachute. At least, I landed first, because I seemed to slip down just before we landed, and he landed full weight on top of me.

Lewis was lucky: Basil Hallam and many more did not live to write memoirs that so mixed farce with pathos. Despite the continued efforts of ingenious inventors like C.G. Spencer, whose Static-Line (Automatic) Parachute added shoulder straps, parachuting still carried a near-suicidal risk. Twisted cords caused a horrific corkscrewing to earth – the notorious 'roman candle'. Gasbags with 30,000cu. ft of flaming hydrogen, now heavier than air, dropped faster than (and on to) an open parachute. Obituaries told bizarre tales of death by ballooning. The happier outcomes became broad slapstick:

> Both observers dropped just as she burst into flames and both parachutes opening beautifully, they landed safely though the Major fell upside down. He came down in the middle of the RAMC camp and was upended so promptly that he was of the opinion the medical people, taking him for a corpse, were going through his pockets [RAMC popularly stood for Rob All My Comrades].[7]

Equipment mixed the primitive with the modern, in a basket two paces wide. Sand ballast in bags was scooped out with a trowel. Aneroid barometers indicated height, but worked too slowly to tell balloonists if they were going up or down; theoretically a 'statometer' did that job, but old hands preferred a simple cigarette paper resting on the palm. Binoculars, mapping boards and battlefield charts to several scales were tools of the trade. Overhead photographs taken by RFC pilots were meaningless for registration of artillery targets without the oblique perspective from the balloon. Balloonists became so familiar with their fixed vista that any movement, however slight, in enemy dispositions was immediately spotted, in a way that wheeling, diving pilots could never register.

GHQ Red Tabs noted the advantages of balloons: they could stay up longer, by day or night; detailed maps could be drawn and vibration-free photographs taken. Best of all, observers could talk to ground crews, answer return questions and take instructions. Communication was by telephone, then a luxury in very few homes; an exchange connected observers to the batteries whose fire they were directing. Artillery gunners took their 'spotters' seriously; observers developed close working relationships, often spending weeks with the batteries, learning their ways.

The latest photographic technology – bulky plate-glass negative cameras – recorded enemy dispositions. Here was a snag: the fragile plates could hardly be dropped by parachute, and could only be developed if the balloon was winched down. Counter-battery work needed speedier intelligence: paper was dropped in weighted canisters. Men with an artistic eye, able to sketch trench systems and chart gun emplacements accurately, were invaluable, as in this account from Serbia:

> Enemy aircraft intervened immediately but did not stop the observers photographing the entire panorama from the Vardar to the Dojran – a mosaic on which the Army based its offensive plans. Cpl Wt Wood an artist, supplemented these pictures with colour sketches of enemy positions as seen from the basket.[8]

Commercial artists now joined the music hall artistes in the Kite Balloon Corps. This is how Robert Jacomb Norris Dale came to join 33 Balloon Section RFC.

Dale was born in 1884 at 22 Talgarth Road, not a fume-laden highway with flyover as now, but a district noted for its artists' studios: Burne-Jones, William Morris and Frank Brangwyn were residents. His father Bernard was 'a neat little company lawyer with a broken nose from playing rugby for Blackheath',[9] whose original

Richardson's field ground belonged to a branch of the family. His hobbies were 'political economy, rugger and cricket averages'. Mother Katharine came from an artistic family of architects and actors – brother George Percy Jacomb-Hood was a fashionable society painter. Robert's childhood was spent with a menagerie of animals, including a baby barn owl. From school at Haileybury (another nursery for Park), Robert followed his father into his law firm, Dale & Company of Cornhill. He enlisted in the Inns of Court OTC in 1910 and served for two years. He also shared Bernard's love of rugby; Robert chose local Rosslyn Park in 1903 after leaving school. Solid middle-class prosperity was assured: by 1911 the family home in Cottenham Park Road, Wimbledon, was a sizeable professional residence.

But the Dale household was divided: Bernard, 'tough upright, opinionated', disliked his wife's family – with some reason, as his brother-in-law business partner 'did him down'. Katharine was as tough: she had a leg amputated by a surgeon on the kitchen table. On the way to her funeral in 1921, Bernard was distracted by a rugger match on Wimbledon Common and stayed behind to watch, in 'locked-up silence'. Younger brother James (who had little love for his father) left Haileybury for the Royal Academy; when his work didn't sell he gave up art to be an actor in 1908 and Bernard 'washed his hands of me for good'. We can only imagine the fatherly reaction to losing his elder son (and legal colleague) to a similar artistic rebellion. By August 1914, both law and rugby were in the past for 30-year-old Robert. His Territorial Force application at Dukes Road on the very first day of war declares him to be a 'designer, printer' in the employ of one Thomas Russell in the West End.

Why the artistic epiphany for Robert Dale? His keen legal mind would surely not expect that his new regiment, the Artists' Rifles (formed in 1860 by art student Edward Sterling), required the credentials of earlier recruits like William Morris, Holman Hunt and Millais. In any case, the pre-Raphaelite brotherhood's motivation was more likely social than military – or aesthetic. Was it a case of *cherchez la femme* – his mother, with her artistic family, or another?

When he met Irene Rose Mawer, the strapping rugby player put aside childish things (like the legal profession and officer training) in favour of his new muse. Irene was a mime artist and classical Greek dancer. She and its foremost exponent, Ruby Ginner, appeared together in *Et Puis Bon Soir*, a play without words. The title, from a poem by Belgian Leon Montenaeken, might aptly describe the brief romance between Irene and Robert:

> La vie est brève, un peu d'espoir
> Un peu de rêve, et puis bonsoir[10]

By November 1914, every dance troupe performance, such as the Red Cross Day held at 'one of London's most delightful beauty spots', Barnes' Ranelagh Club, was a benefit for wounded soldiers. In 1916, with Robert still overseas, Irene joined Ginner's School of Dance as secretary and teacher of mime and voice production. In 1920 it would become the Ginner-Mawer School of Dance and Drama, housed in the Royal Albert Hall. Irene also wrote children's plays and 'word-music' poetry to accompany dance.

Actor brother James joined the King's Liverpool (Scottish) and later wrote: 'Then we went to France to perform.' On 28 October 1914, Robert's Artists' Rifles crossed to France on the SS *Australind* and established an officer training base at Bailleul. Sir John French sent a request for fifty-two other ranks to be made immediate officers, to replace the 'colossal' losses of the 7th Division, which was due back in the line in three days. A two-hour talk by Lt Col May and a copy of the Field Service Pocket Book was all the training they received before having subaltern's stars pinned to their other rank uniforms, to give them immediate authority over the men. When they joined their new companies, many found themselves the only officer – and therefore became company commander. French later commented of the Artists: 'these boys … looked death straight in the face laughing and smiling and earned the soubriquet of "The Suicide Club".'[11]

May wrote later: 'surely they were the most rapidly trained and scantily equipped young officers ever produced by the British Army. General Capper (commanding 7th Division) felt they had "turned out splendidly. Have you any more like them?"'[12] After 'The First Fifty', the stream of officers flowing from the Artists totalled 10,256

– more than the total wartime commissions through Sandhurst. Robert at least had time for training, but remained adamant about his professional calling. By the time he applied for a regular commission, 1656 Private Dale described himself as 'scholar, author, painter' – at 31, the former lawyer had gone determinedly Bohemian. He was commissioned second lieutenant in the New Army's 9th Battalion, the Manchester Regiment, in June 1915, and shipped out to join the 'Ashton Pals' at Gallipoli, where they had been since May.

In Sir Ian Hamilton's plan for the August assault on Sari Bair,[13] a diversion at Helles would distract Turkish attention from the main thrust. It proved a costly failure. The Manchesters were to attack in an area called the Vineyard, 1,000 yards south of Krithia village, and the apex of the British line. After a feeble artillery bombardment the attack to their left was thrown back with heavy losses; the 9th's turn came the next day, against strongly entrenched Turkish positions. Days of Turkish counter-attacks followed and Lt Forshaw won the VC for his forty-one hours of bomb-throwing:

> We decided that we would hold on to the position whatever it cost us for we knew what it meant to us. If we had lost it the whole of the trench would have fallen into the hands of the enemy … The Turks were at it for all they were worth, and they had sap heads right up to my position; but I had a fine supply of bombs, which, by the way, had been made out of jam tins by our Engineers. Obliging little fellows, those Engineers! Fortunately, we had no fewer than 800 of those bombs, but we got rid of the lot during the greatest weekend I have ever spent.[14]

The Manchesters now suffered the disease and blizzards that did for Wilfred Jesson and their numbers dwindled. On 28 December the remainder evacuated from Gallipoli on HMT *Redbreast*, bound for Egypt again, where they had defended the Suez Canal before the Dardanelles campaign. By early January, they were back on guard duty – in comparative comfort and warmth – and spent the rest of 1916 in Egypt, entrenching defensive lines to the east of the canal and Port Said, and on outpost duty. The Turkish threat across the north of Sinai was resisted: the Ottoman invaders were pushed back to the borders of their own empire. In September, Dale was attached to the RFC at Aboukir for two months of 'instruction on aviation'. A planned attack at El Arish was forestalled when the Turks fled, leaving the way open to Palestine. Robert took leave and returned to England to marry Irene.

Suez was finally secured by February 1917 after battles at Rafa and Magdhaba. Having achieved all his objectives, the victorious General Murray quite reasonably expected more resources to continue his push. Instead he lost the key 42nd Division to the Western Front where a spring offensive was planned. On 4 March, their work in Egypt done, the Manchesters, at an impressive strength of thirty-one officers and 1,059 men sailed for Marseilles on HT *Arcadian*. The Embarkation Orders are tribute to the unsung administrators of troop movements, with their attention to detail and discipline:

> Troops should avoid dealing with professional money changers on the quays
> Troops must be prevented from fouling the ground, the ships latrines alone being used
> Lifebelts to be constantly worn except when men turned in, when lifebelts are to be hung up on their hammocks
> Rifles or other articles of steel or iron not to be brought within 20 feet of ships compasses.[15]

Divisional Lt Col Reginald Slaughter, clearly a cavalryman, is particularly fierce on the subject of horses and pack mules:

> All ranks must be warned that SILENCE is absolutely necessary if rapid entrainment is to be effected. The practice of shouting at unruly animals cannot be too strongly deprecated; animals already frightened are not soothed and rendered more tractable by noise. All men must be warned to lead animals straight into the railway trucks; on no account should they face their animals or look at them whilst trying to lead into trucks.

It was two years since Robert had been in France. On arrival at Marseilles, his men were issued with extra blankets for the journey to the colder north. Their train's departure at 10 p.m. was precisely as planned in Egypt, but 'issue of rations at 0400 was difficult due to darkness'. Orange, Macon and Montereau sped past the rattling carriages. He caught fleeting glimpses of the springtime *paysage* before the fifty-seven-hour journey ended at Pont Remy on the Somme, early on 14 March. The battalion marched to billets east of Amiens. After years in tropical 'pith' helmets the men were now issued with their first Brodie 'tin hats' for their Western Front debut. By 8 April they were in training for a style of trench warfare new to them; Lt Dale, in charge of scouts and snipers, took a course of instruction at the Army Telescopic Sights School. At dusk on 22 April, they occupied a section of the front at Epehy.

By July, they were back in reserve. Rest and recreation included winning the brigade football competition – by this stage, soccer was compulsory exercise. The War Diary catalogues the routine minutiae of bombing courses, new drafts, departures on leave; Major Nowell, temporary battalion CO, made a popular decision to suspend training on account of painful inoculations. Robert seized his chance for ten days' precious leave with his bride, but was back by 8 August. The division took over an Ypres sector almost a mile long, enduring appalling weather and constant shellfire.

The 9/Battalion came out of the line in late September and took over coastal defence at Nieuport, a 'quiet sector' under artillery bombardment and aerial attack. Robert, by now battalion Intelligence Officer, reported sick, but did not return to the Manchesters; on his release from hospital he was 'accepted on probation as balloon observer RFC & struck off strength'.[16] He was now a balloonatic in the Western Front asylum.

As the battles around Passchendaele bogged down, General Haig heard alarming news from the south. In October 1917, the Italian Army faced Austrians backed by six German divisions, each with a *Feld Luftschiffer Abteilung* (FLA) balloon unit. The Austrians came down from the mountain like a wolf on the fold – over 20,000 Italian troops died at Caporetto. Double that number deserted despite (or perhaps because of) summary executions by order of General Luigi Cadorna, who had revived the ancient Roman practice of 'decimation', randomly choosing victims in units which showed signs of weakness. If Italy should follow Serbia and Romania (and imminently Russia) out of the war, the Central Powers could turn their full might against a single front. So Britain and France sent a joint Expeditionary Force under General Sir Herbert Plumer to bolster the *arrestamento* of headlong Italian retreat. Four British infantry divisions and four RFC squadrons were dispatched by train; the French sent six divisions and three air squadrons.

On Boxing Day 1917, the balmy south beckoned again to Robert Dale. After the gunmetal grimness of northern European winter trenches, the train journey to Italy would have been a riot of colour and unseasonal warmth. One RFC lieutenant wrote to his mother:

> The last few hours I have seen the most beautiful scenery in all my life whilst travelling along the coast from Marseille into Italy. Nice and Monte Carlo are beautiful towns and as we pass through we are given a great reception ... The climate here is beautiful and warm just like one of our English summers in August although really it is winter here ... Have seen for the first time oranges growing on the trees.[17]

They arrived at Padua on 30 December and then moved forward to Villalta. Army command was determined that this should not be seen as a holiday posting: standing orders issued in Italy prohibited the sending home of picture postcards of Italian towns, the possession of a camera, the purchase of spirits and liqueurs, purchase or acceptance of wines, or purchase of bread by troops from local bakeries.

Robert Dale, self-proclaimed 'scholar, author and painter', was tantalisingly close to the glories of Italian art and architecture of Tiepolo and Palladio. But there was no leave granted for sightseeing. Officers were not allowed to visit Venice until much later and it was forever out of bounds to other ranks. A no-fly zone prohibited planes for 5 miles around La Serenissima, further enforced by a curtain of steel cables suspended between barrage balloons. But the new Franco-British line would staunchly defend its treasures – and those of Verona, Vicenza and Padua. They were at the western edge of the Venetian plain, surrounded by mountains which had seen bitter fighting in dire alpine conditions. Defensive lines were held by a web of rivers flowing south-east across the plain to the Adriatic: the Piave, Monticano, Tagliamento and Isonzo, where multiple battles had raged, culminating in the Twelfth – better known as Caporetto.

British troops now took up positions on the south bank of the Piave, a river that was now a trickle but could turn into a torrent in spring. RFC planes (mainly RE8s) were kept busy photographing the broad plain and bombing railheads and junctions, power stations, depots, camps and airfields, while the kite balloons, shepherded by Sopwith Camels, searched for targets and directed gunnery fire. The Italian front became a ground/air war with constant raids, counter-raids and bombing by all four air forces: the British mostly bombed by day, the Germans at night, while the Italians and Austrians, not to be outdone, did both. With so few balloons available, the crews spent long stretches at the front, without the relief spells granted to the infantry.

Balloons on both sides were tempting targets for gung-ho flying aces. It was great sport for pilots to 'eat a sausage before breakfast', defying the attendant risks from 'Archies' and fighter escorts: Belgian ace Willy Coppens claimed a record thirty-seven balloon kills. Canadian Captain William Barker of 28 Squadron RFC found an outlet in Italy for his aggressive brand of flying and claimed forty-six kills of all types in his Camel B6313 – the single most successful air-craft of the war. His missions, not always officially authorised, were often logged as 'Machine-Gun testing'. For downing two balloons at Conegliano in December he received a second bar to his Military Cross; he already had the DSO and would collect another bar – and the Victoria Cross – in October 1918. His MC citation read: 'When leading patrols he on one occasion attacked eight hostile machines, himself shooting down two, and on another occasion seven, one of which he shot down. In two months he himself destroyed four enemy machines and drove down one, and burned two balloons.'[18]

Barker and his wingman, 2/Lt Hudson, decided to 'test guns' again on Christmas Day: they attacked an Austrian airfield at Motta 10 miles behind the lines, setting one hangar ablaze, 'shooting up personnel on the ground' and damaging four enemy aircraft before dropping a painted placard wishing them a 'Merry Xmas'.[19] This controversial raid was fictionalised by Ernest Hemingway, who was an ambulance driver at the front. His fiction is not reportage and his version may have condensed two raids: on 24 January, the pair took a *Ballonzug* by surprise, destroyed its two balloons and strafed a column of wagons for good measure. Hemingway's writer Harry recounts a less heroic view of Barker:

> … that cold, bright, Christmas day with the mountains showing across the plain that Barker had flown across the lines to bomb the Austrian officers' leave train, machine gunning them as they scattered and ran. He remembered Barker afterwards coming into the mess and starting to tell about it. And how quiet it got and then somebody saying, 'You bloody murderous bastard'.[20]

Barker's maverick arrogance required a response from the proud German fliers. It was not long before tit followed tat, and Lieutenant Robert Dale was to be the unhappy victim of the retaliation.

The pilot responsible was Leutnant Hans von Freden of Jagdstaffel 1, operating from San Fior. He was taking revenge for the two bags burnt by Barker and Hudson on the 24th and, if Hemingway is to be believed, for a much greater insult. Dale's Balloon No. 33 was the second of his three kills in eight days. His final tally was twenty, nine of which were balloons, qualifying him for the *Pour le Mérite*, better known as the Blue Max. It didn't stop influenza carrying him off in 1919. Air Mechanic Harry Green left the only eyewitness record of Dale's death in the afternoon. The diary entry is stark and factual. The final poignant note, in a story full of pathos, is Robert's name, wrongly spelled:

> 29 January 1918. No 34 balloon brought down in flames by German plane. Observer landed safely.
> 30 January 1918. Ballooning. Hostile aircraft around balloon. No damage. All-night duty.
> 31 January 1918. Misty day. At 4pm No. 33 balloon brought down in flames. Lieut Bale was killed.

Green does not mention the fate of Dale's fellow observer. However, the case notes of Maghull Military Hospital (where W.H. Rivers of

Craiglockhart fame first practised) reveal a man much damaged by his experience and Robert's death:

> Neurasthenia: 2 Lt James Baxter, 33rd Kite Balloon Section, RFC 40 year old man with 21 years of service behind him. Was a balloon observer. Broke his upper denture and became unable to masticate his food at the Front. Suffered much in consequence and finally suffered a nervous breakdown after his balloon was brought down and he had to witness the violent death of his friend. He has suffered from insomnia and distressing dreams, dizziness and headaches.[21]

For all its humour and grim slapstick, kite ballooning held terrors which threatened the sanity of its observers.

No. 33 Section remained, depleted, in Italy for the duration of the war; so too did Robert Dale. He lies there still, in Giavera British Cemetery, Arcade, beneath his uniform white headstone; here at least his name is correct. Irene, his dancing muse, received the fatal telegram in their Kensington flat; Robert's will left her £464 8s, enough to buy Bourne Stream, a cottage overlooking the harbour at Boscastle, Cornwall. After the war, 'when time seemed to stand still between the shattered past and the unknown future',[22] she requested his medals be sent there – a memento of their fleeting shadow of a wartime marriage.

Et puis bonsoir.

ARTHUR HARRISON
CLOSE THE WALL UP WITH OUR ENGLISH DEAD

Lieutenant Commander Arthur Leyland Harrison VC, Royal Navy.

On Wimbledon Common, bordering the road to naval Portsmouth, is a playing field. This was established by Mr Richardson Evans to protect a Great War memorial from the 1920s ribbon development spreading along the busy highway now called the A3. As a result of his benevolence, the memorial cross sits in a quiet grove ringed by holly and hawthorn, an oasis of green in the metropolis.

Every March, the peace is disturbed by 7,000 young boys and girls in the world's largest rugby tournament – the Rosslyn Park National Schools Sevens. The memorial has watched silently as they noisily carve budding reputations on the field: among them Gareth Edwards, Keith Jarrett, Will Carling, Matt Dawson and Rory Underwood. Engraved on its granite panels are the names of two decorated Englishmen from Rosslyn Park: Humphrey Dowson MC, who died on the Somme, and Arthur Leyland Harrison VC.

Arthur Harrison led with his chin. He clearly took pride in his prominent jawline: in the uniform of a lieutenant commander in the Royal Navy, he turns his profile to the camera rather than the customary direct gaze – the firm chin juts as far forward as the peak of his cap. The distinctive bulldog jaw, this time under a leather scrumcap, is easily spotted in a photo of the France international of April 1914, when he won his second and last cap. A bleak day at Les Colombes with leafless trees, Harrison is at the rear of the lineout, waiting for the ball to descend. Scrapping for possession ahead of him is the lanky Frenchman de Beyssac.

The same chin appears in that season's Park XV photograph. The rangy second-row forward looks slight alongside burly giants like John Rosher, but his fearless play earned him his England debut against Ireland, aged 28. He was in familiar company with United Services and navy halfbacks Oakley and Davies, as well as the glamour boys Cyril Lowe and Ronnie Poulton Palmer, with their public school pedigrees and Oxbridge Blues. Although E.H.D. Sewell praises Harrison in strictly yeoman-like terms as 'strong and tireless … his game was the sturdy, bustling type, and he was quite a good place-kicker', he acknowledges that 'though past the age at which men receive their first National Cap, he was so fit that he would have played many more times for England but for the War'.[1]

The 'donkeys' of the second row are not meant to be stars: their job is the grunt and grind of the scrum, although lineout lifting has latterly encouraged an unsuspected athleticism. But selfless, uncomplaining toil in the engine room has made many leaders: Martin Johnson, John Eales, Willie John McBride and Bill Beaumont are all men who rarely took a backward step. Arthur Harrison may not have gained gilded laurels on the pitch, but his leadership qualities earned him a distinction unique among England rugby internationals (although three Irishmen, including Alec Todd's friends Tommy Crean and Robert Johnston would share it). He would win his country's highest award for valour: the Victoria Cross.

Many deaths in this volume are sudden: they come from the unseen sniper's bullet or the whizz-bang shell flung from artillery far behind enemy lines. Technology increasingly distanced the combatants, and their deaths rarely came in direct confrontation. Sad and senseless all of them, but rarely can they be termed heroic. By 1918, war seemed endless and volunteers had been replaced by conscripts with no choice. Arthur Harrison, however, would jump at the chance of a mission of extreme danger and would meet his death at close quarters and against impossible odds, in the sure knowledge that his chance of survival was nil. That's heroism, by most standards.

Once more, the famous jawline was squarely to the fore. Like a heavyweight boxer, Harrison would prove vulnerable to a telling blow to his promontory of a chin – that April night it would not come from a leather-gloved fist. He would be knocked cold by a shell fragment which smashed his jaw, as he waited to charge across gangplanks on to the harbour mole at Zeebrugge, Belgium. He hit the deck unconscious, and his body was taken below – yet another casualty under the point-blank fire from German guns just yards away. Harrison's death was a serious blow to his men: he had trained them in fitness for this mission and he was to have led the assault on the mole and its guns. But his story was not yet over.

It began thirty-two years earlier, on 3 February 1886. This son of a Royal Fusiliers colonel was not destined for the army: Arthur Harrison heard the siren call of the ocean at his birthplace in seaside Torquay, Devon. He spent five years from 1895 at Dover College – within sniffing distance of the salty Channel – then returned to Devon, and the Britannia Royal Naval College, in May 1901. As a teenage cadet, he would not sleep in the imposing building now at Dartmouth (not completed until 1905), but on the ageing wooden hulks *Britannia* and *Hindostan*, moored on the River Dart. His captain described the 16-year-old midshipman as 'zealous and energetic'; when promoted sub-lieutenant at 18, he was declared 'physically very strong … most reliable and capable'. In 1908, with pilotage, gunnery and torpedo exams successfully navigated, he was promoted again to lieutenant and his first command at Portsmouth.

At the naval base, Arthur naturally played his rugby for the United Services Club. He made his debut at 20 and was a regular for eight years. Harrison's parents were now Wimbledon residents and he chose younger brother Percy's Rosslyn Park as his occasional London club over two seasons when on leave. 'HM *Torpedo Boat No16*, Portsmouth' is a residential address hard to equal in any club ledger. He played the recruiting sergeant too, bringing along naval colleagues from HMS *Lion* and *Colossus*. At Park he had his first contact with 'Continental opposition'. The club had long been a rugby pioneer in Europe with its fixtures against Stade Français and Bordeaux. Now Harrison went into Europe: in June 1913, Park played two games on German soil, against the Hanover '87 Club and a representative north Germany side at the Hanover Sports Festival.

Germany was an unusual rugby destination: although rugby had been played there since the 1890s, the Hanover club, formerly captained by Park skipper and tour organiser T.R. Treloar, had never yet played an English side. Much of the banter, however, would have a familiar ring as several players on both sides were Old Uppinghamians. This 'great European challenge' would have the accent of an English public school house match, although one authentically Teutonic note is sounded by Hanover's marvellously named Gutbeer – surely a member of the front-row union. Both games ended in convincing English victories and the 'team had a great time owing to the wonderful hospitality of the Germans'.[2] Harrison would wait five years before he next got his hands on German opposition and enjoyed more of their 'hospitality'. It would not go as well for him.

In the immediate pre-war years, he caught the eye of the England selectors when playing county rugby for Hampshire. His first game for his country was the 1914 Valentine's Day game against Ireland at Twickenham, the first match attended by rugby fan King George V since his coronation in 1910. Accompanying him was Prime Minister Asquith. The debate on Irish Home Rule was raging and their attendance was a strong conciliatory statement; international sport has always been inextricably linked with politics, more by politicians than sportsmen. Ireland kicked off with characteristic Gaelic fervour and soon led by seven points. England, playing more conservatively, overhauled the tiring Irish to win by seventeen points to twelve. Harrison, the only new cap, was mentioned in dispatches alongside his army namesake Harold 'Dreadnought' Harrison, a prop built like a battleship. *The Times* noted that 'the English forwards, stiffened in the scrummage by the two Harrisons, did better than against Wales', a victory narrowly squeaked by ten points to nine, after the Welsh pack had dominated.

Harrison shook the royal hand again three weeks later. The 'Officers of the Royal Navy played the Officers of the Army (services rugby was not yet ready for other ranks) at Queen's Club, Kensington, better known today for tennis. Fog and rain settled about the ground, which had an infamous microclimate, but so enthusiastic was the king that he sat in the open without an umbrella, drawing approval for his consideration and hardiness from his spectating subjects.

Perhaps playing to his dampened regal gallery, referee Mr Potter-Irwin encouraged a fast, open game by playing advantage rather than awarding penalties. 'Seldom has a better game of good clean, hard football been played', applauded *The Times*, avowing that 'the vigour of the play was such that had not every man been as hard as nails he would have been in the dock for repairs'. The weighty Army pack with five internationals proved too much for the lighter Navy forwards. Down by eighteen points to three at half-time, the Navy twice hauled themselves back to within seven points, before finally being sunk by twenty-six points to fourteen. The small matter of who scored the Army's final try was uncertain as 'the players were so clothed in mud and mist that identification was doubtful'.

Duty came first for Lieutenant Harrison and the Calcutta Cup match was sacrificed to the Royal Navy's call. But he returned for the Grand Slam victory in Paris. While Poulton Palmer's backs starred with five tries, *Sporting Life* praised the forwards who 'worked the scrums infinitely better than did the French eight'. Proof, if ever doubted, that forwards win games and backs decide by how much. There was time afterwards for liquid celebration and a consoling arm around the broad shoulders of his opposing lock, de Beyssac. Four months later, as his civilian teammates flocked to recruiting halls and commissions, the career navy officer was already steaming into action.

On 28 August, a British raiding force attacked German destroyers at Heligoland Bight. A trap had been sprung, and the force commander had to summon help from Admiral Beatty's three battle-cruisers, *Princess Royal*, *Queen Mary* and Harrison's *Lion*. Four German ships were sunk and more damaged; first blood at sea went to the British. At Dogger Bank in January, *Lion* took heavy fire and was forced to withdraw from the engagement. Two of Harrison's England teammates, centre James Watson on HMS *Hawke* and submariner scrum-half Frank Oakley, were already in watery graves. But the real Big Match came in May 1916 at Jutland, off the Danish coast.

This was the only meeting between the British Grand Fleet and the German High Seas Fleet; 250 ships and over 70,000 seamen made it the biggest naval clash of the war. Previous encounters had been cagey: the Germans were still overawed by the majestic power of the Royal Navy, which in turn was nervous of the unthinkable consequences of defeat. Churchill famously called Admiral Jellicoe 'the only man on either side who could have lost the war in an afternoon'. The Battle of Jutland predictably enough ended in an indeterminate result.

The 'score' of ships sunk pointed to a 14-11 German victory, especially as British losses included prestigious battlecruisers like the *Indefatigable*, *Invincible* (apparently not) and *Lion*'s sister, *Queen Mary*, with 1,300 men drowned. Jellicoe had twice in an hour 'crossed the T', bringing his fleet's guns broadside on to Admiral Scheer's columns, but the Germans turned away in time to avoid obliteration. The eventual German withdrawal on 1 June allowed Jellicoe to claim the triumph. His navy thereafter dominated the North Sea and tightened the noose of blockade around Germany's neck. Harrison's *Lion* was badly mauled by the enemy gunners. She took twelve direct hits, more than any surviving ship except the battleship *Warspite*. But she continued to engage the enemy despite a destroyed turret and 145 casualties. Harrison was Mentioned in Dispatches and promoted to Lieutenant Commander in October.

Jutland changed naval warfare. The bruised High Seas Fleet avoided any rematch. Big battleships would never again slug it out, and submarines and aircraft carriers would dominate the next war. Harrison's game was effectively called off at half-time, while he sucked on his orange after a vigorous first period. The navy life became dull. One frustrated officer, W. W. Childs, recalled:

… things were inclined to become monotonous in the Grand Fleet. The usual routine, gunnery drills etc, which makes a ship efficient, intermingled with recreation became stale. The same old drills day in and day out got on one's nerves. Occasionally there was the usual order 'Raise Steam with all possible speed and report when ready', which meant the same old convoys to Norway which necessitated manning the guns all day and night in case of emergency, putting to sea in the worst possible weather with never a sign of a German ship, but the occasional rumours that there was 'something doing'.[3]

Not one to kick his heels, Arthur used his leave to play in the rugby matches held around the country to boost morale and war charities; he was 'very much to the fore in scratch games played at the Old Deer Park, Richmond'.[4] But expending energy on his old Rosslyn Park stamping ground was not enough for a man keen to close with the opposition, as he had in Hanover. An offer of a second chance for Harrison came in 1917, as Park Secretary Burlinson reported to the thirty-eighth AGM on 20 October, with a wartime mixture of gloom and cheer: 'casualties still continue to be very heavy, but on the brighter side, our members continue to gain various Decorations for their gallantry.'[5]

A brief order pinned up at Scapa Flow asked for volunteers for a 'show'; it specified all must be single and athletic. Harrison was both qualified and intrigued. He was told to report to HMS *Hindustan* (the name, if not the vessel, familiar from Dartmouth) in Chatham Docks, with officers and men from all quarters of the navy. Another from the Rosslyn Park ranks was the handsome Captain Charles Phelps Tuckey, of the Royal Marines Light Infantry. He was second-in-command of Portsmouth Company in a 4th Battalion specially formed for the operation. As volunteers converged at Holborn station, excited clusters of men quizzed each other for gen. As one Royal Marines Light Infantry private noted in his diary:

> We can plainly see there is an air of mystery about this whole stunt.
> What the devil do they want going to the expense of sending 950
> marines over to France for two and a half hours work, when they
> have millions of men there already, is what puzzles some of us.[6]

Vice Admiral Roger Keyes, architect of the 'show', greeted the officers at Chatham with a frank briefing:

It was very interesting to watch their reaction when I told them
that their enterprise would be hazardous, and finally said the best
chance of escape I could offer them after it was a German prison
until the end of the war. With one exception only, they appeared
to be simply delighted and most grateful for the honour I had
done then in offering such a wonderful prospect![7]

Commander W.A. Bury wrote: Keyes 'filled us with enthusiasm in
his extraordinary quiet way, told each officer off for his particular
job, and left us with a strong sense of assurance'.[8] The enthusiasm of
the naval men for action contrasted with the battle-fatigued troops
on the Western Front, whose appetite had been dulled by the attrition and inhuman conditions of Passchendaele. Those who still lived
had simply seen too much. The major battles were now numbered
(Third Ypres, Twelfth Isonzo) in sure proof of one definition of
General Staff madness: repeatedly performing the same action, yet
expecting a different outcome.

When Keyes stated cryptically that 'the command might well
pass rapidly', it took special officers to volunteer for this 'hazardous enterprise'. He did not specify the reason, and the hand-picked
force of 1,000 marines, blue-jackets and Grand Fleet men was blind
to the nature of their secret mission. That it was dangerous was clear
from their various nicknames, gleefully adopted: 'The Suicide Club',
'Death or Glory Boys', 'Jellicoe's Light Horse'. One 19-year-old
rejoiced in the sudden celebrity of being in the gang: 'I never knew
I was so popular; even old sailors of twenty-one and abouts who had
hitherto passed me by with disdain gave me fatherly advice.'[9]

Harrison, tireless international rugby player, was put in charge
of physical fitness, while instructors from the Middlesex Regiment
taught the volunteers grisly close-quarters work with bayonet, rifle
butt and pistol, and even martial ju-jitsu. They trained near Dover
on a replica of 'a position in France' rumoured to be a fortified
ammunition dump. They were also issued with naval cutlasses – a
throwback to the boarding parties of a century ago – which also
made useful cricket stumps. This was to be no sortie from earth-
bound trenches, but a naval raid in the old buccaneering style. At
the end of March, as the army reeled before Ludendorff's Spring

Offensive and the public at home recoiled in shock, the daring plan was finally revealed.

The target was not in France, but Belgium, at the port of Zeebrugge. Its breakwater protected the channel to the U-boat pens at Bruges. The plan was to scuttle concrete-filled ships to block its entrance. The curved stone arm of the mole, reaching out into the North Sea, was nearly 2 miles long and fortified with the same defensive imagination and thoroughness as the Siegfried Line trench systems. A 10ft-thick sea wall reared 16ft above the landward roadway. A lighthouse, a Very light cannon and a fearsome arsenal of a dozen big guns guarded any attack from the sea. To repel other incursions there were two anti-aircraft emplacements, a walled trench and a machine-gun position. The thousand-man garrison lived in reinforced concrete sheds ringed with barbed wire.

For the blockships *Thetis*, *Intrepid* and *Iphigenia* to penetrate the inner harbour and reach the canal mouth, the defensive guns had to be neutralised or at least distracted. So the marines and sailors would storm the mole from two requisitioned Mersey ferries, *Iris* and *Daffodil*, and an obsolete cruiser *Vindictive*, whose 'hull sat aggressively on the water like a landlady at a paying guest's tea-party'.[10] Spared from the scrapyard, she was specially modified to be a 'death-trap fitted with all the ingenious contrivances of war that human brain could think of':[11] shelter barricades padded with splinter-proof mattresses, a false deck at the same height as the mole parapet and sixteen steel gangways that would lower on to it. Calculating the tide was crucial: too low and the gangways would not reach the mole wall. Unable to land, men would be at the mercy of the German guns. If they got ashore, the drop to the roadway was too high to jump laden with weapons and demolition equipment, so ladders would have to be carried. The raiders would descend and attack the batteries before the defending machine-gunners could react.

Keyes' planning for Operation Z.O. was meticulous. The light-house would illuminate them at night, so he asked technical wizard Wing Commander Frank Brock to create a flameless smokescreen. Brock, of the famous fireworks family, was a serial inventor and lifetime 'mad scientist' – he had blown up a stove in his Dulwich

College room. Tommies often likened the dazzling but deadly artillery displays above their trenches to 'Brock's benefits'. His was the incendiary bullet used by John Harman's RFC against Zeppelins, the Dover flare used in anti-submarine warfare and the ingenious 'artificial fog' created for this mission by squirting a chlorosulphonic acid mixture on to hot exhausts or funnel interiors. He used 63 tons of a chemical found in the sweetener *saxin*, which mysteriously disappeared from British teacups for weeks. On Friday 19 April, Brock was on leave with his family but returned bringing a box marked 'Highly Explosive Do Not Open'; it contained bottles of vintage port for the men.

The seventy vessels of the convoy slipped anchor at 4.53 p.m. on 22 April. The German *Kaiserschlacht* offensive gave this tactical raid a far greater significance. Only ten days earlier Haig had warned that 'with our backs to the wall, and believing in the justice of our cause, each one of us must fight on to the end. The safety of our homes and the freedom of mankind depend alike upon the conduct of each one of us at this moment.' Realising that their attack was timed for the small hours of St George's Day, Keyes sent a succinct signal to the fleet, wishing them luck: 'St George for England.' Alfred Carpenter, captain of *Vindictive*, replied, 'May we give the dragon's tail a damned good twist'. Harrison's great chin stands out again in a final photo taken hours before departure, next to the funnels of *Vindictive*. He is grinning cheerfully with other officers. These same funnels will reappear after the raid, pockmarked and battered in souvenir postcards. One can only imagine the effect of shells and shrapnel on the men on the deck.

The *Flandern MarineKorps* on the mole, thinking themselves impregnably safe, ignored the first bombardments – nothing out of the ordinary – until a sudden change of wind direction blew away Brock's 'fog' and revealed *Vindictive* bearing down hard on them. As she closed to within 50 yards – just half a rugby pitch away – the mole guns could not miss. Childs, the Lewis-gunner, described these four minutes under intense fire: 'It seemed like hell let loose. The shrapnel and pieces of funnel caused havoc among the men, and the air was full of the cries of the wounded and dying. The Huns were hitting us every time they fired.'

It was a bloody massacre at point-blank range. W.A. Bury later recalled: 'the length of time that several lived who had large pieces of their heads blown away … we had no room to separate the dead from amongst the living, so thickly were they packed.'[12] The laconic Commander Rosoman, fighting a deck fire of Stokes mortar rounds, 'got a bit of something through my right knee which stung a bit, but I joined [Petty Officer] Youlton, who was trying to stamp it out, and threw what I thought was a sandbag on it. It wasn't, as I knew when I lifted it.'[13] *Vindictive* became a butcher's shop of horrors.

By one minute past midnight *Vindictive* was alongside the mole. All but two of the gangways were shattered. Lt Cmdr George Bradford made desperate attempts swinging on a grappling iron from a davit to secure her to the mole. He was blasted into the churning water by a machine-gun burst. Lt Claude Hawkings climbed up a scaling ladder and was swung over to the parapet by his men. He was immediately rushed by defenders, fired his revolver, but was never seen again. It was left to *Iris* to nuzzle the cruiser closer to the mole. As Keyes had promised, command was indeed passing rapidly, as successive officers fell. The leader of the naval storming party, Captain Halahan, and the two senior marines, Elliott and Cordner, were all killed aboard by gunfire. Arthur Harrison's jaw was ripped apart by a shell; he was taken for dead and his body rushed below.

The only officer left standing, Lt Cmdr Bryan Adams, led the charge: 'up into the night went one huge yell, all the pent-up feeling of the years of war and hatred and the lust for killing.'[14] As the raiders swarmed on to the mole, Adams realised they were 300 yards short of their battery target, and blocked by the trench barrier and machine-gun emplacement. The waiting Germans sneered, 'Here come the footballers!', in scorn at Nevill's exploit at the Somme.[15] Adams back-tracked to collect as many as he could for a further assault and was astonished to find Harrison, risen from the dead, staggering along the parapet. He had merely been knocked unconscious and on coming round, brushed off the medics and immediately made his way to where he belonged – at the head of his men. He knew how important the distraction of the shore batteries was to the success of the raid. This was a bloody-minded refusal to leave the field of play while there was a job to be done.

Harrison sent Adams back to gather more men, then turned to the task before him. At 32 he was the senior man in every sense; once again he became England's pack leader in a forward rush cherished from his rugby days. He led by example, his actions louder than the words which could hardly escape his smashed jaw. But this massive man, caught in the brilliant glare of Very lights, made the biggest of targets: 'Gathering together a handful of his men, Harrison led the charge along the parapet in the face of heavy machine-gun fire. He was killed at the head of his men, all but two of whom were also killed.'[16]

The two were able seamen, Eaves and McKenzie: Eaves tried to carry back Harrison's body, but was cut down by fire and later taken prisoner; McKenzie fired his Lewis gun until it was blown out of his hands, then smashed the broken stock into a German face, before retreating 'pushing, kicking and kneeing every German who got in the way'.[17] As an official German telegram acknowledged, 'On the narrow high wall of the Mole both parties fought with the utmost fierceness'.[18]

The inventive Frank Brock was later described as 'a good all-rounder at sport whether it was boxing, football or shooting, the sort of man who would never dream of going back. I can imagine him being on the Mole at Zeebrugge, and if he lost his revolver, fighting on with his fists.'[19] Also a rugby player (for Richmond), he lived by his Dulwich school song, 'fifteen fellows fighting full out for death and glory'. The belligerent boffin was determined to investigate the secret Goertz sound-ranging system used on the mole. Confused accounts place him fighting with cutlass and pistol with a Matrose Künne or 'punching the heads of German gunners', but he then disappeared.

The storming party had achieved its objectives: the main battery at the mole head never opened fire, the blockships slipped past. *Thetis* became entangled in nets, but *Iphigenia* and *Intrepid* scuttled themselves successfully in the throat of the canal. The recall signal ('K' in Morse) was repeatedly sounded on *Daffodil*'s siren (*Vindictive*'s was shot away), and the storming parties dragged their wounded and dead back across the gangways. Captain Charles Tuckey 'was missing and later reported killed and when last seen was at the foot of the ladders helping men up'.[20] Shells and bullets continued to smack into the three ships as they withdrew; *Iris* took a direct hit below decks which killed seventy-five men sheltering with hot soup.

The final toll was 188 killed, 384 wounded, with 16 missing, for whom hopes were not high. While the nation exulted, the survivors returning to Dover were chastened by the loss of so many comrades. The boost to national morale, however, was huge, while in Germany there was both consternation and grudging admiration for the raid's daring execution. Even the Kaiser visited the scene and interviewed a captured marine. Churchill would later eulogise the exploit 'as the finest feat of arms of the Great War, and certainly an episode unsurpassed in the history of the Royal Navy', a tribute all the more generous as he had nothing to do with it. The raid was a propaganda triumph, but the success was as short lived as any 'bite and hold' sortie in Flanders. At high tide on 25 April, submarine *UB16* quietly slipped through a channel dredged from the silt and carried on business as usual in the North Sea.

Remarkably, for all the mayhem on the mole, the British had brought back most of their dead: of the entire strength of almost 1,700 on the mission, only forty-nine did not return either dead or alive. Some fell into the sea; others who had stayed with the seriously wounded were taken prisoner. Arthur Harrison's body did not return to Dover; nor did those of Brock, Hawkings or Tuckey. The Royal Marine's grave in Zeebrugge churchyard is at least identified, while speculation swirls around seventeen unidentified plots, with the remains of Brock and Harrison somewhere amongst them.

The single men on this raid had been ardent volunteers from the outset. Keyes weeded out those who 'overlooked' their own marriages. Extraordinary efforts from deception to bribery had been made to join the gang. The 'skeleton' crews on the blockships' final run put on considerable extra flesh when the steaming crews for the crossing 'accidentally' missed their point of disembarkation. It seemed therefore appropriate that when medals were handed out, some should be awarded by acclaim of the participants. The desire to celebrate this flash of light in a dark hour of threatened defeat had to be carefully measured against the unsung daily heroism on the retreating Western Front. The solution invoked was the democratic Clause 13 of the original Victoria Cross warrant: in cases where an entire unit shows outstanding bravery, the recipient may be elected by his companions present at the action.

Eight Victoria Crosses were awarded, one of the four elected by ballot going to AB McKenzie who had tried to bring Harrison's body back. Distinguished Service Orders, Crosses, Medals and Mentions in Dispatches were awarded in the hundreds and Keyes was ennobled. The *London Gazette* of 17 March 1919 records Harrison's own posthumous award:

> For most conspicuous gallantry at Zeebrugge on the night of the 22nd–23rd April 1918. This officer was in command of the Naval storming parties embarked in *Vindictive*. Immediately before coming alongside the Mole Lt Cdr Harrison was struck on the head by a fragment of shell which broke his jaw and knocked him senseless. Recovering consciousness he proceeded on to the Mole and took over command of his party, who were attacking the seaward end of the Mole. The silencing of the guns on the Mole was of the first importance, and though in a position fully exposed to the enemy's machine gun fire Lt Cdr Harrison gathered his men together and led them to the attack. He was killed at the head of his men, all of whom were either killed or wounded. Lt Cdr Harrison, though already severely wounded and in great pain, displayed indomitable resolution and courage of the highest order in pressing his attack, knowing as he did that any delay in silencing the guns might jeopardise the main object of the expedition, i.e. the blocking of the Zeebrugge-Bruges Canal.

The Victoria Cross, presented to his mother Adelaide by King George at Buckingham Palace, was donated to the Britannia Royal Naval College at Dartmouth by surviving relatives in 1967. He is honoured in the county of his birth by a memorial at Roundham Head, Paignton.

In Captain Carpenter's 1921 account, his equation of war with sport seemed entirely natural. Today the rhetoric is less comfortable:

Harrison's charge down that narrow gangway of death was a worthy finale to the large number of charges which, as a forward of the first rank, he had led down many a rugby football ground. He has 'played the game' to the end ... with Harrison's death the Navy lost an officer who was as popular and as keen as he had been invaluable to the success of this particular operation.[21]

Harrison was the twenty-sixth England international to die in the war, and the last of six from the 1914 Ireland victory watched by the king. There would be still one more and a last would die of his wounds afterwards. Looking back after the Armistice, a journalist commented of that 1914 team that 'they might have hailed their distinguished spectator, only too appropriately, with the ancient gladiator's cry, "Morituri te salutant"'.[22]

The close-combat fighting at Zeebrugge had lasted less time than the eighty or so minutes of an average rugby match. For Arthur Harrison it was his last game for his country.

CHARLES BUTTON
THE THIN RED STRIPE

Lieutenant Charles Augustus Button, Royal Field Artillery. *(Jimmy Button)*

The Great War was one long crescendo of artillery fire. From the quiet opening bars when British offensives (and the command of Sir John French) petered out from lack of shells, the volume built noisily towards its climax with peak projectile delivery of a deafening 945,052 rounds on the night of 28/29 September 1918. For all the new technology of tanks, submarines, airships and aeroplanes, this was above all an artillery war.

The Royal Regiment of Artillery grew to be the dominant military arm with its Horse, Field and Garrison Artillery. From its 1914 start point of only 1,352 guns, no mortars or anti-aircraft guns and precious few howitzers, the regiment grew exponentially in numbers, killing power and sheer intimidatory terror. In one historian's view, 'artillery was the battle-winner, artillery was what caused the greatest loss of life, the most dreadful wounds and the deepest fear'.[1] By the Armistice, almost 12,000 pieces of ordnance were directed by over half a million men, double the entire number of the BEF in 1914. Tens of thousands died blasting their way toward eventual peace. Charles Sergeant Jagger's colossal Royal Artillery Memorial at Hyde Park Corner stands 'in proud remembrance of the Forty-Nine Thousand & Seventy Six of All Ranks' who gave their lives.

The Royal Field Artillery (RFA) was the most numerous arm in the regiment. Its mainstay was the Quick-Firing (QF) 18-pounder, which had been in service since 1905, and was drawn by six horses. In 1914 it was effectively a huge shotgun with its ammunition scattering 375 lead and antimony balls, designed to cut swathes through cavalry columns and infantry. High-Explosive shells to blast wire and trenches apart were added, but even by the first day of the Somme, three-quarters of the 18-pounder shells fired at La Boisselle by III Corps batteries were still shrapnel. The unbroken wire hanging with ragged scraps of the Tyneside Irish told its own tale.

Gun detachments of six highly trained RFA men on top form could fire thirty rounds a minute over a range that improved from 6,500 to 9,300 yards over the course of the war. An 18-pounder stationed in Trafalgar Square could lob a shell as far as Rosslyn Park's current ground in Roehampton – although this would hardly be popular with Saturday's spectators, even less so with the team on the pitch. That the 60-pounder, weighing 5 tons, could only reach some 3,000 yards further (so pulverising local rivals Richmond or London Scottish) suggests that, pound for pound, the mobile 'Eighteen' was the artillery's weapon of choice.[2]

In the early days, the guns were galloped right up to the front and fired over open sights at visible targets. The infantry felt reassured by their close physical presence, if not the shattering racket. It was not long, however, before the targets went underground and out of sight; it made corresponding sense to retire out of range of small arms and sight of opposing guns and spotters to covered positions, usually on the reverse slope of ridges. Warfare became a fight between two half-blind heavyweights slugging it out at the unseen limits of their reach, with deadly plunging howitzers throwing inverted uppercuts directly into the trench lines. The calibres on both sides grew larger, and their range longer: two British railway guns *Boche Buster* and *Scene Shifter* hurled 14in missiles over 21 miles (or one stride in 7-league boots). Measured from Nelson's Column, that would mean friendly bombs dropping not just on Slough, but on Maidenhead, Reigate or Welwyn Garden City.

The lighter mobile field guns stayed closer to the action and the infantry they protected. Theirs was the job of laying the barrage, static or creeping, that preceded every plodding advance across no-man's-land and – in theory only – kept the enemy machine-gunners' heads down until the last moment. Their HE shells were not really trench-busters and made little impression on the thickets of wire, as thousands discovered on a sunny Saturday morning in July 1916. But their versatility would also see them defending home lines by engaging attacking infantry. Their steel shields belonged to the direct-fire days when rifle bullets could still reach them, but now offered shelter from incoming shrapnel and shell fragments.

A battery of six guns was commanded by a major with five other officers and some 200 men. A lieutenant had a section of two guns, each under command of a sergeant. In the siege conditions of the middle years of the war, counter-battery fire was the biggest threat: no gun crew was photographed with personal weapons, as close-quarters fighting was rarely part of the job description. There were no 'better 'oles', but the gunners' positions behind the front line were safer than most. On the murderous Somme, first-day artillery casualties were just 170 of the 59,000 total. By 1918, however, the fast-moving storm-trooper tactics of the German Spring Offensive would change all that: RFA gunnery officers like 2/Lt Charles Button would find themselves overrun and would face steel that was cold, not molten.

Charles Augustus Button grew up at the westernmost end of the Great Western Railway, in Pembrokeshire, South Wales. In 1853, the GWR began to lay a double track from Swansea to Carmarthen, followed by a single-track extension to Neyland, then just a small fishing village of 200 souls, two chapels and two pubs. Measured by railway mileposts as 285 miles, 27 chains from London, Neyland was the pivot in Isambard Kingdom Brunel's grand vision of travel to New York: passengers purchasing a single ticket at Paddington could travel through, transferring at Neyland onto his SS *Great Eastern* steamship. In the spring of 1857, the new gateway to the United States of America opened – at Milford Haven. Brunel then christened the terminus and town 'New Milford', a snub to old Milford (just to confuse matters, the modern town of Milford Haven) where he had refused to take his line. Real prosperity came from a much shorter sea passage when parliament granted powers for the GWR to operate ships in 1871; the company took over the route between Neyland and the Irish ports of Waterford and Cork.

The protected haven at Milford, a naval anchorage since medieval times, harbouring the Royal Navy Dockyard at Pembroke, also gave birth to the Victorian era's greatest passenger ship. Brunel's New York vision was not fulfilled in his lifetime (he died in 1859), but between 1860 and 1886 his accident-prone *Great Eastern* was a regular visitor to Milford Docks – for lengthy repairs and painting. The leviathan towered over the terraced streets and dominated the economy of the town. Charles' father, John Button, a young marine engineer from Llanmadoc in Glamorgan, moved west for the work. Years later his sons would ride 'God's Wonderful Railway' in the opposite direction with very much the same idea. In booming Neyland, John married Elizabeth Holland, a local girl from Narberth, who would bear him six daughters and five sons, with Charles arriving at (inevitably) Great Eastern Terrace, Number 11, in 1884.

In a town where marine or railway engineers were kings, John was a prominent citizen, Freemason and church warden to the parish of Llanstadwell. His death in 1896 aged 47 left the large Button family without its breadwinner. By 1901 Elizabeth was running a grocer's shop, eldest son Matthew was a journeyman baker and John Holland Button, at 14, was apprenticed to a marine engineer. Twelve-year-old twins, Frank and Frederick, were living away from Pembroke at the Royal Masonic School, established in north London 'for clothing and educating sons of needy Freemasons'. Seventeen-year-old Charles, educated at Bowden's private school at Pembroke Dock, was drawn eastwards by the pervasive influence of the GWR to be a railway clerk, boarding at Railway Terrace in Resolven, Glamorgan.

Neyland died its own early death in 1906 when the Ireland terminus moved to Fishguard. When Elizabeth died in 1911, her many Buttons were scattered across the country. Jane, the eldest, was a married mother in Doncaster; Annie took over the grocery shop with sister Nellie. Lilian cared for an ageing aunt in Llanmadoc, Eudora taught in nearby Goodwick and Maud boarded at Cheltenham College for Ladies. Matthew worked as a bookstall clerk in Leominster; John's apprenticeship had come to nothing and he was now a general labourer in a tinworks. Three of the boys had become bank clerks: Frederick stayed in Welsh Pontypridd, while Frank and Charles took the GWR to London and settled in its suburbs. It is here that Charles, an outsider from South Wales living alone in a succession of boarding houses (40 Gordon Avenue, St Margaret's, 53 Creswell Road, Twickenham, and finally 37 Onslow Road, Richmond) found companionship in the great metropolis through his love of rugby. But it did mean special permission to leave early as bank closing time on Saturdays was 3 p.m.

His hometown club was founded in 1885, the year after his birth. In 1935, three members of the touring New Zealand All Blacks turned out for Neyland (Jerry Collins was doing nothing new with Barnstaple second XV in 2007) and earned it the right to wear the silver fern and all-black strip – still one of only two teams in the world to do so. Today's clashes between the Pembrokeshire All Blacks and the Pembroke Dock Harlequins are as keenly fought as Rugby World Cup finals. His brothers (excepting polio sufferer Matthew) played for Neyland, but Charles played his rugby as an exile in England. The wandering London Welsh club was the natural choice for a Welshman in London, but its ground was hardly convenient: it had played variously at the Queen's Club, Kensington, in Leyton and West Ham and was now at the Heathfield Ground in Wandsworth. The imposing Charles, 6ft and almost 14 stone, therefore chose to play for Rosslyn Park, nearer to his lodgings; his walk home from Old Deer Park after Saturday games would take him past the White Cross and White Swan, two bustling public houses where he could relax with an ale next to the Thames boatyards at Richmond and feel at home.

It was in London too that the 30-year-old Charles took his oath at Armoury House in the City to join the Honourable Artillery Company as a gunner in A Battery Special Reserve in September 1914. He had not lost touch with his Welsh roots and his attestation is signed by Reverend Davies, vicar of his home parish, Llanstadwell. A posed photograph taken on leave shows him in uniform with John, Matthew and Frank – Fred was 'overseas'. Promoted to bombardier in January 1916, he was 'accepted for admission to an Officer Cadet Artillery Brigade, Royal Horse

Artillery, St John's Wood'[3] in September. The following January saw him commissioned as second lieutenant[4] and posted to France with 8th Division, joining the 5th Battery/45 Brigade in April. The battery already had a proud and ancient history and Charles would add to its reputation in one of its most renowned actions.

Button's baptism of fire was at Pilkem Ridge, the opening salvo of the prolonged Third Battle of Ypres. His battery contributed to a huge Allied bombardment from 16 to 31 July when over 4 million shells were launched (compare 1.5 million in the celebrated Somme barrage). On the last day of July, heavy rain began to fall and would continue until November. The British infantry advance began at 3.50 a.m.; 3km of ground was gained at the cost of some 32,000 casualties in three days of battle. The slaughter monster paused for breath then moved to Langemarck for another three days of annihilation in August.

Charles thankfully took his ten days' allotted leave from 21 July. He was reunited in Neyland with his brothers, all of whom were serving, except for the disabled Matthew who was doing clerical war work. Charles now wore his RFA officer's uniform complete with horseman's spurs. To his left sits his strapping brother L/Cpl John Holland Button, serving with the King's Liverpool Regiment, who had already been awarded the Military Medal for bravery in the field at the Somme[5] and who would survive the war. Charles would also be given a high award for gallantry, but would never receive or wear it. This family photograph in the summer garden might be taken in calmer Edwardian days before the storm, but for the uniforms. However, the gathering is sombre, with few smiles.

Back at the Salient, he was lightly wounded in October, early in the first push for the village of Passchendaele, when two ANZAC corps and five British divisions floundered in the waterlogged terrain. Supply and movement problems in the atrocious weather meant that insufficient artillery was brought to bear in protecting the infantry advance. The ground they trudged over bore as much malice as the machine guns they faced. Exhausted men, harshly shelled during their long approach march at night and drenched by pouring rain, were sucked, helpless and heavy with equipment, into the quagmire. They drowned in putrid pools.

There was some respite during the freezing winter, but in 1918 8th Division was once again heavily involved when Germany launched Operation Michael, or the *Kaiserschlacht* (Kaiser's battle), on 21 March at St Quentin. Strengthened by nearly fifty divisions transferred from the East after Russia's surrender and the Treaty of Brest-Litovsk, Germany targeted a BEF weakened by its life-sapping ordeals of 1917, in an attempt to achieve a decisive victory before men and matériel poured in from America. Fresh battles at Rosières and Villers-Bretonneux churned the graveyard ground of the old battlefields. The new German gunnery and infantry tactics imported from the Eastern Front changed life for the 'back-room boys' in the artillery. They would now dance to a new and deadly tune.

First came the *Feuerwalze* (Waltz of Fire), a pattern of artillery bombardment also styled the 'Bruchmüller Concerto', after the colonel who composed its deadly score. The customary intensive shelling before an attack now concentrated not on forward infantry positions, but on the rear – artillery and machine-gun posts, command headquarters, telephone exchanges and rail heads. This deep barrage aimed to destroy any British capability to repel advancing German infantry – the Waltz of Fire became a funeral march. A last brisk battering of the forward positions would signal the first assault. Small groups of elite 'shock troops' (*Stoßtruppen*) were trained to 'infiltrate', exploiting gaps and moving swiftly, leaving any obstacles or pockets of resistance to be mopped up by following waves.

The British reeled before the new storm-trooper tactics of Operation Michael, and April's Operation George on the Lys river in Flanders kept the German territorial momentum flowing. The next full-scale attack in Ludendorff's Spring Offensive was code-named *Blücher-Yorck*, after the Prussian generals of the Napoleonic era. This time the surprise target was the French Sixth Army holding the Chemin des Dames ridge on a line between Rheims and Soissons in Champagne; Ludendorff reckoned that victory at the River Aisne would threaten Paris and force the Allies to divert troops from Flanders to defend the capital. This would then allow renewed German progress in the north.

The Aisne defenders were not just Frenchmen: four British divisions of IX Corps, badly depleted by the desperate onslaughts of spring, had been withdrawn to rest, refit and absorb their raw conscript replacements, under the command of General Denis Duchêne. For the French, the Chemin des Dames had long been a slaughterhouse to rival Verdun, passing back and forth until the costly Nivelle offensive of 1917 finally recaptured it for France. The 'Ladies Way' was built by Louis XV in 1770 to speed his daughters from the royal palace at Compiègne to the rural residence of their former governess. Napoleon was victorious at Craonne in 1814 and the area enjoyed symbolic prominence in French minds. Over lunch, a French colonel handing over his sector gave an impassioned address, reminding the British of the sacrifice that had won this ground. In reply the brigadier 'in very halting and extremely bad French gave the French the assurance that their "sacred ground" would not be left by the British except over their dead bodies'.[6] In this at least, the brigadier proved perspicacious.

To the relief of weary IX Corps the sector, according to a newly arrived staff officer, was 'renowned for its quietude. The French boasted that they had three casualties in two months, and the trenches and dugouts were in wonderful condition: 'We had at brigade headquarters a splendid deep dugout *en cas de bombardement*, but we lived in quiet attractive little rooms at ground level.'[7] One Northumberland officer recalled a beauty which would soon be defiled:

> The Aisne canal became a favourite bathing-place, and in the generous warmth of the excellent weather helped us to forget the dark days of the previous months. Reims, with its Cathedral glorious even in ruins, was not far to the East of us … the villages, such at any rate as had escaped the devastation of war, were things of beauty … The clustering houses, with the quaint old Church set in the midst, were bathed in the full light of a gorgeous moon, and the silver and shadows created a magic scene. Scarcely had we passed the village than from the thickets and hedgerows came the thrilling notes of a score of nightingales, singing away in the silence and the moonlight a sad song whose ecstasy touched us almost to tears.[8]

They would not enjoy such tranquillity for long: the British had exchanged the frying pan for the furnace. Among them was Charles Button's 5/Battery RFA.

In an earlier incarnation, the battery had fought at the siege of Gibraltar over four long years from 1779 to 1783 (although the battle honour was not awarded until 1934). Endurance was in the regimental blood, as was the 'offensive spirit' much cherished by the generals. Their role at the Rock was not confined to gunnery: the bombardiers had pressed a daring attack on foot to spike the opposing Spanish guns.[9] This fighting spirit would be revived in 1918 and remains today: in Afghanistan in 2007, 5/Battery guns, when not escorted by infantry in armoured Viking and Mastiff vehicles, were in charge of their own protection.[10]

In the Great War, before Button's arrival, the battery had first deployed as part of the BEF in November 1914 and fought at Neuve Chapelle, Loos and the Somme. After three long years and their latest exertions in retreat during early 1918, 5/Battery deserved their rest near Pontavert on the Aisne. They moved to Bois des Buttes, north of the river on 12 May. South of the river, unseen by reconnaissance from the newly amalgamated Royal Air Force, a storm was quietly building.

Ludendorff planned to concentrate his attack on a 37-mile section of the Allied line. He took great precautions to conceal his intent. Troops, guns, ammunition and supplies moved at night to avoid detection, and by the eve of attack he had amassed one battery for every 100 yards of frontage. The Allies would have been completely taken by surprise if it were not for two German prisoners who revealed under interrogation the plan for 27 May. Duchêne hastily rushed up reserves, including 2/Devonshires, which moved just forward of 5/Battery.

Battery Commander Major Griffiths had gone back to rest with the horses and gun limbers, leaving Capt. John Massey in command and two lieutenants stationed in outlying observation posts. Under Massey's direction the battery had prepared itself defensively in two sections of three with gun and ammunition pits dug for each gun, as well as defence trenches for the position. 2/Lt Charles Button commanded one section and Lt Charles Large the other. From 9 p.m.

on 26 May, with the crews wearing gas masks, their guns directed harassing fire on to likely enemy approach routes. They had ammunition enough to fire throughout the night of the imminent attack. The German guns, however, were strangely silent. The old gunnery hands, with little taste for Bruchmüller's tempo, were uneasy as the clock ticked past midnight.

At 1 a.m. precisely the 3,719 massed guns of the German artillery began their own orchestrated barrage of high explosives and gas shells 'as a roar of applause might follow a single speaker, drowning and obliterating it in a moment'.[11] It was a roar that lasted fully five and a half hours. Their aim seemed uncannily accurate: acoustic sound-ranging techniques using forward listening posts meant that their firing earlier in the evening had betrayed the British battery locations. One Division HQ captain described the first moments:

> Within a second, a thousand guns roared out their iron hurricane. The night was rent with sheets of flame. The earth shuddered under the avalanche of missiles, leapt skywards in dust and tumult. Even above the din screamed the fierce crescendo of approaching shells, ear splitting crashes as they burst ... all the time the dull thud, thud, thud of detonations and drum fire. Inferno raged and whirled round the Bois des Buttes. The dug outs rocked, filled with the acrid fumes of cordite, the sickly-sweet tang of gas. Timbers started: earth showered from the roof. Men rushed for shelter, seizing kits, weapons, gas masks, message pads as they dived for safety. It was a descent into hell.[12]

To keep sufficient men alive to sustain 5/Battery's return fire during this inferno, Capt. Massey organised a relief rota: an NCO and two gunners per gun at any one time, while the rest took cover until their turn came. Lt Large and 2/Lt Button helped man the guns while Massey moved from gun to gun, encouraging the men and reminding them of the battery's historic feats. According to a survivor's account, 'a steady rate of fire was continued during what seemed an interminable night'. Lt Large lost most of his right foot to a shell but refused to leave the battery.

The Devonshires in front lost telephone communications and had little artillery support due to the large number of guns destroyed by unerring counter-battery fire. They faced the best-trained German assault troops supported by tanks and even, it seemed, by the weather: the dense mist which had risen to help the Germans with almost magical regularity during the spring of 1918 obscured their view. The fast-moving attackers hurled grenades into dugouts and trenches and moved on, leaving the battalion a besieged island. The Devonshires battled for three hours to defend the bridge at Pontavert against overwhelmingly superior numbers, as their colonel told them: 'Your job for England, men, is to hold the blighters as much as you can, to give our troops a chance on the other side of the river. There is no hope of relief. We have to fight to the last.'[13]

The colonel was killed, but his men fought on to a final despairing charge by just twenty-three men. Their last-ditch stand allowed French and British troops to withdraw across the bridge. Refusing to surrender, the whole battalion of 581 officers and men was wiped out or forcibly taken prisoner. Amongst the dead was 2/Lt Cyril Pells who had survived the torpedoing of the *Lusitania*, only to die on French soil.

At 6.30 a.m. artillery fire on the 5/Battery position ceased and the barrage lifted just as large numbers of German infantrymen were spotted just 200 yards away. Capt. Massey ordered his guns to fire directly at them and, under cover of this fire, took a Lewis gun and four gunners armed with rifles and set off to drive back the attackers and protect their own flank.

The swarming Germans broke into the rear of the position, hurling their 'potato-masher' grenades. Despite his wounds, Lt Large took command, while Button dashed to burn the maps and documents at the command post. The detachment was now fighting with personal weapons as well as keeping the guns firing. With the position hopeless, Lt Large ordered that the breech blocks and dial sights be destroyed; as he shouted, he was shot through the lungs and died. Charles Button, last seen moving off to help Capt. Massey, was killed moments later and left 'lying dead in the trench shot to pieces'.[14]

Button was posted as missing. By March 1919 the War Office informed Matthew as next of kin that 'no further report had been received concerning 2/Lt CA Button RFA' and that he must be presumed dead. The compassionate network of the bereaved, in its search for closure, knew better: Matthew received word from Captain Massey's mother of a Bombardier Birley, taken prisoner as the position was overrun, 'who has stated that he saw my brother lying dead'. In a letter forwarded to Matthew with 'expression of sympathy' by the War Office in May, Birley added more detail in a breathless stream of vivid memory:

> The Capt. and Lieut. with me as the Boche made for the guns put 73 Sub-Section gun out of action I being the No1 of the Detachment, picking up a rifle we made for a communication trench in rear both Officers armed with revolvers and ammunition, hotly pressed the Capt. made for the wood further to the rear followed by Mr. Button and myself we were flanked on both sides by the Boche so made a fight for it.
>
> Mr. Button was shot through the heart and myself through the right breast the same bullet struck Capt. Massey above the heart I dropped in a trench where I lay for a time then I got up and made for the Officers to see if anything could be done finding Mr. Button dead I turned to Capt. Massey forcing some water in his mouth. Whilst doing this I was made to get up and walk along with other prisoners to a Dressing Station 17 kilometres behind the Boche line. While laying there I saw Capt. Massey brought in and calling that he was put next to me on a stretcher. Now each case of wounded was inoculated and a Serjeant who came to inoculate me, I asked him if there was any possibility of Capt. Massey living but he said no.[15]

The remainder of the battery fought hand to hand to an end which must have been both bitter and terrifying. Of the three officers and forty-six NCOs and men, only six escaped death or capture – Gunner Sowerbutts and Sergeant Schofield fought their way out with rifles and four unarmed gunners escaped. Schofield later died of his wounds; Sowerbutts was awarded the Military Medal for his efforts to get him to safety. Capt. Massey died at the German dressing station where Birley last saw him. His body was only identified in 1935.

The German attack was a startling success: the first day tore a hole over 35 miles wide in the Allied lines and penetrated 12 miles beyond the broken front. The stubborn Duchêne had defied instructions from his commander-in-chief Pétain by massing his troops in forward positions. Once units like the Devonshires – 'isolated and without hope of assistance'[16] – were overrun, there were no reserves or deep defences to delay the enemy's headlong advance. A French gendarme attached to the British described the chaotic night:

> Boche airplanes come over and machine gun the roads, we still don't know what's happening. No one knows what to do and we wait for orders to leave. A group of artillery men arrive saying that all their guns are lost. We realize that things are bad. At 4am we tell people to leave although they can stay if they want to. Two thirds leave but the others prefer to stay. At 5am we receive the order to leave, the 8th [Division] stay. The road is swept by shell fire. The road is choked with refugees, pushing handcarts, horse-drawn carts and so on. What a sad spectacle.[17]

The rout continued through the dying days of May: 50,000 Allied soldiers were taken prisoner and over 800 guns seized. In June the Allies were pushed back to the Marne and Paris was once again threatened. But Ludendorff had overreached himself in what was intended only as a diversionary attack; with Crown Prince Wilhelm leading the *sturmtruppen*, observed by his father, the Kaiser, it was difficult to restrain the unexpected momentum. Fatigue, severe losses and stretched supply lines did that for him. Counter-attacks, at Belleau Wood by US Marines of the newly arrived American Expeditionary Force, and later at Château-Thierry finally halted the German advance. The British IX Corps had suffered 15,000 fatal casualties and was withdrawn from the front in early July.

For his conduct on 27 May 2/Lt Charles Augustus Button was posthumously awarded the French *Croix de Guerre*, as was his fellow lieutenant Large, the Madras planter who had returned to fight in 1915. Captain Massey was also awarded the honour, as well as the Military Cross by his own nation. The entire 5/Battery RFA and 2/Devonshire battalion were commended by General Berthelot,

GOC of the Fifth French Army for the *Croix de Guerre avec Palmes en Bronze*, the highest category of the medal, in *Ordre General No. 351* of 16 July 1918. The corresponding British IX Corps Special Order is signed by a major on the General Staff, one Bernard Montgomery. Today the battery remains fiercely proud of the honour, awarded formally at Tournai in December 1918. The green ribbon with red stripes from the 1918 *Croix* is still worn today, as authorised by Army Order 118: 'At the top of both sleeves of Service Dress, Number 1, 2, & 3 Dress and later Mess Dress. The ribbon is also worn on the left side of the Service Dress Cap above the button by Officers and Warrant Officers and on the beret below the issued badge.'[18]

The repeated hammer blows of the Spring Offensives – Michael, George, Blücher-Yorck and Gneisenau – badly damaged the Allies, but had their own impact on the German Army. Its elite assault troops suffered crippling losses. Those still alive were on their knees with exhaustion. The regular units, stripped of the fittest men, were left only with the old, the very young and those unfit for front-line fighting. Casualties on both sides were appallingly high and alike in number, belying the apparent German territorial success. American 'doughboys' in their prime, eager for the fight, now helped to turn the tide and the British Army showed an extraordinary ability to bounce back. Despite its losses, 5/Battery was reconstituted and fought on at the second Battle of Arras in August and the taking of Douai in October. Charles Button's body was never found; his name appears on the Soissons Memorial along with most of his battery and 4,000 others with no known grave. The 'Last Stand of the 5th (Gibraltar) Battery' was later immortalised by artist Terence Cuneo. Jimmy Dingle's epitaph was in a poem, Charles Button's in oils.

The Royal Artillerymen of the Great War have their lasting memorial at Hyde Park. The gigantic 9.2in howitzer, its stone muzzle reputedly trained on the Somme, is surrounded by four bronze gunners, massive and uncompromising in their realism. Sculptor Charles Jagger, who was severely wounded at Gallipoli and earned two more wound stripes and the Military Cross on the Western Front, resisted the conventional symbolism of the previous century, insisting that this was a *war* memorial (not, in Sassoon's phrase, a 'pile of peace-complacent stone') and that his 'experience in the trenches persuaded me of the necessity for frankness and truth'.[19] Galsworthy's Soames Forsyte agreed:

> … nothing high-flown about that gun – short, barking brute of a thing; or those dark men – drawn and devoted under those steel hats. Nothing pretty-pretty about that memorial – no angels' wings there! No Georges and dragons, nor horses on the prance; no panoply and no panache! … squatted like a great white toad on the nation's life. Concreted thunder.[20]

Its four monumental figures, shrouded in their capes and greatcoats, are resolutely human, not heroic. Their eyes are downward cast, not raised to the skies. One reads a letter from home, another leans for support against the stonework, and one lies dead, his face covered, his Brodie on his chest like the helmed crown of a warrior king on his catafalque. Its inscription from *Henry V* reads: 'Here was A Royal Fellowship of Death.'

The Great War changed the way the nation's artists and architects thought about war and how it should be remembered. Of all wars, this was not to be marked by statues of generals. They moved on from Victorian military adventure heroes, like Charles Bayly's great-uncle General Gordon, to solid, unsentimental structures like Lutyens' Cenotaph and Thiepval, or Jagger's memorial. Its bas-reliefs, details now decaying in the poisoned air of this huge traffic island, combine technical precision with battlefield chaos. Straining sinews of horse and man, heads and bodies glimpsed in part but rarely whole; they are a Guernica in sooty Portland stone. In their massive implacability, the bronze gunners exude the fortitude and unblinking endurance of the ordinary soldiers who saw it through to the end.

The story of our fifteen rugby players started with one statue and ends with another. In November 1922, three years before the Artillery Memorial, a single Jagger bronze was unveiled at Paddington station, terminus of the Great Western Railway that carried Charles Button from Neyland to London and war. It is a memorial to the 2,524 GWR men who were killed. Churchill described the statue to 6,000 listening relatives:

It depicts a fighting man, though at the moment in no fighting humour, for he is reading a letter from his dear ones at home. I can only hope that when you gaze upon it you may find some solace in the remembrance of those many letters that you wrote to your loved ones at the front, and that you will realise not only what a comfort they were to them, but also how they imbued them with fresh strength and fresh spirit to endure the many horrors and hardships of war.[21]

No letters from the front have survived from Charles Button. No words of his own are left to tell his story or preserve his memory. For the fifteen men and more in this book, these words are humbly offered in their stead.

THE GAME THAT WON THE WAR

In 1919, an anonymous headmaster sent *The Times* his end of term report on the war and the 'National value of Rugby Football'. He declared: 'one game at any rate has been justified triumphantly, not only as a pastime, but as an instrument of true education, and that is Rugby Football … unequalled by any other game as a school of true manhood and leadership.' Like an enthusiastic head of games, he argued:

> It is above all others a team game, where the individual is merged in his side. If he is a forward, he is one of pack that must know how to form together in a moment, each man in his right place, and get down to their work like one man, that must know how to break up together, wheel together, and go down the field together with the ball at their feet, each man helping the other. If he is outside the scrummage, he is one of a line which succeeds only by perfect combination, and is ruined by individualism, however brilliant.[1]

He warms to his task: not only is rugby a game of team cohesion, but it inspires the finest individual qualities, both of command and obedience:

> Rugby football is a game which more than any other calls for instantaneity of decision: in the rapidity of its changes opportunity offers but for the briefest moment, and in that fraction of a moment it must be taken, and a choice made between several possible alternatives. It is a game in which, in the midst of confusion and often of great noise from spectators, every player must be quick and alert to obey his leader, to catch his command, to combine. Fifteen youths

combine to transfer a leather-cased bladder to a position which 15 others seek to deny them, and in that irrational process cooperation, quickness of decision, resource, courage, honour, unselfishness and good temper are all developed.

Triumphantly, he scores his point, citing a day school (presumably his own) whose Old Boys all dutifully went to war, yet distinctions 'fell in a most marked degree to those who had played for the fifteens':

... if it were possible to analyse the records of the many thousands of young officers who, in this war, have won the Military Cross, or have died in an act of brilliant leadership, it is probable and many would say certain that the lion's share of honour would be claimed by those who learned great lessons when they were 'muddied oafs at the goal'.

Of Rosslyn Park's 350 muddied oafs, 63 were awarded the MC – our headmaster was clearly on to something.

As the signature sport of pre-war public schools, rugby was increasingly an identifier of adult potential. In business circles, rugby players were felt to have the right stuff. *Boys' Own Paper* columnists passed on careers advice from the City: 'During a boom on the Exchange, if a fellow couldn't stand his ground with a lot of fellows pushing and elbowing through a crowd, he would be of no use to him. The chap who could pile up a scrum at Rugger was just the man he wanted.'

Physicality at the Stock Exchange may have waned with screen-based trading, but the principle prevailed until professionalism offered a sporting wage in the 1990s – a Harlequins jersey was long a passport to Square Mile pinstripes.

The schools also nurtured the administrators of empire and the colonial mines and plantations that returned wealth to Britain. Rugby joined cricket in the 'civilising' drive to ensure that no wayward native traditions or rival incursions by imperialist continentals would challenge Her Majesty's Britannic model of society. Rugby even tried to conquer territories closer to home with expeditionary forays into Europe; Rosslyn Park pioneered as the first English club in Europe, playing Stade Français in April 1892. London news-papers fretted that this might lead to 'International Complications'. In France, Baron Pierre de Coubertin, rugby cup final referee and devotee of English school sports, was a prime mover in organising the match, and even wrote a match report under the byline 'Pierre le Vieux'. Inspired by this new international Corinthianism, he made his first public call that year to revive the ancient Olympics. The first modern Games took place in Athens in 1896; Rosslyn Park can surely claim a part in their inspiration, just as its mini players would later help the International Rugby Board's pitch for rugby sevens as an Olympic sport for 2016.

Park won in Paris through 'superior science and training'[2] and repeated their visit in 1893, 1900 and 1912. There is no evidence of a return game in London, although a mixed Stade/Racing team toured London under the colours of Coubertin's *Union des Sociétés Françaises de Sports Athlétiques* (USFSA) in 1893. Their jerseys carried two linked rings of red and blue – see where he was going there? Perhaps the Park motive was less international diplomacy, more the champagne pleasures of touring 'gay Paree'. Ditto the later exchange of fixtures with wine-rich Bordeaux, as Park's sophisticates spurned traditional tour destinations in Wales and the West Country.

In 1893, a London newspaper report on the USFSA match hoped that the growing popularity of rugby would have a pacifying effect on the old warring enmities of Europe: 'Judging by the number of clubs springing up not only in France but Germany we may, in a few years hence, see friendly football fights between those old rivals in less agreeable warfare, and also between the continental and British nations.'[3]

By 1912, Park was boldly carrying the gospel to the Central Powers, bringing light to benighted nations not only sadly ignorant of rugby football but also rattling sabres in the general direction of England: 'The tour originated from a visit to England by an Hungarian Association football team which saw Rugby Football played and wanted to introduce it in their country.'[4] The necessary finance was found (the hosts put up £400 and the club £100 – good business) and, bolstered by reinforcements from universities, services and hos-pitals, forty-two players toured Austria-Hungary with 3,000 miles travelled in ten April days. Two sides, named Rosslyn Park and London Nomads, played against each other in distinctive uniform colours.

Despite European press fears that such a violent game must 'inevitably lead to an increase in duelling', rugby was a huge popular success: 'Both Austrian and Hungarian crowds were very lavish in their applause and at the conclusion of each match much laughter was caused when some of the younger onlookers raced onto the field and started forming scrums and trying to collar one another.'[5]

The first exhibition in Prague attracted 'a large enthusiastic crowd, who although very amused at the scrum formation, thoroughly appreciated the various points of the game and heartily applauded every clever piece of play, especially the keen tackling'. The circus moved to Budapest, where 'many spectators were evidently conversant with Rugby rules'. The missionaries were making conversions: their hosts announced that a 'Rugby Club would shortly be formed in Buda-Pesth'. A final match was played at Vienna, where a 'very handsome silver cup' was presented to the captain of the winning team, E.H. Mitchell, who returned thanks.

We can only speculate (entirely fatuously) whether a homeless 23-year-old Austrian art student witnessed this last game in Vienna. What if he had channelled his frustration at rejection by the academy into becoming a chippy scrum-half rather than fanatical dictator? Even in a largely middle-class sport, you will find grizzled forwards with flattened noses who freely admit that the amateur game – like the fabled boxing gyms of London's East End – gave them an outlet that stopped them going to the bad. On this occasion, it was not to be; nor in 1913, when two further intrepid expeditions were made to Hanover. Both the Habsburg Empire and *Deutsches Reich* remained unconquered – rugby's proselytising spirit failed to avert the First World War, let alone the second.

In a journalistic warm-up for the column inches to come in wartime, the *Times* correspondent in Vienna, in smug imperialist tone, hinted at flaws in the opposition's national psyche:

> The unanimous verdict of today's Press is that the game, although amusing and even comical as a spectacle, is totally unfitted to the Austrian temperament and ought not to be taken up. The Austrian

writers praise highly the self-control and sportsmanlike spirit of the English players but confess unreservedly that such virtues are at present beyond Austrian footballers, and seem inclined to the verdict that, however excellent the Rugby game may be a form of violent exercise, it is not football.[6]

Arch propagandist Lord Northcliffe later recycled this sentiment in urging America to join the fight in 1917. The problem with your German, you see, is that he is not a good sport:

> Our soldiers are individual. They embark on little individual enterprises. The German ... is not so clever at these devices. He was never taught them before the war, and his whole train-ing from childhood upwards has been to obey, and to obey in numbers. He has not played individual games. Football, which develops individuality, has only been introduced into Germany in comparatively recent times.[7]

Rugby players were certainly quick off the mark when the whistle blew in 1914. Physique helped: the minimum height for a volunteer at the outbreak of war was 5ft 8in. Only three months later, 5ft 3in would do for cannon fodder, and bantam battalions took even smaller men. Well-nourished public schoolboys who had played sport were often 5in or 6in taller than their men, who looked up to them in every way.

Paul Jones, former first XV captain of Dulwich, admitted that 'in my heart and soul I have always longed for the rough and tumble of war as for a football match'.[8] He was later to ask before his death in 1917: 'do you realise what a fine part amateur sportsmen are playing in this war? I doubt if there will be many great athletes left if things go on as they are doing.' The poet Rupert Brooke, one half of a doomed Rugby School centre partnership with Ronnie Poulton, was the early cheerleader for these young men. Rugby players were still stepping forward in 1918 when the call went out for volunteers for a suicidal tour to Zeebrugge.

Recruiters were eager that 'British athletes' follow the rugby lead. A poster trumpets the 'glorious example' of 'Rugby Union Footballers Doing their Duty – over 90% have enlisted'.

The determined features of a scrum-capped international are also framed under a peaked military cap, the leather ball in his hands exchanged for a Lee-Enfield. Lord Roberts, stern advocate of conscription, declares, 'this is no time to play Games'. Punching home his argument with a statistical hook, the copywriter quotes November's *Times*: 'Every player who represented England in Rugby International matches last year has joined the colours.'

Twenty-seven England players would die in four years. Behind the choice quotations lies one of the early controversies of the war. Gentlemen's Rugby Union (not the breakaway Northern Union, and certainly not association football) claimed the high moral ground over its sporting competitors. Many battles would be fought in this war, not all of them at the front. Rugby would emerge victorious.

The RFU was wrong-footed by the declaration of war. On 13 August, Secretary C.J.B. Marriott instructed clubs to play on, but the amateur players had other ideas and were already trying on new uniforms and training regimens. Club committees swiftly convened to decide that the 'greater game' to be played in Europe demanded the sacrifice of the 1914/15 season. The decision was already out of their hands: many players had already signed up, like Park's Sandhurst contingent and Territorials, or Harlequins' England heroes Stoop and Poulton, both 'Terriers'. The playing strength of clubs simply evaporated before the season could start.

By 4 September, the RFU bowed to the inevitable and cancelled all club, county and international matches. Marriott floated the idea of a rugby battalion too late – players had already taken commissions. England's Edgar Mobbs, initially too old for an officer at 32, joined the ranks and gathered 250 like-minded volunteers in Northampton. But there was never to be an oval-ball version of the footballers' battalions and even the broader sportsmen's battalions contained few rugby men. At a Special General Meeting on 18 September at Carr's Restaurant in the Strand, Park Secretary Burlinson stated 'that owing to the great crisis in which this Country was involved, a very exceptional state of affairs existed which would entirely alter the whole of the programme arranged for the ensuing season'.[9] For three of sixteen attendees – Noel Houghton, Conway Hart and Neil Shoobert – the 'great crisis' would be fatal.

Professional sport, with its commercial imperative, tried to keep the turnstiles open: the Football League and Northern Union continued playing against a growing media outcry. Doggerel poetess Jessie Pope denounced association football in the *Daily Mail*:

> Football's a sport, and a rare sport too
> Don't make it a source of shame
> To-day there are worthier things to do
> Englishmen, play the game![10]

Even Mr Punch weighed in, glaring at a footballer:'No doubt you can make money in this field, my friend, but there's only one field to-day where you can get honour.'The cartoon caption explains: 'The Council of the Football Association apparently proposes to carry out the full programme of the Cup Competition, just as if the country did not need the services of all its athletes for the serious business of War.'[11] Press invective was directed not just at wage-earning players, but at the crowds of 'loafers and shirkers' who preferred to watch football rather than fight. Genteel ladies pressed white feathers on spectators outside grounds in public shaming; sometimes they picked on wounded soldiers on leave and simply looking for some relaxation. Eventually, professional football was officially banned in the spring of 1915. But the stain on its character made it vulnerable to rugby's prompt patriotism, with lasting post-war consequences.

War did not put an end to rugby, just to its club sides. Rugby simply continued in military guise as men donned khaki; it was both recreation and fitness training. On its formation in 1914, the 16th Northumberland (Newcastle Commercials) quickly raised a side:

> The moment the battalion was settled down in billets for 'rest' the old rugger ball (an integral part of the regimental kit which was entrusted as a precious possession to the care of the Regimental Q.M.S), was produced, and scratch games within the battalion were arranged and thoroughly enjoyed.[12]

They played their first match against the 6th Northumberland Fusiliers and, with half the team being county players, they won a decisive victory. However, they would face terrible defeat at the Somme: only one of that 1914 team took the field again after 1 July.

Matches were played at training camps across the country. In December, the Barbarians skippered by England lock Harold Harrison played Shoreham Camp, captained by Edgar Mobbs, in aid of 'Lady Jellicoe's Sea Fleet Comforts Fund'. Four Rosslyn Park players[13] featured at Shoreham, and a fifth may be claimed. Baa-Baas fullback James Urquhart was a Northampton Grammar school teacher and Cambridge University soccer player who had signed amateur forms for Grimsby Town. He joined Mobb's team and his 7th (Service) Battalion and was elected a Barbarian in 1915, giving Rosslyn Park as his club, but never represented it on the field. He died at Loos the day after Charles Vaughan. Mobbs himself, now commanding the battalion he raised, died at Zillebeke in 1917; the memorial match inaugurated in his honour in 1921 was until 2011 the longest-standing Barbarian fixture.

Public matches were also arranged 'outside the wire' to boost morale of troops and civilians alike. Kitchener's New Armies were training hard for France and up to ten military sides were looking for fixtures. As casualty lists grew, the matches also offered fresh recruiting opportunities: when the Canadian Cavalry played the Gloucesters, 'it would not be easy for any able-bodied young man, without overpowering reasons for holding back, to avoid catching some contagion of military enthusiasm'. Games drew spectators as well as players from the forces: 'rows and rows of khaki caps and khaki figures leaning forward with hands on knees, rows of canes waving in time to the tunes of war-cries that rose and fell.'[14] The *Times* writer was gravely conscious of reports from the away game across the Channel:

> This is not the time for describing football matches and it is enough to say that the UPS just won by 13 points to 11. It was a really good game, but even if it had not been the afternoon of watching would have been an eminently encouraging one and the best of antidotes to gloominess.

Antidote or entertainment, rugby matched the country's bellicose mood: a crowd of 20,000 watched the Canadians at Leicester on New Year's Day 1915.

At Old Deer Park, Rosslyn Park's committee was determined to do its bit. In November 1915 journalist Arthur Podmore ('Poddy') approached the secretary, Harry Burlinson ('Burly' – rugby nicknames have gained little originality in a century of change), with a view to reviving the holiday matches for public schoolboys, which had lapsed in the first months of the war. The club took on the 'serious financial responsibility' of £120 for ground rental, because it 'wished to do everything in its power to keep the game going to the fullest extent possible'.[15] Members like John Bodenham were pursued for their subscriptions, even if they happened to be 'somewhere in France' at the time. The first scratch XV of London schools played 'The Rest', with gate monies donated to war charities, chiefly the Star and Garter home for war invalids. After the holidays, the boys returned to their military training; the Public Schools Services XV was formed 'to cater for any officer or man on leave who had no service unit team available, and not to confine itself to those who had just left school'.

During 1916–17 games were played weekly between a curious mix of representative sides, often raised by peacetime Park regulars now in uniform (and dusting off their old pre-war hooped jerseys as makeshift team strip). Hartlepool Garrison or the Royal Warwickshires might play Cambridge ('a team composed of medical students') or the 2/10th Manchesters who were 'mostly amnestied Northern Unionists'. There were now three sets of goalposts at the Old Deer Park, 'which partly eased the scarcity of grounds in or near London'. On one day in January 1917 seventy-five 'boys' took part in two games, with 450 in all playing that year.

Games were now organised on club lines:

… although the cancellations of leave and sudden movements of troops caused many hitches, the main object – to supply officers and men of the forces with the opportunities they needed – was achieved from now until the end of the 1918–19 season, when the matches automatically ceased, leaving as a legacy the schools holiday games which continue.[16]

The 'Public Schools, Past and Present' team, kitted out in an improbable allsorts patchwork of club, county and national shirts, also played against sides of Australians and New Zealanders, both 'teams of convalescents … some of them playing without boots'. The casual press condescension to the colonial visitors is breathtaking: 'the authorities have permitted a number of New Zealanders to leave the front and play a brief series of games in this country for the benefit of the Red Cross.'[17] As well as filling charitable coffers, rugby took a lead in rehabilitating men with scars, both physical and psychological. New Zealander Captain H.M. Chrystall, before his return to France in January 1918, wrote: 'I will very much miss the pleasant Saturday afternoon recreation. The games have got me thoroughly fit in wind and limb, after being a physical wreck through shell-shock and given up by the doctors.'[18]

Rugby was a training ground as good as any drill square. One paper commented: 'the war has proved the value of games generally, and of football in particular, as training for the grim business of the battlefield.'[19] As subalterns succumbed to their short life expectancy, a fresh supply of officers was constantly needed. In 1917, Robert Graves of 2/Royal Welch Fusiliers, who had turned out at fullback in a match in France, was an instructor with 4th Officer Cadet Battalion at Oxford. He thought that rugger was useful in identifying the right sort: 'Those who played rough but not dirty and had quick reactions were the sort we needed, and we spent most of our spare time playing games with them.'[20] But then, this is a poet who could write in 1924:

> In Rugby football I have killed more men,
> Playing full-back and tackling with ill-will,
> Killed them, I mean, in murderous intention,
> Than ever I killed at Loos or Passchendaele.[21]

The 'rough sport' was also seen to inculcate the correct manly attitude to the perils of wounding and the stoical endurance with which a chap must face its horror and pain. In *Journey's End*, the fatally wounded subaltern James Raleigh is comforted by his school idol Captain Dennis Stanhope, who knows he is done for. Raleigh shows a brave face to his skipper: 'I'll be better if I get up and walk about. It happened once before – I got kicked in just the same place at Rugger; it – it soon wore off. It – it just numbs you for a bit.'[22]

A century later, when a Parachute Regiment corporal was blown up by an improvised explosive device (IED) in Afghanistan, he echoed Raleigh with deft understatement: 'it felt like being hit by a hard rugby tackle.'[23] This tackle cost him an arm and both his legs were later amputated above the knee.

It is a matter of macho pride in rugby that players would rather lose an ear than leave the field of play, while soccer players are derided for feigning injury. In amateur days, bandages were a luxury, stitches an interruption to post-match bar activity. The Harlequins 'Bloodgate' affair dealt a body blow to this *omertà*: it offended against a code nurtured since the Great War that the rugby man was impervious to mere flesh wounds which were, after all, an occupational hazard. If a doctor was insistent, stitches were taken like a man, without anaesthetic, and their number counted as a badge of pride. When Tom Williams left the field at the Stoop Memorial Ground gushing a suspicious scarlet from the mouth, here was evidence that a player would feign injury with stage blood to gain a tactical advantage in a tight game. In a telegraphed move, the RFU appointed the uncompromising Lawrence Dallaglio to head a commission to restore rugby's reputation for integrity – and manliness.

Before the war, rugby's association with the armed forces had to fight against the success of soccer: in 1906 the army and navy had 758 association teams between them. The Army/Navy rivalry in rugby was revived by a challenge match in 1905 which helped the sport to flourish in the services, endorsed by no less a figure than Admiral Lord Jellicoe: 'Rugby football, to my mind, above all games is one which develops the qualities which go to make good fighting men. It teaches unselfishness, esprit de corps, quickness of decision, and keeps fit those engaged in it.'[24]

In Malins' famous film of the Somme, General Beauvoir de Lisle addresses the Lancashire Fusiliers; in the background is a set of rugby posts improvised from gnarled trees – a bit twisty, less than white, but posts nonetheless. Rugby was the officers' game: Paul Jones wrote resignedly in 1915 that 'the Tommies … think soccer the only game, so one must cut one's cloth to one's opportunities'.[25] By 1917, however, the official ball of the Western Front was round and every platoon was issued with one. In *Journey's End* they talk of rugby football at home, but play association at the front. All ranks knew the rules and it caused fewer injuries: one Rifle Brigade battalion commander broke his collarbone playing rugby on the eve of the Somme.

The 18/London Irish reportedly kicked the first football across no-man's-land as they attacked at Loos on 25 October 1915.[26] More famously, Captain Nevill of the East Surreys, although from Twickenham and a keen rugby player at Dover College, did the same at Montauban Ridge and gained instant celebrity (and death):

> The captain … had provided four footballs, one for each platoon, urging them to keep up a dribbling competition all the way over the mile and a quarter of ground they had to traverse. As the company formed on emerging from the trench, the platoon commanders kicked off, and the match against Death commenced. The gallant captain himself fell early in the charge, and men began to drop rapidly under the hail of machine-gun bullets. But still the footballs were booted onwards, with hoarse cries of encouragement or defiance, until they disappeared in the dense smother behind which the Germans were shooting. Then, when the bombs and bayonets had done their work, and the enemy had cleared out, the Surrey men looked for their footballs, and recovered two of them in the captured traverses.[27]

British newspapers hailed the plucky charge, but the Germans thought it downright bonkers. They might have a point, as a letter from Nevill written during the seven-day softening-up bombardment has the barking tone of Lieutenant the Honourable George Colthurst St Barleigh in *Blackadder*: 'As I write the shells are fairly haring over; you know one gets just sort of bemused after a few million, still it'll be a great experience to tell one's children about.' Another letter from a fellow officer shows that there was both humour and method in the apparent madness of the 21-year-old in command of even younger men:

I am afraid the newspapers didn't give quite the right story of the footballs. There were two footballs, and on one was printed: 'The Great European Cup-Tie Final. East Surreys v Bavarians. Kick off at zero.' On the other in large letters was this: NO REFEREE, which was W.'s way of telling the men they needn't treat the Hun too gently.[28]

When the two balls were returned to England on their way to regimental museum and myth, the Surreys' Colonel Treeby was more comfortable with the language of rugby:

Our men have played and are playing the game. We are still in the scrum, it is true, but the ball is being carried forward, and we doubt not that in God's good providence the goal for which we are fighting – the goal of freedom, justice and lasting peace – will soon be won.[29]

Sadly (for this author anyway) there is no widespread evidence of rugby balls being kicked or dribbled, probably with good reason; as any fullback will tell you, the unpredictable bounce of the leather oval makes it highly unsuited for the purpose. But the game had at least one determined band of adherents at the front: at Thiepval the rugby-mad '16/Northumberland Fusiliers launched two companies behind a rugby football, drop-kicked in a high arc from the assembly trench'.[30]

Rugby kept right on to the end of the road. On Armistice Day itself proof of its enduring appeal in wartime can be seen in the summary of results pictured below.

When the final whistle blew, the clubs counted their dead. In the hour of victory people did not speak of 'the pity of war' – Owen's poems were not published in his lifetime (cut short a week before the Armistice) and only gained widespread notice in Sassoon's 1930 edition. Pride was the watchword. At Rosslyn Park's AGM in September 1919, Burlinson reported that the total of past and present members serving in the war 'slightly exceeded 350'. The death toll was declared (erroneously as we now know) at sixty-six, with six more missing. No names are mentioned, but the secretary was most punctilious about the honours won: 'VCs 2, DSO 11, with bar, 2, Military Cross 63, DSC 4, DFC 3, Croix de Guerre 2, DCM 1, Military Medal 1, OBE1, KBE1 and 54 mentioned in despatches.'[31] The paucity of other ranks' medals tells its own story of the English rugby class. To Burly's even greater delight, however, despite the losses, rugby was already resurgent: 'no less than 100 new members have been elected this year.'

Many clubs and schools would list similar catalogues of decorated heroism. Our anonymous headmaster is clear why this should be:

> The services of the Officers training Corps have been great, but it is not the military drill that has given the country the product of which it is proud. Nor would any amount of physical training, however scientific, and however desirable in itself, yield the same moral result. Natural leaders will be produced in plenty wherever Rugby football is played, and the virtues which it develops are as valuable for peace as for war, for the work of the Empire in every continent as much as for the trenches of France.

He has little time for the 'less inspiring and the less severe discipline of Association'. With rhetoric rising in crescendo, as if addressing school on speech day, he avers that for the good of secondary education:

RUGBY FOOTBALL.

SATURDAY'S RESULTS.

New Zealand Headquarters Staff beat Australian Headquarters Staff, at Herne Hill, on Saturday, by two tries (6 points) to nothing.

A Machine Gun School side beat a Public Schools' Services' side, at Richmond, by two goals, one dropped goal, and five tries (29 points) to nothing.

South Africans beat London Canadians, at Richmond, by two goals, two dropped goals, one penalty goal, and two tries (27 points) to nothing.

Royal Military Academy beat Guy's Hospital, at Woolwich, by two goals and one penalty goal (13 points) to two tries (6 points).

Cardiff and Pill Harriers played a drawn game, at Cardiff, neither side having scored.

... it is timely to press forward the claims of the greatest game of all. It is not only national but imperial; it is the game of the most vigorous of our Colonies; it is the game of the Army that has won the hardest and grimmest of all wars; it should be the universal game of our new educational system because it is a maker of men.

Despite its losses, rugby was prepared to make the sacrifice again, or so its proponents vowed: E.H.D. Sewell praised the 'glorious deaths for King, for Empire and for the Right' and declared that 'whenever [England] calls again, Rugby Football will be the first to line out; bending forward eager for the moment the fight begins, and ready to "stick it", come what may'. For Sewell, and many others, victory in the war confirmed the staying power of values that had taken so many men willingly to the front and to eventual death. Haig himself judged in 1919 that team games required 'decision and character on the part of the leaders, discipline and unselfishness among the led, and initiative and self-sacrifice on the part of all'.[32] The affirmation of these values and the claims made for rugby's key role in Britain's hard-fought triumph saw many correspondents join our headmaster on *The Times*' letters page. One, in rose-tinted hindsight, praised: 'the way in which all Rugby clubs, aided very fully by the Rugby Union, almost ordered all players to the colours in August 1914, realising that the game for which they had been preparing for so many years had begun, made a deep impression on the country.'[33]

As club and country returned to the field, with England under Wavell Wakefield notably successful in the 1920s, rugby enjoyed a boom. Tectonic plates shifted on school sports fields, as soccer nets increasingly gave way to rugby posts. Radley, Malvern, City of London and Rossall joined the scrum during or immediately after the war. The campaign for rugby at Winchester was led by Brigadier General Godfrey Meynell, a veteran of Delville Wood, who wrote from France in February 1919, where he was still with the BEF: 'Rugby is the most character-forming sport in the world.' He also warned non-rugby schools like Harrow, who 'from the experience of the last war, will consider now the advisability of changing their game, and if not there are "other schools"'.[34] Harrow abandoned soccer for rugby in 1926, the year of the General Strike when suspicion of the working class – and its associated professional game – was at its height.

In their aspiration to the public-school model, middle-class grammar schools now rushed to rugby. By 1929, the number of schools affiliated to the RFU had more than quadrupled to 133. Rugby-playing school and university graduates then began to fill the professions and settled in suburbia, where the local club was a pillar of the social structure. For a young man wanting to get ahead, rugger was the way. As it led to well-paid and secure positions, Rugby Union was able to stay resolutely amateur and look down its nose at 'trade' professionals in league or association, who were simply trying to scrape a living.

Publishing in the 1920s saw an explosion of coaching manuals alongside the outpouring of war memoirs. Titles like *Rugby football and How to play it*, *Rugby for beginners* and *Rugby Football – How to succeed* were self-help handbooks to the social and business advancement craved by the upwardly mobile. Authors took an increasingly academic tone: not content with his *Text Book on Rugby Football*, Irish international I.M.B. Stuart published a *Theory of Modern Rugby Football* in 1930. *Rugby – The Game* by the pseudonymous Scot 'Ompax' advised on the development of rugby, how to play, and even how to watch it. Writers as diverse as England's Wakefield, Lions skipper Cove-Smith, Park's own rugby-playing Reverend H.G. Marshall and RFU secretary Marriott delivered techniques, tips and tales to a market hungry for rugger. War had been good for the game and a lasting association with sacrifice was permanently fixed, much in the way that national remembrance is now enshrined on the eleventh hour, day and month. In 1991, rugby's world cup adopted as its anthem Holst's musical setting of diplomat Sir Cecil Spring-Rice's 1908 poem 'I vow to thee my country'. He revised its words in 1918, in response to wartime losses:

> The love that asks no question, the love that stands the test,
> That lays upon the altar the dearest and the best;
> The love that never falters, the love that pays the price,
> The love that makes undaunted the final sacrifice.

Rugby and war now shared not only a common vocabulary but a soundtrack.

Affinity between rugby and the military continues, although Josh Lewsey may have been the last former army officer to play for England. In a distant echo of those wartime scratch games at Old Deer Park in aid of the Red Cross in 1917, rugby raised over £1 million for the charity Help for Heroes in a 2008 challenge match at Twickenham (repeated in 2011). Lawrence Dallaglio, described as a man who 'would be equally at home leading business or men into battle', carefully avoided the easy rhetoric that equates battlefield and sports field:

> Often sports men and women are put on a pedestal as being kind of heroes, but let's be honest, the real heroes of our country are the people that put their lives at risk ... When we go out on the pitch we put our reputation on the line. Service men and women put their lives on the line.[35]

Rugby may borrow the language of warfare, but in war injury time may last a whole lifetime and not all of the team go home after a shower and a beer.

Rosslyn Park Great War Roll of Honour

Name	Rank/Unit	School
Allen, Wellesley Roe	Capt., RAMC	Uppingham
Ash, Basil Claudius	Lt, 2/Sherwood Foresters	Uppingham
Atkins, Herbert de Carteret	Lt, 15/Durham Light Infantry	Uppingham
Bayly, Charles George Gordon	Lt, Royal Engineers and RFC	St Paul's
Beamish, John Spread Hamilton	Lt, 2/King's Shropshire LI	Haileybury
Bodenham, John Edward Cyril	Rifleman, Queen's Westminster Rifles	Ratcliffe/Ampleforth
Bruce, Jonathan Maxwell	Major, 107th Indian Pioneers	Haileybury
Burdekin, Sydney	2/Lt, Royal Field Artillery	Armidale
Button, Charles Augustus	2/Lt, Royal Field Artillery	Bowden's
Calthrop, Edward Spencer	Surgeon, RN, Royal Marines Div., RND	N/K
Coburn, Charles Isaacs	2/Lt, 18/King's Royal Rifle Corps	St Paul's

Died	Date	Grave/Memorial
Cairo	11/03/19	Cairo
Aisne	20/09/14	Chauny
Le Treport (wounded Loos)	10/10/15	Le Treport
Enghien	22/08/14	Tournai
London (suicide)	02/11/15	Brookwood
Gommecourt	01/07/16	Thiepval
Festubert	24/11/14	Bethune
Loos	28/09/15	Loos
Aisne	27/05/18	Soissons
London (illness)	30/07/17	Sutton
Ypres	31/07/17	Menin Gate

Cole, Humphrey Porteous	2/Lt, 9/Devonshire	Marlborough
Conilh de Beyssac, Jean-Jacques	Sous-Lieut, 501eme de Chars	Inst Ste Marie, Bordeaux
Corban-Lucas, Percival	Capt., 1/Royal Sussex att. 9/Worcs	Bedford
Costin, Bruce Duffus	Lt, 1/Prince of Wales' Own West Yorks Regt	Bedford
Crosley, Cecil	2/Lt, 5/Royal Irish Fusiliers	Uppingham
Cruttwell, Hugh Lockwood	2/Lt, Royal Garrison Artillery	Denstone
Cull, Arthur Tulloch	Capt., Royal Flying Corps	Uppingham
Dale, Robert Jacomb Norris	Lt, Royal Flying Corps, 33 KBS	Haileybury
De la Cour, Herbert Hyde Hedges	Lt, Royal North Devon Hussars	Bedford
De la Mothe, Claude Douglas Fenelon	Lt, RNVR	Tonbridge
Dingle, Arthur James	Capt., 6/East Yorks	Durham
Dowson, Humphrey, MC	Capt., 9/King's Royal Rifle Corps	Uppingham
du Maurier, Guy, DSO	Lt Col, 3/Royal Fusiliers	Marlborough
Fairbairn, George Eric	2/Lt, 10/Durham Light Infantry	Eton
Falle, Bertram Vernon	Capt., Princess Victoria's (Royal Irish Fusiliers)	Tonbridge
Farquharson-Roberts, Donald, MC	Capt., 7/East Surrey att. 4/Bn	Bedford

Corbie (of wounds, Somme)	03/04/16	Corbie
St Remy en l'Eau	13/06/18	St Remy en l'Eau
Mesopotamia	15/12/16	Basra
Ypres	24/10/14	Boulogne
Keretech Tepe	16/08/15	Helles
Ypres	12/10/17	The Huts, Dikkebusch
Arras	11/05/17	Arras
Piave	31/01/18	Giavera
London (of wounds)	03/12/19	Mitcham
Ancre	13/11/16	Ancre
Gallipoli	22/08/15	Helles
Somme	15/09/16	Longueval
Ypres (Kemmel)	09/03/15	Kemmel
Bailleul	20/06/15	Bailleul
Gallipoli	16/08/15	Helles
Cambrai	20/11/17	Louverval

Fazan, Roy	2/Lt, 5/Royal Sussex	Epsom
Fischel, Claude Henry	Capt., RAMC att. 7/Leics	Sutton Valence
Geary-Smith, Alexander	Capt., 9/West Yorks Rgt (Prince of Wales' Own)	Uppingham
Glover, Richard Bowie Gaskell	Capt., 1/London Fusiliers	Uppingham
Gray, George Ernest Marshall	2/Lt, 14/Northumberland Fusiliers	Sherborne
Harman, John Augustus	Lt, Royal Flying Corps	Uppingham
Harris, Hubert Alfred	Capt., RAMC att. RFA 74/Bde	Bedford
Harrison, Arthur Leyland, VC	Lt Cmdr, Royal Navy	Dover
Harrison, Maurice Cazalet	Capt., 1/Royal Warwickshire	Dover
Hart, Conway John	Lt, 16/Sherwood Foresters	N/K
Haslam, Wilfred Henry Westcott	Lt, 4/Queen's Own Royal West Kents	Marlborough
Hickling, John Christopher	2/Lt, 9/Middlesex att. Seaforths	Uppingham
Horsley, Claude Cressy	Lt, 4/North Staffordshire	Oakham
Houghton, Noel	Lt Col, 16/Sherwood Foresters	Glenalmond
Huckett, Arnold Walter	Lt, 5/Wiltshire	St George's, Harpenden
Hudson, Eric Donald Brereton	Private, Royal Fusiliers	N/K

Aubers Ridge	09/05/15	Le Touret
Somme	14/09/18	Manancourt
Lala Baba, Suvla Bay	07/08/15	Helles
Armentieres	05/11/15	Sailly
Somme	14/07/16	Thiepval
Lincolnshire	17/11/17	Gainsborough
Elverdinghe	31/07/17	Bleuet Farm
Zeebrugge	23/04/18	Zeebrugge
Somme	12/10/16	Thiepval
Somme	10/10/16	Mill Road
Mesopotamia	07/02/16	Basra
Kut	11/04/16	Basra
Wimereux (of wounds Ypres)	28/11/17	Wimereux
Ypres	13/09/17	La Clytte
Gallipoli	10/08/15	Helles
Somme	05/08/16	Thiepval

Jesson, Robert Wilfred Fairey	Major, 5/Wiltshire	Sherborne
Jourdain, Ernest Nevill	Capt., 1/Suffolk	Haileybury
Juckes, George Francis	2/Lt, 6/Rifle Brigade att. 1/Bn	King's Canterbury
Kerr, Arthur Douglas Kerr Odell	2/Lt, 10/Middx, att.1/5 Lancs Fusiliers	Uppingham
Kirton, Ralph Imray, AFC	Lt, Royal Flying Corps/RAF	King's Canterbury
Legard, Ralph Hawkesworth	Capt., 4/Durham Light Infantry att. 2/Bn	Durham & Dulwich
Llarena, Eustace Femando	2/Lt, 2/Suffolk	Dulwich
Lloyd Jones, John MC	Capt., 2/Yorks	Uppingham
Lomax, Gerald David	2/Lt, 3/Welsh, att. 2/Royal Berks	Marlborough
Lucas, William Herbert	Lt, 8/North Staffs	Dover & Chesterfield
MacGregor Whitton, Percy William	Capt., 2/Royal Scots Fusiliers	Morrisons Academy
McDermott, Robert Keith	Capt., 3/Seaforth Highlanders att. 1/Bn	Charterhouse
Monaghan, Denis Laurence	Capt., Tank Corps	Uppingham
Moore, Roger Ludovic	Lt, 1/Somerset Light Infantry	Uppingham
Ormsby, Francis James	2/Lt, 14/Royal Sussex	N/K
Oxland, Nowell	Lt, 6/Borders	Durham
Parry-Jones, Owen Guy	Capt., RAMC, att. 3/Suffolks	Sherborne
Paterson, Robert Denzil	Lt, 20/King's (Liverpool)	Birkenhead

Mesopotamia	22/02/17	Basra
Ypres	16/02/15	Menin Gate
Ypres	06/07/15	Talana Farm
Somme	03/08/16	Thiepval
Aldershot	22/11/18	Camberwell
Hooge	09/08/15	Menin Gate
Ypres	18/06/15	Menin Gate
Wales (illness)	11/03/16	Llanwnda
Fromelles	11/05/15	Estaires
Bethune	21/01/16	Merville
Somme	09/07/16	Thiepval
Beit Lid, Palestine	20/09/18	Jerusalem
Cambrai	24/11/17	Louverval
Ploegsteert	20/12/14	Lon Rifle Bde Cem.
Somme	03/09/16	Hamel
Gallipoli	09/08/15	Green Hill
Somme	29/09/16	Puchevillers
Somme	12/10/16	Caterpillar Valley

Pennefather, Charles Lewis	Capt., 2/Rifle Brigade	Marlborough
Pickering, Tom	2/Lt, 7/Gloucesters	Uppingham
Pinfield, Guy Vickery	2/Lt, 8/King's Royal Irish Hussars	Marlborough
Purser, Frank Dulcken	Lt, RNVR	Uppingham
Rutherford, John Douglas	Surgeon, RN, HMS *Theseus*	(Bart's Hospital)
Scholey, Charles Harry Norman	Capt., 9/Rifle Brigade	Uppingham
Silcock, Bertram Baker	2/Lt, 7/Royal Welsh Fusiliers	Blundells
Shoobert, Neil	Lt, 23/Middlesex	St Paul's
Stafford, Arthur Darrell	Lt, 1/Royal Warwicks	St Paul's
Stevenson, Harry Burnett	Capt., Queen Victoria's Own Rajput LI	Uppingham
Teague, Charles Middlemore	L/Cpl, 14/London (Scottish)	QEGS Crediton
Todd, Alexander Findlater	Capt.,1/Norfolk att. 4/Bn	Mill Hill
Tomlin, Charles Geoffrey	Lt, 22/Londons	Uppingham
Townsend-Green, Henry Russell	Capt., 1/16 London, Queen's Westminster Rifles	Uppingham
Tovey, Harry Turner	Major, Royal Field Artillery	St Paul's
Trenchard, Frederick Alfred	Lt, Royal Field Artillery	Oundle
Trinder, John Robert, MC	Major, 18/London (Irish Rifles)	Wellington

Fromelles	14/06/16	Aveluy
Alexandria	01/11/15	Alexandria (Chatby)
Dublin	24/04/16	Dublin
Cambrai	27/12/17	Villers Pluich
Lemnos	11/09/17	Mudros
Ypres	25/09/15	Menin Gate
Suvla Bay	10/08/15	Helles
Ypres	31/07/17	Menin Gate
Rouen (of wounds)	20/05/18	St Sever Rouen
Gallipoli	06/08/15	Helles
Loos	13/10/15	Loos
Ypres	21/04/15	Poperinghe
Bethune	09/07/16	Barlin
Armentieres sector	03/03/15	Cité Bonjean
Ypres	22/04/18	Mendinghem
Ypres	24/05/15	La Brique
Somme	15/09/16	Flatiron Mametz

Tuckey, Charles Phelps	Capt., 4/Royal Marine Light Infantry	RNC Greenwich
Urquhart, James Laurence	Lt, 7/Northants	Grimsby Municipal College
Vaughan, Charles Alvarez	2/Lt, 7/Seaforth Highlanders	Harrow
Veitch, Dawyk Moberley	Capt., RFC	Bedford/Uppingham
Vintcent, Charles Aubrey	2/Lt, 4/Rifle Brigade	Uppingham
Wallis, Edward Percy	Capt., King's Own Royal Lancs att. 8/Royal Sussex	Marlborough
Walker, Walter Arthur Beaumont	2/Lt, 3/Bedfords att. 2/Bn	Bedford Grammar
Wynne, Edward Ernest	Capt., 1/5 Leicesters	Uppingham
Young, Colin Turner	Capt., 3/Duke of Wellington's West Riding	N/K

Zeebrugge	23/04/18	Zeebrugge
Loos	26/09/15	Loos
Loos	25/09/15	Loos
East of Arras	08/07/16	Arras
Ypres	13/04/15	Menin Gate
Somme	18/10/16	Bapaume Post
La Bassee/Havre	30/10/14	Bethune Town
Arras	08/06/17	Bully Grenay
Somme	24/04/17	Fins

NOTES

The Final Whistle

1 Bishop & Bostridge (eds), *Letters from a Lost Generation: First World War letters of Vera Brittain and Four Friends* (Virago, 2008), p. 299.
2 *The Graphic*, 17 May 1879.
3 www.cwgc.org.
4 Eighty-seven names as of January 2012.
5 Rex Alston, *One Hundred Years of Rugby Football at Rosslyn Park 1879–1979* (club archive).
6 Letter to Howard Sturgis in Percy Lubbock (ed.), *Letters of Henry James*, Vol. 2 (Scribner, New York, 1920).
7 *London Gazette*, 24 April 1918.

The Boys Who Won the War

1 *My World as in My Time: Memoirs of Sir Henry Newbolt, 1862–1932* (Faber & Faber, London, 1932).
2 *Harrow Memorials of the Great War*, Vol. 3.
3 Coincidentally, roughly the same number were in service, regular, reserve or territorial in 1914.
4 84 of 350, as at January 2012.
5 Wemyss (ed.), *Barbarian Football Club* (Playfair, London, 1955).
6 Capt. Eric Fazan Diary, Royal Sussex Regimental Museum. See Paul Reed's *Great War Lives* (Pen & Sword, Barnsley, 2010).
7 Preface to the Ukrainian translation of *Animal Farm* (1947, reprinted by Penguin, 2000).
8 George Orwell, *England Your England and other essays* (Secker & Warburg, London, 1953).
9 Bishop & Bostridge, op. cit., p. 113.
10 Letter to *The Elizabethan*, XIV.
11 'War Service in Perspective', in *Promise of Greatness*, edited by George Panichas (Cassell, London, 1968).
12 *The Elizabethan*, October 1915.
13 'The English Public Schools in the War', in Panichas, op. cit.

14 Peter Parker, *The Old Lie; the Great War and the Public School Ethos* (Constable, 1987) p. 159.

15 Panichas, op. cit.

16 A.M. Burrage (ex-Pte 'X'), *War is War* (Gollancz, London, 1930).

17 John Lewis-Stempel's *Six Weeks* covers this subject masterfully.

18 *The Cheltonian*, September 1915.

19 R.C. Sherriff, *Journeys End*, Act II Sc. I (Penguin, 2009).

20 Siegfried Sassoon, 'Suicide in the Trenches', in *Counter-Attack and Other Poems* (Dutton, New York, 1918).

Chapter 1: Charles George Gordon Bayly

1   *The Pauline*, 1906.

2   *The Pauline*, 1910.

3   *The Guy's Hospital Gazette*, 4 November 1916.

4   Maurice Baring, *Flying Corps Headquarters 1914–18* (Bell, London, 1920).

5   Walter Bloem, *The Advance from Mons 1914: The Experiences of a German Infantry Officer* (Helion & Company, 2004).

6   Patrick Loodts, *Médécins de Grande Guerre*, www.1914-1918.be.

7   *The Times*, 29 September 1914.

8   *Morning Post*, 1 September 1914.

9   Sir John French's fourth dispatch, *London Gazette*, 27 November 1914.

10 De Ruvigny, *Roll of Honour 1914–18* (London, 1919).

Chapter 2: Guy du Maurier

1   Daphne du Maurier (ed.), *The Young George du Maurier: A Selection of his letters 1860–67* (Doubleday, New York, 1952).

2   C.C. Hoyer Millar, *Fifty Years of Rosslyn Park* (Wyman, 1929).

3   Daphne du Maurier, *The du Mauriers* (Gollancz, London, 1937).

4   Rex Alston, *One Hundred Years of Rugby Football at Rosslyn Park 1879–1979* (club archive).

5   Hoyer Millar, op. cit., p. 236.

6   Letter to his mother, 6 May 1901, by kind permission of Andrew Birkin.

7   Ibid.

8   *London Gazette*, 29 July 1902.

9   *London Gazette*, 31 October 1902.

10 Letter from Schoon Spruit, 22 April 1902.

11 See *J.M. Barrie and the Lost Boys* by Andrew Birkin (Constable, London, 1979).

12 Pottle & Ledingham, *We Hope to Get Word Tomorrow: The Garvin Family Letters* (Frontline, 2009).

13 J. Twells Brex, *Scaremongerings from the Daily Mail 1896–1914* (London, 1915).

14 Spenser Wilkinson, *Britain at Bay* (New York, 1909).

15 See Chapter 12.

16 *New York Times*, 31 January 1909.

17 Andrew Birkin, *J.M. Barrie and the Lost Boys* (Constable, London, 1979), p. 172.

18 C.B. Davis, *Adventures and Letters of RH Davis 1864–1916*, letter, 23 February 1909, www.gutenberg.org.

19 *Southampton Times & Hampshire Express*, 15 May 1909.

20 *Norfolk News*, 15 May 1909.

21 *New York Times*, 4 April 1909.

22 *Times Literary Supplement*, 30 June 1909.

23 Stanley Casson, *Steady Drummer* (Bell & Sons, London, 1935).

24 *Letters from Lt Col GLB Du Maurier DSO to his Wife* (Bumpus, London, 1915). I am indebted to Andrew Birkin for sight of his personal copy.

25 *Memoirs of an Infantry Officer* (Faber & Faber, London, 1930).

26 G.A. Burgoyne, *The Burgoyne Diaries*, edited by C. Davison (Thomas Harmsworth, 1985), p. 47.

27 H.C. O'Neill, *The Royal Fusiliers in the Great War* (Heinemann, 1922).

28 Birkin, op. cit., p. 267.

29 Burgoyne, op. cit.

30 Birkin, op. cit., p. 242.

31 Courtesy of Jeremy Banning.

32 Still alive/And in my missing her/More beautiful.

33 Geoffrey Winthrop Young, *The Grace of Forgetting* (Country Life, London, 1953), p. 226.

Chapter 3: Alec Todd

1   Since first publication, this clock has now been restarted at the behest of bicycling Boris Johnson, Mayor of London, who was late for a meeting.

2   *The Wine Trade Review*, 9 November 1934.

3   *British Medical Journal*, 3 September 1910.

4   C.C. Hoyer Millar, *Fifty Years of Rosslyn Park* (Wyman, 1929), p. 61.

5   In 1913 Blackheath offered an annual fixture and half the gate – a huge compliment.

6   Obituary, *Morning Post*, 24 April 1915.

7   *African Review*, 27 June 1896.

8   *The Sportsman*, 22 June 1896.

9   Ibid.

10 *African Review*, 27 June 1896.

11 Unpublished letter, 14 July 1896. My thanks to David Byass for these unpublished family letters.

12 Unpublished letter, 6 July 1896.

13 *Athletic Review*, July 1896.

14 *Cape Times*, 10 July 1896.

15 *Cape Times*, 11 July 1896.

16 Letter from Kimberley, 20 July 1896.

17 Letter from Johannesburg, 17 August 1896.

18 *African Review*, 27 June 1896.

19 *Cape Times*, 15 July 1896.

20 Letter from Cape Town, 14 July 1896.

21 Letter from Cape Town, 2 September 1896.

22 Clem Thomas, *The History of the British Lions* (Mainstream, Edinburgh, 1997).

23 *Cape Times*, 7 September 1896.

24 Thomas, op. cit.

25 *African Review*, 3 October 1896.

26 *London Gazette*, 12 February 1901.

27 Arthur Conan Doyle, *The Great Boer War* (Smith, Elder & Co., London, 1902).

28 Letter from James Todd, 25 April 1901.

29 *London Gazette*, 11 February 1902.

30 I am grateful here to Patricia Moorhead, Tommy's great-niece.

31 *The Times*, 4 December 1902.

32 National Archives WO339/28441.

33 E.H.D. Sewell, *Rugby Football Internationals Roll of Honour 1914–1918* (Jack, London, 1919).

34 Frank Keating, *Rugby World*, August 2010.

Chapter 4: Eric Fairbairn

1 G.C. Drinkwater & T.R.B. Saunders, *The University Boat Race Official Centenary History* (Cassell, 1929).

2 www.theboatrace.org.

3 Donald S. Garden, 'Fairbairn, George (1816–1895)', *Australian Dictionary of Biography* (Melbourne University Press, 1972).

4 *The Times*, 29 June 1915.

5 *The Graphic*, 25 March 1911.

6 F. Brittain & H.B. Playford, *The Jesus College Boat Club, Cambridge* (Heffer, Cambridge, 1928).

7 Ibid.

8 *History of Magdalen College Boat Club*, www.srcf.ucam.org.

9 Issue 49, Lent Term 1909, pp. 36–7.

10 *The Times*, editor's comment on letters on rowing theory, 11 January 1933.

11 *Vanity Fair*, 13 March 1907.

12 Drinkwater & Saunders, op. cit.

13 Drinkwater & Saunders, op. cit., p. 121.

14 Theodore Andrea Cook, *The Fourth Olympiad, Being the Official Report* (British Olympic Association, London, 1908).

15 Brittain & Playford, op. cit., pp. 39–46.

16 *The Sportsman*, 18 May 1911.

17 *Truth*, 31 May 1911.

18 *Chanticlere*, Issue 56, May Term 1911.

19 Ernest Parker, *Into Battle* (Longmans, London, 1964).

20 Wilfred Miles, *Durham Forces in the Field 1914–18*, Vol. 2 (Cassell, 1920).

21 *Chanticlere*, Issue 66, Michaelmas Term 1919.

22 Brittain & Playford, op. cit., p. 92.

Chapter 5: Nowell Oxland

1 The mystery has now been solved but the detective must tell the story first.

2 'Cumberland' from *Poems and Stories*, privately published 1917.

3 Col H.C. Wylly CB, *The Border Regiment in the Great War* (Aldershot, 1924).

4 Rupert Brooke, *Peace from 1914 and Other Poems* (Sidgwick & Jackson, London, 1915).

5 Hindi *degci*, an all-purpose mess tin for cooking.

6   Claude Burton, *The Isthmus* (Essex Regimental Museum, Chelmsford).
7   *Cumberland and Westmorland Herald*, 11 September 1915.
8   *Poems and Stories*, op. cit.
9   G. Keynes (ed.), *Brooke, The Letters* (Faber & Faber, London, 1968).
10 Térèse Radic, *Race Against Time: the Diaries of F.S. Kelly* (National Library of Australia, 2004).
11 *The Times*, 26 April 1915.
12 Sir Ian Hamilton, Diary, www.gutenberg.org.
13 Kevin Fewster (ed.), *Gallipoli Correspondent, The Frontline Diary of CEW Bean* (George Allen & Unwin, Sydney, 1983).
14 Wylly, op. cit., p. 52.
15 'I saw a man this morning', in *Anthem for Doomed Youth*, edited by Lyn Macdonald (Folio, London, 2003).
16 Wylly, op. cit., p. 53.
17 Broadrick letters from *Glory is no Compensation* by Ralph May (Silverlink, 2003), by permission of Cumbria's Military Museum.
18 Lt C.K. James, twice awarded the DSO, was killed commanding the battalion in 1918, aged 26.
19 May, op. cit.
20 Wylly, op. cit., p. 55.
21 Ibid., p. 56.
22 Capt. Drury, 6/Royal Dublin Fusiliers, Diary 7607-69,Vol. 1, National Army Museum.
23 May, op. cit., p. 145.
24 Lt C.K. James quoted by Amy Hawthorn to F.J. Lys, 27 December 1915, courtesy of the Provost and Fellows of Worcester College, Oxford.
25 Ibid.
26 W.N. Hodgson, 'Ascension Morning', in *Verse and Prose in Peace and War* (Smith, Elder & Co., London, 1916), pp. 82–5.
27 Sgt John Hargrave, *At Suvla Bay*, www.gutenberg.org.
28 May, op. cit.
29 Hawthorn to F.J. Lys, 18 December 1915.
30 *The Times*, 26 April 1915.
31 Hawthorn to F.J. Lys, 10 January 1916. Dispatch in *London Gazette*, 6 January 1916.
32 *Oxford Magazine*, 5 November 1915.
33 *Cumberland and Westmorland Herald*.
34 *The Times*, 27 August 1915, p. 6.

Chapter 6: Jimmy Dingle

1   W.N. Hodgson, 'Durham Cathedral', in *Verse and Prose in Peace and War* (Smith, Elder & Co., London, 1916), p. 37.
2   *The Times*, 13 December 1911.
3   Fred Lister, *History of Hartlepool Rovers 1879–1939* (1939).
4   C.B. Cowell & E.W. Moses, *Durham County Rugby Union 1876–1936* (1936).
5   *The Times*, 10 February 1913.
6   Ibid., 22 March 1914.

7   *The Times*, 30 January 1913.

8   E.H.D. Sewell, *Rugby Football Internationals Roll of Honour 1914–1918* (Jack, London, 1919).

9   Also as, since 2010, the A.J. Dingle Trophy for the 'Veterrimi IV' competition between the four oldest rugby schools: Durham, Cheltenham College, Rugby and Sherborne.

10 Letters from *The Dunelmian*, 18 December 1915, pp. 236–41, by permission of John Malden, archivist, Durham school.

11 *Poems in Captivity* (Bodley Head, London, 1919).

12 National Archives WO95/4299.

13 Sgt John Hargrave, *At Suvla Bay*, Gutenberg Library, www.gutenberg.org.

14 National Archives WO95/4298.

15 *London Gazette*, 6 January 1916.

16 Ibid.

17 *The Times*, 30 October 1923.

18 Unpublished letter, courtesy of a member of the Great War online forum.

19 *The Times*, 14 February 1925.

20 *Wipers Times*, No. 5 Vol. 2, 22 January 1918.

21 Hargrave, op. cit.

22 National Archives WO339/11893.

Chapter 7: Syd Burdekin

1   Burdekin House can be seen at www.collection.hht.net.au, including a glimpsed portrait of Catherine, reflected in the mirror.

2   National Archive WO339/52112.

3   *Australian Dictionary of Biography*, Vol. 3 (Melbourne, 1969), pp. 297–99.

4   *Bulletin*, 8 January 1881.

5   Jim Graham, *A School of Their Own: the History of The Armidale School* (1994).

6   Online at www.as.edu.au.

7   Sir Henry Newbolt, *A Perpetual Memory and other Poems* (John Murray, London, 1939).

8   *The Times*, 9 May 1905.

9   *Otago Witness*, December 1908.

10 Rupert Brooke, *Peace from 1914 and other Poems* (Sidgwick & Jackson, London, 1915).

11 My thanks to Peter Walker, in whose collection Syd's sword is now sheathed.

12 Len Smith, *Drawing Fire* (Collins, London, 2009).

13 Brig. Gen. Sir J.E. Edmonds (ed.), *Official History of the Great War 1914–18: France & Belgium*, Vol. 2 1915 (London, 1928).

14 Ibid.

15 War Diary, National Archives WO95/1983.

16 *Harrow Memorials of the Great War*, Vol. 3 (Harrow School, Philip Lee Warner, 1920).

17 Edmonds, op. cit.

18 Quoted in *The Donkeys, A History of the British Expeditionary Force in 1915* by Alan Clark (Hutchinson, London, 1961).

19 Letter to Sir Ian Hamilton, 17 August 1915.

20 Sgt John Hargrave, *At Suvla Bay*, www.gutenberg.org.

21 Charles Bean, *The Official History of Australia in the War of 1914–1918*, Vol. 1, The Story of Anzac: The First Phase (1921), pp. 4–7.

22 J.G. Gilbert writing in 1963.
23 *Daily Telegraph*, 7 June 2005.
24 ECB Press Release, 28 June 2009.
25 *The Times*, 7 September 2007.

Chapter 8: Guy Pinfield

1   The name survives in a hard-touring club side at Rosslyn Park.
2   Quoted in Max Arthur, *Forgotten Voices of the Great War* (Ebury Press, London, 2003).
3   Owen Dudley Edwards & Fergus Pyle Owen (eds), 'Sheehy-Skeffington', in *1916: The Easter Rising* (London, 1968).
4   'The Provisional Government to the Citizens of Dublin' in *Weekly Irish Times: Sinn Fein Rebellion Handbook* (Dublin, 1917).
5   *The National Review*, Vol. 86 (1925), p. 746.
6   Peter de Rosa, *Rebels: the Irish rising of 1916* (Bantam Press, 1990).
7   Quoted in Edwards & Pyle, op. cit.
8   *Weekly Irish Times: Sinn Fein Rebellion Handbook* (Dublin, 1917).
9   Royal Commision: Enhanced British Parliamentary Papers on Ireland 1801–1922, Southampton University.
10 John F. Lucy, *There's a Devil in the Drum* (1938).
11 My thanks to Jimmy Taylor.
12 Royal Commission, op. cit., p. 4; also *Sinn Fein Rebellion Handbook*.
13 Max Caulfield, *The Easter Rebellion* (4Square, London, 1964).
14 Edwards & Owen (eds), op. cit.
15 National Archives WO30/67.
16 *New York Times*, 17 October 1917.
17 *James Joyce Quarterly*, Vol. 20, No. 1 (1982), pp. 120–4.
18 Edwards & Owen (eds), op. cit.
19 Hansard HC Deb, 19 October 1916, Vol. 86, c705.
20 National Archives WO71/1027.
21 National Archives WO256/14.
22 National Archives WO339/23591.
23 *The Times*, 24 April 1917.
24 *The Times*, 14 May 1962.
25 Michael Parsons, *Irish Times*, 23 February 2011.
26 'Experiences of a VAD', *Blackwoods Magazine*, Issue 200, 1916.

Chapter 9: John Bodenham

1   www.florislondon.com.
2   My thanks to John Bodenham for these unpublished private papers.
3   Lawrence Dallaglio, *It's in the Blood* (Headline, London, 2007).
4   A mistaken view – see Chapter 10.
5   Peter Davies, 'Charles Edmonds', in *A Subaltern's War* (London, 1929).
6   Len Smith, *Drawing Fire* (Collins, London, 2009).
7   R.C. Sherriff, *Journey's End*, Act II, Sc. I (Penguin, 2009).

8   Supplement to *London Gazette*, 18 June 1917.

9   Alan MacDonald, *Pro Patria Mori: 56th (1st London) Division at Gommecourt, 1st July 1916* (Iona Books, 2008).

10 Cecil Chesterton (ed.), *New Witness*, 29 June 1916.

11 J. Q. Henriques *War History of the Queen's Westminster Rifles*, Medici, London 1923.

12 Rifleman N.H. Lockhart, London Rifle Brigade, quoted in MacDonald, op. cit.

13 Quoted in John Ellis, *Eye Deep in Hell* (Fontana, London, 1977).

Chapter 10: Wilfred Jesson

1   *The Times*, 10 July 1907.

2   *The Times*, 2 September 1907.

3   www.cricketarchive.com.

4   *Daily Princetonian*, 20 January 1910, reported in *New York Times*, 21 January 1910.

5   Rosslyn Park Club Archive.

6   *The Times*, 4 November 1909.

7   National Archives WO339/11984.

8   See Paula Perry, *A History of the 5th (Service) Battalion, Wiltshire Regt 1914–19* (The Rifles Wardrobe and Museum Trust, Salisbury, 2007).

9   Paddy Storrie, 'Here I am; send me', in *The War Dead of St George's School 1914–18* (2004).

10 R. W.F.J. personal account 1915–16, by kind permission of Ann Gammie.

11 Jessie Pope, *More War Poems* (Grant Richards, London, 1915).

12 *Wadham College Gazette*, October 1915.

13 Pte W.J. Gronow, 4/South Wales Borderers, was awarded the DCM.

14 War Diary, The Rifles Museum (Berks & Wilts) Salisbury and online www.thewardrobe.org.uk.

15 L.A. Carlyon, *Gallipoli* (Bantam, 2003).

16 Major A.C. Temperley, Norfolk Regiment, Brigade Major, NZ Infantry Brigade. *A Personal Narrative of the Battle of Chunuk Bair, August 6th–10th, 1915*, MS0017, Q.E.II Army Museum, Waiouru, New Zealand.

17 See Perry, op. cit., pp. 179–81.

18 Letter Pte S.B. Ayling, quoted in Perry, op. cit., p. 215.

19 War Diary, 28 November 1915.

20 Wellcome Library, www.wellcome.ac.uk.

21 National Archives WO339/11984.

22 *4 Month Diary of Henry Woolley*, The Great War Archive, University of Oxford (www.oucs.ox.ac.uk/ww1lit/gwa) © Ruth E Bartlett.

23 Ibid.

24 *The Times*, 19 July 1916.

25 Title of A.J. Barker's 1967 campaign history.

26 War Diary, op. cit.

27 Major R.I. Scorer MC, *Mesopotamia 1916–19* (The Rifles Museum (Berkshire & Wiltshire), Salisbury).

28 Brig. Gen. F.J. Moberley, *Official History of the War, Mesopotamia Campaign*, Vol. 3 (HMSO, London, 1924).

29 National Archives WO339/11984.

tt2tttt

Chapter 11: John Augustus Harman

1   Rhoda Gilman, 'Zeppelin in Minnesota: A Study in Fact and Fable', in *Minnesota History* 39, 1965, pp. 278–85.
2   Christopher Chant, *The Zeppelin: The History of German Airships from 1900–1937* (David & Charles, 2001).
3   Maria Bach Dunn/Rhoda Gilman, *Minnesota History* 40, pp. 265–78.
4   Gilman, op. cit.
5   *Sheffield Telegraph*, 13 May 1909.
6   *Peterborough Advertiser*, 27 March 1909.
7   *Daily Express*, 14 May 1909.
8   *Evening Star*, 15 May 1909.
9   *Daily Mail*, 21 May 1909.
10 Vera Brittain (ed.), *Chronicle of Youth: the War Diary 1913–17* (Bishop & Smart, Morrow, New York, p. 135).
11 Quoted in Wilbur Cross, *Zeppelins of World War 1* (Paragon House, London, 1991).
12 *The Times*, 21 January 1915.
13 David Forsyth, *RAF Spirit of the Air*, Vol. 1, No. 4, 2006.
14 Ian Castle, *London 1914–17 The Zeppelin Menace* (Osprey), p. 13.
15 Quoted in Cross, op. cit., p. 36.
16 H.G. Castle, *Fire over England* (Secker & Warburg, London, 1982).
17 Cross, op. cit., p. 36.
18 Vera Brittain, op. cit., p. 270.
19 E.M. Horsley (ed.), *Lady Cynthia Asquith Diaries 1915–18* (Knopf, New York, 1969), p. 34.
20 Ibid., p. 87.
21 Reginald & Charles Fair, *Marjorie's War: Four families in the Great War 1914–18* (Menin House, 2011).
22 National Archives WO339/36130.
23 Ibid.
24 Ibid.
25 R.F. Scott, *Voyage of the Discovery*, Vol. 1 (Macmillan, London, 1905), p. 468.
26 H.G. Castle, op. cit., p. 136.
27 Quoted by Jay Winter, *Sites of Memory, Sites of Mourning* (New York, Cambridge University Press, 1995), p. 193.
28 Fair, op. cit.
29 *Flight Magazine*, 12 December 1952.
30 C. Cole and E.F. Cheeseman, *The Air Defence of Britain 1914–18* (Putnam, 1984), pp. 344–7.
31 Ian Castle, op. cit., p. 87.
32 National Archives WO339/36130.
33 *Flight Magazine*, 13 December 1917.
34 *Gainsborough News* 23 November 1917.

Chapter 12: Denis Monaghan & J.J. Conilh de Beyssac

1   *Eyewitness* (Hodder & Stoughton, London, 1932).
2   David Lloyd George, *War Memoirs* (Nicholson & Watson, London, 1933–36).
3   Richard Haigh, *Life in a Tank* (Houghton Mifflin, Boston, 1918).
4   1 July 1690 under the Julian calendar, now celebrated on 12 July.
5   Quoted by Robert Kershaw, *Tank Men* (Hodder & Stoughton, London, 2008).
6   Basil Henriques, *Indiscretions of a Warden* (Methuen, London, 1937).
7   *The Times*, 29 September 1916.
8   Richard Haigh, op. cit.
9   John Griffiths, *The Phoenix Book of International Rugby Records* (Phoenix House, 1987).
10 Bernard Busson, *Héros du Sport – Héros de France* (Atos, 1947 (author's translation)).
11 Ibid.
12 C.C. Hoyer Millar, *Fifty Years of Rosslyn Park* (Wyman, 1929), p. 144.
13 IWM Sound Archive 9752 Capt. N.M. Dillon, Tank Corps.
14 Clough & Amabel Williams-Ellis, *The Tank Corps* (Country Life, 1919).
15 IWM Docs 82/22/1 Pte Reginald Beall, typescript.
16 David Fletcher (ed.), *Tanks and Trenches* (The History Press, Stroud, 2009).
17 War History 9th Bn Tank Corps, © Tank Museum Bovington.
18 Major R.F.G. Maurice, *Tank Corps Book of Honour* (London, 1919).
19 Fletcher, op. cit.
20 Heinz Guderian, *Achtung-Panzer!* (1937, trans. Duffy, Arms & Armour Press, London, 1992).
21 IWM Docs J.K. Wilson papers *c.* 1970 PP/MCR/100.
22 Ibid.
23 Ibid.
24 IWM Docs J.K. Wilson papers, Letter from Parsons to Wilson, 1969.
25 *The Times*, 20 November 1916.
26 R.F.G. Maurice, op. cit.

Chapter 13: Robert Dale

1   *Those Magnificent men in their Flying Machines*, lyric: Richard Kaufman.
2   Godric Hodges, *Memoirs of an old Balloonatic* (William Kimber, London, 1972).
3   W.S. Lewis, 'In a Kite Balloon', in *Everyman at War* ed. C.B. Purdom (London, 1930).
4   Quote by Harold Macmillan, *The Winds of Change* (Macmillan, London, 1966).
5   *The Times*, 24 August 1916.
6   W.S. Lewis, op. cit.
7   Alan Morris, *The Balloonatics* (Jarrold, London, 1970).
8   Ibid.
9   James Dale, *Pulling faces for a living* (Gollancz, London, 1970). He became Dr Jim Dale in radio's *Mrs Dale's Diary*.
10 Life is short, a little hope/ A little dream and then good night.
11 Preface to *Regimental Roll of Honour and War Record* (1922).
12 Col H.A.R. May, *Memoirs of the Artists Rifles* (Howlett, London, 1929).
13 See Chapter 10.
14 *Ashton Reporter*, 16 October 1915, from www.ashtonpals.webs.com.

15 National Archives WO95/4595, War Diary 1/9 Manchester Regt.
16 National Archives WO95/4595.
17 Letters, Lt E. Trevor Evans, 34 Squadron, courtesy of Chris Myers www.staff-shomeguard.co.uk.
18 Supplement to the *London Gazette*, 16 September 1918.
19 Norman Macmillan, *Offensive Patrol* (Jarrold, London, 1973).
20 Ernest Hemingway, 'The Snows of Kilimanjaro', in *Collected Stories* (Everyman, 1995).
21 Joshua Levine, *On a Wing and a Prayer* (Collins, 2008).
22 Unpublished memoir by Irene Mawer, NRCD Archive, Guildford University.

Chapter 14: Arthur Harrison

1   E.H.D. Sewell, *Rugby Football Internationals Roll of Honour 1914–1918* (Jack, London, 1919), p. 66.
2   C.C. Hoyer Millar, *Fifty Years of Rosslyn Park* (Wyman, 1929), p. 134.
3   Philip Warner, *The Zeebrugge Raid* (Kimber, London, 1978).
4   E.H.D. Sewell, op. cit., p. 66.
5   Rosslyn Park No. 3 Minute Book.
6   Quoted by Warner, op. cit.
7   Roger Keyes, *The Naval Memoirs of Admiral of the Fleet Sir Roger Keyes* (Thornton Butterworth, London, 1936), p. 220.
8   Warner, op. cit.
9   W. Wainwright RN from *Everyman at War*, ed. C.B. Purdom (London, 1930).
10 Barrie Pitt, *Zeebrugge* (Cassell, London, 1958).
11 Wainwright, op. cit.
12 Warner, op. cit.
13 Ibid.
14 Wainwright, op. cit.
15 Deborah Lake, *The Zeebrugge and Ostend Raids 1918* (Leo Cooper, Barnsley, 2002), p. 113.
16 Captain Alfred Carpenter VC, *The Blocking of Zeebrugge* (Herbert Jenkins, London, 1921).
17 Letter from A.B. McKenzie, www.mckenzie.uk.com, with kind permission of Colin McKenzie.
18 Telegram Berlin to Amsterdam, reprinted in *The Times*, 25 April 1918.
19 Sir Roger Keyes.
20 Gen. Sir H.E. Blumberg KCB, *Britain's Sea Soldiers: A Record of the Royal Marines during the War 1914–1919* (Swiss & Co., Devonport, 1927).
21 Carpenter, op. cit.
22 *The Times*, 30 December 1918.

Chapter 15: Charles Button

1   John Terraine, *White Heat – the New Warfare 1914–18* (Sidgwick & Jackson, London, 1982).
2   See Gordon Corrigan, *Mud, Blood and Poppycock* (Cassell, 2003), p. 123.
3   National Archives WO339/77786.

4   *London Gazette*, 30 January 1917.

5   *London Gazette*, 19 September 1916.

6   IWM Sound Archive 4214, Captain Sidney Rogerson, *c.* 1963.

7   IWM Docs 7313, Diary of Capt. P.A. Ledward MC. HQ 23rd Bde.

8   Rev. Wilfrid Callin, *When the Lantern of Hope burned low* (Hexham, 1919), www. archive.org.

9   Brigadier W.F.K. Thompson, 'The Great Siege of Gibraltar 1779–1783', in *Journal of the Royal Artillery* CVI No. 2, September 1979.

10 Major Luker presentation, Royal Artillery Historical Society, 23 April 2008.

11 IWM Docs 3381, Diary of Capt. P.H.B. Lyon, Durham Light Infantry.

12 Captain Sydney Rogerson, quoted in Lt Colonel J.H. Boraston and C.E.O. Bax, *Eighth Division in War 1914–18* (1922).

13 Col Anderson-Morshead, quoted in R.A. Colwill, *Through Hell to Victory* (Torquay, 1927).

14 H.C.C. Uniacke, *Royal Artillery War Commemoration Book* (Bell & Sons, London, 1920).

15 National Archives WO339/77786.

16 General Berthelot speech, 6 November 1921, at unveiling of memorial at Bois des Buttes, Devonian Year Book 1922.

17 Letter from personal collection with translation courtesy of Lawrence Brown.

18 *Materiel Regulations for the Army*, Vol. 3: Clothing, Pamphlet No. 15, November 1995, Annex C to Section 6, Serial 11.

19 *Daily Express*, quoted by Ann Compton. The Sculpture of Charles Sargeant Jagger, Ashgate, 1985.

20 John Galsworthy, *Swan Song* (Heinemann, London, 1928).

21 *The Great Western Railway Magazine*, December 1922, pp. 537–40.

The Game that Won the War

1   *The Times*, 26 February 1919.

2   *The Graphic*, 30 April 1892.

3   *The Sketch*, 22 February 1893.

4   C.C. Hoyer Millar, *Fifty Years of Rosslyn Park* (Wyman, 1929), p. 132.

5   Ibid., p. 132.

6   *The Times*, 16 April 1912.

7   Alfred Harmsworth, *Lord Northcliffe's War Book* (Northcliffe, New York, 1917).

8   Paul Jones, *War Letters of a Public Schoolboy* (Cassell, London, 1918).

9   Rosslyn Park No. 3 Minute Book.

10 *Daily Mail*, 11 September 1914.

11 *Punch*, 21 October 1914.

12 C.H. Cooke, *Historical Records 16th (Service) Battalion Northumberland Fusiliers* (1923).

13 One Henry Grierson was the last to join Park before the war and survived.

14 *The Times*, 14 December 1914.

15 Hoyer Millar, op. cit., p. 148.

16 Ibid., p. 150.

17 *The Graphic*, 24 February 1917.

18 Hoyer Millar, op. cit., p. 153.

19 *The Graphic*, 24 February 1917.

20 Robert Graves, *Goodbye to all that* (Cassell, London, 1958).

21 'At the Games', in *The Sportsman's Hornbook*, edited by Charles Grayson (Random House, 1933).

22 Act 3, Sc. 3 (Penguin, 2009).

23 *The Times*, 28 February 2010.

24 E.H.D. Sewell, *The Log of a Sportsman* (London, 1923).

25 Paul Jones, op. cit.

26 Ed Harris, *The Footballer of Loos: A Story of the London Irish Rifles in the First World War* (The History Press, 2010).

27 *Daily Telegraph*, 12 July 1916.

28 2/Lt C.W. Alcock, from Ruth Elwin Harris, *'Billie' – The Nevill Letters 1914–16* (Julia Macrae Books, London, 1991).

29 Harris, op. cit.

30 A.H. Farrar-Hockley, *The Somme* (Batsford, 1954).

31 Hoyer Millar, op. cit. p. 155.

32 Address to University of St Andrews, 14 May 1919.

33 *The Times*, 4 March 1919.

34 *The Times*, 6 February 1919.

35 *Sunday Times*, 21 September 2008.

SELECT BIBLIOGRAPHY

This is not an exhaustive list of the works consulted in the writing of this book, but is a personal selection chosen to inform or entertain the interested reader.

Arthur, Max, *Forgotten Voices of the Great War* (Ebury Press, 2003)

Badsey, Stephen, *The British Army in Battle and its Image 1914–18* (Birmingham War Studies, 2009)

Barker, Ralph, *The RFC in France, Vol. 1, Mons to the Somme* (Constable, 1994)

Beard, Richard, *Muddied Oafs: the Last Days of Rugger* (Yellow Jersey Press, 2003)

Birkin, Andrew, *JM Barrie and the Lost Boys* (Constable, 1979)

Bishop & Bostridge (eds), *Letter from a Lost Generation: First World War letters of Vera Brittain and Four Friends* (Virago, 2008)

Brown, Malcolm, *Somme* (Pan, 1997)

Blunden, Edmund, *Undertones of War* (Penguin, 2000)

Campbell, Christy, *Band of Brigands: the First Men in Tanks* (Harper, 2007)

Carlyon, L.A., *Gallipoli* (Bantam, 2003)

Castle, H.G., *Fire over England* (Secker & Warburg, 1982)

Castle, Ian, *The Zeppelin Menace, London 1914–17* (Osprey, 2008)

Caulfield, Max, *The Easter Rebellion* (Four Square, 1965)

Clark, Alan, *The Donkeys* (Hutchinson, 1961)

Collins, Tony, *A Social History of English Rugby Union* (Routledge, 2009)

Corrigan, Gordon, *Mud, Blood and Poppycock* (Cassell, 2003)

Cross, Wilbur, *Zeppelins of World War 1* (Paragon House, 1991)

De Ruvigny, *Roll of Honour 1914–18* (reprinted by N&MP)

Dyer, Geoff, *The Missing of the Somme* (Hamish Hamilton, 1994)

Ellis, John, *Eye-Deep in Hell: Life in the Trenches 1914–18* (Fontana, 1977)

Farrar-Hockley, Anthony, *The Somme* (Batsford, 1954)

Ferguson, Niall, *The Pity of War* (Penguin, 1999)

Fewster, Kevin (ed.), *Gallipoli Correspondent: the frontline diary of CEW Bean* (Allen & Unwin, 1983)

Foley, Michael, *Hard as Nails: the Sportsmen's Battalion of World War One* (Spellmount, 2007)

Fussell, Paul, *The Great War and Modern Memory* (Oxford University Press, 1975)

Gliddon, Gerald, *The Battle of the Somme: a Topographical History* (Sutton, 1998)

Graves, Robert, *Goodbye to all that* (Cassell, 1957)

Griffiths, John, *The Phoenix Book of International Rugby Records* (Phoenix, 1987)

Haigh, Richard, *Life in a Tank* (Houghton Mifflin, Boston, 1918)

Hammond, Bryn, *Cambrai 1917: the Myth of the first Great Tank Battle* (Orion, 2009)

Hart, Peter, *1918: a Very British Victory* (Weidenfield & Nicholson, 2008)

Harris, Clive & Whippy, Julian, *The Greater Game: Sporting Icons who fell in the Great War* (Pen & Sword, 2008)

Hodges, Godric, *Memoirs of an Old Balloonatic* (Kimber, 1972)

Holmes, Richard, *Shots from the Front* (Harper, 2008)

Hoyer Millar, Charles, *Fifty Years of Rosslyn Park* (Wyman, 1929)

Hunter, Adrian, *Renaissance of the Rose: the Rise of English Rugby 1909–14* (Emp3Books, 2010)

Hurst, Steve, *The Public Schools Battalion in the Great War* (Pen & Sword, 2007)

Jenkins, Rebecca, *The First London Olympics 1908* (Piatkus, 2008)

Jones, Nigel, *The War Walk: a Journey along the Western Front* (Cassell, 2004)

Keegan, John, *The First World War: an Illustrated History* (Hutchinson, 2001)

Kershaw, Robert, *Tank Men* (Hodder & Stoughton, 2008)

Lake, Deborah, *The Zeebrugge and Ostend Raids 1918* (Leo Cooper, 2002)

Levine, Joshua, *On a Wing and a Prayer* (Collins, 2008)

Lewis-Stempel, John, *Six Weeks* (Weidenfeld & Nicolson, 2010)

Macdonald, Alan, *Pro Patria Mori: the 56th Division at Gommecourt, 1st July 1916* (Iona Books, 2008)

Macdonald, Lyn (ed.), *Anthem for Doomed Youth: Poets of the Great War* (Folio, 2000)

———, *To the Last Man: Spring 1918* (Penguin, 1998)

May, Ralph, *Glory is no Compensation* (Cumbria Military Museum/Silverlink, 2003)

Medomsley, Jack, *William Noel Hodgson: the Gentle Poet* (MEL, Durham, 1989)

Middlebrook, Martin, *The First Day on the Somme* (Penguin, 1984)

Moorehead, Alan, *Gallipoli* (Hamish Hamilton, 1956)

Morris, Alan, *The Balloonatics* (Jarrold, 1970)

Mortimer, Gavin, *Fields of Glory* (Deutsch, 2001)

Orr, Philip, *The Road to the Somme* (Blackstaff, Belfast, 1987)

Panichas, George (ed.), *Promise of Greatness* (London, 1968)

Parker, Ernest, *Into Battle 1914–18* (Longmans, 1964)

Parker, Peter, *The Old Lie: the Great War and the Public School Ethos* (Constable, 1987)

Parsons, I.M. (ed.), *Men who March Away: Poems of the First World War* (Chatto & Windus, 1978)

Perry, Paula, *History of the 5th (Service) Battalion, Wiltshire Regiment 1914–19* (The Rifles (Berks & Wilts) Museum, 2007)

Pitt, Barrie, *Zeebrugge: Eleven VCs before Breakfast* (Cassell, 1958)

Purdom, C.B. (ed.), *Everyman at War* (Everyman, 1930)

Rawson, Andrew, *The British Army Handbook 1914–18* (Sutton, 2006)

Read, Paul, *Great War Lives: a Guide for Family Historians* (Pen & Sword, 2010)

Rhodes James, Robert, *Gallipoli* (Pimlico, 1999)

Rogerson, Sydney, *Twelve days on the Somme* (Greenhill, 2006)

Sheffield, Gary & Bourne, John (eds), *Douglas Haig: War Diaries and Letters 1914–18* (Weidenfeld & Nicolson, 2005)

Sassoon, Siegfried, *Memoirs of an Infantry officer* (Faber & Faber, 1930)

Sellers, Leonard, *The Hood Battalion* (Leo Cooper, 1995)

Sewell, E.H.D., *Rugger: the Man's Game* (Hollis & Carter, 1947)

Smith, Len, *Drawing Fire* (Collins, 2009)

Smith, Sean, *The Union Game: A Rugby History* (BBC Books, 1999)

Spiring, Paul (ed.), *Rugby Football during the Nineteenth Century* (MX, 2010)

Steel, Nigel & Hart, Peter, *Tumult in the Clouds: the British Experience of the War in the Air 1914–18* (Hodder & Stoughton, 1997)

Terraine, John, *White Heat: the New Warfare 1914–18* (Sidgwick & Jackson, 1982)

Thomas, Clem, *History of the British & Irish Lions* (Mainstream, Edinburgh, 2005)

Travers, Tim, *Gallipoli 1915* (Tempus, 2004)

Warner, Philip, *The Zeebrugge Raid* (Kimber, 1978)

Watson, W.H.L., *A Company of Tanks* (Blackwood (N&MP Reprint))

Wemyss, A., *Barbarians Football Club 1890–1955* (Playfair, 1955)

ACKNOWLEDGEMENTS

Like the best rugby victories, the researching of this book has been a team effort. The stories of these men could not have been written without the willing help, encouragement and detailed knowledge shared by a host of teammates.

Above all my appreciation goes to Richard Cable, who kicked off the original research and made the first hard yards. Without him this book would not be.

It is my fortune and privilege to have been granted access to personal papers, photographs and memories by family members. My grateful thanks, in chapter order, go to: David Byass and Patricia Moorhead (Alec Todd); Tessa Montgomery (Guy du Maurier); John Bodenham of Floris Ltd for the letters and diary of his namesake; Edward Bodenham for his help with the photographs; Ann Gammie, John Gay, Richard Gay, Peter Lucas and Paul Blunt (Wilfred Jesson); Sir Jeremiah and Charles Harman ('Uncle Jack' Harman); Eileen Laird, who completed the photographic jigsaw with Robert Dale; and Jimmy Button for material on his Great-Uncle Charles.

Through the miracle of the internet the kindness of strangers has furnished me with many details great and small, but always significant to an author groping blindly into the past. I cannot do justice to them all, but must mention in dispatches the following: Pam and Ken Linge, Andrew Birkin, Paula Perry, Charles Fair, Dominic Walsh, John Hamblin, Bill MacCormick, Jimmy Taylor, Linda Corbett, Michael Parsons, David Huckett, Gavin Mortimer, Jeremy Banning, Philip Barker, Ruaridh Greig, Merv Brown, Mark Bazalgette, Paul Reed, Anne Pedley, Russell Ash, Nick Balmer, Paul Wapshott, Gwyn Prescott, David Lester, John Lee, Ajax Bardrick, Ray Smith, Nigel Marshall, Brian Budge, Alexander Findlater, David Grant, Ann Willmore, Tim Fox-Godden, Lawrence Brown, Charlotte Zeepvat, and John Lewis-Stempel.

A host of archivists and historians have been unfailingly patient and helpful with my enquiries. First amongst equals is David Whittam, tireless archivist and stalwart at Rosslyn Park FC, but deserved gratitude also goes to: Simon May and Alexandra Aslett of St Paul's school; Vernon Creek at the RAF Museum; David Underdown at Kew; Dr Frances Willmoth of Jesus College, Cambridge; Emma Goodrun and the provost and fellows of Worcester College, Oxford; Christine Leighton of Cheltenham College; Toby Parker of Haileybury; John Malden, Old Dunelmians archivist; Dave Allen of Hampshire CCC; Jim Graham, Donna Jackson and Anne White of TAS; Alastair Robertson of the Alston Historical Society; Sharon Maxwell of the NRCD, Guildford; Michael Harte and Heather Woodward of Wadhurst Historical Society; Julian Reid, archivist of Merton & Corpus Christi Colleges, Oxford; Janice Tait at the Tank Museum; Jonathan Smith of Trinity College, Cambridge; Stuart Eastwood at Cumbria's Military Museum; Judy Faraday and Linda Moroney of the John Lewis Partnership; Kate Jarvis, Wandsworth

Heritage Service; Katie Ormerod, St Bart's Hospital; Tracy Wilkinson, King's College, Cambridge; Elizabeth Stratton of Clare College; Anselm Cramer of Ampleforth Abbey; Sue Chan, National Library of Australia; and Katherine Lindsay at the Oxford University Great War Archive.

Additional help and photographs have been kindly provided by Rosemary Fitch, Francis de Look, Chas Keyes, Robert Smith, Peter Bradshaw, Carole Cuneo, Peter Walker, John Black, Ian Lewis, Louise Lawson, Stephen May, Barbara Evans, Nik Boulting, Jenny Hopkins, Ian Metcalfe, Francesca Hunter, Andrew Dawrant of the Royal Aero Club Trust, Christine de Poortere and Great Ormond Street Hospital Children's Charity.

My gratitude is also due to the staff at the Commonwealth War Graves Commission, National Archives, British Library and Imperial War Museum. These national treasures deserve all possible recognition and support. Also to Alison McDonald of Richmond Libraries for her persistence in tracking down obscure volumes in the lending system. Another man-made wonder is Chris Baker's website, the 'Long, Long Trail' with its associated Great War forum, an online meeting house and depositary for knowledgeable enthusiasts, many known to me only by their *nom de guerre*. My grateful thanks to all who freely helped and encouraged.

My thanks also to my classical authority Andrew Maynard, to my Australian correspondents, Ian Johnstone and Michael Durey, and to Major General Dair Farrar-Hockley MC for their unflagging enthusiasm. *Merci mille fois à mon copain rugby*, Frédéric Humbert.

To Penny Hoare for starting me on the road to publication and to Jo de Vries, Chrissy McMorris and the team at The History Press for the map and driving lessons.

For permission to quote from their copyright work, my thanks to Bill MacCormick, Paula Perry and The Rifles Museum, Paddy Storrie, Stuart Eastwood at Cumbria's Military Museum, Colonel Tim Collins, Charles Fair, Robert Kershaw, Paddy Storrie, and Chris Myers.

For Faber & Faber Ltd for permission to quote from the letters of Rupert Brooke.

Quotations from Vera Brittain are included by permission of Mark Bostridge and Timothy Brittain-Catlin, Literary Executors for the Estate of Vera Brittain 1970; quotes from George Orwell's *Animal Farm* and *England, Your England And Other Essays* are reproduced by kind permission of Bill Hamilton as the Literary Executor of the Estate of the Late Sonia Brownell Orwell; from *Journey's End* by permission of the Estate of R.C. Sherriff; from *The Burgoyne Diaries* with permission from Thomas Harmsworth Publishing Company; from Siegfried Sassoon copyright by kind permission of the Estate of George Sassoon. Excerpt from *The Snows of Kilimanjaro* by Ernest Hemingway, published by Vintage Books, reprinted by permission of The Random House Group Limited; from Robert Graves by permission of Carcanet Press Ltd. Extract from *The Donkeys: A History of the BEF in 1915* by Alan Clark reprinted by permission of Peters Fraser & Dunlop on behalf of the Estate of Alan Clark; also for the extract from *White Heat: the new Warfare 1914–18* by John Terraine, on behalf of the Estate of John Terraine.

Every effort has been made to trace copyright holders and the author and publisher welcome correspondence on this matter from any sources where it has not been possible to obtain permission to quote.

It is my hope that I have breathed life back into these players. This book too is a living memorial, which must go on growing; I welcome any further facts about any of the men and apologise where I have drawn conclusions in their absence.

This is a work of personal passion more than historical erudition, and I trust that true historians will forgive me. Where I have consulted experts, they have corrected me. As in my brief and undistinguished playing career, the errors are all mine.

INDEX